KV-606-646

References

Article Licenses

Jean Simmons

Jean Simmons	
Studio publicity shot	
Born	Jean Merilyn Simmons January 31, 1929 Lower Holloway, London, England, United Kingdom
Died	January 22, 2010 (aged 80) Santa Monica, California, United States
Cause of death	Lung Cancer
Nationality	British, American
Alma mater	Aida Foster School of Dance
Occupation	Actress, dancer
Years active	1944–2009
Spouse(s)	Stewart Granger (1950–60) (divorced) 1 child Richard Brooks (1960–77) (divorced) 1 child
Parents	Charles Simmons, Winifred (Loveland) Simmons

Jean Merilyn Simmons, OBE (January 31, 1929 – January 22, 2010) was a British-American actress.[1][2] She appeared predominantly in films, beginning with those films made in Great Britain during and after World War II – she was one of J. Arthur Rank's 'well-spoken young starlets' – followed mainly by Hollywood films from 1950.[3]

Early life and career

Simmons was born in Lower Holloway, London, England, to Charles Simmons and his wife, Winifred (Loveland) Simmons. Jean was the youngest of four children with siblings Edna, Harold and Lorna. She began acting at the age of 14. During World War II, the Simmons family was evacuated to Winscombe in Somerset.[4] Her father, a physical education teacher (who had represented Great Britain in the 1912 Summer Olympics),[5] taught briefly at Sidcot School, and sometime during this period Simmons followed her elder sister on to the village stage and sang songs such as "Daddy Wouldn't Buy Me a Bow Wow". Returning to London and just enrolled at the Aida Foster School of Dance, she was spotted by the director Val Guest, who cast her in the Margaret Lockwood vehicle *Give Us the Moon*.[6] Small roles in several other films followed including the high profile *Caesar and Cleopatra*, produced by Gabriel Pascal. Pascal saw potential in Simmons and in 1945 he signed her to a seven-year contract.[7] Prior to moving to Hollywood, she played the young Estella in David Lean's version of *Great Expectations* (1946) and Ophelia in Laurence Olivier's *Hamlet* (1948), for which she received her first Oscar nomination. It was the experience of working on *Great Expectations* that caused her to pursue an acting career more seriously:

Please return/renew this item by the last date
above. You can renew on-line at

www.lbhf.gov.uk/libraries

Topic releva   or by phone   :inted
and shipped      **0303 123 0035**

Hammersmith & Fulham Libraries

Combine th   con-
venience of

A portion of the proceeds of each book will be donated to the Wikimedia
Foundation to support their mission: to empower and engage people around
the world to collect and develop educational content under a free license or in
the public domain, and to disseminate it effectively and globally.

The content within this book was generated collaboratively by volunteers.
Please be advised that nothing found here has necessarily been reviewed by
people with the expertise required to provide you with complete, accurate
or reliable information. Some information in this book maybe misleading
or simply wrong. The publisher does not guarantee the validity of the information found here. If you need specific advice (for example, medical, legal,
financial, or risk management) please seek a professional who is licensed or
knowledgeable in that area.

Sources, licenses and contributors of the articles and images are listed in the
section entitled "References". Parts of the books may be licensed under the
GNU Free Documentation License. A copy of this license is included in the
section entitled "GNU Free Documentation License"

All used third-party trademarks belong to their respective owners.

Contents

Articles

> I thought acting was just a lark, meeting all those exciting movie stars, and getting £5 a day which was lovely because we needed the money. But I figured I'd just go off and get married and have children like my mother. It was working with David Lean that convinced me to go on.[8]

Playing Ophelia in Olivier's *Hamlet* made her a star, although she was already well known for her work in other British films, including her first starring role in the film adaptation of *Uncle Silas*, and *Black Narcissus* (both 1947). Olivier offered her the chance to work and study at the Bristol Old Vic, advising her to play anything they threw at her to get experience; she was under contract to the Rank Organisation who vetoed the idea.[9] Rank was unhappy at this time also that Stewart Granger was pursuing his young star and, (according to the actor's account), confronted Granger ("a shop-worn thirty-four"), at a meeting at the Dorchester Hotel saying that what was going on was wrong since he was a married man with two children. Granger told Rank he had been divorced for six months, and left.[10] In 1949 Simmons starred with Granger in *Adam and Evelyne*. In 1950 Rank sold Simmons's contract to Howard Hughes, who then owned the RKO studio in Hollywood. That year she was voted the fourth most popular star in Britain.[11]

In 1950 she married the English actor Stewart Granger, with whom she appeared in several films, successfully making the transition to an American career. She made four films for Hughes, including *Angel Face*, directed by Otto Preminger. According to David Thomson "if she had made only one film – *Angel Face* – she might now be spoken of with the awe given to Louise Brooks."[12] A court case freed her from the contract with Hughes in 1952.[12] In 1953 she starred alongside Spencer Tracy in *The Actress*, a film that was one of her personal favourites. Among the many films she appeared in during this period were *The Robe* (1953), *Young Bess* (1953), *Désirée* (1954), *The Egyptian* (1954), *Guys and Dolls* (1955) – "in which she's delightfully proper (and improper) as the Salvation Army officer Sarah Brown" [13] – *The Big Country* (1958), *Elmer Gantry* (1960), (directed by her second husband, Richard Brooks), *Spartacus* (1960), *All the Way Home* (1963) – a film of James Agee's novel, *A Death in the Family* – and *The Happy Ending* (1969), again directed by Brooks and for which she received her second Oscar nomination. In the opinion of film critic Philip French, a film of 1958, *Home Before Dark*, saw her give "perhaps her finest performance as a housewife driven into a breakdown in Mervyn LeRoy's psychodrama."[14]

By the 1970s Simmons turned her focus to stage and television acting. She toured the United States in Stephen Sondheim's well-reviewed musical *A Little Night Music*, then took the show to London, and thus originated the role of Desirée Armfeldt on the West End.[15] Doing the show for three years, she said she never tired of Sondheim's music; "No matter how tired or *off* you felt, the music would just pick you up."

She portrayed Fiona Cleary, Cleary family matriarch, in the 1983 mini-series, *The Thorn Birds*; she won an Emmy Award for her role.

In 1985 and 1986 she appeared in *North & South*, again playing the role of the family matriarch as Clarissa Main.

In 1988 she starred in *The Dawning* with Anthony Hopkins and Hugh Grant, and in 1989 she again starred in a mini-series, this time a version of *Great Expectations*, in which she played the role of Miss Havisham, Estella's adoptive mother. Simmons made a late career appearance in the *Star Trek: The Next Generation* episode "The Drumhead" as a retired Starfleet admiral and hardened legal investigator who conducts a witch-hunt. In 1991 she appeared in the short-lived revival of the 1960s daytime series *Dark Shadows*, in roles originally played by Joan Bennett. From 1994 until 1998 Simmons narrated the A&E documentary television series, *Mysteries of the Bible*. In 2004 Simmons voiced the lead-role of Sophie in the English dub of *Howl's Moving Castle*.

Personal life

Jean Simmons was married and divorced twice. She married Stewart Granger in Tucson, Arizona, on 20 December 1950. In 1956 she and Granger became U.S. citizens; they divorced in 1960. On 1 November 1960, she married director Richard Brooks; they divorced in 1977. Although both men were significantly older than Simmons, she denied she was looking for a father figure. Her father had died when she was just 16 but she said: "They were really nothing like my father at all. My father was a gentle, soft-spoken man. My husbands were much noisier and much more opinionated ... it's really nothing to do with age ... it's to do with what's there – the twinkle and sense of humour."[8] And in a 1984 interview, given in Copenhagen at the time she was shooting the film *Yellow Pages*, she elaborated slightly on her marriages, stating,

> It may be simplistic, but you could sum up my two marriages by saying that, when I wanted to be a wife, Jimmy [Stewart Granger] would say: 'I just want you to be pretty.' And when I wanted to cook, Richard would say: 'Forget the cooking. You've been trained to act – so act!' Most people thought I was helpless – a clinger and a butterfly – during my first marriage. It was Richard Brooks who saw what was wrong and tried to make me stand on my own two feet. I'd whine: 'I'm afraid.' And he'd say: 'Never be afraid to fail. Every time you get up in the morning, you are ahead.'

She had two daughters, Tracy Granger and Kate Brooks, one by each marriage – their names bearing witness to Simmons' friendship with Spencer Tracy[16] and Katharine Hepburn. Simmons moved to the East Coast of the US in the late 1970s, briefly owning a home in New Milford, Connecticut near her longtime friend Rex Reed. Later she moved to Santa Monica, California, where she lived until her death from lung cancer. She died at home on 22 January 2010, nine days before her 81st birthday, surrounded by her family.[17]

Throughout her life Simmons spoke out publicly about her own struggle with addiction, and in 2003 became the patron of the UK drugs and human rights charity Release. She was an active supporter of their campaigns for just, humane and effective drug policies, recognising that many of those with drug problems cannot afford the luxurious facilities available to celebrities. In 2005 Simmons signed a petition to the British Prime Minister Tony Blair asking him not to upgrade cannabis from a class C drug to a class B.[18] Because cannabis was legal in California, Simmons was able to use medical cannabis to ease her pain and suffering during the last months of her life.

She was cremated in Santa Monica and her ashes buried in North London in Highgate Cemetery West.

Filmography

Year	Film	Role	Notes
1944	*Sports Day*	Peggy[19]	
	Give us the Moon	Heidi[20]	
	Mr. Emmanuel	Sally Cooper[21]	Billed as Jean Simmonds
1945	*Kiss the Bride Goodbye*	Molly Dodd[22]	
	Meet Sexton Blake	Eva Watkins[23]	
	The Way to the Stars	A singer	
	Caesar and Cleopatra	harpist	
1946	*Great Expectations*	Estella as a girl	
1947	*The Woman in the Hall*	Jay	
	Uncle Silas	Caroline Ruthyn[24]	
	Black Narcissus	Kanchi	
	Hungry Hill	Jane Brodrick	
1948	*Hamlet*	Ophelia	Nominated — Academy Award for Best Supporting Actress
1949	*The Blue Lagoon*	Emmeline Foster	
	Adam and Evelyne	Evelyne Kirby	

1950	*So Long at the Fair*	Vicky Barton	
	Cage of Gold	Judith Moray[25]	
	Trio: "*Sanatorium*"	Evie Bishop	
1951	*The Clouded Yellow*	Sophie Malraux	
1952	*Angel Face*	Diane Tremayne	
	Androcles and the Lion	Lavinia	
1953	*Young Bess*	Princess Elizabeth	
	Affair with a Stranger	Carolyn Parker[26]	
	The Robe	Diana	
	The Actress	Ruth Gordon Jones	National Board of Review Award for Best Actress
1954	*She Couldn't Say No* (AKA *Beautiful but Dangerous*)	Corby Lane	
	Demetrius and the Gladiators	Diana	Appeared in a clip from *The Robe*
	The Egyptian	Meryt	
	A Bullet Is Waiting	Cally Canham[27]	
	Désirée	Désirée Clary	
1955	*Footsteps in the Fog*	Lily Watkins	
	Guys and Dolls	Sergeant Sarah Brown	Awarded — Golden Globe for Best Musical/Comedy Actress Nominated — BAFTA for Best Actress
1956	*Hilda Crane*	Hilda Crane	
1957	*This Could Be the Night*	Anne Leeds	Nominated — Golden Globe for Best Musical/Comedy Actress
	Until They Sail (1957)	Barbara Leslie Forbes	
1958	*The Big Country*	Julie Maragon	
	Home Before Dark	Charlotte Bronn[28]	Nominated — Golden Globe for Best Drama Actress
1959	*This Earth Is Mine*	Elizabeth Rambeau[29]	
1960	*Elmer Gantry*	Sharon Falconer	Nominated — BAFTA for Best Actress Nominated — Golden Globe for Best Drama Actress
	Spartacus	Varinia	
	The Grass Is Greener	Hattie Durant	
1963	*All the Way Home*	Mary Follett	
1965	*Life at the Top*	Susan Lampton[30]	
1966	*Mister Buddwing* (1966)	The Blonde	
1967	*Divorce American Style*	Nancy Downes	
	Rough Night in Jericho	Molly Lang	
1968	*Heidi*	Fräulein Rottenmeier	
1969	*The Happy Ending*	Mary Spencer	Nominated — Academy Award for Best Actress
1971	*Say Hello to Yesterday*	Woman	
1975	*Mr. Sycamore*	Estelle Benbow	

1978	*The Dain Curse* (TV)	Aaronia Haldorn	
	Dominique	Dominique Ballard	
1979	*Beggarman, Thief* (TV)	Gretchen Jordache Burke[31]	
1981	*A Small Killing* (TV)	Margaret Lawrence[32]	
1983	*The Thorn Birds* (TV)	Fee Cleary	Awarded — Emmy for Outstanding Supporting Actress
1984	*December Flower* (TV)	Etta Marsh[33]	
1985	*Midas Valley* (TV)	Molly Hammond[34]	
	North and South	Clarissa Gault Main	
1986	*North and South Book II*	Clarissa Gault Main	
1987	*Perry Mason: The Case of the Lost Love*	Laura Robertson [35]	
1988	*Yellow Pages*	Maxine de la Hunt[36]	
	The Dawning	Aunt Mary	
1989	*Great Expectations*	Miss Havisham	
	Murder She Wrote Episode: "Mirror, Mirror on the Wall"		Nominated — Emmy for Outstanding Guest Actress, Drama Series
1991	*Star Trek: The Next Generation* Episode: "The Drumhead"	Rear Admiral Norah Satie	
	Dark Shadows	Elizabeth Collins Stoddard / Naomi Collins	
	They Do It with Mirrors	Carrie-Louise Serrocold	
1995	*How to Make an American Quilt*	Em Reed	
	Daisies in December	Katherine Palmer[37]	
2001	*Final Fantasy: The Spirits Within*	Council Member 2 (voice)	
2003	*Winter Solstice*	Countess Lucinda Rhives[38]	Released in Germany as *Wintersonne*
2004	*Jean Simmons: Rose of England*	Herself	
	Howl's Moving Castle	Grandma Sophie (voice)	
2005	*Thru the Moebius Strip*	Shepway (voice)[39]	
2009	*Shadows in the Sun*	Hannah [40]	

Box Office Ranking

For a number of years, British film exhibitors voted her among the top ten British stars at the box office via an annual poll in the *Motion Picture Herald*.

- 1949 - 4th[41] (9th most popular over all)[42]
- 1950 - 2nd (4th most popular over all)[43]
- 1951 - 3rd[44]

Awards and nominations

Awards

- Emmy for Outstanding Supporting Actress - Series/Special, *The Thorn Birds* (1983)
- Golden Globe for Best Musical/Comedy Actress, *Guys and Dolls* (1956)

Nominations

- Academy Award for Best Actress, *The Happy Ending* (1969)
- Academy Award for Best Supporting Actress, *Hamlet* (1948)
- BAFTA for Best Actress, *Guys and Dolls* (1956)
- BAFTA for Best Actress, *Elmer Gantry* (1960)
- Emmy for Outstanding Guest Actress - Drama Series, *Murder, She Wrote* (1989)
- Golden Globe for Best Drama Actress, *Home Before Dark* (1959)
- Golden Globe for Best Drama Actress, *Elmer Gantry* (1961)
- Golden Globe for Best Drama Actress, *The Happy Ending* (1970)
- Golden Globe for Best Musical/Comedy Actress, *This Could Be the Night* (1958)
- Golden Globe for Best Supporting Actress - Miniseries, *The Thorn Birds* (1984)

References

[1] Obituary *Los Angeles Times*, 23 January 2010.
[2] Obituary *London Independent*, 26 January 2010.
[3] Aljean Harmetz (January 23, 2010). "Jean Simmons, Actress, Dies at 80" (http://www.nytimes.com/2010/01/24/movies/24simmons. html). *The New York Times*. . Retrieved January 24, 2010. "Jean Simmons, the English actress who made the covers of Time and Life magazines by the time she was 20 and became a major mid-century star alongside strong leading men like Laurence Olivier, Richard Burton and Marlon Brando, often playing their demure helpmates, died on Friday at her home in Santa Monica, California. She was 80. The cause was lung cancer, according to Judy Page, her agent. ..."
[4] *Picturegoer* 2 August 1947 'Are They Being Fair To Jean Simmons?'
[5] as told to Gloria Hunniford in *Sunday, Sunday* television interview LWT, autumn 1985
[6] Val Guest *So You Want to be in Pictures?* p.58.ISBN 1-90311-115-3
[7] Jean Simmons, The Biography Channel
[8] *Woman's Weekly*, Christmas 1989
[9] French, Philip (24 January 2010). "Jean Simmons: an unforgettable English rose" (http://www.guardian.co.uk/uk/2010/jan/23/ the-unforgettable-jean-simmons). *The Observer*. .
[10] Stewart Granger, Sparks Fly Upward, Granada 1981, p.132
[11] "Critics Praise Drama: Comedians Win Profits." (http://nla.gov.au/nla.news-article18193224). *The Sydney Morning Herald* (NSW: National Library of Australia): p. 3. 29 December 1950. . Retrieved 24 April 2012.
[12] Thomson, David (25 January 2010). "Jean Simmons obituary" (http://www.guardian.co.uk/film/2010/jan/24/jean-simmons-obituary). *The Guardian*. .
[13] Philip French, Screen Legends, No.11 (http://www.guardian.co.uk/film/2008/apr/06/1)
[14] French, Philip (6 April 2008). "Philip French's screen legends - No 11: Jean Simmons 1929-" (http://www.guardian.co.uk/film/2008/ apr/06/1). *The Observer*. .
[15] Sondheim Guide - A Little Night Music (http://www.sondheimguide.com/night.html)
[16] *Picture Show and TV Mirror, 2 July 1960, p.7. Simmons says her daughter was named after Spencer Tracy in interview, but adds, "Jimmy (Stewart Granger) says he got the name from the role Katharine Hepburn played in* The Philadelphia Story *"*

[17] "British-born Hollywood actress Jean Simmons dies at 80" (http://news.bbc.co.uk/1/hi/uk/8476400.stm). BBC. 2010-01-23. . Retrieved 23 January 2010.

[18] Goodchild, Sophie (2005-12-18). "Sting leads campaign against Blair's plan to reclassify cannabis" (http://www.independent.co.uk/news/uk/politics/sting-leads-campaign-against-blairs-plan-to-reclassify-cannabis-519959.html). *The Independent* (London). . Retrieved 17 March 2010.

[19] "*Sports Day* (1944)" (http://www.imdb.com/title/tt0037305/). IMDb. .

[20] "*Give Us the Moon* (1944)" (http://www.imdb.com/title/tt0035945/). IMDb. .

[21] "*Mr. Emmanuel* (1944)" (http://www.imdb.com/title/tt0037093/fullcredits#cast). IMDb. .

[22] "*Kiss the Bride Goodbye* (1945)" (http://www.imdb.com/title/tt0036985/). IMDb. .

[23] "*Meet Sexton Blake* (1945)" (http://www.imdb.com/title/tt0037061/fullcredits#cast). IMDb. .

[24] "*Uncle Silas* (1947)" (http://www.imdb.com/title/tt0039492/). IMDb. .

[25] "*Cage of Gold* (1950))" (http://www.imdb.com/title/tt0042295/). IMDb. .

[26] "*Affair with a Stranger* (1953)" (http://www.imdb.com/title/tt0045477/). IMDb. .

[27] "*A Bullet Is Waiting* (1954)" (http://www.imdb.com/title/tt0046812/). IMDb. .

[28] "*Home Before Dark* (1958)" (http://www.imdb.com/title/tt0051732/). IMDb. .

[29] "*This Earth is Mine* (1959)" (http://www.imdb.com/title/tt0053355/). IMDb. .

[30] "*Life at the Top* (1965)" (http://www.imdb.com/title/tt0059389/). IMDb. .

[31] "*Beggarman, Thief* (1979)" (http://www.imdb.com/title/tt0078839/). IMDb. .

[32] "*A Small Killing* (1981)" (http://www.imdb.com/title/tt0083095/). IMDb. .

[33] "*December Flower* (1984)" (http://www.imdb.com/title/tt0397051/). IMDb. .

[34] "*Midas Valley* (1985)" (http://www.imdb.com/title/tt0089592/). IMDb. .

[35] "*Perry Mason: The Case of the Lost Love* (1987)" (http://www.imdb.com/title/tt0093722/). IMDb. .

[36] "*Yellow Pages* (1988)" (http://www.imdb.com/title/tt0095233/). IMDb. .

[37] "*Katherine Palmer* (1995)" (http://www.imdb.com/title/tt0112781/). IMDb. .

[38] "*Winter Solstice* (2003)" (http://www.imdb.com/title/tt0354213/). IMDb. .

[39] "*Through the Moebius Stip* (2005)" (http://www.imdb.com/title/tt0267024/). IMDb. .

[40] "*Shadows in the Sun* (2009)" (http://www.imdb.com/title/tt1065124/). IMDb. .

[41] "Bob Hope Takes Lead from Bing In Popularity." (http://nla.gov.au/nla.news-article2759831). *The Canberra Times (ACT : 1926 - 1954)* (ACT: National Library of Australia): p. 2. 31 December 1949. . Retrieved 27 April 2012.

[42] "TOPS AT HOME." (http://nla.gov.au/nla.news-article49700937). *The Courier-Mail (Brisbane, Qld. : 1933 - 1954)* (Brisbane, Qld.: National Library of Australia): p. 4. 31 December 1949. . Retrieved 27 April 2012.

[43] "BOB HOPE BEST DRAW IN BRITISH THEATRES." (http://nla.gov.au/nla.news-article26748158). *The Mercury (Hobart, Tas. : 1860 - 1954)* (Hobart, Tas.: National Library of Australia): p. 4. 29 December 1950. . Retrieved 27 April 2012.

[44] "Vivien Leigh Actress Of The Year." (http://nla.gov.au/nla.news-article63397098). *Townsville Daily Bulletin (Qld. : 1885 - 1954)* (Qld.: National Library of Australia): p. 1. 29 December 1951. . Retrieved 27 April 2012.

External links

- Jean Simmons (http://www.imdb.com/name/nm1739/) at the Internet Movie Database
- Jean Simmons (http://en.wikipedia.org/wiki/Memoryalpha:jean_simmons) at Memory Alpha (a Star Trek wiki)
- Jean Simmons (http://tcmdb.com/participant/participant.jsp?participantId=177854) at the TCM Movie Database
- Jean Simmons (http://movies.yahoo.com/movie/contributor/1800017941) at Yahoo! Movies
- The Jean Simmons Memorial YouTube Page (http://www.youtube.com/user/JeanSimmonsMemorial)
- Jean Simmons - A Fan Resource (http://jeansimmons.netfirms.com/)
- Jean Simmons 1946 newsreel footage (http://www.britishpathe.com/record.php?id=48279) from British Pathe (newsreel search (http://www.britishpathe.com/results.php?search="jean+simmons"))
- Jean Simmons in motorboat Britlsh Pathe (http://www.britishpathe.com/video/jean-simmons-in-motorboat)
- BBC obituary (http://news.bbc.co.uk/1/hi/uk/3516771.stm)
- Telegraph obituary (http://www.telegraph.co.uk/news/obituaries/culture-obituaries/film-obituaries/7061131/Jean-Simmons.html)
- Obituary (http://www.nytimes.com/2010/01/24/movies/24simmons.html) in *The New York Times* (January 23, 2010)
- Biography (http://www.reelclassics.com/Actresses/Simmons/simmons-bio.htm)

- In Appreciation of Jean Simmons (1929-2010) (http://moviemorlocks.com/2010/01/27/ in-appreciation-of-jean-simmons-1929-2010.htm)
- Photographs and literature (http://www.virtual-history.com/movie/person/1603/jean-simmons)

A Bullet Is Waiting

A Bullet Is Waiting	
Directed by	John Farrow
Starring	Rory Calhoun Jean Simmons Brian Aherne
Release date(s)	1954
Country	United States
Language	English

A Bullet Is Waiting is a 1954 film directed by John Farrow.

External links

- *A Bullet is Waiting* [1] at IMDB

References

[1] http://www.imdb.com/title/tt0046812/

A Death in the Family

A Death in the Family	
1st edition cover	
Author(s)	James Agee
Country	United States
Language	English
Genre(s)	Novel
Publisher	McDowell, Obolensky
Publication date	1957
Media type	Print (hardcover)
Pages	339 pp
OCLC Number	123180486 [1]

A Death in the Family is an autobiographical novel by author James Agee, set in Knoxville, Tennessee. He began writing it in 1948, but it was not quite complete when he died in 1955. It was edited and released posthumously in 1957 by editor David McDowell. Agee's widow and children were left with little money after Agee's death and McDowell wanted to help them by publishing the work. Agee won the Pulitzer Prize for Fiction in 1958 for the novel. The novel was included on *Time*'s 2005 list of the 100 best English-language novels written since 1923.[2]

Plot

The novel is based on the events that occurred to Agee in 1915 when his father went out of town to see his own father, who had had a heart attack. During the return trip, Agee's father was killed in a car accident. The novel provides a portrait of life in Knoxville, Tennessee, showing how such a loss affects the young widow, her two children, her atheist father and the dead man's alcoholic brother.

New version

University of Tennessee professor Michael Lofaro claimed the version published in 1957 was not the version intended for print by the author. He discussed his work at a conference that was part of the Knoxville James Agee Celebration (April 2005). Lofaro tracked down the author's original manuscripts and notes and has reconstructed a version he says is more authentic. Lofaro's version of the novel, *A Death in the Family: A Restoration of the Author's Text*, was published in 2007 as part of a 10-volume set, *The Collected Works of James Agee* (University of Tennessee Press). Lofaro is also the author of *Agee Agonistes: Essays on the Life, Legend, and Works of James Agee* (2007).

Differences

According to Lofaro, McDowell altered the original text in a number of ways:

- Removed the original opening, a nightmare scene, and instead started the novel with "Knoxville: Summer of 1915," a previously published short work of Agee's that was not intended as part of the novel.
- Altered the order of the book, which was intended to be chronological.
- Some chapters were removed.
- Some chapters were chopped up.
- Some chapters were moved and presented as flashbacks.
- The number of chapters was changed from 44 short chapters to 20.

Adaptations

The novel was adapted into *All the Way Home*, a 1961 Pulitzer Prize-winning play by Tad Mosel.

The movie, *All The Way Home* (1963), was adapted by Philip H. Reisman, Jr. from the Agee novel and the Mosel play. It was filmed in the same neighborhood where Agee grew up in Knoxville. Produced by David Susskind and directed by Alex Segal, it stars Robert Preston, Jean Simmons and Pat Hingle.

Samuel Barber wrote *Knoxville: Summer of 1915* (1947, revised 1950) on commission from the American soprano Eleanor Steber, who had asked for a work for soprano with orchestra. Barber's piece is about childhood, the reminiscence of childhood fashioned from Agee's *A Death in the Family* is poetic in novelistic terms but unusually long-limbed for vocal setting. Barber's contemplative monologue turns Agee's irregular prose rhythms into simple musical meters, bringing intensity to phrases that were casual in the prose telling, and emphasizing two undercurrents: nostalgia and intimations of mortality. The scene is still viewed through the eyes of a child, but the mature voice of the writer is also there, emerging especially in the elements of fore-knowledge which give the setting a special poignance.

References

[1] http://worldcat.org/oclc/123180486
[2] Grossman, Lev; Richard Lacayo (2005). "All-Time 100 Novels: The Complete List" (http://www.time.com/time/2005/100books/the_complete_list.html). *Time.* .

External links

- Photos of the first edition of A Death in the Family (http://www.pprize.com/BookDetail.php?bk=40)

A Little Night Music

	A Little Night Music	
	original Broadway production poster	
Music	Stephen Sondheim	
Lyrics	Stephen Sondheim	
Book	Hugh Wheeler	
Basis	1955 Ingmar Bergman film *Smiles of a Summer Night*	
Productions	1973 Broadway 1975 West End 1977 Film 1989 West End revival 1990 New York City Opera 1995 Royal National Theatre 2002 Kennedy Center 2003 NYCO revival 2008 London revival 2009 Broadway revival International productions	
Awards	Tony Award for Best Musical Tony Award for Best Book Tony Award for Best Original Score Drama Desk Awards, Outstanding Book of a Musical, Outstanding Music, Outstanding Lyrics	

A Little Night Music is a musical with music and lyrics by Stephen Sondheim and book by Hugh Wheeler. Inspired by the Ingmar Bergman film *Smiles of a Summer Night*, it involves the romantic lives of several couples. Its title is a literal English translation of the German name for Mozart's Serenade No. 13 for strings in G major, *Eine kleine Nachtmusik*. The musical includes the popular song "Send in the Clowns".

Since its original 1973 Broadway production, the musical has enjoyed professional productions in the West End, by opera companies, in a 2009 Broadway revival, and elsewhere, and it is a popular choice for regional groups. It was adapted for film in 1977, with Harold Prince directing and Elizabeth Taylor, Len Cariou, Lesley-Anne Down and Diana Rigg starring.

Synopsis

Act One

The setting is Sweden, around the year 1900. One by one, the Quintet – five singers who comment like a Greek chorus throughout the show – enter, tuning up. Gradually, their vocalizing becomes an overture blending fragments of "Remember," "Soon," and "The Glamorous Life," leading into the first "Night Waltz". The other characters enter waltzing, each uncomfortable with their particular partner. After they drift back off, the aging and severe Madame Armfeldt and her solemn granddaughter, Fredrika, enter. Madame Armfeldt tells the child that the summer night "smiles" three times: first on the young, second on fools, and third on the old. Fredrika vows to watch the smiles occur. Middle aged Fredrik Egerman is a successful lawyer. He has recently married an 18-year-old trophy wife, Anne, a vain girl who is in love with Fredrik, but too immature to grasp the concept of marriage. The two have been married for eleven months, but Anne still protects her virginity. Fredrik laments his inability to make love to his wife

("Now"). Meanwhile, his son Henrik, a year older than his stepmother, is feeling extremely frustrated. He is a seminary student and everyone is always teasing him, never taking him seriously or letting him talk ("Later"). Anne is intrigued by him, but fails to understand his real meaning. Anne promises her husband that she will consent to have sex shortly ("Soon"). Anne's maidservant Petra, an experienced and forthright girl, slightly older than the teen herself, offers her worldly but crass advice.

Desiree Armfeldt is a prominent and glamorous actress who is now reduced to touring in small towns. Madame Armfeldt, Desiree's mother, has taken over the care of Desiree's daughter Fredrika. Fredrika misses her mother, but Desiree continually puts off going to see her, preferring, somewhat ironically, "The Glamorous Life". She is performing near Fredrik's home, and he brings Anne to see the play. While there, Desiree notices Fredrik; the two were lovers years before. Anne, suspicious and annoyed because of Desiree's amorous glances, demands that Fredrik bring her home immediately. Meanwhile, Petra has been trying to seduce Henrik.

That night, as Fredrik remembers his past with Desiree, he sneaks out to see her; the two share a happy but strained reunion, as they "Remember". They reflect on their new lives, and Fredrik tries to explain how much he loves Anne ("You Must Meet My Wife"). Desiree responds sarcastically, boasting of her own adultery, as she has been seeing the married dragoon, Count Carl-Magnus Malcolm. Upon learning that Fredrik has gone for eleven months without sex, she agrees to accommodate him as a favor for an old friend.

Madame Armfeldt offers advice to young Fredrika. The elderly woman reflects poignantly on her own checkered past, and wonders what happened to her refined "Liaisons". Back in Desiree's apartment, Count Carl-Magnus Malcolm proclaims his unannounced arrival in his typical booming voice. Fredrik and Desiree fool the gullible Count into believing that their disheveled appearance was entirely innocent, but he is still suspicious. He instantly dislikes Fredrik and returns to his wife, Countess Charlotte. Charlotte is quite aware of her husband's infidelity, but Carl-Magnus is too absorbed in his suspicions of Desiree to talk to her ("In Praise of Women"). When she persuades him to blurt out the whole story, a twist is revealed—Charlotte's little sister is a school friend of Anne's.

Charlotte visits Anne, who is talking with Petra. Charlotte describes Fredrik's meeting with Desiree; Anne reacts with shock and horror. The older woman explains to Anne that such is the lot of a wife, and that marriage brings pain ("Every Day A Little Death"). Meanwhile, Desiree asks Madame Armfeldt to host a party for Fredrik, Anne, and Henrik. Though reluctant, Madame Armfeldt agrees. She sends out a personal invitation; its receipt sends the women into a frenzy, imagining "A Weekend in the Country". Anne does not want to accept the invitation, but Charlotte convinces her to do so to heighten the contrast between the older woman and the young teenager. Meanwhile, the Count has plans of his own — as a birthday present to his wife, the pair will attend the party uninvited. Carl-Magnus plans to challenge Fredrik to a duel, while Charlotte hopes to seduce the lawyer to make her husband jealous and end his philandering. The day of the party dawns.

Act Two

Armfeldt's country estate is bathed in the golden glow of perpetual summer sunset at this high latitude ("Night Waltz One and Two"). Everyone arrives, each carrying their own amorous purposes and desires—even Petra, who catches the eye of Armfeldt's fetching manservant, Frid. The women begin to act against each other. Fredrik is astonished to learn the name of Desiree's daughter. Henrik meets Fredrika, and confesses his deep love for Anne to her. Meanwhile, in the garden, Fredrik and Carl-Magnus reflect on how difficult it is to be annoyed with Desiree, agreeing "It Would Have Been Wonderful" had she not been quite so wonderful. Dinner is served, and the characters' "Perpetual Anticipation" enlivens that meal.

At dinner, Charlotte attempts to flirt with Fredrik, while Anne and Desiree trade insults. Soon, everyone is shouting and scolding everyone else, except for Henrik, who finally stands up for himself. He shrieks at them for being completely amoral, and flees the scene. Stunned, everyone reflects on the situation and wanders away. Fredrika tells Anne of Henrik's secret love, and the two dash off searching for him. Meanwhile, Desiree meets Fredrik and asks if he still wants to be "rescued" from his life. Fredrik answers honestly that he loves Desiree, but only as a dream. Hurt and bitter, Desiree can only reflect on the nature of her life ("Send in the Clowns"). Anne finds Henrik, who is attempting to commit suicide. The clumsy boy cannot complete the task, and Anne tells him that she has feelings for him, too. The pair begins to kiss, which leads to Anne's first sexual encounter. Meanwhile, not far away, Frid sleeps in Petra's lap. The maid thinks of the joy and freedom that she longs for before becoming trapped in marriage ("The Miller's Son"). Henrik and Anne, happy together, run away to start their new life. Charlotte confesses her plan to Fredrik, and the two commiserate on a bench. Carl-Magnus, preparing to romance Desiree, sees this and challenges Fredrik to Russian Roulette, at which a nervous Fredrik misfires and simply grazes his own ear. Victorious, Carl-Magnus begins to romance Charlotte, granting her wish at last.

After the Count and Countess leave, Fredrika and Madame Armfeldt discuss the chaos of the recent turns-of-events. The elderly woman then asks Fredrika a surprising question: "What is it all for?" Fredrika thinks about this, and decides that it "must be worth it". Madame Armfeldt is surprised, ruefully noting that she rejected love for material wealth at Fredrika's age. She praises her granddaughter and remembers true love's fleeting nature.

Fredrik finally confesses his love for Desiree, acknowledges that Fredrika is his daughter, and the two promise to start a new life together ("Finale"). Armfeldt sits alone with Fredrika. Fredrika tells her grandmother that she has watched carefully, but still has not seen the night smile. Armfeldt laughs and points out that the night has indeed smiled twice: Henrik and Anne, the young, and Desiree and Fredrik, the fools. As the two wait for the "third smile", on the old, Armfeldt closes her eyes, and dies peacefully.

Musical numbers

Act 1	Act 2
• Overture — Mr. Lindquist, Mrs. Nordstrom, Mrs. Anderssen, Mr. Erlanson and Mrs. Segstrom	• Entr'acte — Orchestra
• Night Waltz — Company	• Night Waltz I (The Sun Won't Set) — Mr. Lindquist, Mrs. Nordstrom, Mrs. Anderssen, Mr. Erlanson and Mrs. Segstrom
• Now — Fredrik Egerman	• Night Waltz II (The Sun Sits Low) — Mr. Lindquist, Mrs. Nordstrom, Mrs. Anderssen, Mr. Erlanson and Mrs. Segstrom
• Later — Henrik Egerman	• It Would Have Been Wonderful — Fredrik Egerman and Count Carl-Magnus Malcolm
• Soon — Anne Egerman, Frederik Egerman and Henrik Egerman	• Perpetual Anticipation — Mrs. Nordstrom, Mrs. Segstrom and Mrs. Anderssen
• The Glamorous Life — Fredrika Armfeldt, Desiree Armfeldt, Madame Armfeldt and Quintet	• Dinner Table Scene — Orchestra
• Remember? — Mr. Lindquist, Mrs. Nordstrom, Mrs. Anderssen, Mr. Erlanson and Mrs. Segstrom	• Send in the Clowns — Desiree Armfeldt
• You Must Meet My Wife — Desiree Armfeldt and Fredrik Egerman	• The Miller's Son — Petra
• Liaisons — Madame Armfeldt	• Reprises ("Soon", "You Must Meet My Wife", "A Weekend in the Country", and "Every Day a Little Death") — Mr. Lindquist, Mrs. Nordstrom, Mrs. Anderssen, Mr. Erlanson and Mrs. Segstrom
• In Praise of Women — Count Carl-Magnus Malcolm	• Send in the Clowns (reprise) — Desiree Armfeldt, Fredrik Egerman
• Every Day a Little Death — Countess Charlotte Malcolm and Anne Egerman	• Last Waltz — Orchestra
• Weekend in the Country — Company	

Additional musical numbers

Stage:

• Two Fairy Tales — Henrik and Anne Egerman (cut for time)
• Silly People — Frid (cut for time)
• Bang! — Count Carl-Magnus Malcolm (replaced by 'In Praise of Women')
• My Husband the Pig — Countess Charlotte Malcolm (replaced by the second half of 'In Praise of Women')

Screen:

- Love Takes Time - Company (lyrics added to Night Waltz)
- The Glamorous Life - Fredrika (solo version)

Characters

- **Fredrik Egerman**: A successful widowed middle-aged lawyer. He is married to the 18-year-old Anne and has one son from his previous marriage, Henrik.
- **Anne Egerman**: Fredrik's new, naive wife.
- **Henrik Egerman**: Fredrik's son, 20 years old and Anne's stepson. He is serious but confused, as he reads the works of philosophers and theologians as he studies for the Lutheran priesthood.
- **Petra**: Anne's maid and closest confidante.
- **Desiree Armfeldt**: Self-absorbed, once-successful actress, now touring the country-side in what is clearly not the "glamorous life".
- **Fredrika Armfeldt**: Desiree's thirteen-year-old daughter, who may or may not be the product (unbeknownst to Fredrik) of the actress's and Fredrik's affair.
- **Madame Armfeldt**: Desiree's mother, who has had "liaisons" with royalty.
- **Count Carl-Magnus Malcolm**: A military dragoon who is Desiree's latest lover.
- **Charlotte Malcolm**: Carl-Magnus' wife.
- **Frid**: Madame Armfeldt's manservant.
- **The Quintet**: Mr. Lindquist, Mrs. Nordstrom, Mrs. Anderssen, Mr. Erlanson and Mrs. Segstrom. A group of five singers that act as a Greek chorus. Sometimes referred to as the Liebeslieder Singers although Sondheim and Wheeler did not script them to have that title, using Quintet instead. The first usage of Liebeslieders for the Quintet came during the 1990 New York Opera production. Prince said that these characters represent "people in the show who aren't wasting time ... the play is about wasting time."
- **Malla**: Desiree's maid, with her constantly

[1]

Productions

Original Broadway production

A Little Night Music opened on Broadway at the Shubert Theatre on February 25, 1973, and closed on August 3, 1974 after 601 performances and 12 previews. It moved to the Majestic Theatre on September 17, 1973 where it completed its run. It was directed by Harold Prince with choreography by Patricia Birch and design by Boris Aronson. The cast included Glynis Johns (Desiree Armfeldt), Len Cariou (Fredrik Egerman), Hermione Gingold (Madame Armfeldt), Victoria Mallory, Judith Kahan, Mark Lambert, Laurence Guittard, Patricia Elliott, George Lee Andrews, and D. Jamin Bartlett. It won the New York Drama Critics' Circle Award and the Tony Award for Best Musical.

United States tour

A US national tour began on February 26, 1974 at the Forrest Theatre, Philadelphia, and ended on February 13, 1975 at the Shubert Theatre, Boston. Jean Simmons as Desiree Armfeldt, George Lee Andrews as Fredrik Egerman and Margaret Hamilton as Madame Armfeldt headed the cast.[2]

West End premiere

The musical premiered in the West End at the Adelphi Theatre on April 15, 1975 and starred Jean Simmons, Joss Ackland, David Kernan, Liz Robertson, and Diane Langton, with Hermione Gingold reprising her role as Madame Armfeldt. It ran for 406 performances. During the run, Angela Baddeley replaced Gingold, and Virginia McKenna replaced Simmons.

1989 West End revival

A revival opened in the West End on October 6, 1989 at the Piccadilly Theatre, directed by Ian Judge, designed by Mark Thompson, and choreographed by Anthony Van Laast. It starred Lila Kedrova as Madame Armfeldt, Dorothy Tutin as Desiree Armfeldt, Peter McEnery as Fredrick, and Susan Hampshire. The production ran for 144 performances, closing on February 17, 1990.

1995 London revival

A revival by the Royal National Theatre opened at the Olivier Theatre on September 26, 1995. It was directed by Sean Mathias, with set design by Stephen Brimson Lewis, costumes by Nicky Gillibrand, lighting by Mark Henderson and choreography by Wayne McGregor. It starred Judi Dench (Desiree), Siân Phillips (Madame Armfeldt), Joanna Riding (Anne Egerman), Laurence Guittard (Fredrik Egerman), Patricia Hodge (Countess Charlotte) and Issy van Randwyck (Petra). The production closed on August 31, 1996. Dench received the Olivier Award for Best Actress in a Musical.[3]

2008 London revival

The third London revival ran at the Menier Chocolate Factory from November 22, 2008 until March 8, 2009. The production was directed by Trevor Nunn, with choreography by Lynne Page, sets and costumes by David Farley and new orchestrations by Jason Carr. The cast included Hannah Waddingham as Desiree, Alexander Hanson as Frederik, Jessie Buckley (Anne), Maureen Lipman (Mme. Armfeldt), Alistair Robins (the Count), Gabriel Vick (Henrik), Grace Link and Holly Hallam (shared role Fredrika) and Kasia Hammarlund (Petra).[4] This critically acclaimed[5][6][7] production transferred to the Garrick Theatre in the West End for a limited season, opening on March 28, 2009 running until July 25, 2009.[8] This production transferred to Broadway on December 13, 2009, starring Catherine Zeta-Jones as Desiree and Angela Lansbury as Madame Armfeldt. Alexander Hanson again played Frederik.

2009 Broadway revival

The 2008 Menier Chocolate Factory production opened on Broadway at the Walter Kerr Theatre in previews on November 24, 2009 and officially on December 13, 2009, with the same creative team. The original cast starred Angela Lansbury as Madame Armfeldt and, in her Broadway debut, Catherine Zeta-Jones as Desiree. Also featured were Alexander Hanson as Frederik,[9] Ramona Mallory as Anne, Hunter Ryan Herdlicka as Henrik, Leigh Ann Larkin as Petra, Erin Davie as the Countess, Aaron Lazar as the Count, and Bradley Dean as Frid. Zeta-Jones won the Tony for Best Leading Actress in a Musical for 2010.[10]

The production temporarily closed on June 20, 2010 when the contracts of Zeta-Jones and Lansbury ended and resumed on July 13, with new stars Bernadette Peters as Desiree Armfeldt and Elaine Stritch as Madame

Armfeldt.[11][12] In an interview, Peters said that Sondheim had "proposed the idea to her this spring and urged the producers of the revival to cast her."[13] Trevor Nunn directed rehearsals with the two new stars, and the rest of the original cast remained.[14][15] Peters and Stritch extended their contracts until January 9, 2011, when the production closed with 20 previews and 425 regular performances.[16] Before the production closed it recouped its initial investment.[17]

Europe

Zarah Leander played Madame Armfeldt in the original Austrian staging (in 1975) as well as in the original Swedish staging in Stockholm in 1978 (here with Jan Malmsjö as Fredrik Egerman), performing *Send In The Clowns* and *Liaisons* in both stagings. The successful Stockholm-staging was directed by Stig Olin. In 2010 the musical was scheduled to return to Stockholm and the Stockholm Stadsteater. The cast included Pia Johansson, Dan Ekborg, Yvonne Lombard and Thérèse Andersson.

The Théâtre du Châtelet, Paris production ran from February 15, 2010 through February 20, 2010. Lee Blakeley directed and Andrew George was the choreographer.[18] Italian-born actress Greta Scacchi played Désirée, and Leslie Caron played Madame Armfeldt.[19]

Opera companies

The musical has also become part of the repertoire of a few opera companies. Michigan Opera Theatre was the first major American opera company to present the work in 1983, and again in November 2009. Light Opera Works (Evanston, IL) produced the work in August 1983. New York City Opera staged it in 1990, 1991 and 2003, the Houston Grand Opera in 1999, and the Los Angeles Opera in 2004. New York City Opera's production in August 1990 and July 1991 (total of 18 performances) won the 1990 Drama Desk Award for Outstanding Revival and was telecast on the PBS show "Live at Lincoln Center" on November 7, 1990. The cast included both stage performers: Sally Ann Howes and George Lee Andrews as Desiree and Frederick and opera regular Regina Resnik as Madame Armfeldt (in 1991).[20] The 2003 production featured a young Anna Kendrick as Fredrika Armfeldt, alongside Jeremy Irons as Frederick and Marc Kudisch as Carl-Magnus.[21]

Opera Australia presented the piece in Melbourne in May 2009, starring Sigrid Thornton as Desiree Armfeldt and Nacye Hayes as Madame Armfeldt. The production returned in 2010 at the Sydney Opera House with Anthony Warlow taking on the role of Fredrik Egerman. The production was directed by Stuart Maunder, designed by Roger Kirk, and conducted by Andrew Greene.[22] Opera Theatre of Saint Louis performed the musical in June 2010. Designer Isaac Mizrahi directed and designed the production, with a cast that starred Amy Irving, Siân Phillips, and Ron Raines.[23]

The piece has also become a popular choice for amateur musical theatre and light opera companies.

Film adaptation

In 1977, a film version of *A Little Night Music* was released, starring Elizabeth Taylor, Lesley-Anne Down and Diana Rigg, with Len Cariou, Hermione Gingold and Laurence Guittard reprising their Broadway roles. The setting for the film was moved from Sweden to Austria. Stephen Sondheim wrote lyrics for the "Night Waltz" theme ("Love Takes Time") and wrote an entirely new version of "The Glamorous Life", which has been incorporated into several subsequent productions of the stage musical. However, other songs, including "In Praise of Women", "The Miller's Son" and "Liaisons", were cut and remain heard only as background orchestrations. The film marked Broadway director Hal Prince's second time as a motion picture director. Critical reaction to the film was mostly negative, with much being made of Taylor's wildly fluctuating weight from scene to scene.[24] Some critics talked more positively of the film, with *Variety* calling it "an elegant looking, period romantic charade".[25] There was praise for Diana Rigg's performance, and orchestrator Jonathan Tunick received an Oscar for his work on the score. A soundtrack recording was released on LP, and a DVD release was issued in June 2007.[26]

Music analysis

The score for *A Little Night Music* has elements not often found in musical theater, presenting challenges for performers, with complex meters, pitch changes, polyphony, and high notes for both males and females. The difficulty is heightened when songs merge, as in "Now"/"Later"/"Soon", because all three have to be performed in the same key, limiting the ability to pick a comfortable key for each singer. Critic Rex Reed noted that "The score of 'Night Music' ...contains patter songs, contrapuntal duets and trios, a quartet, and even a dramatic double quintet to puzzle through. All this has been gorgeously orchestrated by Jonathan Tunick; there is no rhythm section, only strings and woodwinds to carry the melodies and harmonies aloft."[27]

Sondheim's engagement with threes extends to his lyrics. He organizes trios with the singers separated, while his duets are sung together, about a third person.[28]

Another of the show's signature elements is that many songs end on a single brief note played by one or more instruments.

The work is performed as an operetta in many professional opera companies. For example, it was added to the New York City Opera Company repertoire in 1990.[29]

3/4 time

Virtually all of the music in the show is written in waltz time (3/4). Some parts adopt compound meter, with a time signature such as 12/8.[28] Passages in "Overture", "Glamorous Life", "Liaisons", and "The Miller's Son" are in duple meter.[30]

Counterpoint and polyphony

At several points, Sondheim has multiple performers each sing a different song simultaneously. This use of counterpoint maintains coherence even as it extends the notion of a round, familiar in songs such as the traditional "Frère Jacques", into something more complex. Sondheim said: "As for the three songs... going together well, I might as well confess. In those days I was just getting into contrapuntal and choral writing...and I wanted to develop my technique by writing a trio. What I didn't want to do is the quodlibet method...wouldn't it be nice to have three songs you don't think are going to go together, and they do go together... The trick was the little vamp on "Soon" which has five-and six-note chords."[31] Steve Swayne comments that the "contrapuntal episodes in the extended ensembles... stand as testament to his interest in Counterpoint."[31]

"Send In The Clowns"

The show's best-known and Sondheim's biggest hit song was almost an afterthought, written several days before the start of out of town tryouts.[32] Sondheim initially conceived Desiree as a role for a more-or-less non-singing actress. When he discovered that the original Desiree, Glynis Johns, was able to sing (she had a "small, silvery voice"[33]) but could not "sustain a phrase", he devised the song "Send in the Clowns" for her in a way that would work around her vocal weakness, e.g., by ending lines with consonants that made for a short cut-off.[33] "It is written in short phrases in order to be acted rather than sung...tailor-made for Glynis Johns, who lacks the vocal power to sustain long phrases."[34]

In analyzing the text of the song, Max Cryer wrote that it "is not intended to be sung by the young in love, but by a mature performer who has seen it all before. The song remains an anthem to regret for unwise decisions in the past and recognition that there's no need to send in the clowns-they're already here."[35]

Influences

There is a Mozart reference in the title—*A Little Night Music* is an occasionally used translation of *Eine kleine Nachtmusik*, the nickname of Mozart's Serenade No. 13 for strings in G major, K. 525. The elegant, harmonically-advanced music in this musical pays indirect homage to the compositions of Maurice Ravel, especially his *Valses nobles et sentimentales*[36] (whose opening chord is "borrowed" for the opening chord of the song "Liaisons"); part of this effect stems from the style of orchestration that Jonathan Tunick used.

Cast recordings

In addition to the original Broadway and London cast recordings, and the motion picture soundtrack (no longer available), there are recordings of the 1990 studio cast, the 1995 Royal National Theatre revival (starring Judi Dench), and the 2001 Barcelona cast recording sung in Catalan. In 1997 an all-jazz version of the score was recorded by Terry Trotter.[37]

The 2009 Broadway revival with Catherine Zeta-Jones and Angela Lansbury recorded a cast album on January 4, 2010 which was released on April 6.[38]

Critical response

In his review of the original 1973 Broadway production, Clive Barnes in the *New York Times* called the musical "heady, civilized, sophisticated and enchanting." He noted that "the real triumph belongs to Stephen Sondheim...the music is a celebration of 3/4 time, an orgy of plaintively memorable waltzes, all talking of past loves and lost worlds...There is a peasant touch here." He commented that the lyrics are "breathtaking".[39]

In its review of the 1989 London revival, the reviewer for *The Guardian* wrote that the "production also strikes me as infinitely superior to Harold Prince's 1975 version at the Adelphi. Mr Judge's great innovation is to transform the Liebeslieder Singers from the evening-dressed, after-dinner line-up into 18th century ghosts weaving in and out of the action...But Mr Judge's other great realisation is that, in Sondheim, the lyrics are not an adornment to a song but their very essence: understand them and the show will flow. Thus Dorothy Tutin as Desiree, the touring thesp eventually reunited with her quondam lover, is not the melting romantic of previous productions but a working mother with the sharpness of a hat-pin."[40]

The *Independent* review of the 1995 National Theatre revival praised the production, writing "For three hours of gloriously barbed bliss and bewitchment, Sean Mathias's production establishes the show as a minor miracle of astringent worldly wisdom and one that is haunted by less earthy intimations." The review went on to state that "The heart of the production, in both senses, is Judi Dench's superb Desiree Armfeldt...Her husky-voiced rendering of "Send in the Clowns" is the most moving I've ever heard."[41]

In reviewing the 2008 Menier Chocolate Factory production, *The Telegraph* reviewer wrote that "Sondheim's lyrics are often superbly witty, his music here, mostly in haunting waltz-time, far more accessible than is sometimes the case. The score positively throbs with love, regret and desire." But of the specific production, the reviewer went on to note: "But Nunn's production, on one of those hermetic sets largely consisting of doors and tarnished mirrors that have become such a cliché in recent years, never penetrates the work's subtly erotic heart. And as is often the case with this director's work, the pace is so slow and the mood so reverent, that initial enchantment gives way to bored fidgeting."[7]

In his *New York Times* review of the 2009 Broadway production, Ben Brantley noted that "the expression that hovers over Trevor Nunn's revival...feels dangerously close to a smirk...It is a smirk shrouded in shadows. An elegiac darkness infuses this production." The production is "sparing on furniture and heavy on shadows", with "a scaled-down orchestra at lugubriously slowed-down tempos..." He goes on to write that "this somber, less-is-more approach could be effective were the ensemble plugged into the same rueful sensibility. But there is only one moment in this production when all its elements cohere perfectly. That moment, halfway through the first act, belongs to Ms. Lansbury, who has hitherto been perfectly entertaining, playing Madame Armfeldt with the overripe aristocratic condescension of a Lady Bracknell. Then comes her one solo, "Liaisons", in which her character thinks back on the art of love as a profession in a gilded age, when sex 'was but a pleasurable means to a measurable end.' Her face, with its glamour-gorgon makeup, softens, as Madame Armfeldt seems to melt into memory itself, and the wan stage light briefly appears to borrow radiance from her. It's a lovely example of the past reaching out to the present..."[42]

Steven Suskin, reviewing the new Broadway cast for *Variety*, wrote "What a difference a diva makes. Bernadette Peters steps into the six-month-old revival of 'A Little Night Music' with a transfixing performance, playing it as if she realizes her character's onstage billing -- "the one and only Desiree Armfeldt"—is cliched hyperbole. By figuratively rolling her eyes at the hype, Peters gives us a rich, warm and comedically human Desiree, which reaches full impact when she pierces the facade with a nakedly honest, tears-on-cheek 'Send in the Clowns.'"[43]

Awards and nominations

Original Broadway production

Year	Award Ceremony	Category	Nominee	Result
1973	Drama Desk Award	Outstanding Book of a Musical	Hugh Wheeler	Won
		Outstanding Music	Stephen Sondheim	Won
		Outstanding Lyrics		Won
		Outstanding Actress in a Musical	Glynis Johns	Nominated
			Patricia Elliott	Won
		Outstanding Director	Harold Prince	Won
		Most Promising Performer	D'Jamin Bartlett	Won
	Grammy Award	Best Musical Show Album		Won
	Theatre World Award		Laurence Guittard	Won
			Patricia Elliott	Won
			D'Jamin Bartlett	Won
	Tony Award	Best Musical		Won
		Best Book of a Musical	Hugh Wheeler	Won
		Best Original Score	Stephen Sondheim	Won
		Best Performance by a Leading Actor in a Musical	Len Cariou	Nominated
		Best Performance by a Leading Actress in a Musical	Glynis Johns	Won
		Best Performance by a Featured Actor in a Musical	Laurence Guittard	Nominated
		Best Performance by a Featured Actress in a Musical	Patricia Elliott	Won
			Hermione Gingold	Nominated
		Best Costume Design	Florence Klotz	Won
		Best Scenic Design	Boris Aronson	Nominated
		Best Lighting Design	Tharon Musser	Nominated
		Best Direction of a Musical	Harold Prince	Nominated

1995 London revival

Year	Award Ceremony	Category	Nominee	Result
1995	Laurence Olivier Award	Best Actress in a Musical	Judi Dench	Won
		Best Performance in a Supporting Role in a Musical	Siân Phillips	Nominated
		Best Theatre Choreographer	Wayne McGregor	Nominated
		Best Costume Design	Nicky Gillibrand	Nominated

2009 Broadway revival

Year	Award Ceremony	Category	Nominee	Result
2010	Drama Desk Award	Outstanding Revival of a Musical		Nominated
		Outstanding Actress in a Musical	Catherine Zeta-Jones	Won
		Outstanding Featured Actress in a Musical	Angela Lansbury	Nominated
	Outer Critics Circle Award	Outstanding Revival of a Musical		Nominated
		Outstanding Actress in a Musical	Catherine Zeta-Jones	Won
		Outstanding Featured Actress in a Musical	Angela Lansbury	Nominated
	Tony Award	Best Revival of a Musical		Nominated
		Best Performance by a Leading Actress in a Musical	Catherine Zeta-Jones	Won
		Best Performance by a Featured Actress in a Musical	Angela Lansbury	Nominated
		Best Sound Design	Dan Moses Schreier and Gareth Owen	Nominated
2011	Grammy Award[44]	Best Musical Show Album		Nominated

References

[1] Gussow, Mel, "Prince Revels in 'A Little Night Music'", *The New York Times*, p. 54, March 27, 1973

[2] "'A Little Night Music' tour, 1974" (http://www.sondheimguide.com/night.html#BWP) sondheimguide.com, accessed March 13, 2011

[3] "Olivier Winners 1996" (http://www.officiallondontheatre.co.uk/olivier_awards/past_winners/view/item98530/Olivier-Winners-1996/) officiallondontheatre.co.uk, retrieved June 14, 2010

[4] Benedict, David. "Waddingham to star in 'Night Music'" (http://www.variety.com/article/VR1117993701.html?categoryid=15&cs=1), *Variety*, October 10, 2008

[5] (http://www.nightmusiclondon.com/news_and_reviews/) nightmusiclondon.com

[6] Nightingale, Benedict. "'A Little Night Music' at the Menier Chocolate Factory, London SE1" (http://entertainment.timesonline.co.uk/tol/arts_and_entertainment/stage/theatre/article5289255.ece) December 5, 2008

[7] Spencer, Charles. "'A Little Night Music' at the Menier Chocolate Factory" (http://www.telegraph.co.uk/culture/theatre/drama/3687085/A-Little-Night-Music-at-the-Menier-Chocolate-Factory.html)*The Telegraph*, December 4, 2008

[8] Shenton, Mark. "Isn't It Rich?: Menier 'A Little Night Music' Arrives in the West End March 28" (http://www.playbill.com/news/article/127812.html), playbill.com, March 28, 2009

[9] Hernandez, Ernio and Gans, Andrew. "A Little Night Music, With Zeta-Jones and Lansbury, Begins on Broadway" (http://www.playbill.com/news/article/134767-A-Little-Night-Music-With-Zeta-Jones-and-Lansbury-Begins-on-Broadway). Playbill.com, November 24, 2009

[10] "Tony Award nominees, 2009-2010" (http://www.tonyawards.com/en_US/nominees/index.html). . Retrieved May 13, 2010.

[11] Gans, Andrew. "'Isn't It Bliss?' Bernadette Peters and Elaine Stritch Open in Night Music Revival Aug. 1 (http://www.playbill.com/news/article/141676-Isnt-It-Bliss-Bernadette-Peters-and-Elaine-Stritch-Open-in-Night-Music-Revival-Aug-1). Playbill, August 1, 2010

[12] McBride, Walter. "Photo Coverage: Bernadette Peters and Elaine Stritch Open in 'A Little Night Music'" (http://www.broadwayworld.com/article/Photo_Coverage_Bernadette_Peters_and_Elaine_Stritch_Open_in_A_LITTLE_NIGHT_MUSIC_20100714). Broadwayworld.com, July 14, 2010

[13] Healy, Patrick. "Peters, Stritch To Join 'Night Music' Cast" (http://artsbeat.blogs.nytimes.com/2010/06/07/peters-stritch-to-join-night-music-cast/). *The New York Times*, June 7, 2010

[14] Rizzo, Frank. "Elaine Stritch: She's Still Here – in West Hartford" (http://www.courant.com/features/ hc-rizzo-ticker-0610-20100610,0,1197922.column). *The Hartford Courant*, June 10, 2010

[15] "A Little Night Music Sets Closing Date; Peters and Stritch Extend" (http://www.broadway.com/shows/little-night-music/buzz/153809/ a-little-night-music-sets-closing-date-peters-and-stritch-extend/). Broadway.com

[16] Gans, Andrew. "Bernadette Peters and Elaine Stritch Extend Run in Broadway's A Little Night Music" (http://www.playbill.com/news/ article/143644-Bernadette-Peters-and-Elaine-Stritch-Extend-Run-in-Broadways-A-Little-Night-Music). Playbill.com, October 5, 2010

[17] Gans, Andrew. Broadway's A Little Night Music, with Bernadette Peters and Elaine Stritch, Recoups" (http://www.playbill.com/news/ article/146428-Broadways-A-Little-Night-Music-with-Bernadette-Peters-and-Elaine-Stritch-Recoups). Playbill, January 6, 2011

[18] Gans, Andrew and Jones, Kenneth. "Kristin Scott Thomas and Leslie Caron to Star in 'A Little Night Music' in France" (http://www. playbill.com/news/article/130840-Kristin_Scott_Thomas_and_Leslie_Caron_to_Star_in_A_Little_Night_Music_in_France) playbill.com, July 6, 2009

[19] Hetrick, Adam. "Scacchi and Caron Sing 'A Little Night Music' in Paris Beginning Feb. 15" (http://www.playbill.com/news/article/ 136884-Scacchi-and-Caron-Sing-A-Little-Night-Music-in-Paris-Beginning-Feb-15) playbill.com, February 15, 2010

[20] 1990 New York City Opera Production (http://www.sondheimguide.com/night.html#1990NYCO) sondheimguide.com, accessed October 21, 2012

[21] 2003 New York City Opera Production (http://www.sondheimguide.com/night.html#2003NYCO) sondheimguide.com, accessed October 21, 2012

[22] *A Little Night Music* (http://www.opera-australia.org.au/scripts/nc.dll?OPRA:PRODUCTION:0:pc=PC_90107), Opera Australia

[23] Hetrick, Adam. "Mizrahi-Helmed 'Night Music', with Irving, Phillips and Raines, Opens in St. Louis" (http://www.playbill.com/news/ article/140075-Mizrahi-Helmed-Night-Music-with-Irving-Phillips-and-Raines-Opens-in-St-Louis). Playbill.com, June 6, 2010

[24] Canby, Vincent. "Review: A Little Night Music (1977)" (http://movies.nytimes.com/movie/ review?res=9E0CEEDA1F3EE632A2575BC0A9659C946990D6CF), *The New York Times*, March 8, 1978

[25] (http://www.variety.com/review/VE1117792646.html?categoryid=31&cs=1) variety.com

[26] *A Little Night Music* (http://www.imdb.com/title/tt0076319/) at the Internet Movie Database

[27] Deutsch, Didier C. "'A Little Night Music' Liner Notes, Song List and Synopsis" (http://www.masterworksbroadway.com/music/ a-little-night-music) masterworksbroadway.com, retrieved June 9, 2010

[28] Sondheim, Stephen; Prince, Hal; Tunick, Neal (November 30, 1973). *A Little Night Music (Libretto)* (http://books.google.com/ books?id=90jK8A_nzqUC&dq=A+Little+Night+Music&printsec=frontcover#v=onepage&q=&f=false). . Retrieved December 2009.

[29] Green, Kay. "Broadway Musicals, Show By Show" (1996). Hal Leonard Corporation. ISBN 0-7935-7750-0, p. 237

[30] Citron, p. 204

[31] Swayne, Steve. *How Sondheim Found His Sound*, University of Michigan Press, 2007, ISBN 0-472-03229-1, p. 251

[32] Citron, p. 207

[33] Secrest, Meryle. "Stephen Sondheim: A Life" (1998). Dell Publishing. ISBN 0-385-33412-5, pp. 251-252

[34] Sondheim, S., Shevelove, B., Gelbart, L., Wheeler, H., and Lapine, J. "Four by Sondheim, Wheeler, Lapine, Shevelove and Gelbart" (2000). Hal Leonard Corporation. ISBN 1-55783-407-5, p. 170

[35] Cryer, Max. *Love Me Tender: The Stories Behind the World's Best-loved Frances Lincoln Ltd, 2008, ISBN 0-7112-2911-2, p. 171*

[36] Citron, Stephen. pp. 200, 203

[37] "Recordings, 'A Little Night Music'" (http://www.sondheimguide.com/nightrecs.html) sondheimguide.com, retrieved June 8, 2010

[38] Hetrick, Adam and Jones, Kenneth. "'A Little Night Music' CD Released April 6; Sondheim and Co. Host Signing" (http://www.playbill. com/news/article/138450-A-Little-Night-Music-CD-Released-April-6-Sondheim-and-Co-Host-Signing) playbill.com, April 6, 2010

[39] Barnes, Clive, "The Theater:'A Little Night Music", *The New York Times*, February 26, 1973, p. 26

[40] Billington, Michael. "Arts: Night of the short memories - 'A Little Night Music'", *The Guardian* (London)., October 23, 1989 (no page number)

[41] Taylor, Paul and Seckerson, Edward. "Double Take: Reviews: 'A Little Night Music'" (http://www.independent.co.uk/life-style/ double-take-reviews-a-little-night-music-1603205.html)*Independent', September 1995*

[42] Brantley, Ben. "A Weekend in the Country With Eros and Thanatos" (http://theater.nytimes.com/2009/12/14/theater/reviews/14little. htm) *The New York Times*, December 14, 2009

[43] Suskin, Steven. "'A Little Night Music' Review", *Variety*, August 2, 2010

[44] Gans, Andrew. "Idiot, Fela!, Night Music, Promises and Sondheim Are Grammy-Nominated" (http://www.playbill.com/news/article/ 145450-Idiot-Fela-Night-Music-Promises-and-Sondheim-Are-Grammy-Nominated) playbill.com, December 1, 2010

Bibliography

- Citron, Stephen. "Sondheim and Lloyd-Webber: The New Musical" (2001). Oxford University Press US. ISBN 0-19-509601-0

External links

- *A Little Night Music* (http://www.ibdb.com/show.asp?id=1162) at the Internet Broadway Database
- *A Little Night Music* on The Stephen Sondheim Reference Guide (http://www.sondheimguide.com/night.html)
- MTI Shows (http://www.mtishows.com/show_home.asp?ID=000048)
- A Little Night Music info page on StageAgent.com (http://stageagent.com/Shows/View/735) - A Little Night Music plot summary & character descriptions
- Little Night Music (http://www.nightmusiconbroadway.com"A) - A Little Night Music Broadway Revival

Academy Award for Best Actress

Academy Award for Best Actress	
Awarded for	Best Performance by an Actress in a Leading Role
Presented by	Academy of Motion Picture Arts and Sciences
Country	United States
Currently held by	Meryl Streep, *The Iron Lady* (2011)
Official website	http://www.oscars.org

Performance by an Actress in a Leading Role is one of the Academy Awards of merit presented annually by the Academy of Motion Picture Arts and Sciences (AMPAS) to recognize an actress who has delivered an outstanding performance while working within the film industry. Prior to the 49th Academy Awards ceremony (1976), this award was known as the Academy Award of Merit for Performance by an Actress. Since its inception, however, the award has commonly been referred to as the Oscar for **Best Actress**. While actresses are nominated for this award by Academy members who are actors and actresses themselves, winners are selected by the Academy membership as a whole.

History

Throughout the past 84 years, accounting for ties and repeat winners, AMPAS has presented a total of 85 Best Actress awards to 70 different actresses. Winners of this Academy Award of Merit receive the familiar Oscar statuette, depicting a gold-plated knight holding a crusader's sword and standing on a reel of film. The first recipient was Janet Gaynor, who was honored at the 1st Academy Awards ceremony (1929) for her performances in *Seventh Heaven*, *Street Angel*, and *Sunrise*. The most recent recipient was Meryl Streep, who was honored at the 84th Academy Awards ceremony (2012) for her performance in *The Iron Lady*.

In the first three years of the Academy Awards, individuals such as actors and directors were nominated as the best in their categories. Then all of their work during the qualifying period (as many as three films, in some cases) was listed after the award. However, during the 3rd Academy Awards ceremony (1930), only one of those films was cited in each winner's final award, even though each of the acting winners had had two films following their names on the ballots. For the 4th Academy Awards ceremony (1931), this unwieldy and confusing system was replaced by the current system in which an actress is nominated for a specific performance in a single film. Such nominations are limited to five per year. Until the 8th Academy Awards ceremony (1936), nominations for the Best Actress award were intended to include all actresses, whether the performance was in either a leading or supporting role. At the 9th Academy Awards ceremony (1937), however, the Best Supporting Actress category was specifically introduced as a distinct award following complaints that the single Best Actress category necessarily favored leading performers with the most screen time. Currently, Performance by an Actor in a Leading Role, Performance by an Actress in a Leading Role, Performance by an Actor in a Supporting Role, and Performance by an Actress in a Supporting Role constitute the four Academy Awards of Merit for acting annually presented by AMPAS.

Other awards for acting

Actors have also received special awards, or Academy Honorary Awards, for acting in specific films (such as in the case of James Baskett, who received a special honorary award for Disney's *Song of the South*). Child actors have also been awarded the Academy Juvenile Award.

Winners and nominees

Following the Academy's practice, the films below are listed by year of their Los Angeles qualifying run, which is usually (but not always) the film's year of release. For example, the Oscar for Best Actress of 1999 was announced during the award ceremony held in 2000.

For the first six ceremonies, the eligibility period spanned two calendar years. For example, the 2nd Academy Awards presented on April 3, 1930, recognized films that were released between August 1, 1928 and July 31, 1929. Starting with the 7th Academy Awards, held in 1935, the period of eligibility became the full previous calendar year from January 1 to December 31.

Winners are listed first in **bold**, followed by the other nominees.

1920s

Year	Actress	Film	Character
1927/28 (1st)	**Janet Gaynor**	***Seventh Heaven***	**Diane**
		Street Angel	**Angela**
		Sunrise	**The Wife – Indre**
	Louise Dresser	*A Ship Comes In*	Mrs. Pleznik
	Gloria Swanson	*Sadie Thompson*	Sadie Thompson
1928/29 (2nd)	**Mary Pickford**	***Coquette***	**Norma Besant**
	Ruth Chatterton	*Madame X*	Jacqueline Floriot
	Betty Compson	*The Barker*	Carrie
	Jeanne Eagels (posthumous nomination)	*The Letter*	Leslie Crosbie
	Corinne Griffith	*The Divine Lady*	Emma, Lady Hamilton
	Bessie Love	*The Broadway Melody*	Hank Mahoney

1930s

Year	Actress	Film	Character
1929/30 (3rd)	**Norma Shearer**	***The Divorcee***	**Jerry Bernard Martin**
	Nancy Carroll	*The Devil's Holiday*	Hallie Hobart
	Ruth Chatterton	*Sarah and Son*	Sarah Storm
	Greta Garbo	*Anna Christie*	Anna Christie
	Greta Garbo	*Romance*	Madame Rita Cavallini
	Norma Shearer	*Their Own Desire*	Lucia 'Lally' Marlett
	Gloria Swanson	*The Trespasser*	Marion Donnell
1930/31 (4th)	**Marie Dressler**	***Min and Bill***	**Min Divot, Innkeeper**
	Marlene Dietrich	*Morocco*	Mademoiselle Amy Jolly
	Irene Dunne	*Cimarron*	Sabra Cravat
	Ann Harding	*Holiday*	Linda Seton
	Norma Shearer	*A Free Soul*	Jan Ashe
1931/32 (5th)	**Helen Hayes**	***The Sin of Madelon Claudet***	**Madelon Claudet**
	Marie Dressler	*Emma*	Emma Thatcher Smith
	Lynn Fontanne	*The Guardsman*	The Actress
1932/33 (6th)	**Katharine Hepburn**	***Morning Glory***	**Eva Lovelace**
	May Robson (2nd)	*Lady for a Day*	Apple Annie
	Diana Wynyard (3rd)	*Cavalcade*	Jane Marryot
1934 (7th)	**Claudette Colbert**	***It Happened One Night***	**Ellie Andrews**
	Grace Moore	*One Night of Love*	Mary Barrett
	Norma Shearer (2nd)	*The Barretts of Wimpole Street*	Elizabeth Barrett
	Bette Davis (write-in) (3rd)	*Of Human Bondage*	Mildred Rogers
1935 (8th)	**Bette Davis**	***Dangerous***	**Joyce Heath**
	Elisabeth Bergner	*Escape Me Never*	Gemma Jones
	Claudette Colbert	*Private Worlds*	Dr. Jane Everest
	Katharine Hepburn (3rd)	*Alice Adams*	Alice Adams
	Miriam Hopkins (2nd)	*Becky Sharp*	Becky Sharp
	Merle Oberon	*The Dark Angel*	Kitty Vane
1936 (9th)	**Luise Rainer**	***The Great Ziegfeld***	**Anna Held**
	Irene Dunne	*Theodora Goes Wild*	Theodora Lynn
	Gladys George	*Valiant Is the Word for Carrie*	Carrie Snyder
	Carole Lombard	*My Man Godfrey*	Irene Bullock
	Norma Shearer	*Romeo and Juliet*	Juliet – Daughter to Capulet

1937 (10th)	Luise Rainer	*The Good Earth*	O-Lan
	Irene Dunne	*The Awful Truth*	Lucy Warriner
	Greta Garbo	*Camille*	Marguerite Gautier
	Janet Gaynor	*A Star Is Born*	Esther Victoria Blodgett, aka Vicki Lester
	Barbara Stanwyck	*Stella Dallas*	Stella Martin Dallas
1938 (11th)	**Bette Davis**	*Jezebel*	**Julie Marsden**
	Fay Bainter	*White Banners*	Hannah Parmalee
	Wendy Hiller	*Pygmalion*	Eliza Doolittle
	Norma Shearer	*Marie Antoinette*	Marie Antoinette
	Margaret Sullavan	*Three Comrades*	Patricia 'Pat' Hollmann
1939 (12th)	**Vivien Leigh**	*Gone with the Wind*	**Scarlett O'Hara**
	Bette Davis	*Dark Victory*	Judith Traherne
	Irene Dunne	*Love Affair*	Terry McKay
	Greta Garbo	*Ninotchka*	Nina Yakushova 'Ninotchka' Ivanoff
	Greer Garson	*Goodbye, Mr. Chips*	Katherine

1940s

Year	Actress	Film	Character
1940 (13th)	**Ginger Rogers**	*Kitty Foyle*	**Kitty Foyle**
	Bette Davis	*The Letter*	Leslie Crosbie
	Joan Fontaine	*Rebecca*	The Second Mrs. de Winter
	Katharine Hepburn	*The Philadelphia Story*	Tracy Lord
	Martha Scott	*Our Town*	Emily Webb
1941 (14th)	**Joan Fontaine**	*Suspicion*	**Lina McLaidlaw Aysgarth**
	Bette Davis	*The Little Foxes*	Regina Giddens
	Olivia de Havilland	*Hold Back the Dawn*	Emmy Brown
	Greer Garson	*Blossoms in the Dust*	Edna Gladney
	Barbara Stanwyck	*Ball of Fire*	Katherine 'Sugarpuss' O'Shea
1942 (15th)	**Greer Garson**	*Mrs. Miniver*	**Kay Miniver**
	Bette Davis	*Now, Voyager*	Charlotte Vale
	Katharine Hepburn	*Woman of the Year*	Tess Harding
	Rosalind Russell	*My Sister Eileen*	Ruth Sherwood
	Teresa Wright	*The Pride of the Yankees*	Eleanor Twitchell Gehrig

1943 (16th)	**Jennifer Jones**	*The Song of Bernadette*	**Bernadette Soubirous**
	Jean Arthur	*The More the Merrier*	Constance "Connie" Milligan
	Ingrid Bergman	*For Whom the Bell Tolls*	María
	Joan Fontaine	*The Constant Nymph*	Tessa Sanger
	Greer Garson	*Madame Curie*	Marie Curie
1944 (17th)	**Ingrid Bergman**	*Gaslight*	**Paula Alquist Anton**
	Claudette Colbert	*Since You Went Away*	Anne Hilton
	Bette Davis	*Mr. Skeffington*	Fanny Trellis
	Greer Garson	*Mrs. Parkington*	Susie 'Sparrow' Parkington
	Barbara Stanwyck	*Double Indemnity*	Phyllis Dietrichson
1945 (18th)	**Joan Crawford**	*Mildred Pierce*	**Mildred Pierce Beragon**
	Ingrid Bergman	*The Bells of St. Mary's*	Sister Mary Benedict
	Greer Garson	*The Valley of Decision*	Mary Rafferty
	Jennifer Jones	*Love Letters*	Singleton
	Gene Tierney	*Leave Her to Heaven*	Ellen Berent Harland
1946 (19th)	**Olivia de Havilland**	*To Each His Own*	**Josephine 'Jody' Norris**
	Celia Johnson	*Brief Encounter*	Laura Jesson
	Jennifer Jones	*Duel in the Sun*	Pearl Chavez
	Rosalind Russell	*Sister Kenny*	Elizabeth Kenny
	Jane Wyman	*The Yearling*	Orry Baxter
1947 (20th)	**Loretta Young**	*The Farmer's Daughter*	**Katie Holstrom**
	Joan Crawford	*Possessed*	Louise Howell
	Susan Hayward	*Smash-Up, the Story of a Woman*	Angelica Evans Conway
	Dorothy McGuire	*Gentleman's Agreement*	Kathy Lacy
	Rosalind Russell	*Mourning Becomes Electra*	Lavinia Mannon
1948 (21st)	**Jane Wyman**	*Johnny Belinda*	**Belinda McDonald**
	Ingrid Bergman	*Joan of Arc*	Joan of Arc
	Olivia de Havilland	*The Snake Pit*	Virginia Stuart Cunningham
	Irene Dunne	*I Remember Mama*	Martha Hanson
	Barbara Stanwyck	*Sorry, Wrong Number*	Leona Stevenson
1949 (22nd)	**Olivia de Havilland**	*The Heiress*	**Catherine Sloper**
	Jeanne Crain	*Pinky*	Patricia 'Pinky' Johnson
	Susan Hayward	*My Foolish Heart*	Eloise Winters
	Deborah Kerr	*Edward, My Son*	Evelyn Boult
	Loretta Young	*Come to the Stable*	Sister Margaret

1950s

Year	Actress	Film	Character
1950 (23rd)	**Judy Holliday**	***Born Yesterday***	**Emma 'Billie' Dawn**
	Anne Baxter	*All About Eve*	Eve Harrington
	Bette Davis	*All About Eve*	Margo Channing
	Eleanor Parker	*Caged*	Marie Allen
	Gloria Swanson	*Sunset Boulevard*	Norma Desmond
1951 (24th)	**Vivien Leigh**	***A Streetcar Named Desire***	**Blanche DuBois**
	Katharine Hepburn	*The African Queen*	Rose Sayer
	Eleanor Parker	*Detective Story*	Mary McLeod
	Shelley Winters	*A Place in the Sun*	Alice Tripp
	Jane Wyman	*The Blue Veil*	Louise Mason
1952 (25th)	**Shirley Booth**	***Come Back, Little Sheba***	**Lola Delaney**
	Joan Crawford	*Sudden Fear*	Myra Hudson
	Bette Davis	*The Star*	Margaret Elliot
	Julie Harris	*The Member of the Wedding*	Frances 'Frankie' Addams
	Susan Hayward	*With a Song in My Heart*	Jane Froman
1953 (26th)	**Audrey Hepburn**	***Roman Holiday***	**Princess Ann**
	Leslie Caron	*Lili*	Lili Daurier
	Ava Gardner	*Mogambo*	Eloise "Honey Bear" Kelly
	Deborah Kerr	*From Here to Eternity*	Karen Holmes
	Maggie McNamara	*The Moon Is Blue*	Patty O'Neill
1954 (27th)	**Grace Kelly**	***The Country Girl***	**Georgie Elgin**
	Dorothy Dandridge	*Carmen Jones*	Carmen Jones
	Judy Garland	*A Star Is Born*	Vicki Lester / Esther Blodgett
	Audrey Hepburn	*Sabrina*	Sabrina Fairchild
	Jane Wyman	*Magnificent Obsession*	Helen Phillips
1955 (28th)	**Anna Magnani**	***The Rose Tattoo***	**Serafina Delle Rose**
	Susan Hayward	*I'll Cry Tomorrow*	Lillian Roth
	Katharine Hepburn	*Summertime*	Jane Hudson
	Jennifer Jones	*Love Is a Many-Splendored Thing*	Dr. Han Suyin
	Eleanor Parker	*Interrupted Melody*	Marjorie 'Margie' Lawrence

1956 (29th)	**Ingrid Bergman**	*Anastasia*	**Anna Koreff / Anastasia**
	Carroll Baker	*Baby Doll*	Baby Doll Meighan
	Katharine Hepburn	*The Rainmaker*	Lizzie Curry
	Nancy Kelly	*The Bad Seed*	Christine Penmark
	Deborah Kerr	*The King and I*	Anna Leonowens
1957 (30th)	**Joanne Woodward**	*The Three Faces of Eve*	**Eve White / Eve Black / Jane**
	Deborah Kerr	*Heaven Knows, Mr. Allison*	Sister Angela
	Anna Magnani	*Wild Is the Wind*	Gioia
	Elizabeth Taylor	*Raintree County*	Susanna Drake
	Lana Turner	*Peyton Place*	Constance MacKenzie
1958 (31st)	**Susan Hayward**	*I Want to Live!*	**Barbara Graham**
	Deborah Kerr	*Separate Tables*	Sibyl Railton-Bell
	Shirley MacLaine	*Some Came Running*	Ginnie Moorehead
	Rosalind Russell	*Auntie Mame*	Mame Dennis
	Elizabeth Taylor	*Cat on a Hot Tin Roof*	Margaret 'Maggie the Cat' Pollitt
1959 (32nd)	**Simone Signoret**	*Room at the Top*	**Alice Aisgill**
	Doris Day	*Pillow Talk*	Jan Morrow
	Audrey Hepburn	*The Nun's Story*	Sister Luke (Gabrielle van der Mal)
	Katharine Hepburn	*Suddenly, Last Summer*	Violet Venable
	Elizabeth Taylor	*Suddenly, Last Summer*	Catherine Holly

1960s

Year	Actress	Film	Character
1960 (33rd)	**Elizabeth Taylor**	*BUtterfield 8*	**Gloria Wandrous**
	Greer Garson	*Sunrise at Campobello*	Eleanor Roosevelt
	Deborah Kerr	*The Sundowners*	Ida Carmody
	Shirley MacLaine	*The Apartment*	Fran Kubelik
	Melina Mercouri	*Never on Sunday*	Ilya
1961 (34th)	**Sophia Loren**	*Two Women*	**Cesira**
	Audrey Hepburn	*Breakfast at Tiffany's*	Holly Golightly
	Piper Laurie	*The Hustler*	Sarah Packard
	Geraldine Page	*Summer and Smoke*	Alma Winemiller
	Natalie Wood	*Splendor in the Grass*	Wilma Dean 'Deanie' Loomis

1962 (35th)	**Anne Bancroft**	***The Miracle Worker***	**Annie Sullivan**
	Bette Davis	*What Ever Happened to Baby Jane?*	Baby Jane Hudson
	Katharine Hepburn	*Long Day's Journey Into Night*	Mary Tyrone
	Geraldine Page	*Sweet Bird of Youth*	Alexandra Del Lago
	Lee Remick	*Days of Wine and Roses*	Kirsten Arnesen Clay
1963 (36th)	**Patricia Neal**	***Hud***	**Alma Brown**
	Leslie Caron	*The L-Shaped Room*	Jane Fossett
	Shirley MacLaine	*Irma la Douce*	Irma La Douce
	Rachel Roberts	*This Sporting Life*	Margaret Hammond
	Natalie Wood	*Love with the Proper Stranger*	Angie Rossini
1964 (37th)	**Julie Andrews**	***Mary Poppins***	**Mary Poppins**
	Anne Bancroft	*The Pumpkin Eater*	Jo Armitage
	Sophia Loren	*Marriage Italian-Style*	Filumena Marturano
	Debbie Reynolds	*The Unsinkable Molly Brown*	Molly Brown
	Kim Stanley	*Séance on a Wet Afternoon*	Myra Savage
1965 (38th)	**Julie Christie**	***Darling***	**Diana Scott**
	Julie Andrews	*The Sound of Music*	Maria von Trapp
	Samantha Eggar	*The Collector*	Miranda Grey
	Elizabeth Hartman	*A Patch of Blue*	Selina D'Arcy
	Simone Signoret	*Ship of Fools*	La Contessa
1966 (39th)	**Elizabeth Taylor**	***Who's Afraid of Virginia Woolf?***	**Martha**
	Anouk Aimée	*A Man and a Woman*	Anne Gauthier
	Ida Kaminska	*The Shop on Main Street*	Rozalie Lautmann
	Lynn Redgrave	*Georgy Girl*	Georgina 'Georgy' Parkin
	Vanessa Redgrave	*Morgan!*	Leonie Delt
1967 (40th)	**Katharine Hepburn**	***Guess Who's Coming to Dinner***	**Christina Drayton**
	Anne Bancroft	*The Graduate*	Mrs. Robinson
	Faye Dunaway	*Bonnie and Clyde*	Bonnie Parker
	Edith Evans	*The Whisperers*	Maggie Ross
	Audrey Hepburn	*Wait Until Dark*	Susy Hendrix
1968 (41st)	**Barbra Streisand (tie)**	***Funny Girl***	**Fanny Brice**
	Katharine Hepburn (tie)	***The Lion in Winter***	**Eleanor of Aquitaine**
	Patricia Neal	*The Subject was Roses*	Nettie Cleary
	Vanessa Redgrave	*Isadora*	Isadora Duncan
	Joanne Woodward	*Rachel, Rachel*	Rachel Cameron

1969 (42nd)	Maggie Smith	*The Prime of Miss Jean Brodie*	Jean Brodie
	Geneviève Bujold	*Anne of the Thousand Days*	Anne Boleyn
	Jane Fonda	*They Shoot Horses, Don't They?*	Gloria Beatty
	Liza Minnelli	*The Sterile Cuckoo*	Mary Ann 'Pookie' Adams
	Jean Simmons	*The Happy Ending*	Mary Wilson

1970s

Year	Actress	Film	Character
1970 (43rd)	Glenda Jackson	*Women in Love*	Gudrun Brangwen
	Jane Alexander	*The Great White Hope*	Eleanor Backman
	Ali MacGraw	*Love Story*	Jennifer Cavalleri
	Sarah Miles	*Ryan's Daughter*	Rosy Ryan
	Carrie Snodgress	*Diary of a Mad Housewife*	Tina Balser
1971 (44th)	Jane Fonda	*Klute*	Bree Daniels
	Julie Christie	*McCabe & Mrs. Miller*	Constance Miller
	Glenda Jackson	*Sunday Bloody Sunday*	Alex Greville
	Vanessa Redgrave	*Mary, Queen of Scots*	Mary, Queen of Scots
	Janet Suzman	*Nicholas and Alexandra*	Empress Alexandra / Alix of Hesse Darmstadt
1972 (45th)	Liza Minnelli	*Cabaret*	Sally Bowles
	Diana Ross	*Lady Sings the Blues*	Billie Holiday
	Maggie Smith	*Travels with My Aunt*	Augusta Bertram
	Cicely Tyson	*Sounder*	Rebecca Morgan
	Liv Ullmann	*The Emigrants*	Kristina
1973 (46th)	Glenda Jackson	*A Touch of Class*	Vicki Allessio
	Ellen Burstyn	*The Exorcist*	Chris MacNeil
	Marsha Mason	*Cinderella Liberty*	Maggie Paul
	Barbra Streisand	*The Way We Were*	Katie Morosky
	Joanne Woodward	*Summer Wishes, Winter Dreams*	Rita Walden
1974 (47th)	Ellen Burstyn	*Alice Doesn't Live Here Anymore*	Alice Hyatt
	Diahann Carroll	*Claudine*	Claudine Price
	Faye Dunaway	*Chinatown*	Evelyn Cross Mulwray
	Valerie Perrine	*Lenny*	Honey Bruce
	Gena Rowlands	*A Woman Under the Influence*	Mabel Longhetti

1975 (48th)	**Louise Fletcher**	***One Flew Over the Cuckoo's Nest***	**Nurse Mildred Ratched**
	Isabelle Adjani	*The Story of Adele H.*	Adèle Hugo / Adèle Lewry
	Ann-Margret	*Tommy*	Nora Walker
	Glenda Jackson	*Hedda*	Hedda Gabler
	Carol Kane	*Hester Street*	Gitl
1976 (49th)	**Faye Dunaway**	***Network***	**Diana Christensen**
	Marie-Christine Barrault	*Cousin, cousine*	Marthe
	Talia Shire	*Rocky*	Adrian Pennino
	Sissy Spacek	*Carrie*	Carrie White
	Liv Ullmann	*Face to Face*	Dr. Jenny Isaksson
1977 (50th)	**Diane Keaton**	***Annie Hall***	**Annie Hall**
	Anne Bancroft	*The Turning Point*	Emma Jacklin
	Jane Fonda	*Julia*	Lillian Hellman
	Shirley MacLaine	*The Turning Point*	Deedee Rodgers
	Marsha Mason	*The Goodbye Girl*	Paula McFadden
1978 (51st)	**Jane Fonda**	***Coming Home***	**Sally Hyde**
	Ingrid Bergman	*Autumn Sonata*	Charlotte Andergast
	Ellen Burstyn	*Same Time, Next Year*	Doris
	Jill Clayburgh	*An Unmarried Woman*	Erica Benton
	Geraldine Page	*Interiors*	Eve
1979 (52nd)	**Sally Field**	***Norma Rae***	**Norma Rae Webster**
	Jill Clayburgh	*Starting Over*	Marilyn Holmberg
	Jane Fonda	*The China Syndrome*	Kimberly Wells
	Marsha Mason	*Chapter Two*	Jennie MacLaine
	Bette Midler	*The Rose*	Mary Rose Foster

1980s

Year	Actress	Film	Character
1980 (53rd)	**Sissy Spacek**	***Coal Miner's Daughter***	**Loretta Lynn**
	Ellen Burstyn	*Resurrection*	Edna Mae McCauley
	Goldie Hawn	*Private Benjamin*	Pvt. Judy Benjamin
	Mary Tyler Moore	*Ordinary People*	Beth Jarrett
	Gena Rowlands	*Gloria*	Gloria Swenson

1981 (54th)	**Katharine Hepburn**	*On Golden Pond*	**Ethel Thayer**
	Diane Keaton	*Reds*	Louise Bryant
	Marsha Mason	*Only When I Laugh*	Georgia Hines
	Susan Sarandon	*Atlantic City*	Sally Matthews
	Meryl Streep	*The French Lieutenant's Woman*	Anna (Sara Woodruff)
1982 (55th)	**Meryl Streep**	*Sophie's Choice*	**Sophie Zawistowski**
	Julie Andrews	*Victor Victoria*	Victoria Grant
	Jessica Lange	*Frances*	Frances Farmer
	Sissy Spacek	*Missing*	Beth Horman
	Debra Winger	*An Officer and a Gentleman*	Paula Pokrifki
1983 (56th)	**Shirley MacLaine**	*Terms of Endearment*	**Aurora Greenway**
	Jane Alexander	*Testament*	Carol Wetherly
	Meryl Streep	*Silkwood*	Karen Silkwood
	Julie Walters	*Educating Rita*	Rita
	Debra Winger	*Terms of Endearment*	Emma Greenway Horton
1984 (57th)	**Sally Field**	*Places in the Heart*	**Edna Spalding**
	Judy Davis	*A Passage to India*	Adela Quested
	Jessica Lange	*Country*	Jewell Ivy
	Vanessa Redgrave	*The Bostonians*	Olive Chancellor
	Sissy Spacek	*The River*	Mae Garvey
1985 (58th)	**Geraldine Page**	*The Trip to Bountiful*	**Carrie Watts**
	Anne Bancroft	*Agnes of God*	Mother Miriam Ruth
	Whoopi Goldberg	*The Color Purple*	Celie Harris Johnson
	Jessica Lange	*Sweet Dreams*	Patsy Cline
	Meryl Streep	*Out of Africa*	Karen Blixen
1986 (59th)	**Marlee Matlin**	*Children of a Lesser God*	**Sarah Norman**
	Jane Fonda	*The Morning After*	Alex Sternbergen
	Sissy Spacek	*Crimes of the Heart*	Babe Magrath
	Kathleen Turner	*Peggy Sue Got Married*	Peggy Sue Bodell
	Sigourney Weaver	*Aliens*	Ellen Ripley
1987 (60th)	**Cher**	*Moonstruck*	**Loretta Castorini**
	Glenn Close	*Fatal Attraction*	Alex Forrest
	Holly Hunter	*Broadcast News*	Jane Craig
	Sally Kirkland	*Anna*	Anna
	Meryl Streep	*Ironweed*	Helen Archer

1988 (61st)	Jodie Foster	*The Accused*	Sarah Tobias
	Glenn Close	*Dangerous Liaisons*	Marquise Isabelle de Merteuil
	Melanie Griffith	*Working Girl*	Tess McGill
	Meryl Streep	*A Cry in the Dark*	Lindy Chamberlain
	Sigourney Weaver	*Gorillas in the Mist*	Dian Fossey
1989 (62nd)	Jessica Tandy	*Driving Miss Daisy*	Daisy Werthan
	Isabelle Adjani	*Camille Claudel*	Camille Claudel
	Pauline Collins	*Shirley Valentine*	Shirley Valentine-Bradshaw
	Jessica Lange	*Music Box*	Ann Talbot
	Michelle Pfeiffer	*The Fabulous Baker Boys*	Susie Diamond

1990s

Year	Actress	Film	Character
1990 (63rd)	Kathy Bates	*Misery*	Annie Wilkes
	Anjelica Huston	*The Grifters*	Lilly Dillon
	Julia Roberts	*Pretty Woman*	Vivian Ward
	Meryl Streep	*Postcards from the Edge*	Suzanne Vale
	Joanne Woodward	*Mr. and Mrs. Bridge*	India Bridge
1991 (64th)	Jodie Foster	*The Silence of the Lambs*	Clarice Starling
	Geena Davis	*Thelma & Louise*	Thelma Dickinson
	Laura Dern	*Rambling Rose*	Rose
	Bette Midler	*For the Boys*	Dixie Leonard
	Susan Sarandon	*Thelma & Louise*	Louise Sawyer
1992 (65th)	Emma Thompson	*Howards End*	Margaret Schlegel
	Catherine Deneuve	*Indochine*	Eliane Devries
	Mary McDonnell	*Passion Fish*	May-Alice Culhane
	Michelle Pfeiffer	*Love Field*	Lurene Hallett
	Susan Sarandon	*Lorenzo's Oil*	Michaela Odone
1993 (66th)	Holly Hunter	*The Piano*	Ada McGrath
	Angela Bassett	*What's Love Got to Do with It*	Tina Turner
	Stockard Channing	*Six Degrees of Separation*	Ouisa Kittredge
	Emma Thompson	*The Remains of the Day*	Mary Kenton
	Debra Winger	*Shadowlands*	Joy Gresham

1994 (67th)	**Jessica Lange**	*Blue Sky*	**Carly Marshall**
	Jodie Foster	*Nell*	Nell Kellty
	Miranda Richardson	*Tom & Viv*	Vivienne Haigh-Wood
	Winona Ryder	*Little Women*	Jo March
	Susan Sarandon	*The Client*	Reggie Love
1995 (68th)	**Susan Sarandon**	*Dead Man Walking*	**Helen Prejean**
	Elisabeth Shue	*Leaving Las Vegas*	Sera
	Sharon Stone	*Casino*	Ginger McKenna
	Meryl Streep	*The Bridges of Madison County*	Francesca Johnson
	Emma Thompson	*Sense and Sensibility*	Elinor Dashwood
1996 (69th)	**Frances McDormand**	*Fargo*	**Marge Gunderson**
	Brenda Blethyn	*Secrets & Lies*	Cynthia Rose Purley
	Diane Keaton	*Marvin's Room*	Bessie
	Kristin Scott Thomas	*The English Patient*	Katharine Clifton
	Emily Watson	*Breaking the Waves*	Bess McNeill
1997 (70th)	**Helen Hunt**	*As Good as It Gets*	**Carol Connelly**
	Helena Bonham Carter	*The Wings of the Dove*	Kate Croy
	Julie Christie	*Afterglow*	Phyllis Mann
	Judi Dench	*Mrs. Brown*	Queen Victoria
	Kate Winslet	*Titanic*	Rose DeWitt Bukater
1998 (71st)	**Gwyneth Paltrow**	*Shakespeare in Love*	**Viola De Lesseps**
	Cate Blanchett	*Elizabeth*	Elizabeth I
	Fernanda Montenegro	*Central Station*	Dora
	Meryl Streep	*One True Thing*	Kate Gulden
	Emily Watson	*Hilary and Jackie*	Jacqueline du Pré
1999 (72nd)	**Hilary Swank**	*Boys Don't Cry*	**Brandon Teena**
	Annette Bening	*American Beauty*	Carolyn Burnham
	Janet McTeer	*Tumbleweeds*	Mary Jo Walker
	Julianne Moore	*The End of the Affair*	Sarah Miles
	Meryl Streep	*Music of the Heart*	Roberta Guaspari

2000s

Year	Actress	Film	Character
2000 (73rd)	**Julia Roberts**	*Erin Brockovich*	**Erin Brockovich**
	Joan Allen	*The Contender*	Senator Laine Hanson
	Juliette Binoche	*Chocolat*	Vianne Rocher
	Ellen Burstyn	*Requiem for a Dream*	Sara Goldfarb
	Laura Linney	*You Can Count on Me*	Sammy Prescott
2001 (74th)	**Halle Berry**	*Monster's Ball*	**Leticia Musgrove**
	Judi Dench	*Iris*	Iris Murdoch
	Nicole Kidman	*Moulin Rouge!*	Satine
	Sissy Spacek	*In the Bedroom*	Ruth Fowler
	Renée Zellweger	*Bridget Jones's Diary*	Bridget Jones
2002 (75th)	**Nicole Kidman**	*The Hours*	**Virginia Woolf**
	Salma Hayek	*Frida*	Frida Kahlo
	Diane Lane	*Unfaithful*	Constance 'Connie' Sumner
	Julianne Moore	*Far from Heaven*	Cathy Whitaker
	Renée Zellweger	*Chicago*	Roxie Hart
2003 (76th)	**Charlize Theron**	*Monster*	**Aileen Wuornos**
	Keisha Castle-Hughes	*Whale Rider*	Paikea Apirana
	Diane Keaton	*Something's Gotta Give*	Erika Berry
	Samantha Morton	*In America*	Sarah Sullivan
	Naomi Watts	*21 Grams*	Cristina Peck
2004 (77th)	**Hilary Swank**	*Million Dollar Baby*	**Maggie Fitzgerald**
	Annette Bening	*Being Julia*	Julia Lambert
	Catalina Sandino Moreno	*Maria Full of Grace*	María Álvarez
	Imelda Staunton	*Vera Drake*	Vera Rose Drake
	Kate Winslet	*Eternal Sunshine of the Spotless Mind*	Clementine Kruczynski
2005 (78th)	**Reese Witherspoon**	*Walk the Line*	**June Carter**
	Judi Dench	*Mrs Henderson Presents*	Laura Henderson
	Felicity Huffman	*Transamerica*	Sabrina "Bree" Osbourne
	Keira Knightley	*Pride & Prejudice*	Elizabeth Bennet
	Charlize Theron	*North Country*	Josey Aimes
2006 (79th)	**Helen Mirren**	*The Queen*	**Queen Elizabeth II**
	Penélope Cruz	*Volver*	Raimunda
	Judi Dench	*Notes on a Scandal*	Barbara Covett
	Meryl Streep	*The Devil Wears Prada*	Miranda Priestly
	Kate Winslet	*Little Children*	Sarah Pierce

2007 (80th)	Marion Cotillard	La Vie en Rose	Édith Piaf
	Cate Blanchett	Elizabeth: The Golden Age	Elizabeth I
	Julie Christie	Away from Her	Fiona Anderson
	Laura Linney	The Savages	Wendy Savage
	Ellen Page	Juno	Juno MacGuff
2008 (81st)	Kate Winslet	The Reader	Hanna Schmitz
	Anne Hathaway	Rachel Getting Married	Kym Buchman
	Angelina Jolie	Changeling	Christine Collins
	Melissa Leo	Frozen River	Ray Eddy
	Meryl Streep	Doubt	Sister Aloysius Beauvier
2009 (82nd)	Sandra Bullock	The Blind Side	Leigh Anne Tuohy
	Helen Mirren	The Last Station	Sofya Tolstoy
	Carey Mulligan	An Education	Jenny Mellor
	Gabourey Sidibe	Precious	Claireece "Precious" Jones
	Meryl Streep	Julie & Julia	Julia Child

2010s

Year	Actress	Film	Character
2010 (83rd)	Natalie Portman	Black Swan	Nina Sayers
	Annette Bening	The Kids Are All Right	Dr. Nicole "Nic" Allgood
	Nicole Kidman	Rabbit Hole	Becca Corbett
	Jennifer Lawrence	Winter's Bone	Ree Dolly
	Michelle Williams	Blue Valentine	Cindy Heller
2011 (84th)	Meryl Streep	The Iron Lady	Margaret Thatcher
	Glenn Close	Albert Nobbs	Albert Nobbs
	Viola Davis	The Help	Aibileen Clark
	Rooney Mara	The Girl with the Dragon Tattoo	Lisbeth Salander
	Michelle Williams	My Week with Marilyn	Marilyn Monroe
2012 (85th)	TBA	TBA	TBA
	Jessica Chastain	Zero Dark Thirty	Maya
	Jennifer Lawrence	Silver Linings Playbook	Tiffany Maxwell
	Emmanuelle Riva	Amour	Anne Laurent
	Quvenzhané Wallis	Beasts of the Southern Wild	Hushpuppy
	Naomi Watts	The Impossible	Maria Bennett

Superlatives

Superlative	Best Actress		Best Supporting Actress		Overall	
Actress with most awards	Katharine Hepburn	4	Shelley Winters Dianne Wiest	2	Katharine Hepburn	4
Actress with most nominations	Meryl Streep	14	Thelma Ritter	6	Meryl Streep	17
Actress with most nominations without ever winning	Deborah Kerr	6	Thelma Ritter	6	Deborah Kerr Thelma Ritter Glenn Close	6
Film with most nominations	*All About Eve* *Suddenly, Last Summer* *The Turning Point* *Terms of Endearment* *Thelma & Louise*	2	*Tom Jones*	3	*All About Eve*	4
Oldest winner	Jessica Tandy	80	Peggy Ashcroft	77	Jessica Tandy	80
Oldest nominee	Emmanuelle Riva[1][2]	85	Gloria Stuart	87	Gloria Stuart	87
Youngest winner	Marlee Matlin	21	Tatum O'Neal	10	Tatum O'Neal	10
Youngest nominee	Quvenzhané Wallis[1][2]	9	Tatum O'Neal	10	Quvenzhané Wallis	9

Katharine Hepburn, with four wins, has more Best Actress Oscars than any other actress. Twelve women have won two Best Actress Academy Awards; in chronological order, they are Luise Rainer, Bette Davis, Olivia de Havilland, Vivien Leigh, Ingrid Bergman, Elizabeth Taylor, Glenda Jackson, Jane Fonda, Sally Field, Jodie Foster, Hilary Swank and Meryl Streep.

With two Best Actress Oscars and one for Best Supporting Actress, Ingrid Bergman and Meryl Streep are the only actresses, after Katharine Hepburn, to have won three competitive acting Oscars.

Only two actresses have won this award in consecutive years: Luise Rainer (1937 and 1938) and Katharine Hepburn (1967 and 1968).

Five women have won both the Best Actress and the Best Supporting Actress awards: Helen Hayes, Ingrid Bergman, Maggie Smith, Meryl Streep, and Jessica Lange.

Meryl Streep holds the record of 14 nominations in the Best Actress category. Streep has been nominated 17 times (14 for Best Actress and 3 for Best Supporting Actress), which makes her the overall most-nominated performer of all time.

There has been only one tie in the history of this category. This occurred in 1969 when Katharine Hepburn and Barbra Streisand were both given the award. Hepburn and Streisand each received exactly the same number of votes.

Life expectancy of winners

In 2001 Donald A. Redelmeier and Sheldon M. Singh published a study in the Annals of Internal Medicine in which they found that

> "Winning an Academy Award was associated with a large gain in life expectancy for actors and actresses... Winning an Academy Award can increase a performer's stature and may add to their longevity. The absolute difference in life expectancy is about equal to the societal consequence of curing all cancers in all people for all time (22, 23). Moreover, movie stars who have won multiple Academy Awards have a survival advantage of 6.0 years (CI, 0.7 to 11.3 years) over performers with multiple films but no victories. Formal education is not the only way to improve health, and strict poverty is not

the only way to worsen health. The main implication is that higher status may be linked to lower mortality rates even at very impressive levels of achievement."[3]

The authors did an update to 29 March 2006 in which they found 122 more individuals and 144 more deaths since their first publication. Their unadjusted analysis showed a smaller survival advantage of 3.6 years for winners compared to their fellow nominees and costars in the films in which their performance garnered them their award.[4] However, in a 2006 published study by Marie-Pierre Sylvestre, MSc, Ella Huszti, MSc, and James A. Hanley, PhD, the authors found:

> "The statistical method used to derive this statistically significant difference gave winners an unfair advantage because it credited an Oscar winner's years of life before winning toward survival subsequent to winning. When the authors of the current article reanalyzed the data using methods that avoided this "immortal time" bias, the survival advantage was closer to 1 year and was not statistically significant. The bias in Redelmeier and Singh's study is not limited to longevity comparisons of persons who reach different ranks within their profession."[5]

International presence

As the Academy Awards are based in the United States and are centered on the Hollywood film industry, the majority of Academy Award winners have been Americans. Nonetheless, there is significant international presence at the awards, as evidenced by the following list of winners for the Academy Award for Best Actress.

- Australia: Nicole Kidman (Kidman was born in the United States to Australian parents who were temporarily living in Hawaii; she is a citizen of both countries.)
- Canada: Marie Dressler, Mary Pickford, Norma Shearer (Pickford, Shearer, and Dressler won their respective awards in three consecutive years, 1929–1931.)
- France: Claudette Colbert, Marion Cotillard, Simone Signoret (Colbert later became a dual French and American citizen.)
- Germany: Luise Rainer
- Italy: Sophia Loren, Anna Magnani
- Israel: Natalie Portman (Portman, born in Israel, has an Israeli father and an American mother, and is a dual Israeli and American citizen.)
- The Netherlands: Audrey Hepburn (Hepburn had a British father and a Dutch mother; hence, she was a native-born citizen of both countries. Hepburn spent her childhood and teenage years mostly in The Netherlands and Belgium.)
- South Africa: Charlize Theron (Theron later became an American citizen.)
- Sweden: Ingrid Bergman (Bergman became an Italian by marriage.)
- United Kingdom: Julie Andrews, Julie Christie, Olivia de Havilland, Joan Fontaine, Greer Garson, Audrey Hepburn, Glenda Jackson, Vivien Leigh, Helen Mirren, Maggie Smith, Jessica Tandy, Elizabeth Taylor, Emma Thompson, Kate Winslet (Taylor was born in England of American parents who were living there temporarily and who returned to the United States permanently in 1939. Hence, Taylor had dual citizenship and has been eligible to receive a damehood in the United Kingdom.)

There have been two years in which all four of the top acting Academy Awards were presented to non-Americans.

- At the 37th Academy Awards (1964), the winners were Rex Harrison (British), Julie Andrews (British), Peter Ustinov (British), and Lila Kedrova (Russian-born French).
- At the 80th Academy Awards (2007), the winners were Daniel Day-Lewis (British and Irish), Marion Cotillard (French), Javier Bardem (Spanish), and Tilda Swinton (British).

Multiple awards for Best Actress

Katharine Hepburn is the most-honored actress, winning four awards. Twelve actresses have won two awards: Ingrid Bergman, Bette Davis, Olivia De Havilland, Sally Field, Jane Fonda, Jodie Foster, Glenda Jackson, Vivien Leigh, Luise Rainer, Meryl Streep, Hilary Swank, and Elizabeth Taylor.[6]

Multiple nominations for Best Actress

2 nominations[6]

- Isabelle Adjani
- Jane Alexander
- Cate Blanchett
- Leslie Caron
- Ruth Chatterton
- Jill Clayburgh
- Marie Dressler
- Sally Field
- Janet Gaynor
- Holly Hunter
- Jennifer Lawrence
- Vivien Leigh
- Laura Linney
- Sophia Loren
- Anna Magnani
- Bette Midler
- Liza Minnelli
- Helen Mirren
- Julianne Moore
- Patricia Neal
- Michelle Pfeiffer
- Luise Rainer
- Julia Roberts
- Gena Rowlands
- Simone Signoret
- Maggie Smith
- Barbra Streisand
- Hilary Swank
- Charlize Theron
- Liv Ullmann
- Emily Watson
- Naomi Watts
- Sigourney Weaver
- Michelle Williams
- Natalie Wood
- Loretta Young
- Renée Zellweger

3 nominations

- Julie Andrews

- Annette Bening
- Glenn Close
- Claudette Colbert
- Joan Crawford
- Faye Dunaway
- Joan Fontaine
- Jodie Foster
- Nicole Kidman
- Eleanor Parker
- Gloria Swanson
- Emma Thompson
- Debra Winger

4 nominations

- Julie Christie
- Olivia De Havilland
- Judi Dench
- Greta Garbo
- Glenda Jackson
- Jennifer Jones
- Diane Keaton
- Marsha Mason
- Geraldine Page
- Vanessa Redgrave
- Rosalind Russell
- Barbara Stanwyck
- Kate Winslet
- Joanne Woodward
- Jane Wyman

5 nominations

- Anne Bancroft
- Ellen Burstyn
- Irene Dunne
- Susan Hayward
- Audrey Hepburn
- Jessica Lange
- Shirley MacLaine
- Susan Sarandon
- Elizabeth Taylor

6 nominations

- Ingrid Bergman
- Jane Fonda
- Deborah Kerr
- Norma Shearer
- Sissy Spacek

7 nominations

- Greer Garson

10 nominations

- Bette Davis

12 nominations

- Katharine Hepburn

14 nominations

- Meryl Streep

Note: Bette Davis has ten nominations. Her performance in *Of Human Bondage* was not nominated for an Oscar. Several influential people at the time campaigned to have her name included on the list, so for that year (and the following year also) the Academy relaxed its rules and allowed a write-in vote. Technically this meant that any performance was eligible, however, the Academy does not officially recognize this as a nomination for Davis.

Multiple Nominations for Best Actress without winning

2 nominations	3 nominations
• Isabelle Adjani	• Annette Bening
• Jane Alexander	• Glenn Close
• Cate Blanchett†	• Eleanor Parker
• Leslie Caron	• Gloria Swanson
• Ruth Chatterton	• Debra Winger
• Jill Clayburgh	**4 nominations**
• Laura Linney	• Judi Dench†
• Bette Midler	• Greta Garbo‡
• Julianne Moore	• Marsha Mason
• Michelle Pfeiffer	• Vanessa Redgrave†
• Gena Rowlands	• Rosalind Russel‡
• Liv Ullmann	• Barbara Stanwyck‡
• Emily Watson	**5 nominations**
• Sigourney Weaver	• Irene Dunne
• Michelle Williams	**6 nominations**
• Natalie Wood	• Deborah Kerr‡
• Renée Zellweger†	

† Blanchett, Dench, Redgrave and Zellweger have won a Best Supporting Actress Oscar.

‡ Garbo, Kerr, Russell and Stanwyck received an Honorary Oscar.

Multiple awards for Best Actress and Best Supporting Actress combined

2 awards[6]	3 awards
• Bette Davis	• Ingrid Bergman
• Olivia De Havilland	• Meryl Streep
• Sally Field	**4 awards**
• Jane Fonda	• Katharine Hepburn
• Jodie Foster	
• Helen Hayes	
• Glenda Jackson	
• Jessica Lange	
• Vivien Leigh	
• Luise Rainer	
• Maggie Smith	
• Hilary Swank	
• Elizabeth Taylor	
• Dianne Wiest	
• Shelley Winters	

Note: Ingrid Bergman, Helen Hayes, Jessica Lange, Maggie Smith and Meryl Streep have won Oscars in both the Best Actress and Best Supporting Actress categories, while Dianne Wiest and Shelley Winters have both won two Best Supporting Actress Oscars.

Multiple nominations for Best Actress and Best Supporting Actress combined

3 nominations[6]

- Joan Allen
- Julie Andrews
- Fay Bainter
- Kathy Bates
- Claudette Colbert
- Gladys Cooper
- Joan Crawford
- Penélope Cruz
- Faye Dunaway
- Edith Evans
- Sally Field
- Joan Fontaine
- Wendy Hiller
- Celeste Holm
- Anjelica Huston
- Nicole Kidman
- Diane Ladd
- Angela Lansbury
- Piper Laurie
- Laura Linney
- Eleanor Parker
- Michelle Pfeiffer
- Anne Revere
- Julia Roberts

- Gloria Swanson
- Marisa Tomei
- Claire Trever
- Sigourney Weaver
- Dianne Wiest
- Michelle Williams
- Debra Winger
- Natalie Wood
- Teresa Wright
- Renée Zellweger

4 nominations

- Amy Adams
- Jane Alexander
- Ethel Barrymore
- Annette Bening
- Julie Christie
- Jodie Foster
- Greta Garbo
- Lee Grant
- Holly Hunter
- Glenda Jackson
- Diane Keaton
- Frances McDormand
- Marsha Mason
- Helen Mirren
- Julianne Moore
- Agnes Moorehead
- Rosalind Russell
- Barbara Stanwyck
- Maureen Stapleton
- Emma Thompson
- Shelley Winters
- Joanne Woodward
- Jane Wyman

5 nominations

- Anne Bancroft
- Cate Blanchett
- Olivia de Havilland
- Irene Dunne
- Susan Hayward
- Audrey Hepburn
- Jennifer Jones
- Shirley MacLaine
- Susan Sarandon
- Elizabeth Taylor

6 nominations

- Ellen Burstyn
- Glenn Close
- Judi Dench
- Deborah Kerr
- Jessica Lange
- Vanessa Redgrave
- Thelma Ritter
- Norma Shearer
- Maggie Smith
- Sissy Spacek
- Kate Winslet

7 nominations

- Ingrid Bergman
- Jane Fonda
- Greer Garson

8 nominations

- Geraldine Page

10 nominations

- Bette Davis

12 nominations

- Katharine Hepburn

17 nominations

- Meryl Streep

Note: All three nominations received by Cooper, Holm, Ladd, Lansbury, Revere, Tomei, Trevor and Wiest, as well as all four received by Adams, Barrymore, Grant, and Moorehead and all six received by Ritter, were in the Supporting Actress category.

References

[1] "Youngest v oldest actress vie for Oscar as Lincoln leads the pack" (http://www.thetimes.co.uk/tto/arts/film/oscars/article3653450. ece). *The Times*. . Retrieved 2013-01-10.

[2] "Quvenzhané Wallis v Emmanuelle Riva: Best actress Oscar contested by oldest and youngest ever nominees" (http://www.independent. co.uk/arts-entertainment/films/news/ quvenzhan-wallis-v-emmanuelle-riva--best-actress-oscar-contested-by-oldest-and-youngest-ever-nominees-8446248.html). *The Independent*. . Retrieved 2013-01-10.

[3] Redelmeier, Donald A. & Singh, Sheldon M. (15 May 2001), "Survival in Academy Award–Winning Actors and Actresses" (http://www. annals.org/cgi/reprint/134/10/955.pdf), *Annals of Internal Medicine*: 961, , retrieved 14 Jan 2009

[4] Redelmeier, Donald A. & Singh, Sheldon M. (5 Sep 2006), "Reanalysis of Survival of Oscar Winners" (http://www.annals.org/cgi/reprint/ 145/5/392-a.pdf), *Annals of Internal Medicine*: 392, , retrieved 14 Jan 2009

[5] Sylvestre, Marie-Pierre, Huszti, Ella & Hanley, James A. (5 Sep 2006), "Do Oscar Winners Live Longer than Less Successful Peers? A Reanalysis of the Evidence" (http://www.annals.org/cgi/reprint/145/5/361.pdf), *Annals of Internal Medicine*: 361, , retrieved 14 Jan 2009

[6] http://awardsdatabase.oscars.org/ampas_awards/DisplayMain.jsp?curTime=1331103553275

External links

- Oscars.org (http://www.oscars.org/) (official Academy site)
- Oscar.com (http://www.oscar.com/) (official ceremony promotional site)
- The Academy Awards Database (http://www.oscars.org/awardsdatabase/index.html) (official site)
- Photos of the best actress nominees for the 80th Academy Awards (http://www.people.com/people/package/gallery/0,,20168763_20175502,00.html) (People.com)

Academy Award for Best Supporting Actress

Academy Award for Best Supporting Actress	
Awarded for	Best Performance by an Actress in a Supporting Role
Presented by	Academy of Motion Picture Arts and Sciences
Country	United States
First awarded	1937 (for performances in films released in 1936)
Currently held by	Octavia Spencer, *The Help* (2011)
Official website	http://www.oscars.org

Performance by an Actress in a Supporting Role is one of the Academy Awards of Merit presented annually by the Academy of Motion Picture Arts and Sciences (AMPAS) to recognize an actress who has delivered an outstanding performance while working within the film industry. Since its inception, however, the award has commonly been referred to as the Oscar for **Best Supporting Actress**. While actresses are nominated for this award by Academy members who are actors and actresses themselves, winners are selected by the Academy membership as a whole.

History

Throughout the past 76 years, accounting for ties and repeat winners, AMPAS has presented a total of 76 Best Supporting Actress awards to 74 different actresses. Winners of this Academy Award of Merit currently receive the familiar Oscar statuette, depicting a gold-plated knight holding a crusader's sword and standing on a reel of film. Prior to the 16th Academy Awards ceremony (1943), however, they received a plaque. The first recipient was Gale Sondergaard, who was honored at the 9th Academy Awards ceremony (1936) for her performance in *Anthony Adverse*. The most recent recipient was Octavia Spencer, who was honored at the 84th Academy Awards ceremony (2012) for her performance in *The Help*.

Until the 8th Academy Awards ceremony (1935), nominations for the Best Actress award were intended to include all actresses, whether the performance was in either a leading or supporting role. At the 9th Academy Awards ceremony (1936), however, the Best Supporting Actress category was specifically introduced as a distinct award following complaints that the single Best Actress category necessarily favored leading performers with the most screen time. Nonetheless, May Robson had received a Best Actress nomination (*Lady for a Day*, 1933) for her performance in a clear supporting role. Under the system currently in place, an actress is nominated for a specific performance in a single film, and such nominations are limited to five per year. Currently, Performance by an Actor in a Leading Role, Performance by an Actress in a Leading Role, Performance by an Actor in a Supporting Role, and Performance by an Actress in a Supporting Role constitute the four Academy Awards of Merit for acting annually presented by AMPAS.

Winners and nominees

Following the Academy's practice, the films below are listed by year of their Los Angeles qualifying run, which is usually (but not always) the film's year of release. For example, the Oscar for Best Supporting Actress of 1999 was announced during the award ceremony held in 2000. Winners are listed first in **bold**, followed by the other nominees. For a list sorted by actress names, please see List of Best Supporting Actress nominees. For a list sorted by film titles, please see List of Best Supporting Actress nominees (films).

1930s

Year	Actress	Film	Character
1936 (9th)	**Gale Sondergaard**	***Anthony Adverse***	**Faith Paleologus**
	Beulah Bondi	*The Gorgeous Hussy*	Rachel Jackson
	Alice Brady	*My Man Godfrey*	Angelica Bullock
	Bonita Granville	*These Three*	Mary Tilford
	Maria Ouspenskaya	*Dodsworth*	Baroness Von Obersdorf
1937 (10th)	**Alice Brady**	***In Old Chicago***	**Molly O'Leary**
	Andrea Leeds	*Stage Door*	Kay Hamilton
	Anne Shirley	*Stella Dallas*	Laurel "Lollie" Dallas
	Claire Trevor	*Dead End*	Francey
	May Whitty	*Night Must Fall*	Mrs. Bramson
1938 (11th)	**Fay Bainter**	***Jezebel***	**Aunt Belle Massey**
	Beulah Bondi	*Of Human Hearts*	Mary Wilkins
	Billie Burke	*Merrily We Live*	Emily Kilbourne
	Spring Byington	*You Can't Take It with You*	Penny Sycamore
	Miliza Korjus	*The Great Waltz*	Carla Donner
1939 (12th)	**Hattie McDaniel**	***Gone with the Wind***	**Mammy**
	Olivia de Havilland	*Gone with the Wind*	Melanie Hamilton
	Geraldine Fitzgerald	*Wuthering Heights*	Isabella Linton
	Edna May Oliver	*Drums Along the Mohawk*	Sarah McKlennar
	Maria Ouspenskaya	*Love Affair*	Grandmother Janou

1940s

Year	Actress	Film	Character
1940 (13th)	**Jane Darwell**	***The Grapes of Wrath***	**Ma Joad**
	Judith Anderson	*Rebecca*	Mrs. Danvers
	Ruth Hussey	*The Philadelphia Story*	Elizabeth Imbrie
	Barbara O'Neil	*All This and Heaven Too*	Duchesse de Praslin
	Marjorie Rambeau	*Primrose Path*	Mamie Adams
1941 (14th)	**Mary Astor**	***The Great Lie***	**Sandra Kovak**
	Sara Allgood	*How Green Was My Valley*	Beth Morgan
	Patricia Collinge	*The Little Foxes*	Birdie Hubbard
	Teresa Wright	*The Little Foxes*	Alexandra Giddens
	Margaret Wycherly	*Sergeant York*	Mother York

1942 (15th)	**Teresa Wright**	*Mrs. Miniver*	**Carol Beldon**
	Gladys Cooper	*Now, Voyager*	Mrs. Vale
	Agnes Moorehead	*The Magnificent Ambersons*	Fanny Minafer
	Susan Peters	*Random Harvest*	Kitty Chilcet
	May Whitty	*Mrs. Miniver*	Lady Beldon
1943 (16th)[1]	**Katina Paxinou**	*For Whom the Bell Tolls*	**Pilar**
	Gladys Cooper	*The Song of Bernadette*	Sister Marie Therese Vauzous
	Paulette Goddard	*So Proudly We Hail!*	Lt. Joan O'Doul
	Anne Revere	*The Song of Bernadette*	Louise Soubirous
	Lucile Watson	*Watch on the Rhine*	Fanny Farrelly
1944 (17th)	**Ethel Barrymore**	*None but the Lonely Heart*	**Ma Mott**
	Jennifer Jones	*Since You Went Away*	Jane Deborah Hilton
	Angela Lansbury	*Gaslight*	Nancy Oliver
	Aline MacMahon	*Dragon Seed*	Ling Tan's Wife
	Agnes Moorehead	*Mrs. Parkington*	Baroness Aspasia Conti
1945 (18th)	**Anne Revere**	*National Velvet*	**Araminty Brown**
	Eve Arden	*Mildred Pierce*	Ida Corwin
	Ann Blyth	*Mildred Pierce*	Veda Pierce Forrester
	Angela Lansbury	*The Picture of Dorian Gray*	Sibyl Vane
	Joan Lorring	*The Corn is Green*	Bessie Watty
1946 (19th)	**Anne Baxter**	*The Razor's Edge*	**Sophie MacDonald**
	Ethel Barrymore	*The Spiral Staircase*	Mrs. Warren
	Lillian Gish	*Duel in the Sun*	Laura Belle McCanles
	Flora Robson	*Saratoga Trunk*	Angelique Buiton
	Gale Sondergaard	*Anna and the King of Siam*	Lady Thiang
1947 (20th)	**Celeste Holm**	*Gentleman's Agreement*	**Anne Dettrey**
	Ethel Barrymore	*The Paradine Case*	Lady Sophie Horfield
	Gloria Grahame	*Crossfire*	Ginny Tremaine
	Marjorie Main	*The Egg and I*	Ma Kettle
	Anne Revere	*Gentleman's Agreement*	Mrs. Green
1948 (21st)	**Claire Trevor**	*Key Largo*	**Gaye Dawn**
	Barbara Bel Geddes	*I Remember Mama*	Katrin Hanson
	Ellen Corby	*I Remember Mama*	Aunt Trina
	Agnes Moorehead	*Johnny Belinda*	Aggie McDonald
	Jean Simmons	*Hamlet*	Ophelia

1949 (22nd)	Mercedes McCambridge	*All the King's Men*	Sadie Burke
	Ethel Barrymore	*Pinky*	Miss Em
	Celeste Holm	*Come to the Stable*	Sister Scholastica
	Elsa Lanchester	*Come to the Stable*	Amelia Potts
	Ethel Waters	*Pinky*	Dicey Johnson

1950s

Year	Actress	Film	Character
1950 (23rd)	Josephine Hull	*Harvey*	Veta Louise Simmons
	Hope Emerson	*Caged*	Evelyn Harper
	Celeste Holm	*All About Eve*	Karen Richards
	Nancy Olson	*Sunset Boulevard*	Betty Schaefer
	Thelma Ritter	*All About Eve*	Birdie Kumen
1951 (24th)	Kim Hunter	*A Streetcar Named Desire*	Stella Kowalski
	Joan Blondell	*The Blue Veil*	Annie Rawlins
	Mildred Dunnock	*Death of a Salesman*	Linda Loman
	Lee Grant	*Detective Story*	Shoplifter
	Thelma Ritter	*The Mating Season*	Ellen McNulty
1952 (25th)	Gloria Grahame	*The Bad and the Beautiful*	Rosemary Bartlow
	Jean Hagen	*Singin' in the Rain*	Lina Lamont
	Colette Marchand	*Moulin Rouge*	Marie Charlet
	Terry Moore	*Come Back, Little Sheba*	Marie Buckholder
	Thelma Ritter	*With a Song in My Heart*	Clancy
1953 (26th)	Donna Reed	*From Here to Eternity*	Alma "Lorene" Burke
	Grace Kelly	*Mogambo*	Linda Nordley
	Geraldine Page	*Hondo*	Angie Lowe
	Marjorie Rambeau	*Torch Song*	Mrs. Stewart
	Thelma Ritter	*Pickup on South Street*	Moe
1954 (27th)	Eva Marie Saint	*On the Waterfront*	Edie Doyle
	Nina Foch	*Executive Suite*	Erica Martin
	Katy Jurado	*Broken Lance*	Señora Devereaux
	Jan Sterling	*The High and the Mighty*	Sally McKee
	Claire Trevor	*The High and the Mighty*	May Holst

1955 (28th)	**Jo Van Fleet**	***East of Eden***	**Kate**
	Betsy Blair	*Marty*	Clara Snyder
	Peggy Lee	*Pete Kelly's Blues*	Rose Hopkins
	Marisa Pavan	*The Rose Tattoo*	Rosa Delle Rose
	Natalie Wood	*Rebel Without a Cause*	Judy
1956 (29th)	**Dorothy Malone**	***Written on the Wind***	**Marylee Hadley**
	Mildred Dunnock	*Baby Doll*	Rose Comfort
	Eileen Heckart	*The Bad Seed*	Hortense Daigle
	Mercedes McCambridge	*Giant*	Luz Benedict
	Patty McCormack	*The Bad Seed*	Rhoda Penmark
1957 (30th)	**Miyoshi Umeki**	***Sayonara***	**Katsumi**
	Carolyn Jones	*The Bachelor Party*	The Existentialist
	Elsa Lanchester	*Witness for the Prosecution*	Miss Plimsoll
	Hope Lange	*Peyton Place*	Selena Cross
	Diane Varsi	*Peyton Place*	Allison MacKenzie
1958 (31st)	**Wendy Hiller**	***Separate Tables***	**Pat Cooper**
	Peggy Cass	*Auntie Mame*	Agnes Gooch
	Martha Hyer	*Some Came Running*	Gwen French
	Maureen Stapleton	*Lonelyhearts*	Fay Doyle
	Cara Williams	*The Defiant Ones*	Billy's mother
1959 (32nd)	**Shelley Winters**	***The Diary of Anne Frank***	**Petronella Van Daan**
	Hermione Baddeley	*Room at the Top*	Elspeth
	Susan Kohner	*Imitation of Life*	Sarah Jane Johnson (age 18)
	Juanita Moore	*Imitation of Life*	Annie Johnson
	Thelma Ritter	*Pillow Talk*	Alma

1960s

Year	Actress	Film	Character
1960 (33rd)	**Shirley Jones**	***Elmer Gantry***	**Lulu Baines**
	Glynis Johns	*The Sundowners*	Mrs. Firth
	Shirley Knight	*The Dark at the Top of the Stairs*	Reenie Flood
	Janet Leigh	*Psycho*	Marion Crane
	Mary Ure	*Sons and Lovers*	Clara Dawes

1961 (34th)	**Rita Moreno**	*West Side Story*	**Anita del Carmen**
	Fay Bainter	*The Children's Hour*	Amelia Tilford
	Judy Garland	*Judgment at Nuremberg*	Irene Hoffman Wallner
	Lotte Lenya	*The Roman Spring of Mrs. Stone*	Contessa Magda Terribili-Gonzales
	Una Merkel	*Summer and Smoke*	Mrs. Winemiller
1962 (35th)	**Patty Duke**	*The Miracle Worker*	**Helen Keller**
	Mary Badham	*To Kill a Mockingbird*	Jean Louise "Scout" Finch
	Shirley Knight	*Sweet Bird of Youth*	Heavenly Finley
	Angela Lansbury	*The Manchurian Candidate*	Mrs. Eleanor Iselin
	Thelma Ritter	*Birdman of Alcatraz*	Elizabeth Stroud
1963 (36th)	**Margaret Rutherford**	*The V.I.P.s*	**The Duchess of Brighton**
	Diane Cilento	*Tom Jones*	Molly Seagrim
	Edith Evans	*Tom Jones*	Miss Western
	Joyce Redman	*Tom Jones*	Mrs. Waters (Jenny Jones)
	Lilia Skala	*Lilies of the Field*	Mother Maria Marthe
1964 (37th)	**Lila Kedrova**	*Zorba the Greek*	**Madame Hortense**
	Gladys Cooper	*My Fair Lady*	Mrs. Higgins
	Edith Evans	*The Chalk Garden*	Mrs. St. Maugham
	Grayson Hall	*The Night of the Iguana*	Judith Fellowes
	Agnes Moorehead	*Hush… Hush, Sweet Charlotte*	Velma Cruther
1965 (38th)	**Shelley Winters**	*A Patch of Blue*	**Rose-ann D'Arcy**
	Ruth Gordon	*Inside Daisy Clover*	Mrs. Clover / The Dealer
	Joyce Redman	*Othello*	Emilia
	Maggie Smith	*Othello*	Desdemona
	Peggy Wood	*The Sound of Music*	Mother Abbess
1966 (39th)	**Sandy Dennis**	*Who's Afraid of Virginia Woolf?*	**Honey**
	Wendy Hiller	*A Man for All Seasons*	Alice More
	Jocelyne LaGarde	*Hawaii*	Queen Malama
	Vivien Merchant	*Alfie*	Lily
	Geraldine Page	*You're a Big Boy Now*	Margery Chanticleer
1967 (40th)	**Estelle Parsons**	*Bonnie and Clyde*	**Blanche Barrow**
	Carol Channing	*Thoroughly Modern Millie*	Muzzy Van Hossmere
	Mildred Natwick	*Barefoot in the Park*	Ethel Banks
	Beah Richards	*Guess Who's Coming to Dinner*	Mrs. Prentice
	Katharine Ross	*The Graduate*	Elaine Robinson

1968 (41st)	Ruth Gordon	*Rosemary's Baby*	Minnie Castevet
	Lynn Carlin	*Faces*	Maria Forst
	Sondra Locke	*The Heart Is a Lonely Hunter*	Mick Kelly
	Kay Medford	*Funny Girl*	Rose Brice
	Estelle Parsons	*Rachel, Rachel*	Calla Mackie
1969 (42nd)	Goldie Hawn	*Cactus Flower*	Toni Simmons
	Catherine Burns	*Last Summer*	Rhoda
	Dyan Cannon	*Bob & Carol & Ted & Alice*	Alice Henderson
	Sylvia Miles	*Midnight Cowboy*	Cass
	Susannah York	*They Shoot Horses, Don't They?*	Alice LeBlanc

1970s

Year	Actress	Film	Character
1970 (43rd)	Helen Hayes	*Airport*	Ada Quonsett
	Karen Black	*Five Easy Pieces*	Rayette Dipesto
	Lee Grant	*The Landlord*	Joyce Enders
	Sally Kellerman	*MASH*	Maj. Margaret "Hot Lips" Houlihan
	Maureen Stapleton	*Airport*	Inez Guerrero
1971 (44th)	Cloris Leachman	*The Last Picture Show*	Ruth Popper
	Ann-Margret	*Carnal Knowledge*	Bobbie
	Ellen Burstyn	*The Last Picture Show*	Lois Farrow
	Barbara Harris	*Who Is Harry Kellerman and Why Is He Saying Those Terrible Things About Me?*	Allison Densmore
	Margaret Leighton	*The Go-Between*	Mrs. Maudsley
1972 (45th)	Eileen Heckart	*Butterflies Are Free*	Mrs. Baker
	Jeannie Berlin	*The Heartbreak Kid*	Lila Kolodny
	Geraldine Page	*Pete 'n' Tillie*	Gertrude
	Susan Tyrrell	*Fat City*	Oma
	Shelley Winters	*The Poseidon Adventure*	Belle Rosen
1973 (46th)	Tatum O'Neal	*Paper Moon*	Addie Loggins
	Linda Blair	*The Exorcist*	Regan MacNeil
	Candy Clark	*American Graffiti*	Debbie Dunham
	Madeline Kahn	*Paper Moon*	Trixie Delight
	Sylvia Sidney	*Summer Wishes, Winter Dreams*	Mrs. Pritchett

1974 (47th)	**Ingrid Bergman**	*Murder on the Orient Express*	**Greta Ohlsson**
	Valentina Cortese	*Day for Night*	Severine
	Madeline Kahn	*Blazing Saddles*	Lili Von Shtupp
	Diane Ladd	*Alice Doesn't Live Here Anymore*	Flo Castleberry
	Talia Shire	*The Godfather Part II*	Connie Corleone
1975 (48th)	**Lee Grant**	*Shampoo*	**Felicia Karpf**
	Ronee Blakley	*Nashville*	Barbara Jean
	Sylvia Miles	*Farewell, My Lovely*	Jessie Halstead Florian
	Lily Tomlin	*Nashville*	Linnea Reese
	Brenda Vaccaro	*Jacqueline Susann's Once Is Not Enough*	Linda Riggs
1976 (49th)	**Beatrice Straight**	*Network*	**Louise Schumacher**
	Jane Alexander	*All the President's Men*	Judy Hoback
	Jodie Foster	*Taxi Driver*	Iris Steensma
	Lee Grant	*Voyage of the Damned*	Lillian Rosen
	Piper Laurie	*Carrie*	Margaret White
1977 (50th)	**Vanessa Redgrave**	*Julia*	**Julia**
	Leslie Browne	*The Turning Point*	Emilia Rodgers
	Quinn Cummings	*The Goodbye Girl*	Lucy McFadden
	Melinda Dillon	*Close Encounters of the Third Kind*	Gillian Guiler
	Tuesday Weld	*Looking for Mr. Goodbar*	Katherine Dunn
1978 (51st)	**Maggie Smith**	*California Suite*	**Diana Barrie**
	Dyan Cannon	*Heaven Can Wait*	Julia Farnsworth
	Penelope Milford	*Coming Home*	Vi Munson
	Maureen Stapleton	*Interiors*	Pearl
	Meryl Streep	*The Deer Hunter*	Linda
1979 (52nd)	**Meryl Streep**	*Kramer vs. Kramer*	**Joanna Kramer**
	Jane Alexander	*Kramer vs. Kramer*	Margaret Phelps
	Barbara Barrie	*Breaking Away*	Evelyn Stoller
	Candice Bergen	*Starting Over*	Jessica Potter
	Mariel Hemingway	*Manhattan*	Tracy

1980s

Year	Actress	Film	Character
1980 (53rd)	**Mary Steenburgen**	***Melvin and Howard***	**Lynda Dummar**
	Eileen Brennan	*Private Benjamin*	Capt. Doreen Lewis
	Eva Le Gallienne	*Resurrection*	Grandma Pearl
	Cathy Moriarty	*Raging Bull*	Vickie Thailer LaMotta
	Diana Scarwid	*Inside Moves*	Louise
1981 (54th)	**Maureen Stapleton**	***Reds***	**Emma Goldman**
	Melinda Dillon	*Absence of Malice*	Teresa Perrone
	Jane Fonda	*On Golden Pond*	Chelsea Thayer Wayne
	Joan Hackett	*Only When I Laugh*	Toby Landau
	Elizabeth McGovern	*Ragtime*	Evelyn Nesbit
1982 (55th)	**Jessica Lange**	***Tootsie***	**Julie Nichols**
	Glenn Close	*The World According to Garp*	Jenny Fields
	Teri Garr	*Tootsie*	Sandy Lester
	Kim Stanley	*Frances*	Lillian Farmer
	Lesley Ann Warren	*Victor Victoria*	Norma Cassady
1983 (56th)	**Linda Hunt**	***The Year of Living Dangerously***	**Billy Kwan**
	Cher	*Silkwood*	Dolly Pelliker
	Glenn Close	*The Big Chill*	Sarah Cooper
	Amy Irving	*Yentl*	Hadass
	Alfre Woodard	*Cross Creek*	Geechee
1984 (57th)	**Peggy Ashcroft**	***A Passage to India***	**Mrs. Moore**
	Glenn Close	*The Natural*	Iris Gaines
	Lindsay Crouse	*Places in the Heart*	Margaret Lomax
	Christine Lahti	*Swing Shift*	Hazel Zanussi
	Geraldine Page	*The Pope of Greenwich Village*	Mrs. Ritter
1985 (58th)	**Anjelica Huston**	***Prizzi's Honor***	**Maerose Prizzi**
	Margaret Avery	*The Color Purple*	Shug Avery
	Amy Madigan	*Twice in a Lifetime*	Sunny Sobel
	Meg Tilly	*Agnes of God*	Sister Agnes
	Oprah Winfrey	*The Color Purple*	Sofia Johnson
1986 (59th)	**Dianne Wiest**	***Hannah and Her Sisters***	**Holly**
	Tess Harper	*Crimes of the Heart*	Chick Boyle
	Piper Laurie	*Children of a Lesser God*	Mrs. Norman
	Mary Elizabeth Mastrantonio	*The Color of Money*	Carmen
	Maggie Smith	*A Room with a View*	Charlotte Bartlett

1987 (60th)	**Olympia Dukakis**	*Moonstruck*	**Rose Castorini**
	Norma Aleandro	*Gaby: A True Story*	Florencia
	Anne Archer	*Fatal Attraction*	Beth Gallagher
	Anne Ramsey	*Throw Momma from the Train*	Mrs. Lift
	Ann Sothern	*The Whales of August*	Tisha Doughty
1988 (61st)	**Geena Davis**	***The Accidental Tourist***	**Muriel Pritchett**
	Joan Cusack	*Working Girl*	Cyn
	Frances McDormand	*Mississippi Burning*	Mrs. Pell
	Michelle Pfeiffer	*Dangerous Liaisons*	Madame Marie de Tourvel
	Sigourney Weaver	*Working Girl*	Katharine Parker
1989 (62nd)	**Brenda Fricker**	***My Left Foot***	**Mrs. Brown**
	Anjelica Huston	*Enemies, a Love Story*	Tamara Broder
	Lena Olin	*Enemies, a Love Story*	Masha
	Julia Roberts	*Steel Magnolias*	Shelby Eatenton Latcherie
	Dianne Wiest	*Parenthood*	Helen Buckman

1990s

Year	Actress	Film	Character
1990 (63rd)	**Whoopi Goldberg**	***Ghost***	**Oda Mae Brown**
	Annette Bening	*The Grifters*	Myra Langtry
	Lorraine Bracco	*Goodfellas*	Karen Hill
	Diane Ladd	*Wild at Heart*	Marietta Fortune
	Mary McDonnell	*Dances with Wolves*	Stands With A Fist
1991 (64th)	**Mercedes Ruehl**	***The Fisher King***	**Anne Napolitano**
	Diane Ladd	*Rambling Rose*	Mother
	Juliette Lewis	*Cape Fear*	Danielle Bowden
	Kate Nelligan	*The Prince of Tides*	Lila Wingo Newbury
	Jessica Tandy	*Fried Green Tomatoes*	Ninny Threadgoode
1992 (65th)	**Marisa Tomei**	***My Cousin Vinny***	**Mona Lisa Vito**
	Judy Davis	*Husbands and Wives*	Sally
	Joan Plowright	*Enchanted April*	Mrs. Fisher
	Vanessa Redgrave	*Howards End*	Ruth Wilcox
	Miranda Richardson	*Damage*	Ingrid Fleming

1993 (66th)	**Anna Paquin**	*The Piano*	**Flora McGrath**
	Holly Hunter	*The Firm*	Tammy Hemphill
	Rosie Perez	*Fearless*	Carla Rodrigo
	Winona Ryder	*The Age of Innocence*	May Welland
	Emma Thompson	*In the Name of the Father*	Gareth Peirce
1994 (67th)	**Dianne Wiest**	*Bullets Over Broadway*	**Helen Sinclair**
	Rosemary Harris	*Tom & Viv*	Rose Haigh-Wood
	Helen Mirren	*The Madness of King George*	Queen Charlotte
	Uma Thurman	*Pulp Fiction*	Mia Wallace
	Jennifer Tilly	*Bullets Over Broadway*	Olive Neal
1995 (68th)	**Mira Sorvino**	*Mighty Aphrodite*	**Linda Ash**
	Joan Allen	*Nixon*	Pat Nixon
	Kathleen Quinlan	*Apollo 13*	Marilyn Lovell
	Mare Winningham	*Georgia*	Georgia Flood
	Kate Winslet	*Sense and Sensibility*	Marianne Dashwood
1996 (69th)	**Juliette Binoche**	*The English Patient*	**Hana**
	Joan Allen	*The Crucible*	Elizabeth Proctor
	Lauren Bacall	*The Mirror Has Two Faces*	Hannah Morgan
	Barbara Hershey	*The Portrait of a Lady*	Madame Serena Merle
	Marianne Jean-Baptiste	*Secrets & Lies*	Hortense Cumberbatch
1997 (70th)	**Kim Basinger**	*L.A. Confidential*	**Lynn Bracken**
	Joan Cusack	*In & Out*	Emily Montgomery
	Minnie Driver	*Good Will Hunting*	Skylar
	Julianne Moore	*Boogie Nights*	Amber Waves
	Gloria Stuart	*Titanic*	Rose Calvert
1998 (71st)	**Judi Dench**	*Shakespeare in Love*	**Queen Elizabeth I**
	Kathy Bates	*Primary Colors*	Libby Holden
	Brenda Blethyn	*Little Voice*	Mari Hoff
	Rachel Griffiths	*Hilary and Jackie*	Hilary du Pré
	Lynn Redgrave	*Gods and Monsters*	Hanna
1999 (72nd)	**Angelina Jolie**	*Girl, Interrupted*	**Lisa Rowe**
	Toni Collette	*The Sixth Sense*	Lynn Sear
	Catherine Keener	*Being John Malkovich*	Maxine Lund
	Samantha Morton	*Sweet and Lowdown*	Hattie
	Chloë Sevigny	*Boys Don't Cry*	Lana Tisdel

2000s

Year	Actress	Film	Character
2000 (73rd)	**Marcia Gay Harden**	*Pollock*	**Lee Krasner**
	Judi Dench	*Chocolat*	Armande Voizin
	Kate Hudson	*Almost Famous*	Penny Lane
	Frances McDormand	*Almost Famous*	Elaine Miller
	Julie Walters	*Billy Elliot*	Georgia Wilkinson
2001 (74th)	**Jennifer Connelly**	*A Beautiful Mind*	**Alicia Nash**
	Helen Mirren	*Gosford Park*	Jane Wilson
	Maggie Smith	*Gosford Park*	Constance Trentham
	Marisa Tomei	*In the Bedroom*	Natalie Strout
	Kate Winslet	*Iris*	Young Iris Murdoch
2002 (75th)	**Catherine Zeta-Jones**	*Chicago*	**Velma Kelly**
	Kathy Bates	*About Schmidt*	Roberta Hertzel
	Julianne Moore	*The Hours*	Laura Brown
	Queen Latifah	*Chicago*	Matron Mama Morton
	Meryl Streep	*Adaptation.*	Susan Orlean
2003 (76th)	**Renée Zellweger**	*Cold Mountain*	**Ruby Thewes**
	Shohreh Aghdashloo	*House of Sand and Fog*	Nadereh Behrani
	Patricia Clarkson	*Pieces of April*	Joy Burns
	Marcia Gay Harden	*Mystic River*	Celeste Boyle
	Holly Hunter	*Thirteen*	Melanie Freeland
2004 (77th)	**Cate Blanchett**	*The Aviator*	**Katharine Hepburn**
	Laura Linney	*Kinsey*	Clara McMillen
	Virginia Madsen	*Sideways*	Maya Randall
	Sophie Okonedo	*Hotel Rwanda*	Tatiana Rusesabagina
	Natalie Portman	*Closer*	Alice Ayres
2005 (78th)	**Rachel Weisz**	*The Constant Gardener*	**Tessa Quayle**
	Amy Adams	*Junebug*	Ashley Johnsten
	Catherine Keener	*Capote*	Nelle Harper Lee
	Frances McDormand	*North Country*	Glory Dodge
	Michelle Williams	*Brokeback Mountain*	Alma Beers Del Mar

2006 (79th)	Jennifer Hudson	*Dreamgirls*	Effie White
	Adriana Barraza	*Babel*	Amelia
	Cate Blanchett	*Notes on a Scandal*	Sheba Hart
	Abigail Breslin	*Little Miss Sunshine*	Olive Hoover
	Rinko Kikuchi	*Babel*	Chieko Wataya
2007 (80th)	Tilda Swinton	*Michael Clayton*	Karen Crowder
	Cate Blanchett	*I'm Not There*	Jude Quinn
	Ruby Dee	*American Gangster*	Mama Lucas
	Saoirse Ronan	*Atonement*	Briony Tallis
	Amy Ryan	*Gone Baby Gone*	Helene McCready
2008 (81st)	Penélope Cruz	*Vicky Cristina Barcelona*	María Elena
	Amy Adams	*Doubt*	Sister James
	Viola Davis	*Doubt*	Mrs. Miller
	Taraji P. Henson	*The Curious Case of Benjamin Button*	Queenie
	Marisa Tomei	*The Wrestler*	Cassidy/Pam
2009 (82nd)	Mo'Nique	*Precious*	Mary Lee Johnston
	Penélope Cruz	*Nine*	Carla Albanese
	Vera Farmiga	*Up in the Air*	Alex Goran
	Maggie Gyllenhaal	*Crazy Heart*	Jean Craddock
	Anna Kendrick	*Up in the Air*	Natalie Keener

2010s

Year	Actress	Film	Character
2010 (83rd)	Melissa Leo	*The Fighter*	Alice Ward
	Amy Adams	*The Fighter*	Charlene Fleming
	Helena Bonham Carter	*The King's Speech*	Queen Elizabeth
	Hailee Steinfeld	*True Grit*	Mattie Ross
	Jacki Weaver	*Animal Kingdom*	Janine "Smurf" Cody
2011 (84th)	Octavia Spencer	*The Help*	Minny Jackson
	Bérénice Bejo	*The Artist*	Peppy Miller
	Jessica Chastain	*The Help*	Celia Foote
	Melissa McCarthy	*Bridesmaids*	Megan
	Janet McTeer	*Albert Nobbs*	Hubert Page

2012 (85th)	TBA	TBA	TBA
	Amy Adams	*The Master*	Peggy Dodd
	Sally Field	*Lincoln*	Mary Todd Lincoln
	Anne Hathaway	*Les Misérables*	Fantine
	Helen Hunt	*The Sessions*	Cheryl Cohen-Greene
	Jacki Weaver	*Silver Linings Playbook*	Dolores Solitano

Superlatives

Superlative	Best Actress		Best Supporting Actress		Overall	
Actress with most awards	Katharine Hepburn	4	Shelley Winters Dianne Wiest	2	Katharine Hepburn	4
Actress with most nominations	Meryl Streep	14	Thelma Ritter	6	Meryl Streep	17
Actress with most nominations (without ever winning)	Deborah Kerr	6	Thelma Ritter	6	Deborah Kerr Thelma Ritter Glenn Close	6
Film with most nominations	*All About Eve* *Suddenly, Last Summer* *The Turning Point* *Terms of Endearment* *Thelma & Louise*	2	*Tom Jones*	3	*All About Eve*	4

The only actresses to have won the Best Supporting Actress award twice are Shelley Winters and Dianne Wiest. Winters won in 1959 and 1965 (she was also nominated in 1972); Wiest won in 1986 and 1994 (she was also nominated in 1989).

Thelma Ritter had six nominations in this category, more than any other actress in this category. As she never won the award, she also holds the record for the number of unsuccessful nominations.

Multiple nominations

Six nominations
Thelma Ritter

Four nominations
• Amy Adams
• Ethel Barrymore
• Lee Grant
• Agnes Moorehead
• Geraldine Page
• Maggie Smith
• Maureen Stapleton

Three nominations
• Cate Blanchett
• Glenn Close
• Gladys Cooper

- Celeste Holm
- Diane Ladd
- Angela Lansbury
- Frances McDormand
- Anne Revere
- Meryl Streep
- Claire Trevor
- Marisa Tomei
- Dianne Wiest
- Shelley Winters

Two nominations

- Jane Alexander
- Joan Allen
- Fay Bainter
- Kathy Bates
- Beulah Bondi
- Alice Brady
- Dyan Cannon
- Penélope Cruz
- Joan Cusack
- Judi Dench
- Melinda Dillon
- Mildred Dunnock
- Edith Evans
- Marcia Gay Harden
- Ruth Gordon
- Gloria Grahame
- Eileen Heckart
- Wendy Hiller
- Holly Hunter
- Anjelica Huston
- Madeline Kahn
- Catherine Keener
- Shirley Knight
- Elsa Lanchester
- Piper Laurie
- Mercedes McCambridge
- Sylvia Miles
- Helen Mirren
- Julianne Moore
- Maria Ouspenskaya
- Estelle Parsons
- Marjorie Rambeau
- Vanessa Redgrave
- Joyce Redman
- Gale Sondergaard
- Jacki Weaver
- May Whitty
- Kate Winslet
- Teresa Wright

International presence

As the Academy Awards are based in the United States and are centered on the Hollywood film industry, the majority of Academy Award winners have been Americans. Nonetheless, there is significant international presence at the awards, as evidenced by the following list of winners for the Academy Award for Best Supporting Actress.

- Australia: Cate Blanchett
- Canada / New Zealand: Anna Paquin
- France: Juliette Binoche
- Greece: Katina Paxinou
- Republic of Ireland: Brenda Fricker
- Japan: Miyoshi Umeki
- Puerto Rico: Rita Moreno
- Russia: Lila Kedrova
- Spain: Penélope Cruz
- Sweden: Ingrid Bergman
- United Kingdom: Peggy Ashcroft, Judi Dench, Wendy Hiller, Vanessa Redgrave, Margaret Rutherford, Maggie Smith, Tilda Swinton, Rachel Weisz, Catherine Zeta-Jones

There have been two years in which all four of the top acting Academy Awards were presented to non-Americans (Europeans).

- At the 37th Academy Awards (1964), the winners were Rex Harrison (British), Julie Andrews (British), Peter Ustinov (British), and Lila Kedrova (Russian).
- At the 80th Academy Awards (2007), the winners were Daniel Day-Lewis (British and Irish), Marion Cotillard (French), Javier Bardem (Spanish), and Tilda Swinton (British).

See also

- 1936 in film

References

[1] Beginning with the 1943 awards, winners in the supporting acting categories were awarded Oscar statuettes similar to those awarded to winners in all other categories, including the leading acting categories. Prior to this, however, winners in the supporting acting categories were awarded plaques.

External links

- Oscars.org (http://www.oscars.org/) (official Academy site)
- Oscar.com (http://www.oscar.com/) (official ceremony promotional site)
- The Academy Awards Database (http://www.oscars.org/awardsdatabase/index.html) (official site)

Adam and Evelyne

Adam and Evelyne	
Poster with the American title	
Directed by	Harold French
Produced by	Harold French
Written by	Noel Langley (story) George Barraud Nicholas Phipps Lesley Storm
Starring	Stewart Granger Jean Simmons
Studio	Two Cities Films
Release date(s)	May 31, 1949
Running time	70 minutes
Country	United Kingdom
Language	English

Adam and Evelyne, released in the U.S. as *Adam and Evalyn*, is a 1949 romance film starring Stewart Granger and Jean Simmons. According to Robert Osborne, host of Turner Classic Movies, this suited the stars, as they were romantically involved at the time, despite their age difference. They married the next year.

Plot

When jockey Chris Kirby (Fred Johnson) is fatally injured in a horse race, he gets his best friend, gambler Adam Black (Stewart Granger), to promise to take care of his teenage daughter, Evelyne (Jean Simmons), who has been raised apart from her father. Unbeknownst to Adam, Evelyne had been led to believe that Adam is her father in correspondence between parent and child. Adam is unable to tell her the truth; his butler and friend Bill Murray (Edwin Styles) tries and fails as well. Finally, Adam's sometime girlfriend Moira (Helen Cherry) breaks the news to the girl.

Adam sends Evelyne to an exclusive boarding school. When she has grown up, she reappears unexpectedly in his life. Because of the hatred she has for gambling, Adam does not reveal that he stages illegal gambling sessions; instead he tells her that he makes his money on the stock exchange. She begins casually dating Adam's no-good brother Roddy (Raymond Young).

When Adam tells Moira that he is getting out of the business, she accuses him of being in love with his "ward". Roddy has his own grudge against his brother - Adam refuses to finance a shady deal - and the two of them tip off the police about Adam's last operation. Roddy also brings Evelyne to see what Adam really does for a living.

Shocked, she quarrels with Adam and leaves. A kindly gambler, Colonel Bradley (Wilfred Hyde-White), gives her some sage advice and convinces her to reconcile with Adam.

Cast

- Stewart Granger as Adam Black
- Jean Simmons as Evelyne Kirby
- Edwin Styles as Bill Murray
- Raymond Young as Roddy Black
- Helen Cherry as Moira
- Beatrice Varley as Mrs. Parker, a gambler
- Joan Swinstead as Molly
- Wilfred Hyde-White as Colonel Bradley
- Fred Johnson as Chris Kirby
- Geoffrey Denton as Police Inspector Collins
- Peter Reynolds as David

External links

- *Adam and Evelyne* [1] at the Internet Movie Database

References

[1] http://www.imdb.com/title/tt0041089/

Affair with a Stranger

Affair with a Stranger	
Theatrical release poster	
Directed by	Roy Rowland
Produced by	Robert Sparks
Written by	Richard Flournoy
Starring	Jean Simmons Victor Mature Mary Jo Tarola Monica Lewis Jane Darwell Dabbs Greer Olive Carey
Music by	Sam Coslow Roy Webb
Cinematography	Harry J. Wild
Editing by	George Amy
Distributed by	RKO Pictures
Release date(s)	June 20, 1953
Running time	87 minutes
Country	United States
Language	English

Affair with a Stranger is a 1953 American comedy-drama starring Jean Simmons and Victor Mature. It was directed by Roy Rowland, and was originally to be released as ***Kiss and Run***.

The film centres around the rumoured marital troubles of a successful playwright. As various people who came into contact with the couple reminisce about the couple's past, the story of the relationship and the budding affair that is potentially destroying it is told through a series of flashbacks.

Upon release, the film was met with lukewarm reviews, Bosley Crowther of *The New York Times* calling it "a virtual collection of cliches".[1]

References

[1] NYT review (http://movies.nytimes.com/movie/review?res=9F03E1DD173DE23BBC4952DFB1668388649EDE)

External links

- *Affair with a Stranger* (http://www.imdb.com/title/tt0045477/) at the Internet Movie Database

Aida Foster stage school

The **Aida Foster School** was founded by Aida Foster in 1929[1] as a hobby to teach dancing. It expanded over the years to become one of Britain's foremost stage schools. Many of the 20th-century stage and film personalities obtained their professional education from the school, and many their first employment through the school. Run by Aida and later by her daughter, Anita Foster, the school catered for three different groups of students; Those that took dance training only, the younger students that had full education plus both dancing and drama training, and the older students taking drama training only.

Aida Foster school supplied many of the Pantomime "Babes" (Children choruses and parts) for many of the West End Christmas shows in the 1950s.[2] They also obtained modelling contracts for many of the juveniles.

The school was situated on the Finchley Road in Golders Green, London, just north of the junction with Golders Green Road. It closed in 2003.

Alumni

Notable alumni include Jean Simmons,[1] Barbara Windsor,[1] Kate O'Mara,[1] Vicki Michelle,[1] Shirley Eaton,[1] Elaine Paige,[1] Marti Webb, Dilys Laye, and Paul Layton.

References

[1] Freeman, Ian (2 October 2007), "Anita Foster" (http://www.thestage.co.uk/features/obituaries/feature.php/18384/anita-foster), *The Stage*,

[2] Aida Foster Babes (http://www.its-behind-you.com/chorus.html)

External links

- BritishPathe Aida Foster School video newsreel film (http://www.britishpathe.com/record.php?id=315)

Androcles and the Lion (film)

Androcles and the Lion	
DVD cover	
Directed by	Chester Erskine Nicholas Ray (uncredited)
Produced by	Gabriel Pascal
Written by	George Bernard Shaw Ken Englund Chester Erskine
Starring	Jean Simmons Victor Mature Alan Young
Music by	Friedrich Hollaender
Cinematography	Harry Stradling Sr.
Editing by	Roland Gross
Distributed by	RKO
Release date(s)	1952
Running time	98 minutes
Country	United Kingdom
Language	English

Androcles and the Lion is a 1952 RKO film produced by Gabriel Pascal from the George Bernard Shaw play.

This was Pascal's last film, made two years after the death of Shaw, his long-standing friend and mentor, and two years before Pascal's own death.

Plot

Androcles is a fugitive Christian tailor who is on the run from his Roman persecutors. While hiding in the forest he comes upon a wild lion who, instead of attacking the weak and starving slave, approaches him with a wounded paw, which he holds out to Androcles as if to beg his assistance. Androcles sees that the source of the lion's agony is a large thorn embedded in the paw; the slave courageously pulls it out. The lion is greatly relieved but Androcles is arrested and joins a procession of Christian prisoners on their way to the Colosseum in Rome. Eventually he is placed in the arena and the lion is released upon him. It turns out to be none other than the lion which Androcles had helped, and the two embrace each other and begin dancing in front of thousands of aghast people and an astonished Roman Emperor. The Emperor orders an end to the persecution of Christians and allows Androcles and his lion friend "Tommy" to depart in peace.

Cast

- Jean Simmons - Lavinia
- Victor Mature - Captain
- Alan Young - Androcles
- Robert Newton - Ferrovius
- Maurice Evans - Caesar
- Elsa Lanchester - Megaera
- Reginald Gardiner - Lentulus
- Gene Lockhart - Menagerie Keeper
- Alan Mowbray - Editor of Gladiators
- Noel Willman - Spintho
- John Hoyt - Cato
- Jim Backus - Centurion
- Woody Strode - The Lion
- Sylvia Lewis - Chief of the Vestal Virgins

Note that the opening sequence of the film places it during the time of Emperor Antoninus, but the character is only addressed as "Caesar" during the film.

External links

- *Androcles and the Lion* [1] at the Internet Movie Database

References

[1] http://www.imdb.com/title/tt0044355/

Cage of Gold

Cage of Gold is a 1950 British drama film directed by Basil Dearden and starring Jean Simmons, David Farrar and James Donald.[1]

Plot

A young woman deserts her prospective fiance for an old flame who marries her, then leaves her pregnant when he discovers that her father can offer him no financial support. Two years later, when she has married her former fiance, believing her husband to be dead, he reappears and begins to blackmail her.[2]

Critical Responses

"Melodrama of a young girl's tragic infatuation for a worthless bounder who had been her schoolgirl hero. Lavishly staged and efficiently directed, but the characters are somewhat stereotyped."[3]

Cast

- Jean Simmons as Judith Moray
- David Farrar as Bill Glennan
- James Donald as Dr Alan Kearn
- Herbert Lom as Rahman
- Madeleine LeBeau as Marie Jouvet
- Maria Mauban as Antoinette Duport
- Bernard Lee as Inspector Grey
- Grégoire Aslan as Duport
- Gladys Henson as Waddy
- Harcourt Williams as Dr Kearn senior
- Léo Ferré as Victor
- George Benson as Assistant Registrar
- Martin Boddey as Police Sergeant Adams
- Arthur Hambling as Jenkins
- Campbell Singer as Constable

References

[1] http://www.imdb.com/title/tt0042295/
[2] http://explore.bfi.org.uk/4ce2b6a6ec10f
[3] *Picture Show*, vol 55, No 1441

References

December Flower

December Flower	
Directed by	Stephen Frears
Produced by	Roy Roberts
Written by	Judy Allen
Starring	Jean Simmons Mona Washbourne Pat Heywood Bryan Forbes June Ritchie Ann-Marie Gwatkin Richard Warner Richard Hope Christopher Fulford
Studio	Granada Television

December Flower is a British single drama first broadcast at Christmas 1984. It featured the first acting appearance for 17 years by Bryan Forbes.[1]

Plot synopsis

Newly widowed Etta Marsh goes to visit her elderly Aunt, Mary Grey, whom she has never met. (Mary and her sister, Etta's mother, had not seen each other for some 60 years - after Mary "stole" Etta's mother's boyfriend, Harry's father.) Etta finds her 85-year old "Aunt M" being looked after by an inattentive, selfish cook-housekeeper called Mrs. Cullen. Aunt M herself is extremely inattentive and listless because Mrs. Cullen keeps her sedated with pills. Her son is too wrapped up in his own life to be interested and his wife is only waiting for the old woman to die so they will inherit her property. Her granddaughter Jill is the only one, besides Etta, who displays any genuine affection for the old woman.

On the last day of Etta's visit, she and Mrs. Cullen have a row over what the latter has been giving Mrs. Grey to eat - or, rather, what she has *not* been feeding Mrs. Grey but keeping for herself to eat on her own. Mrs. Cullen quits, cousin Harry is distraught, and Etta promises to stay until he can sort out a new cook-housekeeper or Mrs. Cullen agrees to return.

However, once Mrs. Cullen is gone and Aunt M is no longer being fed sleeping pills in place of food, the old woman begins to perk up. She and Etta strike up a tremendous friendship, and Aunt M takes revenge on her snooty daughter-in-law by inviting the family over to admire her new Mickey Mouse telephone and have tea and cakes - served on rotating musical cake stand.

Harry and Etta are both pleased for Etta to stay and look after his mother. Harry's wife is not and drops a vitriolic bombshell: "Mother and *your* mother were adopted. You're not *really* related. You can call her "Aunt" if you want to but she *isn't* your aunt!"

There is some foundation for her concern. When Mary dies, Etta is shocked to learn that Aunt M had made a new will leaving everything to *her* instead of to her son. Etta receives assurances from Mary's attending physician that, her "Aunt died of a massive coronary that was coming in any case. If anything, what you did *prolonged* her life; and you certainly brightened the end of it beyond *all* recognition." Etta then arranges to put most of the money and other assets in trust for her niece, Aunt M's granddaughter, Jill.

The closing scene is in the cemetery where Aunt M is buried. A large white marble statue has been erected in her memory, and the caretaker has instructions to replenish its floral arrangements on a weekly basis. "Only *orange* flowers?" he asks. Etta smiles and replies, "*Orange* flowers, yes!".

References

[1] *TV Times*, Christmas 1984 issue

Demetrius and the Gladiators

Demetrius and the Gladiators	
Original film poster	
Directed by	Delmer Daves
Produced by	Frank Ross
Written by	Philip Dunne Lloyd C. Douglas
Starring	Victor Mature Susan Hayward William Marshall Michael Rennie Debra Paget Anne Bancroft Jay Robinson Ernest Borgnine Barry Jones Richard Egan
Music by	Franz Waxman
Cinematography	Milton R. Krasner
Editing by	Robert Fritch Dorothy Spencer
Distributed by	20th Century Fox
Release date(s)	18 June 1954
Running time	101 min
Country	United States
Language	English
Budget	$1.99 million[1]
Box office	$4.25 million (US rentals)[2][3]

Demetrius and the Gladiators is a 1954 sword-and-sandal drama film and a sequel to *The Robe*. The picture was made by 20th Century Fox, directed by Delmer Daves and produced by Frank Ross. The screenplay was written by Philip Dunne based on characters created by Lloyd C. Douglas in *The Robe*.

The movie presents Victor Mature as Demetrius, a Christian slave made to fight in the Roman arena as a gladiator, and Susan Hayward as Messalina. The cast also features Ernest Borgnine, William Marshall, Michael Rennie, Jay Robinson as depraved emperor Caligula, Debra Paget, a young Anne Bancroft in one of her earlier roles and Julie Newmar as a briefly seen dancing entertainer. The film is in color and Cinemascope.

Plot summary

The film begins with a clip from the previous film, showing its central characters Marcellus and Diana going to be martyred for their Christian beliefs on the order of the Emperor Caligula. Before being executed, Diana hands the robe to Marcellus' servant Marcipor, telling him that it is "for the Big Fisherman," meaning Peter, who was a fisherman before being called as an apostle.

Peter hands the robe to Demetrius while at the funeral of Marcellus and Diana before leaving on a journey to live in 'the north'. Caligula becomes interested in the robe, thinking that it has magic powers and will bring him the 'eternal life' that Jesus had spoken of. He accosts his uncle Claudius, wanting to know what had happened to it.

Demetrius, looking out for his Lucia and the robe and refusing to reveal its location, is arrested for assaulting a Roman soldier, and sentenced to the arena. Meanwhile, Lucia disguises herself to gain entrance to the gladiator school to see Demetrius. However, the two are forcibly separated on orders of Messalina, Claudius' wife. Lucia is then assaulted by Dardanius and the other gladiators, forcibly kissing her and trying to carry her to private chambers. Demetrius in desperation prays for God to save her, and suddenly it appears that Dardanius has broken Lucia's neck. All present are shocked at Lucia's apparent death, especially Demetrius, and he loses all his faith in the god of Jesus Christ. Previously, he had refused to avoided killing anyone in the Emperor's games, because of his religion, but all that now changes. His next time in the arena, not only does he fight, but he ferociously kills all the gladiators that took part in the attack on Lucia. The Roman spectators, including the Emperor, are thrilled. Demetrius is freed, and allowed to join the Praetorian Guard. Caligula asks if Demetrius renounces Christ; he does, and once Demetrius does this, Caligula frees him and inducts him into the guard with the rank of Tribune.

As a Tribune, Demetrius rejects the teachings of Christ (and of Isis when encountering Messalina praying to her statue), beginning an affair with Messalina. When Peter comes to visit them, he turns him away too. The affair continues for several months, and eventually Caligula finds out about it.

Demetrius takes the robe to the Emperor, who takes the robe down below to a prisoner. He has the prisoner killed, and tries to resurrect him. Furious that he cannot, Caligula accuses Demetrius of having brought him a fake, and that both the robe and Christ are frauds. Demetrius is taken back to the arena. When the Emperor tries to have Demetrius executed, the Praetorian Guard (already angry at Caligula over worse pay and conditions) finally turns against Caligula and kills first Macro, the prefect of the Praetorian Guard, then Caligula. Claudius is installed as Emperor by the Praetorian Guard almost immediately after Caligula is killed.

Demetrius is taken to a small house, where he is surprised to find Lucia's body, lying on a bed. He finds out that she never had died, after all, but that when he prayed for God to save her, her sudden coma had accomplished her rescue. Now, months later, she is still unconscious. Demetrius realizes he has made a mistake, prays to the Christian God after placing the robe on Lucia's body, and she wakes up.

Soon after his installation, Claudius says that he is neither a god, nor would he likely become one anytime soon. Claudius says that he maintained the appearance of being weak to survive Caligula's rule, and that he would now take on the role of Emperor to the best of his ability. He gives Demetrius his final orders as a Tribune, to go to Peter and the other Christians, and tell them that as long as they do not act against the Empire that they have nothing to fear from Claudius. Messalina re-vows her constancy to her husband. Demetrius and Glycon (another virtuous gladiator) take the robe to Peter, and they leave the Imperial palace together.

Cast

- Victor Mature - Demetrius
- Susan Hayward - Messalina
- Michael Rennie - Peter
- Debra Paget - Lucia
- Jay Robinson - Caligula
- William Marshall - Glycon
- Ernest Borgnine - Strabo
- Barry Jones - Claudius
- Anne Bancroft - Paula
- Richard Egan - Dardanius
- Charles Evans - Cassius Chaerea
- Everett Glass - Kaeso
- Jeff York - Albus
- Fred Graham - Decurion
- Dayton Lummis - Magistrate
- Paul Stader - Gladiator
- George Eldredge - Chamberlain
- Woody Strode - Gladiator
- Jean Simmons - in clip from *The Robe*
- Richard Burton - in clip from *The Robe*
- Cameron Mitchell as voice of Jesus - in clip from *The Robe*

References

[1] Aubrey Solomon, *Twentieth Century Fox: A Corporate and Financial History*, Scarecrow Press, 1989 p249

[2] Aubrey Solomon, Twentieth Century Fox: A Corporate and Financial History, Scarecrow Press, 1989 p225

[3] 'The Top Box-Office Hits of 1954', *Variety Weekly*, January 5, 1955

External links

- *Demetrius and the Gladiators* (http://www.afi.com/members/catalog/DetailView.aspx?s=&Movie=51179) at the American Film Institute Catalog
- *Demetrius and the Gladiators* (http://www.imdb.com/title/tt0046899/) at the Internet Movie Database

Divorce American Style

Divorce American Style	
Theatrical poster	
Directed by	Bud Yorkin
Produced by	Norman Lear
Written by	Norman Lear Robert Kaufman
Starring	Dick Van Dyke Debbie Reynolds Jason Robards Jean Simmons
Music by	Dave Grusin
Cinematography	Conrad L. Hall
Editing by	Ferris Webster
Studio	Tandem Productions
Distributed by	Columbia Pictures
Release date(s)	• June 21, 1967
Running time	109 minutes
Country	United States
Language	English
Box office	$12,000,000[1]

Divorce American Style is a 1967 American satirical comedy film directed by Bud Yorkin and starring Dick Van Dyke, Debbie Reynolds, Jean Simmons, Jason Robards and Van Johnson. Norman Lear produced the film and wrote the script based on a story by Robert Kaufman. It focuses on a married couple that opts for divorce when counseling fails to help them resolve their various problems, and the problems presented by divorced people by alimony. The title is an *homage* to *Divorce Italian Style* (1961).

Plot

After seventeen years of marriage, affluent Los Angeles suburban couple Richard Harmon (Van Dyke) and his wife Barbara (Reynolds) seem to have it all, but they're constantly bickering. When they discover they can no longer communicate, even to argue, they make an effort to salvage their relationship through counseling. But after catching each other emptying their joint bank accounts, they file for divorce.

Richard finds himself living in a small apartment and trying to survive on $87.30 a week. His take-home income has been cut to ribbons by high alimony. Richard meets a recently divorced man, Nelson Downes (Robards), who introduces him to ex-wife Nancy (Simmons). Nelson wants to marry off Nancy to be free of his alimony burden, so that he can marry his fiancee. Nancy also wishes to marry because she is lonely.

Since Richard now cannot afford to be remarried, Nelson and Nancy plot to set up Barbara with a millionaire auto dealer, Big Al Yearling (Johnson).

Barbara begins a relationship with Big Al, but one night all of the principal characters end up in the audience at a nightclub show. A hypnotist puts Barbara in a trance and coaxes her into doing a mock striptease. But when instructed to kiss her true love, Barbara plants one on Richard, and just like that their marriage problems are resolved.

Nelson, not to be deterred, immediately tries to get Nancy interested in Big Al.

Cast

• Dick Van Dyke as Richard Harmon	• Lee Grant as Dede Murphy
• Debbie Reynolds as Barbara Harmon	• Tom Bosley as Farley
• Jason Robards as Nelson Downes	• Emmaline Henry as Fern Blandsforth
• Jean Simmons as Nancy Downes	• Richard Gautier as Larry Strickland
• Van Johnson as Al Yearling	• Tim Matheson as Mark Harmon
• Joe Flynn as Lionel Blandsforth	• Eileen Brennan as Eunice Tase
• Shelley Berman as David Grieff	• Shelley Morrison as Jackie
• Martin Gabel as Dr. Zenwinn	

Reception

The film earned an estimated $5,150,000 in North American rentals in 1967.[2]

Critical reception

In his review in the *Chicago Sun-Times*, Roger Ebert called the film "a member of that rare species, the Hollywood comedy with teeth in it" and added, "Bud Yorkin has directed with wit and style, and the cast, which seems unlikely on paper, comes across splendidly on the screen . . . The charm of this film is in its low-key approach. The plot isn't milked for humor or pathos: Both emerge naturally from familiar situations."[3]

Variety observed, "Comedy and satire, not feverish melodrama, are the best weapons with which to harpoon social mores. An outstanding example is *Divorce American Style* . . . which pokes incisive, sometimes chilling, fun at US marriage-divorce problems."[4]

New York Times film critic Bosley Crowther disliked the film, saying that "it is rather depressing, saddening and annoying, largely because it does labor to turn a solemn subject into a great big American-boob joke." Crowther criticized Van Dyke's performance, remarking that "He is too much of a giggler, too much of a dyed-in-the-wool television comedian for this serio-comic husband role."[5]

A more recent review in *Time Out New York* cites "Two or three very funny scenes . . . and a first-rate batch of supporting performances."[6]

Awards and honors

Norman Lear and Robert Kaufman were nominated for the Academy Award for Best Original Screenplay but lost to William Rose for *Guess Who's Coming to Dinner*. Lear also was nominated for the Writers Guild of America Award for Best Written American Comedy.

References

Notes

[1] "Divorce American Style, Box Office Information" (http://www.the-numbers.com/movies/1967/0DIAM.php). The Numbers. . Retrieved May 22, 2012.

[2] "Big Rental Films of 1967", *Variety*, 3 January 1968 p 25. Please note these figures refer to rentals accruing to the distributors.

[3] *Chicago Sun-Times* review (http://rogerebert.suntimes.com/apps/pbcs.dll/article?AID=/19670621/REVIEWS/706210301/1023)

[4] *Variety* review (http://www.variety.com/review/VE1117790466.html?categoryid=31&cs=1&p=0)

[5]   Crowther, Bosley (1967-07-20). "The Screen: 'Divorce American Style':Solemn Topic Treated Too Much as Joke" (http://movies.nytimes. com/movie/review?_r=1&res=9803E6D81E3CE731A25753C2A9619C946691D6CF). *The New York Times*. . Retrieved 2009-09-15.

[6]   *Time Out New York* review (http://www.timeout.com/film/newyork/reviews/65544/Divorce_American_Style.html)

External links

- *Divorce American Style* (http://www.imdb.com/title/tt0061581/) at the Internet Movie Database
- *Divorce American Style* (http://www.allrovi.com/movies/movie/v89602) at AllRovi
- *Divorce American Style* (http://tcmdb.com/title/title.jsp?stid=23748) at the TCM Movie Database

Dominique (film)

Dominique	
Directed by	Michael Anderson
Produced by	Andrew Donally (producer) Melvin Simon (executive producer) Milton Subotsky (producer)
Written by	Edward Abraham (writer) Valerie Abraham (writer) Harold Lawlor (story)
Starring	See below
Music by	David Whitaker
Cinematography	Ted Moore
Editing by	Richard Best
Release date(s)	1980
Running time	100 minutes
Country	United Kingdom
Language	English

Dominique is a 1980 British film directed by Michael Anderson.

The film is also known as *Dominique Is Dead* (American reissue title and UK video title).

Plot

Greedy David Ballard (Cliff Robertson) wants to get the money of his wife Dominique (Jean Simmons), so he attempts to drive her insane. He succeeds and she hangs herself, only to come back to haunt him from the afterlife.

Cast

- Cliff Robertson as David Ballard
- Jean Simmons as Dominique Ballard
- Jenny Agutter as Ann Ballard
- Simon Ward as Tony Calvert
- Ron Moody as Dr. Rogers
- Judy Geeson as Marjorie Craven
- Michael Jayston as Arnold Craven
- Flora Robson as Mrs. Davis
- David Tomlinson as Lawyer
- Jack Warner as George
- Leslie Dwyer as Cemetery Supervisor
- Erin Geraghty as Ballard's Secretary
- Brian Hayes as S.T. Reeve
- Ian Holden as Policeman
- Jack McKenzie as John, 1st Chauffeur

- Michael Nightingale as Vicar at Funeral

External links

- *Dominique* [1] at the Internet Movie Database
- *Dominique* [2] is available for free download at the Internet Archive [*more*]

References

[1] http://www.imdb.com/title/tt0077450/
[2] http://www.archive.org/details/Dominique_638

Désirée (film)

Désirée	
Theatrical release poster	
Directed by	Henry Koster
Produced by	Julian Blaustein
Written by	Daniel Taradash Annemarie Selinko (novel)
Starring	Marlon Brando Jean Simmons Merle Oberon Michael Rennie Cameron Mitchell
Music by	Alex North
Cinematography	Milton R. Krasner
Editing by	William H. Reynolds
Distributed by	20th Century Fox
Release date(s)	November 17, 1954
Running time	110 minutes
Country	United States
Language	English
Budget	$2,720,000[1]
Box office	$4.5 million (US rentals)[2]

Désirée is a 1954 historical film biography made by 20th Century Fox. It was directed by Henry Koster and produced by Julian Blaustein from a screenplay by Daniel Taradash, based on the best-selling novel *Désirée* by Annemarie Selinko. The music score was by Alex North and the cinematography by Milton R. Krasner. The film was made in CinemaScope.

It stars Marlon Brando, Jean Simmons, Merle Oberon and Michael Rennie with Cameron Mitchell, Elizabeth Sellars, Charlotte Austin, Cathleen Nesbitt, Carolyn Jones and Evelyn Varden.

The film was nominated for two Academy Awards, for Best Art Direction (Lyle Wheeler, Leland Fuller, Walter M. Scott, Paul S. Fox) and Costume Design.[3]

Plot

In 1794, in Marseille, Désirée Clary (Jean Simmons) makes the acquaintance of a Corsican named Joseph Bonaparte (Cameron Mitchell) and invites him and his brother, General Napoleon Bonaparte (Marlon Brando), to call upon the family the following day. The next day, Julie (Elizabeth Sellars), Désirée's sister and Joseph are immediately attracted to each other, and Napoleon is taken with Désirée. He admits to her that the poor Bonaparte brothers need the rich dowries of the Clary sisters. Later, Désirée learns that Napoleon has been arrested and taken to Paris.

Napoleon eventually returns to Marseille, tells Désirée that he has been cleared of all charges, but has been ordered to track down royalists in Paris. Désirée begs Napoleon to leave the Army and join her brother in business, but he scoffs at the idea and instead proposes marriage. Désirée accepts and lends Napoleon the money to return to Paris.

Napoleon tells her that he will always love her and will return soon for their wedding but, as the months pass, Désirée starts doubting him and goes to the city where she meets General Jean-Baptiste Bernadotte (Michael Rennie). She learns that Napoleon is engaged to the wealthy, Joséphine de Beauharnais (Merle Oberon). Désirée contemplates suicide, Bernadotte, who has fallen in love with her, stops her.

Later, in 1797, Napoleon, now France's leading general, has succeeded in conquering Italy, and Désirée lives in Rome with Julie and Joseph. She soon tires of Rome, however, and decides to return to Paris, where she meets Napoleon, now married to Josephine, who announces that he will be leaving for Egypt. Bernadotte is thrilled to see Désirée again and proposes marriage to her.

By July 4, 1799, Désirée and Bernadotte have happily settled into married life and have a son, Oscar (Nicholas Koster). On November 9, 1799, Napoleon is proclaimed First Consul of the French Republic and asks Bernadotte to join his council of state, and Bernadotte agrees.

Several years later, Napoleon is proclaimed emperor, and at his coronation he takes the crown from the hands of Pope Pius VII and crowns himself.

Five years later, desperate for an heir, Napoleon divorces Josephine, and Désirée comforts her former rival, before Napoleon's upcoming marriage to the 18-year-old Marie Louise of Austria (Violet Rensing). Napoleon involves France in more wars, and Bernadotte is approached by representatives of the king of Sweden, who wishes to adopt him and make him the heir to the throne. Désirée, stunned by the news that she will one day be a queen, nevertheless supports her husband, and eventually Napoleon allows both of them to leave Paris.

In Stockholm, Désirée does not fit in with the royal family and asks to go home. Eight months later, she attends a ball in Paris at which Napoleon shows off his new son. Napoleon makes veiled threats about Bernadotte's alliance with Russia and announces to the crowd that she will be held hostage to ensure Sweden's support while his army marches through Russia to Moscow.

Napoleon's army is defeated, and he visits Désirée, asking her to write a letter to Bernadotte, requesting his help. Désirée realizes that Napoleon still loves her and came more for her than to seek her husband's help. Soon after, Bernadotte leads one of the armies that overwhelms Napoleon, and the triumphant general reunites with Désirée before returning to Sweden.

Napoleon's exile to Elba is short-lived, however, and after the Battle of Waterloo, Napoleon retreats with his personal army to the Château de Malmaison. Representatives of the allied armies ask Désirée to speak with Napoleon, hoping that she can persuade him to surrender. Napoleon agrees to speak with Désirée alon, and muses on what his destiny would have been if he had married her. Napoleon proclaims that he has given his life to protect France, but Désirée gently tells him that he must do as France asks and go into exile on St. Helena. Commenting on how strange it is that the two most outstanding men of their time had fallen in love with her, Napoleon gives Désirée his sword in surrender and assures her that her dowry was not the only reason that he proposed to her many years ago in Marseille.

Cast

- Marlon Brando - Napoleon Bonaparte
- Jean Simmons - Désirée Clary
- Merle Oberon - Joséphine de Beauharnais
- Michael Rennie - Jean-Baptiste Bernadotte
- Cameron Mitchell - Joseph Bonaparte
- Elizabeth Sellars - Julie Clary
- Charlotte Austin - Paulette
- Cathleen Nesbitt - Mme. Bonaparte
- Evelyn Varden - Marie

- Isobel Elsom - Madame Clary
- Alan Napier - Despereaux
- Nicholas Koster - Oscar
- Richard Deacon - Etienne
- Edith Evanson - Queen Hedwig
- Carolyn Jones - Mme. Tallien
- Sam Gilman - Fouché
- Larry Craine - Louis Bonaparte
- Judy Lester - Caroline Bonaparte
- Louis Borell - Baron Morner
- Peter Bourne - Count Brahe
- Dorothy Neumann - Queen Sofia
- John Hoyt - Talleyrand
- Violet Rensing - Marie Louise of Austria

Notes

The story of Désirée was the subject of an earlier film, *Le Destin fabuleux de Désirée Clary* made in 1942 by Sacha Guitry.

References

[1] Solomon, Aubrey. *Twentieth Century Fox: A Corporate and Financial History (The Scarecrow Filmmakers Series)*. Lanham, Maryland: Scarecrow Press, 1989. ISBN 978-0-8108-4244-1. p248

[2] 'The Top Box-Office Hits of 1954', *Variety Weekly*, January 5, 1955

[3] "NY Times: Désirée" (http://movies.nytimes.com/movie/13390/Desiree/details). *NY Times*. . Retrieved 2008-12-21.

External links

- Désirée Clary (http://www.nebula5.org/clary/desiree.html)
- The story of Desiree (http://home.snafu.de/veith/Texte/Napoleon.htm) (ger.)
- *Désirée* (http://www.imdb.com/title/tt0046903/) at the Internet Movie Database

Footsteps in the Fog

Footsteps in the Fog	
Directed by	Arthur Lubin
Produced by	M. J. Frankovich Maxwell Setton
Written by	W. W. Jacobs (short story) Lenore J. Coffee Dorothy Davenport Arthur Pierson
Starring	Stewart Granger Jean Simmons
Music by	Benjamin Frankel
Cinematography	Christopher Challis
Editing by	Alan Osbiston
Release date(s)	June 1955
Running time	90 minutes
Country	United Kingdom
Language	English

Footsteps in the Fog is a 1955 British crime film starring Stewart Granger and Jean Simmons, with a screenplay co-written by Lenore Coffee and Dorothy Davenport, and released by Columbia Pictures. It is based on the short story "The Interruption" by W.W. Jacobs.[1]

Plot

After poisoning his wife, the master of the house (Stewart Granger), is blackmailed by his Cockney maid (Jean Simmons) who demands promotion. As she steadily takes the place of his dead wife, he again attempts murder. While attempting to murder Lily, by following someone that looked like her through the fog, he accidently kills Constable Burke's wife and gets chased by an angery mob which he evades. Lily returns home and Stephen learns of his mistake. Some local bar goers saw him murder Mrs Burke and Stephen is put on trial but their claims are dismissed after it was revealed they drank a lot. Stephen now guilt ridden decides to commit suicide by drinking the poison that he used to kill his own wife and frame Lily who declared her love for him. The plan works and Lily is confused about Stephen never loving her and is arrested for Stephen and his wife's murder.

Cast

- Stewart Granger as Stephen Lowry
- Jean Simmons as Lily Watkins
- Bill Travers as David MacDonald
- Belinda Lee as Elizabeth Travers
- Ronald Squire as Alfred Travers
- Finlay Currie as Inspector Peters
- William Hartnell as Herbert Moresby
- Frederick Leister as Dr. Simpson
- Percy Marmont as Magistrate
- Marjorie Rhodes as Mrs. Park
- Peter Bull as Brasher
- Barry Keegan as Constable Burke
- Sheila Manahan as Rose Moresby
- Norman Macowan as Grimes
- Cameron Hall as Corcoran
- Victor Maddern as Jones
- Arthur Howard as Vicar

Notes

Granger and Simmons were a married couple at the time, "and their scenes together are perversely touching, even as they seek to outwit one another. Simmons delivers another superb performance as one of the most sweetly innocent femme fatales of the big screen, recalling her role in *Angel Face*. The scene where she switches from victim to ruthless avenger when she usurps the power of the loathed housekeeper is brilliantly played." (Alex Davidson B.F.I. British Film Institute).[2] It was the third and final time that Simmons and Granger starred together - after *Adam and Evelyne* and *Young Bess*.

References

[1] "Footsteps in the Fog - Screenplay Info" (http://www.tcm.com/tcmdb/title/27900/Footsteps-in-the-Fog/screenplay-info.html). Turner Classic Movies. . Retrieved 18 July 2011.
[2] *Moviemail* Catalogue November 2008.

External links

- *Footsteps in the Fog* (http://tcmdb.com/title/title.jsp?stid=27900) at the TCM Movie Database
- *Footsteps in the Fog* (http://www.imdb.com/title/tt0048087/) at the Internet Movie Database

Gene Simmons

<table>
<tr><td colspan="2" align="center">Gene Simmons</td></tr>
<tr><td colspan="2" align="center"></td></tr>
<tr><td colspan="2" align="center">Gene Simmons, Los Angeles, California, USA on October 15, 2012</td></tr>
<tr><td colspan="2" align="center">Background information</td></tr>
<tr><td>Birth name</td><td>Chaim Witz (pron.: /ˈxɑːjɪm/; Hebrew: חיים ויץ)</td></tr>
<tr><td>Also known as</td><td>"The Demon"</td></tr>
<tr><td>Born</td><td>August 25, 1949
Tirat HaCarmel, Israel</td></tr>
<tr><td>Genres</td><td>Heavy metal, hard rock</td></tr>
<tr><td>Occupations</td><td>Musician, songwriter, producer, actor, entrepreneur</td></tr>
<tr><td>Instruments</td><td>Bass guitar, vocals, guitar, piano, keyboards, drums</td></tr>
<tr><td>Years active</td><td>1959–present</td></tr>
<tr><td>Associated acts</td><td>Kiss, Wicked Lester</td></tr>
<tr><td>Website</td><td>www.genesimmons.com [1]</td></tr>
<tr><td colspan="2" align="center">Notable instruments</td></tr>
<tr><td colspan="2" align="center">Cort Signature GS-1
Gene Simmons Signature model</td></tr>
</table>

Gene Simmons (born **Chaim Witz** Hebrew: חיים ויץ; August 25, 1949) is an Israeli-born American rock bassist, singer-songwriter, producer, entrepreneur and actor. Known by his stage persona **The Demon**, he is the bassist/co-vocalist of Kiss, a hard rock band he co-founded in the early 1970s. With Kiss, Simmons has sold more than 100 million albums worldwide.

Biography

Early life

Chaim Witz (later Gene Simmons) was born at the Rambam Hospital in Tirat HaCarmel, Haifa, Israel in 1949. With his mother, he emigrated to Jackson Heights, Queens in New York City at the age of eight, speaking no English.[2] His mother Flóra "Florence" Klein (formerly Kovács) was born in Jánd, Hungary. The name Klein, which means "small" in German, is sometimes used informally in Hungarian as *Kis*; this however, did not give the band its name.[3] Florence and her brother, Larry Klein, were the only members of the family to survive the Holocaust. Simmons' father, Feri Witz, also Hungarian-born, remained in Israel, where he had one other son and three daughters. Simmons says the family was "dirt poor," scraping by on bread and milk.[4] In the United States, Simmons changed his name to Eugene Klein (later Gene Klein), adopting his mother's maiden name. He was a part of Yeshiva Torah Vodaath in Williamsburg, Brooklyn as a child, from 7 am to 9:30 pm.[5]

Before his musical career began, Simmons worked a variety of jobs in the New York City area. An "excellent typist", he served as an assistant to an editor of fashion magazine *Vogue* and also spent several months as a sixth-grade instructor in the upper west side.[6]

Kiss

Simmons became involved with his first band, Lynx, then renamed The Missing Links, when he was a teenager. Eventually, he disbanded The Missing Links to form The Long Island Sounds, the name being a play on words relating to the estuary separating Long Island from Westchester County, New York, Connecticut and Rhode Island. While he played in these bands, he kept up odd jobs on the side to make more money, including trading used comic books. Simmons attended Sullivan County Community College in Loch Sheldrake, New York. He then joined a new band, Bullfrog Bheer, and the band recorded a demo, "Leeta"; this was later included on the Kiss box set.

Gene Simmons as "The Demon" onstage with Kiss, 2010

Simmons formed the rock band Wicked Lester in the early 1970s with Stanley Harvey Eisen (now known as Paul Stanley) and recorded one album, which was never released. Dissatisfied with Wicked Lester's sound and look, Simmons and Stanley attempted to fire their band members; they were met with resistance, and they quit Wicked Lester, walking away from their record deal with Epic Records. They decided to form the ultimate rock band, and started looking for a drummer.

Simmons and Stanley found an ad placed by Peter Criscoula, known as Peter Criss, who was playing clubs in Brooklyn at the time; they joined and started out as a trio. Paul Frehley, better known as Ace Frehley, responded to an ad they put in *The Village Voice* for a lead guitar player, and soon joined them. Kiss released its self-titled debut album in February 1974. Stanley took on the role of lead performer on stage, while Simmons became the driving force behind what became an extensive Kiss merchandising franchise. The eye section of his "Vampire" makeup with KISS came from the wing design of comic book character Black Bolt.[7]

In 1983, while Kiss' fame was waning, the members took off their trademark make-up and enjoyed a resurgence in popularity that continued into the 1990s. At this time, Peter Criss, the original drummer, quit the band, and a replacement was sought to fill the drummers vacancy. The drummer who did so was Paul Charles Caravello, who went by the stage name of Eric Carr, and played for KISS from 1980 until his early death at the age of 41 in 1991. The band hosted their own fan conventions throughout 1995, and fan feedback about the original Kiss members reunion influenced the highly successful 1996–1997 Alive Worldwide reunion tour. In 1998, the band released *Psycho Circus*. Since then, the original line-up has once again dissolved, with Tommy Thayer replacing Ace Frehley on lead guitar and Eric Singer (who performed with Kiss from 1992 up through 1996) replacing Peter Criss on drums.

Stage makeup and persona

During an interview in 1999, Simmons was asked about the source and significance of Kiss' stage makeup and personas:

> I've always been a fan of Americana, and Americana has always been about imagery, often above content. I think there's nothing wrong with that. The world worships this culture. Most people only think about America in terms of rock & roll, movies and television. Kiss is very all-American, in the sense that our constituency has never had anything in common with critics... because our power, our lifeblood, our very reason for existence is our fans. Without them, we'd be nothing.

Political views

Simmons was a supporter of the foreign policy of the George W. Bush administration.[8] He supported the 2003 invasion of Iraq, writing on his website: "I'm ashamed to be surrounded by people calling themselves liberal who are, in my opinion, spitting on the graves of brave American soldiers who gave their life to fight a war that wasn't theirs...in a country they've never been to... simply to liberate the people therein".[9] In a follow-up, Simmons explained his position and wrote about his love and support for the United States: "I wasn't born here. But I have a love for this country and its people that knows no bounds. I will forever be grateful to America for going into World War II, when it had nothing to gain, in a country that was far away... and rescued my mother from the Nazi German concentration camps. She is alive and I am alive because of America. And, if you have a problem with America, you have a problem with me."[9]

During the 2006 Lebanon War between Israel and Lebanon, Simmons sent a televised message of support (in both English and Hebrew) to an Israeli soldier seriously wounded in fighting in Lebanon, calling him his "hero."[10]

In 2010, Simmons said he regretted voting for Barack Obama and criticized the 2009 health care reforms.[11] Following Obama's 2011 Mideast speech, in which the President called on Israel and the Palestinians to negotiate a settlement "based on the 1967 lines with mutually agreed swaps,"[12] Simmons told *CNBC* that Obama was gravely misguided. "If you have never been to the moon, you can't issue policy about the moon. For the president to be sitting in Washington D.C. and saying, 'Go back to your '67 borders in Israel' – how about you live there and try to defend an indefensible border – nine miles wide?" Simmons also accused the United Nations of being "the most pathetic body on the face of the earth."[13]

During his visit to Israel in 2011, he stated that the artists refusing to perform in Israel for political reasons are "stupid," referring to artists who canceled planned concerts in Israel.[14]

In an April 2012 interview, Simmons endorsed Republican Mitt Romney for President, stating as well that "America should be in business and it should be run by a businessman."[15]

Personal life

Simmons is a science-fiction and comic book fan and published several science fiction fanzines, among them *Id*, *Cosmos* (which eventually merged with *Stilletto* to become *Cosmos-Stilletto* and then *Faun*), *Tinderbox*, *Sci-Fi Showcase*, *Mantis* and *Adventure*. He also contributed to other fanzines, among them *BeABohema* and *Sirruish*.[16] In the late 1960s, he changed his name to Gene Simmons, after legendary rockabilly performer Jumpin' Gene Simmons.[17] Simmons' legal name after arriving from Israel is **Gene Klein**. Simmons has said that he has never had alcohol or recreational drugs.[18]

Gene Simmons fire breathing.

Simmons lives in Beverly Hills, California, with former Playboy Playmate and actress Shannon Tweed whom he had dated for 28 years. He often joked that he and Tweed were "happily unmarried" for over 20 years. He often stated, "Marriage is an institution, and I don't want to live in an institution." Simmons and Tweed finally wed on October 1, 2011, at the historic Beverly Hills Hotel in Beverly Hills, California.[19][20] They have two children: a son, Nick (born January 22, 1989), and a daughter, Sophie (born July 7, 1992). He formerly had live-in relationships with Cher and Diana Ross.[2] Simmons can speak English, German, Hungarian, and Hebrew.[2]

Homecoming visit to Israel

In March 2011, Simmons visited Israel, where he was born. He described the trip as a "life changing experience". He talked about how he still feels that he is an Israeli: "I'm Israeli. I'm a stranger in America. I'm an outsider".[21] While there, Gene met his half-brother Kobi, and triplet half-sisters Drora, Sharon and Ogenia.[22] Simmons has plans to take his band KISS to Israel. He has always said that he is an ardent supporter of Israel.[23] At a press conference in Israel, he spoke both Hebrew and English.[24]

Controversy

- In February 2002, Simmons was interviewed on the NPR radio show *Fresh Air* and asked about his claim of having had sex with 4,600 women. He told Terry Gross: "If you want to welcome me with open arms, I'm afraid you're also going to have to welcome me with open legs," paraphrasing a lyric from The Who's 1981 hit song "You Better You Bet". Gross replied: "That's a really obnoxious thing to say." At the time, Simmons refused to grant permission to NPR to make the interview available online.[25] However, it appears in print in Gross's book *All I Did Was Ask* (ISBN 1-4013-0010-3) and unauthorized transcripts are available. NPR re-broadcast part of the interview in August 2007.[26] Simmons' bandmate Paul Stanley has frequently used the phrase "... welcomed us with open arms and open legs" in onstage patter during Kiss concerts.

- In 2004, during an interview in Melbourne, Australia, while talking about Islamic extremists, Simmons described Islam as a "vile culture", saying that Muslim women had to walk behind their husbands, were not allowed to be educated or to own houses. He said: "They want to come and live right where you live and they think that you're evil." Amongst ensuing criticism, Australian Muslim of the Year Susan Carland argued that Simmons' stereotyping of Muslims was inaccurate.[27] Simmons later clarified his comments on his website, saying he had been talking specifically about Muslim extremists.

- In 2005, Simmons was sued by a former girlfriend, Georgeann Walsh Ward, who said she had been "defamed" in the VH1 documentary *When Kiss Ruled the World* and portrayed as an "unchaste woman".[28] A settlement was reached in June 2006.[29]

- In 2007, Simmons openly spoke out against music piracy, and called for file-sharers to be sued.[30] A year later, he threatened further lawsuits, and to withhold new recordings, if file-sharing continued.[31] In 2010, Anonymous staged a DDoS on his Web site, prompting Simmons to hit back with provocative comments once he was back online.[31]

- In 2011, Kiss was removed from the lineup for Michael Jackson's tribute concert because of Simmons' allegations and negative comments regarding Jackson's personal life and legal issues.[32]

Instruments

Gene Simmons has used various bass guitars during his career including:

- Axe Bass (Kramer, Jackson, B.C. Rich and now Cort)
- Punisher Bass (B.C.Rich, now made by Cort)
- Spector Gene Simmons Signature
- Pedulla Basses (mainly in the 1980s and early 1990s)
- Gibson Grabber (mainly in Kiss' early years)
- Gibson Ripper (mainly in Kiss' early years)
- Custom lebau bass (Wicked Lester, very early Kiss circa 73–74)
- Cort Guitars Signature GS-1 Bass

Gene Simmons' axe bass at the Hard Rock Cafe in Seattle, Washington

He uses Ampeg SVT CL Series amps with 8x10 cabinets. He uses Silver Herco Flex .75 Nylon Flat Guitar Picks. He uses D'Addario EXL165 Nickel Wound Custom Light .45-.105 Long Scale Bass Strings and Dunlop Electric Bass Guitar Stainless Steel Heavy .050 -.110 strings. In 2010 Gene Simmons collaborated with Cort Guitars to make his own signature bass line called the GS-AXE-2.

Film and television career

Simmons has been involved with such television projects as:

- *My Dad the Rock Star*, a cartoon by the Canadian animation company Nelvana, about the mild mannered son of a Gene Simmons-like rock star;
- *Mr. Romance*, a show created and hosted by Simmons on the Oxygen cable television channel;
- *Rock School*, a reality show in which Simmons tries to make a rock band out of a group of students of Christ's Hospital School in the first season, and in the second, a group of kids from a comprehensive school in Lowestoft;
- *Gene Simmons Family Jewels*,[33] a reality show documenting the personal lives of Simmons, his wife, his son and daughter

On March 9, 2011, Simmons and Kiss co-founder Paul Stanley and E! Entertainment announced that they have finalized a production and development deal to create an as-yet-untitled comedic half-hour kids' television series.[34] Simmons appeared as a psychic working at the Mystic Journey Bookstore in Venice, California on the American hidden camera prank TV series *I Get That a Lot*.[35]

Awards and recognition

On January 28, 2011, Simmons was in Dallas, Texas, to host the Aces & Angels Salute to the Troops charity event. While in Dallas, Simmons was presented the key to the city in Dallas, Texas and a street, Gene Simmons Boulevard, was named for him. Simmons and Tweed also visited Ft. Hood to support the Troops as a part of the Aces & Angels event. On June 15 of the same year he was given the key to the city in Winnipeg, Manitoba. In 2012, Simmons was awarded the *Golden God* award by the Revolver magazine.[36]

Filmography

Year	Film	Role	Bandmates	Miscellaneous
1978	*Kiss Meets the Phantom of the Park*	The Demon	Peter Criss, Ace Frehley, Paul Stanley	TV movie
1984	*Runaway*	Dr. Charles Luther		
1986	*Trick or Treat*	Nuke (radio DJ)		
1986	*Never Too Young to Die*	Carruthers / Velvet Von Ragner		
1987	*Wanted: Dead or Alive*	Malak Al Rahim		
1988	*The Decline of Western Civilization Part II: The Metal Years*	Himself	Paul Stanley	Documentary
1989	*Red Surf*	Doc		
1999	*Detroit Rock City*	Himself	Peter Criss, Ace Frehley, Paul Stanley	Simmons also produced
2002	*The New Guy*	Reverend		
2002	*Wish You Were Dead*	Vinny		
2008	*Detroit Metal City*	Jack lll Dark		Japanese movie
2009	*Extract*[37]	Joe Adler		
2010	*Expecting Mary*	Taylor		
2010	*Rush: Beyond the Lighted Stage*	Himself		Documentary

Television appearances

Year	Show	Episode	Role	Bandmates	Miscellaneous
1974	*The Mike Douglas Show*	June 11, 1974	Himself	Peter Criss, Ace Frehley, Paul Stanley	Kiss' first national television appearance, performed "Firehouse". During the interview segment, comedian Totie Fields, after looking at Simmons in his full Kiss makeup and costume, remarks to Douglas that underneath it all, "he's probably a nice Jewish boy."
1976	*The Paul Lynde Halloween Special*	October 29, 1976	Himself	Peter Criss, Ace Frehley, Paul Stanley	The band performed "Detroit Rock City" "King of the Night Time World" and "Beth"
1979	Tomorrow		Himself	Peter Criss, Ace Frehley, Paul Stanley	
1985	*Miami Vice*	"Prodigal Son"	Newton Blade		
1986	*The Hitchhiker*	"O.D.Feelin'"(Jan.28)	Mr. Big		
1997	*Action League Now!*	"Rock-A-Big-Baby"	Toy version of himself	Peter Criss, Ace Frehley, Paul Stanley	Performed "Rock and Roll All Nite"
1998	*MADtv*[38]	October 31, 1998 (#406)	Himself	Peter Criss, Ace Frehley, Paul Stanley.	Halloween special; performed in five sketches

2001	*Family Guy*	"A Very Special Family Guy Freakin' Christmas"	Animated version of himself	Peter Criss, Ace Frehley, Paul Stanley	
2001	*Who Wants To Be a Millionaire?*	May 27, 2001	Himself		Won $32,000 for a charity
2001	*The Daily Show with Jon Stewart*[39]	June 12, 2001	Himself		Almost licked Jon Stewart's face in response to Jon being unable to explain the difference between pleasure and joy to a man with a 'twelve-inch tongue'
2002	*Family Guy*	"Road to Europe"	Animated version of himself	Peter Criss, Ace Frehley, Paul Stanley	
2002	*The Tonight Show with Jay Leno*	September 6, 2002	Himself		
2003	*King of the Hill*	"Reborn to Be Wild"	Jessie		
2004	*Third Watch*	"Higher Calling"	Donald Mann		
2004	*Third Watch*	"Monsters"	Donald Mann		
2004	*Third Watch*	"More Monsters"	Donald Mann		
2005	*American Idol*	"Auditions: New Orleans"	Himself- guest judge		
2005	*Family Guy*	"Don't Make Me Over"	Animated version of himself/ Prisoner No. 3		
2005	*Mind of Mencia*	Episode #1.7	Himself		
2006	*The View*	August 1, 2006	Himself		Gene Simmons Family Jewels
2007	*SpongeBob SquarePants*	"20,000 Patties Under the Sea"	Sea Monster		
2007	*Shrink Rap*	"Gene Simmons"	Himself		UK's More4 show
2008	*Entertainment Tonight*	January 2, 2008	Himself		
2008	*Jimmy Kimmel Live!*	January 18, 2008	Himself		
2008	*Rachael Ray*	March 11, 2008	Himself		
2008	*Criss Angel Mindfreak*	"Mindfreaking with the Stars"	Himself		
2008	*Ugly Betty*	"The Kids Are Alright"	Himself		
2008	*Ugly Betty*	"A Thousand Words by Friday"	Himself		
2008	*Are You Smarter Than a 5th Grader?*	Episode #3.9	Himself		Won $500,000 for the Elizabeth Glaser Pediatric AIDS Foundation charity
2008	*The Celebrity Apprentice*	First three episodes	Himself		Won $20,000 for the Elizabeth Glaser Pediatric AIDS Foundation charity; Fired in the third episode
2008	*Jingles*[40]		Celebrity judge		Mark Burnett reality show

2009	Glenn Martin DDS	Glenn Gary, Glenn Martin	himself		
2009	American Idol	Season Finale	Himself	Eric Singer, Tommy Thayer, Paul Stanley	Performed medley of 3 songs with contestant Adam Lambert
2009	The Fairly OddParents	"Wishology – Part 1: The Big Beginning"	Animated version of himself	Eric Singer, Tommy Thayer, Paul Stanley	
2009	The Fairly OddParents	"Wishology – Part 3: The Final Ending"	Animated version of himself	Eric Singer, Tommy Thayer, Paul Stanley	
2010	I Get That a Lot	Episode 2	As Himself		Simmons appeared as a psychic working at the Mystic Journey Bookstore in Venice, California
2010	Extreme Makeover: Home Edition	Episode 160	As Himself		The band Kiss made a personal appearance during the Wagstaff family's vacation in Disneyland and honored them as special guests at one of their concerts. Kiss also made a personal appearance at a local school where a donation of new musical instruments was made in the Wagstaff family's name.
2010	I'm in a Rock 'n' Roll Band!	Episode 1 And 5	As Himself		Discussing the requirements of being in a rock band.
2011	Castle	To Love and Die in LA	As Himself		

Music video appearances

In 2007, he appeared alongside other celebrities, as well as regular people, in the music video for "Rockstar" by Nickelback.

Video game appearances

Gene Simmons is a playable character in *Tony Hawk's Underground*, unlocked when completing the story mode on Normal difficulty, and also appears with his Kiss bandmates in the Hotter Than Hell level to play one of three songs upon collecting the four K-I-S-S letters.

Gene Simmons' Kiss character, The Demon, is a playable character in *Kiss: Psycho Circus: The Nightmare Child*. Simmons also has a large role in the 2010 music video game *Guitar Hero: Warriors of Rock*. In addition to narrating the main storyline and doing advertising for the game, the Kiss song "Love Gun" is playable.

Discography

Solo

- *Gene Simmons* (1978)
- *Sex Money Kiss* (audiobook CD, 2003)
- *Asshole* (2004)
- *Speaking in Tongues* (spoken word CD, 2004)

Publishing career

In 2002, Simmons launched *Gene Simmons' Tongue*, a men's lifestyle magazine.[41] The magazine lasted five issues before being discontinued.

Other ventures

In the mid-2000s, Simmons was a principal investor in "Gene Simmons' Toyota" in Newbridge, New Jersey. As a public service, he would discuss the dealership and give financial advice on a local high school radio station. [42]

Published works

- *Kiss and Make-Up*, Gene Simmons (ISBN 0-609-81002-2)
- *Sex Money Kiss*, Gene Simmons (ISBN 1-893224-86-4)
- *Kiss: The Early Years*, Gene Simmons and Paul Stanley (ISBN 0-609-81028-6)
- *Kiss: Behind the Mask*, David Leaf and Ken Sharp (ISBN 0-446-96524-6)
- *Ladies of the Night: A Historical and Personal Perspective on the Oldest Profession in the World*, Gene Simmons (ISBN 1-59777-501-0)

References

[1] http://www.genesimmons.com

[2] Biography (http://www.genesimmons.com/bio2.html). GeneSimmons.com. Retrieved on February 1, 2011.

[3] Message Board – AETV Community – Real Life. Drama (http://boards.aetv.com/topic/Meet-The-Simmons/Gene-Honors-His/700001881). Boards.aetv.com. Retrieved on February 1, 2011.

[4] Associated, The (March 22, 2011). "Lead singer of Kiss Gene Simmons slams Israel boycotters" (http://www.haaretz.com/jewish-world/lead-singer-of-kiss-gene-simmons-slams-israel-boycotters-1.351197). *Haaretz*. Israel. . Retrieved August 10, 2011.

[5] *.Kiss and Make-Up* (Simmons' autobiography)

[6] Lewis, Barbara (June 4, 1978). "Gene Simmons Was Sixth Grade Teacher" (http://news.google.com/newspapers?nid=1346&dat=19780604&id=sJJNAAAAIBAJ&sjid=yvoDAAAAIBAJ&pg=5422,1350574). *The Lakeland Ledger*. .

[7] Gene Simmons Family Jewels – Under the Knife? – Wednesday, Nov 3, 2010 – mReplay Livedash TV Transcript – Livedash – Search what is being mentioned across national TV (http://www.livedash.com/transcript/gene_simmons_family_jewels-(under_the_knife_)/6120/AETVP/Wednesday_November_3_2010/328010/). Livedash. Retrieved on February 1, 2011.

[8] News (http://www.genesimmons.com/news/082004.html). GeneSimmons.com. Retrieved on February 1, 2011.

[9] News (http://www.genesimmons.com/news/042003.html). GeneSimmons.com. Retrieved on February 1, 2011.

[10] "Gene Simmons hails Israeli soldier" (http://www.washingtonpost.com/wp-dyn/content/article/2006/08/26/AR2006082600502.html). *The Washington Post*. Associated Press. August 26, 2006. . Retrieved May 12, 2010.

[11] Gavin, Patrick (December 6, 2010). "Gene Simmons Knocks President Obama" (http://www.politico.com/click/stories/1012/gene_simmons_knocks_obama.html). *The Politico*. . Retrieved December 6, 2010.

[12] Remarks by the President on the Middle East and North Africa (http://www.whitehouse.gov/the-press-office/2011/05/19/remarks-president-middle-east-and-north-africa), Barack Obama, *The White House*, May 19, 2011

[13] Ben Gedalyahu, Tzvi (May 22, 2011). "Video of Rock Star Gene Simmons: Obama Doesn't Have a Clue" (http://www.israelnationalnews.com/News/News.aspx/144384). *Israel National News*. . Retrieved June 1, 2011.

[14] "ישראל מחרימי הוצרים" :סימונס ג'ין – טיפשים"" (http://www.ynet.co.il/articles/0,7340,L-4046360,00.html). YNet. March 23, 2011. . Retrieved March 23, 2011.

[15] "Kiss Frontman Gene Simmons Voices Support For Mitt Romney, Regrets Voting For Obama In '08" (http://www.mediaite.com/tv/kiss-frontman-gene-simmons-voices-support-for-mitt-romney-regrets-voting-for-obama-in-08/). Mediaite. 2012-04-03. . Retrieved 2012-04-25.

[16] "Gene Simmons: 60's Fanzine Publisher" (http://www/genesimmons.com/news/102008.html), October 2008

[17] Lollar, Michael (June 14, 2009). "Tongues were wagging as KISS star Gene Simmons visited Memphis" (http://www.commercialappeal.com/news/2009/jun/14/kiss-star-gets-ducky-during-02/). Memphis Commercial Appeal. . Retrieved June 14, 2009.

[18] http://www.thedenverchannel.com/entertainment/31258255/detail.html

[19] "Gene Simmons is married" (http://www.people.com/people/article/0,,20533363,00.html). The People. October 1, 2011. . Retrieved October 2, 2011.

[20] "Gene Simmons and long term girlfriend marry" (http://wonderwall.msn.com/entertainment/gene-simmons-and-longtime-girlfriend-marry-1644963.story). MSN - Wonderwall. October 1, 2011. . Retrieved October 2, 2011.

[21] Josef Federman. "AP Interview: Simmons blasts Israel boycotters" (http://news.yahoo.com/s/ap/20110322/ap_en_mu/ml_israel_people_gene_simmons). Yahoo!. .

[22] Late Night Rocker (March 31, 2011). "Kiss Mask Webzine: Meet Gene Simmons' Brother and Sisters" (http://kissmaskwebzine.blogspot.com/2011/03/meet-gene-simmons-brother-and-sisters.html). Kissmaskwebzine.blogspot.com. . Retrieved August 10, 2011.

[23] Brinn, David (March 23, 2011). "Kiss rocker Gene Simmons back in Israel after 51 years" (http://www.jpost.com/VideoArticles/Video/Article.aspx?id=213425). *Jerusalem Post*. . Retrieved August 10, 2011.

[24] Gene Simmons in Israel / ‮ג"ין סימונס בישראל‬ (https://www.youtube.com/watch?v=FhnTbJNH0Wo) on YouTube

[25] "Terry Gross interview with Gene Simmons" (http://www.archive.org/details/TerryGrossInterviewWithGeneSimmons). *Internet Archive.* . Retrieved August 13, 2009.

[26] The Unpredictable Gene Simmons (http://www.npr.org/templates/story/story.php?storyId=14081542). NPR. Retrieved on February 1, 2011.

[27] "Outrage as KISS player mouths off on Muslims" (http://www.smh.com.au/articles/2004/05/14/1084289868279.html). *Sydney Morning Herald*, May 14, 2004

[28] KISS Singer's Motion to Dismiss Defamation Suit Denied (http://www.law.com/jsp/article.jsp?id=1131640457086). Law.com. Retrieved on February 1, 2011.

[29] Kiss's Gene Simmons Settles Defamation Suit by Ex-Girlfriend – Music I Songs I Country I Rap (http://www.foxnews.com/story/0,2933,201436,00.html). FOXNews.com (June 28, 2006). Retrieved on February 1, 2011.

[30] Billboard Q&A: Gene Simmons, 12 Nov 2007 (http://www.billboard.biz/bbbiz/others/billboard-q-a-gene-simmons-1003671447.story)

[31] ArsTechnica 28 Oct 2010 - Gene Simmons vs. Anonymous: Who's the bigger tool? (http://arstechnica.com/tech-policy/news/2010/10/gene-simmons-vs-anonymous-whos-the-bigger-asshole.ars)

[32] "KISS Added, Then Removed, From Michael Jackson Tribute" (http://www.upvenue.com/article/1456-kiss-added-to-michael-jackson-s-tribute-despite-controversy.html). *UpVenue.* August 17, 2011. . Retrieved 2011-08-17.

[33] Gene Simmons Family Jewels – A&E TV (http://www.aetv.com/gene-simmons-family-jewels/). Aetv.com. Retrieved on February 1, 2011.

[34] > News > Kissonline.com; News (http://www.kissonline.com/news/News/4). Kissonline.Com. Retrieved on February 1, 2011.

[35] "Gene Simmons poses as psychic for US prank show" (http://www.metrolyrics.com/2010-gene-simmons-poses-as-psychic-for-us-prank-show-news.html). January 7, 2010. . Retrieved January 14, 2010.

[36] 'Revolver' Golden Gods Awards Winners Announced! (http://www.revolvermag.com/goldengods/revolver-golden-gods-awards-winners-announced/). *revolvermag.com.* April-16-2012. Retrieved April 21, 2012.

[37] "Gene Simmons To Appear In 'Extract' Film" (http://www.roadrunnerrecords.com/BLABBERMOUTH.net/news.aspx?mode=Article&newsitemID=119334). Blabbermouth.net. May 3, 2009. . Retrieved August 14, 2009.

[38] "Planet MADtv – *Episode No. 406 (Aired October 31, 1998)*" (http://www.planetmadtv.com/forum/showthread.php?t=2129#1). . Retrieved June 5, 2009.

[39] "The Daily Show-*Gene Simmons*" (http://www.thedailyshow.com/watch/tue-june-12-2001/gene-simmons). . Retrieved February 20, 2011.

[40] "Gene Simmons to judge Burnett's 'Jingles'." (http://www.thrfeed.com/2008/07/gene-simmons-ji.html). . Retrieved March 14, 2009.

[41] Tongue is cheeky / Kiss' Gene Simmons combines sex, showmanship in his men's magazine (http://www.sfgate.com/cgi-bin/article.cgi?file=/chronicle/archive/2002/08/28/DD82104.DTL). Sfgate.com (August 28, 2002). Retrieved on February 1, 2011.

[42] Tom interviews Gene Simmons (http://www.wfmu.org/listen.ram?show=13401&archive=17115) WFMU.org (December 7, 2004). Retrieved on January 29, 2013.

External links

- Official website (http://www.genesimmons.com)
- Gene Simmons (http://www.imdb.com/name/nm0005430/) at the Internet Movie Database

Guys and Dolls (film)

Guys and Dolls	
theatrical poster	
Directed by	Joseph L. Mankiewicz
Produced by	Samuel Goldwyn
Screenplay by	Joseph L. Mankiewicz Ben Hecht
Based on	*Guys and Dolls* by Abe Burrows Jo Swerling Frank Loesser Damon Runyon
Starring	• Marlon Brando • Jean Simmons • Frank Sinatra • Vivian Blaine • Stubby Kaye • Regis Toomey
Music by	Frank Loesser
Cinematography	Harry Stradling
Editing by	Daniel Mandell
Studio	Samuel Goldwyn Productions
Distributed by	Metro-Goldwyn-Mayer
Release date(s)	• November 3, 1955
Running time	150 minutes
Country	United States
Language	English
Box office	$20 million

Guys and Dolls is a 1955 musical film starring Marlon Brando, Jean Simmons, Frank Sinatra and Vivian Blaine. The film was made by Samuel Goldwyn Productions and distributed by MGM. It was directed by Joseph L. Mankiewicz, who also wrote the screenplay. The film is based on the 1950 Broadway musical by composer and lyricist Frank Loesser, with a book by Jo Swerling and Abe Burrows based on "The Idyll Of Miss Sarah Brown" and "Blood Pressure", two short stories by Damon Runyon.[1]

Upon Samuel Goldwyn's and Joseph L. Mankiewicz's requests, Frank Loesser wrote three new songs for the film: "Pet Me Poppa", "(Your Eyes Are the Eyes of) A Woman in Love", and "Adelaide", the last written specifically for Sinatra. Five songs in the stage musical were omitted from the movie: "A Bushel and a Peck" (heard instrumentally as background music), "My Time of Day", "I've Never Been In Love Before", "More I Cannot Wish You" and "Marry the Man Today".

Plot

Although there are detail differences between the stage and movie versions, the plot is essentially based on the activities of New York petty criminals and professional gamblers in the late 1940s.

Gambler Nathan Detroit (Frank Sinatra) is under pressure from all sides. He has to organize an unlicensed crap game but the police, led by Lieutenant Brannigan (Robert Keith), are "putting on the heat". All the places where Nathan usually holds his games refuse him entry due to Brannigan's intimidating pressure. The owner of the Biltmore garage does agree to host the game provided Nathan pays him $1000 in cash in advance. The garage owner will not even accept a "marker" or IOU, he insists on having the money itself. Adding to Nathan's problems, his fiancée, Miss Adelaide (Vivian Blaine), a nightclub singer, wants to bring an end to their 14-year engagement and actually tie the knot. She also wants him to go straight, but organizing illegal gambling is the only thing he's good at.

Trying to obtain the money for the garage, Nathan meets an old acquaintance, Sky Masterson (Marlon Brando), a gambler willing to bet on virtually anything and for high amounts. Nathan proposes a $1000 bet by which Sky must take a girl of Nathan's choosing to dinner in Havana, Cuba. The bet seems impossible for Sky to win when Nathan nominates Sergeant Sarah Brown (Jean Simmons), a straight-walking sister at the Save a Soul Mission (based on the Salvation Army) which opposes gambling.

Sarah herself has problems. She has been in charge of the Broadway branch of the Mission for some time now and no drunks or gamblers have come in to confess or reform. To approach Sarah, Sky pretends that he is a gambler who wants to change. Sarah sees how expensively dressed he is and she is suspicious: "It's just so unusual for a successful sinner to be unhappy about sin."

Seeing that the Mission is and has been empty and unsuccessful, "a store full of repentance and no customers", Sky suggests a bargain. He will get a dozen sinners into the Mission for her Thursday night meeting in return for her having dinner with him in Havana. With General Matilda Cartwright (Kathryn Givney) threatening to close the Broadway branch for lack of participation, Sarah has little choice left, and agrees to the date.

Meanwhile, confident that he will win his bet with Sky, Nathan has gathered together all the gamblers, including a visitor that tough-guy Harry the Horse (Sheldon Leonard) has invited: Big Jule (B.S. Pully), a Chicago mobster. When Lieutenant Brannigan appears and notices this gathering of "senior delinquents", all gathered at Mindys, Nathan's sidekick, Benny Southstreet (Johnny Silver), covers it up by claiming that they are celebrating the fact that Nathan is getting married to Adelaide. Nathan is shocked by this, but is forced to play along. Later, when he notices the Save a Soul Mission band passing by and sees that Sarah is not among them, he collapses on the realization that he has lost his bet with Sky. He has no money and nowhere to house the crap game, and, since Adelaide was present at the "wedding announcement" Benny Southstreet dreamed up, he is now apparently committed to actually marrying Adelaide. He does love Adelaide, but is uneasy about going straight, either maritally or lawfully.

Over the course of their short stay in Cuba, Sky manages to break down Sarah's social inhibitions, partly through disguised alcoholic drinks (several glasses of milk with Bacardi added "as a preservative"), and they begin to fall in love with one another. He even confesses that the whole date was part of a bet, but she forgives him as she realizes that his love for her is sincere.

They return to Broadway at dawn and meet the Save a Soul Mission band which, on Sky's advice, has been parading all night. At that moment police sirens can be heard, and before they know it the gamblers led by Nathan Detroit are hurrying out of a back room of the Mission, where they took advantage of the empty premises to hold the crap game.

The police arrive too late to make any arrests, but Lieutenant Brannigan finds the absence of Sarah and the other Save a Soul members too convenient to have been a coincidence. He implies that it was all Sky's doing: "Masterson, I had you in my big-time book. Now I suppose I'll have to reclassify you — under shills and decoys". Sarah is equally suspicious and she dumps Sky there and then, refusing to accept his denials.

But Sky still has to make good his arrangement with Sarah to provide sinners to the Mission. Sarah would rather forget the whole thing, but Uncle Arvide Abernathy (Regis Toomey), who acts as a kind of father figure to her, warns Sky that "If you don't make that marker good, I'm going to buzz it all over town you're a welcher."

Nathan has continued the crap game in a sewer. With his revolver visible in its shoulder holster, Big Jule, who has lost all his money, forces Nathan to play against him while he cheats, cleaning Nathan out. Sky enters and knocks Big Jule down and removes his pistol. Sky, who has been stung and devastated by Sarah's rejection, lies to Nathan that he lost the bet about taking her to Havana, and pays Nathan the $1000. Nathan tells Big Jule he now has money to play him again, but Harry the Horse says that Big Jule can't play without cheating because "he cannot make a pass to save his soul". Sky overhears this, and the phrasing inspires him to make a bold bet: He will roll the dice, and if he loses he will give all the other gamblers $1000 each; if he wins they are all to attend a prayer meeting at the Mission.

The Mission is near to closing when suddenly the gamblers come parading in, taking up most of the room. Sky won the roll. They grudgingly confess their sins, though they show little sign of repentance: "Well ... I was always a bad guy. I was even a bad gambler. I would like to be a good guy and a good gambler. I thank you." Even Big Jule declares: "I used to be bad when I was a kid. But ever since then I've gone straight, as I can prove by my record — 33 arrests and no convictions." Nicely-Nicely Johnson (Stubby Kaye) however, recalling a dream he had the night before, seems to have an authentic connection to the Mission's aim, and this satisfies everyone.

When Nathan tells Sarah that Sky lost the Cuba bet, which she knows he won, she hurries off in order to make up with him.

It all ends with a double wedding in the middle of Times Square, with Sky marrying Sarah, and Nathan marrying Adelaide, who is given away by Lieutenant Brannigan. Arvide Abernathy performs the dual ceremony. Nicely-Nicely has joined the Save a Soul Mission, and he and General Matilda Cartwright are sweet on each other. As the film closes, the two newlywed couples are escorted from the wedding to their respective love nests inside police cars, with lights festively flashing and sirens blaring.

Notes

- There is a suggestion that Nathan Detroit may be Jewish, due to his frequent use of Yinglish phrases, especially in the song "Sue Me" which includes "nu" (an interjection roughly meaning *well*, as of expectation), and turns of phrase such as "What can you do me?" and Gesundheit.
- When "Angie the Ox" tells Nathan to guess who he saw having a "steak breakfast", Nathan sarcastically mutters "Hitler". Part of the sarcasm is that Hitler is widely believed to have been vegetarian.

Casting the movie

Robert Alda had originated the role of Sky Masterson on Broadway in 1950. For the movie, Gene Kelly, then one of the screen's greatest dancers, at first seemed a serious candidate for the part. Instead it went to Marlon Brando, one of the screen's greatest actors, partly because MGM would not loan Kelly for the production, but also because Goldwyn wanted to cast Brando, the world's biggest box office draw at that moment. The film ended up being distributed by MGM, Kelly's home studio.[2]

Another contender for the part of Sky was Sinatra himself.[2] Sinatra had also been considered for the part of Terry Malloy in *On the Waterfront*;[3] both roles went to Brando.

Marilyn Monroe and Grace Kelly were also considered for the parts of Adelaide and Sarah respectively. Mankiewicz refused to work with Monroe, probably as a result of his experiences while filming *All About Eve*, in which she had appeared.[2]

The musical scenes for Jean Simmons and Marlon Brando were sung by the actors themselves (no dubbing).[4][5]

Robert Keith plays police Lieutenant Brannigan, and one of his targets is Sky Masterson. Keith had matched wits with Brando before in the part of a sheriff facing Brando's reckless biker in *The Wild One*.

Stubby Kaye, Vivian Blaine, B.S. Pully, and Johnny Silver all repeated their Broadway roles in the film.

Cast

- Marlon Brando as Sky Masterson
- Jean Simmons as Sister Sarah Brown
- Frank Sinatra as Nathan Detroit
- Vivian Blaine as Miss Adelaide
- Stubby Kaye as Nicely-Nicely Johnson
- Robert Keith as Lieutenant Brannigan
- Sheldon Leonard as Harry the Horse
- Regis Toomey as Arvide Abernathy
- B.S. Pully as Big Jule
- Johnny Silver as Benny Southstreet
- The Goldwyn Girls as the Hot Box Girls (uncredited), including June Kirby, Pat Sheehan and Larri Thomas.[6]

Awards and nominations

- **Academy Awards**[7]
    - Nominated for Best Art Direction: Oliver Smith, Joseph C. Wright, Howard Bristol; Best Cinematography: Harry Stradling, Best Costume Design: Irene Sharaff; Best Music, Scoring of a Musical Picture: Jay Blackton and Cyril J. Mockridge.
- **BAFTA Awards**
    - Nominated for Best Film from any Source
    - Nominated for Best Foreign Actress: Jean Simmons
- **Golden Globe Awards**
    - Best Motion Picture - Musical/Comedy
    - Best Motion Picture Actress - Musical/Comedy: Jean Simmons

In 2004, the AFI ranked the song Luck Be a Lady at #42 on their list of the 100 greatest film songs, AFI's 100 Years... 100 Songs. In 2006 *Guys and Dolls* ranked #23 on the American Film Institute's list of best musicals.

Critical reception and commercial success

Guys and Dolls opened on November 3, 1955 to mostly good reviews. Review aggregator Rotten Tomatoes reports that 86% of critics have given the film a positive review, with a rating average of 6.9/10. Casting Marlon Brando has long been somewhat controversial, although *Variety* wrote "The casting is good all the way." This was the only Samuel Goldwyn film released through MGM. With an estimated budget of over $5 million, it went on to gross in excess of $13 million. *Variety* ranked it as the #1 moneymaking film of 1956, netting a profit of $9,000,000.[8] *Guys and Dolls* went on to gross $1.1 million in the UK, $1 million in Japan, and over $20 million dollars globally.

However, the film has been criticized by some critics and by the surviving family of Frank Loesser, who wrote the music and lyrics. Loesser had a very public disagreement with Sinatra, considering him totally wrong for the role of Nathan Detroit, who, in the stage version, was played by the gruff-voiced Sam Levene, who was not really a singer. Loesser felt that Sinatra was too slick for the role of Nathan and strongly disliked the way he "crooned" Nathan's songs. This resulted in Loesser and Sinatra never speaking to each other again after the film was finished. Others have criticized the smooth, mellow-voiced gambler Sky Masterson being played by the non-singer Brando, who, according to a biography of Samuel Goldwyn by Arthur Marx, was cast simply because he was then the hottest rising star in Hollywood. Nevertheless, Brando sings in the film and received praise for his vocal performance.

References

[1] "Damon Runyon" (http://www.ebooks-library.com/author.cfm/AuthorID/900). *Authors*. The eBooks-Library. . Retrieved 2008-07-20.

[2] Guys and Dolls (1955/I) - Trivia (http://www.imdb.com/title/tt0048140/trivia)

[3] On the Waterfront (1954) - Trivia (http://www.imdb.com/title/tt0047296/trivia)

[4] Jean Simmons (I) - Biography (http://imdb.com/name/nm0001739/bio)

[5] http://abcnews.go.com/Entertainment/wireStory?id=9641368

[6] Kurtti, Jeff (1996). *The Great Hollywood Musical Trivia Book*. New York: Applause Books. p. 41. ISBN 1-55783-222-6.

[7] "NY Times: Guys and Dolls" (http://movies.nytimes.com/movie/21198/Guys-and-Dolls/awards). *NY Times*. . Retrieved 2008-12-22.

[8] Steinberg, Cobbett (1980). *Film Facts*. New York: Facts on File, Inc.. p. 22. ISBN 0-87196-313-2. When a film is released late in a calendar year (October to December), its income is reported in the following year's compendium, unless the film made a particularly fast impact (p. 17)

External links

- *Guys and Dolls* (http://www.imdb.com/title/tt0048140/) at the Internet Movie Database
- *Guys and Dolls* (http://www.allrovi.com/movies/movie/v21198) at AllRovi
- *Guys and Dolls* (http://www.rottentomatoes.com/m/guys_and_dolls/) at Rotten Tomatoes
- *Guys and Dolls* (http://tcmdb.com/title/title.jsp?stid=77180) at the TCM Movie Database
- *Variety* Review (http://www.variety.com/review/VE1117791435.html?categoryid=31&cs=1&p=0)

Hugh Grant

Hugh Grant	
 Hugh Grant in March 2011	
Born	Hugh John Mungo Grant 9 September 1960 Hammersmith, London, UK
Alma mater	New College, Oxford
Occupation	Actor, film producer
Years active	1982–present
Partner(s)	Elizabeth Hurley (1987–2000) Jemima Khan (2004–2007)
Children	Tabitha Grant (2011)

Hugh John Mungo Grant[1] (born 9 September 1960) is a British actor and film producer. He has received a Golden Globe Award, a BAFTA, and an Honorary César. His films have earned more than US$2.4 billion from 25 theatrical releases worldwide.[2] Grant achieved international stardom after appearing in Richard Curtis's successful *Four Weddings and a Funeral* (1994).[3] He used this breakthrough role as a frequent cinematic persona during the 1990s, delivering comic performances in mainstream films like *Mickey Blue Eyes* (1999) and *Notting Hill* (1999). By the turn of the 21st century, he had established himself as a leading man skilled with a satirical comic talent.[4] Grant has expanded his oeuvre with critically acclaimed turns as a cad in *Bridget Jones's Diary* (2001), *About A Boy* (2002), *Love Actually* (2003), and *American Dreamz* (2006).[5] He later played against type with multiple cameo roles in the epic drama film *Cloud Atlas* (2012).

Within the film industry, Grant is cited as an anti-film star who approaches his roles like a character actor, and attempts to make his acting appear spontaneous.[6] Hallmarks of his comic skills include a nonchalant touch of irony/sarcasm and studied physical mannerisms as well as his precisely-timed dialogue delivery and facial expressions. The entertainment media's coverage of Grant's life off the big screen has often overshadowed his work as a thespian.[7][8] He has been vocal about his disrespect for the profession of acting, and in his disdain towards the culture of celebrity and hostility towards the media.[9][10] In a career spanning 30 years, Grant has repeatedly claimed that acting is not a true calling but just a job he fell into.[11]

Early life and ancestry

Grant was born at Charing Cross Hospital in Hammersmith, London, the second son of Fynvola Susan MacLean (b. Wickham, Hampshire, 11 October 1933; d. Hounslow, London, July 2001)[12] and Captain James Murray Grant (b. 1929). Genealogist Antony Adolph has described Grant's family history as "a colourful Anglo-Scottish tapestry of warriors, empire-builders and aristocracy,"[13] including William Drummond, 4th Viscount Strathallan and Dr. James Stewart.[13][14][15] John Murray, 1st Marquess of Atholl, Heneage Finch, 1st Earl of Nottingham, Rt. Hon. Sir Evan Nepean, and a sister of former British Prime Minister Spencer Perceval, are a few of his notable maternal ancestors.[16] Grant's grandfather, Major James Murray Grant, DSO, a native of Inverness in Scotland, was decorated for bravery and leadership at Dunkirk during World War II.[17]

Grant's father was trained at Sandhurst and served with the Seaforth Highlanders for eight years in Malaya, Germany and Scotland.[18] He ran a carpet firm, pursued hobbies such as golf and painting watercolours, and raised his family in Chiswick, west London, where the Grants lived next to Arlington Park Mansions on Sutton Lane.[19][20] In September 2006, a collection of Capt. Grant's paintings was hosted by the John Martin Gallery in a charity exhibition, organised by his famous son, called "James Grant: 30 Years of Watercolours."[21] His mother worked as a schoolteacher and taught Latin, French and music for more than 30 years in the state schools of west London.[22] She died at the age of 65,[12] 18 months after being diagnosed with pancreatic cancer.[23]

Grant's accent is an inheritance from his mother and, on *Inside the Actors Studio* in 2002, he credited her with "any acting genes that [he] might have."[20] Both his parents were children of military families,[24] but, despite his parents' backgrounds, Grant has stated that his family was not always affluent while he was growing up.[25] Grant spent his childhood summers shooting and hunting with his grandfather in Scotland.[19] Grant's elder brother, James "Jamie" Grant, is a successful banker as managing director, Head of Healthcare, Consumer, & Retail Investment Banking Coverage, at JPMorgan Chase in New York.[26]

Education

Grant started his education at Hogarth Primary School in Chiswick but then moved to St Peter's Primary School in Hammersmith. From 1969 to 1978, he attended the independent Latymer Upper School in Hammersmith on a scholarship and played 1st XV rugby, cricket and soccer for the school.[27][28] He also represented Latymer on the popular quiz show, *Top of the Form*, an academic competition between two teams of four secondary school students each.[29] Chris Hammond, his form teacher in 1975 and later the assistant head of Latymer, told *People* magazine that Grant was "a clever boy among clever boys."[28][30] In 1979, he won the Galsworthy scholarship to New College, Oxford where he starred in his first film, *Privileged*, produced by the Oxford University Film Foundation, OUFF [31]. He studied English literature and graduated with 2:1 honours.[32] Actress Anna Chancellor, who met Grant while she was still at school, has recalled, "I first met Hugh at a party at Oxford. There was something magical about him. He was a star even then, without having done anything."[33] He received an offer from the Courtauld Institute of Art, University of London to pursue a PhD in the history of art, but decided not to take the offer because he failed to secure a grant. Viewing acting as nothing more than a creative outlet,[34] he joined the Oxford University Dramatic Society and starred in a successful touring production of *Twelfth Night*.[35] Hugh Grant funds The Fynvola Grant Scholarship [36] at Latymer Upper School in memory of his mother who was a teacher in West London.

Young earner

After making his debut as Hughie Grant in the Oxford-financed *Privileged* (1982), Grant dabbled in a variety of jobs: he wrote book reviews,[37] worked as assistant groundsman at Fulham Football Club,[38] tried his hand at tutoring, wrote comedy sketches for TV shows,[39] and was hired by Talkback Productions to write and produce radio commercials for products such as Mighty White bread and Red Stripe lager.[40] To obtain his Equity card, he joined the Nottingham Playhouse, a regional theatre, and lived for a year at Park Terrace in The Park Estate, Nottingham.[41] Bored with small acting parts, he created his own comedy revue called The Jockeys of Norfolk with friends Chris Lang and Andy Taylor. The group toured London's pub comedy circuit with stops at *The George IV* in Chiswick, *Canal Cafe Theatre* in Little Venice and *The King's Head* in Islington.[42] Starting on a low note, The Jockeys of Norfolk eventually proved a hit at the Edinburgh Festival after their sketch on the Nativity, told as an Ealing comedy, gained them a spot on the BBC2 TV show called *Edinburgh Nights*.[43] During this time, Grant also appeared in theatre productions of plays such as *An Inspector Calls*, *Lady Windermere's Fan*, and *Coriolanus*.

Career

Grant at the Cannes film festival, 1997

Grant's first leading film role came in Merchant-Ivory's Edwardian drama, *Maurice* (1987), adapted from E. M. Forster's novel, in which he played the homosexual Clive Durham. He and co-star James Wilby shared the Volpi Cup for best actor at the Venice Film Festival for their portrayals of lovers Clive Durham and Maurice Hall, respectively. During the late 1980s and early 1990s, Grant balanced small roles on television with rare film work, which included a supporting role in *The Dawning* (1988), opposite Anthony Hopkins and Jean Simmons and a turn as Lord Byron in a Goya Award-winning Spanish production called *Remando al viento* (1988). He also portrayed some other real life figures during in his early career such as Charles Heidsieck in *Champagne Charlie* and as Hugh Cholmondeley in BAFTA Award-nominated *White Mischief*.

In 1990, he made a cameo appearance in the sport/crime drama *The Big Man*, opposite Liam Neeson, and in which Grant assumed a Scottish accent. The film explores the life of a Scottish miner (Neeson) who becomes unemployed during a union strike. In 1991, he played Julie Andrews' gay son in the ABC made-for-television film *Our Sons*.

In 1992, he appeared in Roman Polanski's film *Bitter Moon*, portraying a fastidious and proper British tourist who is married, but finds himself enticed by the sexual hedonism of a seductive French woman and her embittered, paraplegic American husband. The film was called an "anti-romantic opus of sexual obsession and cruelty" by the *Washington Post*.[44] His other work in period pieces such as Ken Russell's horror film, *The Lair of the White Worm* (1988), award-winning Merchant-Ivory drama *The Remains of the Day* (1993) and (as Frédéric Chopin in) *Impromptu* (1991) went largely unnoticed. He later called this phase of his career "hilarious," referring to his early films as "Europuddings, where you would have a French script, a Spanish director, and English actors. The script would usually be written by a foreigner, badly translated into English. And then they'd get English actors in, because they thought that was the way to sell it to America."[45]

At 32, Grant claimed to be on the brink of giving up the acting profession but was surprised by the script of *Four Weddings and a Funeral* (*FWAAF*).[4] "If you read as many bad scripts as I did, you'd know how grateful you are when you come across one where the guy actually is funny," he later recalled.[3] Released in 1994, *FWAAF* became the highest-grossing British film to date with a worldwide box office in excess of $244 million,[46] making Grant an overnight international star. The film was nominated for two Academy Awards, and among numerous awards won by its cast and crew, it earned Grant his first and only Golden Globe Award for Best Actor - Motion Picture Musical or Comedy and a BAFTA Award for Best Actor in a Leading Role. It also temporarily typecast him as the lead character, Charles, a bohemian and debonair bachelor. Grant and Curtis saw it as an inside joke that the star, due to the parts he played, was assumed to have the personality of the screenwriter, who is known for writing about himself and his own life.[45][47] Grant later expressed:

> ❝Although I owe whatever success I've had to *Four Weddings and a Funeral*, it did become frustrating after a bit that people made two
> assumptions: One was that I was that character – when in fact nothing could be further from the truth, as I'm sure Richard would tell you – and
> the other frustrating thing was that they thought that's all I could do. I suppose, because those films happened to be successful, no one, perhaps❞
> understandably, ... bothered to rent all the other films I'd done.[4]

In July 1994, Grant signed a two-year production deal with Castle Rock Entertainment and by October, he became founder and director of the UK-based Simian Films Limited.[48] He appointed his then-girlfriend, Elizabeth Hurley, as the head of development to look for prospective projects. Simian Films produced two Grant vehicles in the 1990s and lost a bid to produce *About a Boy* to Robert De Niro's TriBeCa Productions.[49] The company closed its U.S. office in 2002 and Grant resigned as director in December 2005.[50] Grant was one of the choices to play James Bond in 1995's GoldenEye, but eventually lost out to Pierce Brosnan.

Grant's first studio-financed Hollywood project was Chris Columbus's comedy *Nine Months*. Though a hit at the box office, it was almost universally panned by critics. The *Washington Post* called it a "grotesquely pandering caper" and singled out Grant's performance, as a child psychiatrist reacting unfavourably to his girlfriend's unexpected pregnancy, for his "insufferable muggings."[51] The same year, he played leading roles as Emma Thompson's suitor in Ang Lee's Academy Award-winning adaptation of Jane Austen's *Sense and Sensibility* and as a cartographer in 1917 Wales in *The Englishman Who Went Up a Hill But Came Down a Mountain*. In the same year he performed in the Academy Award-winning *Restoration*.

Before the release of *Four Weddings and a Funeral*, Grant reunited with its director, Mike Newell, for the tragicomedy *An Awfully Big Adventure* that was labelled a "determinedly off-beat film" by *The New York Times*.[52] Grant portrayed a bitchy, supercilious director of a repertory company in post-World War II Liverpool. Critic Roger Ebert wrote, "It shows that he has range as an actor,"[53] but the *San Francisco Chronicle* disapproved on grounds that the film "plays like a vanity production for Grant."[54] Janet Maslin, praising Grant as "superb" and "a dashing cad under any circumstances," commented, "For him this film represents the road not taken. Made before *Four Weddings and a Funeral* was released, it captures Mr. Grant as the clever, versatile character actor he was then becoming, rather than the international dreamboat he is today."[52] Grant made his debut as a film producer with the 1996 thriller *Extreme Measures*, a commercial and critical failure.

After a three-year hiatus, in 1999 he paired with Julia Roberts in *Notting Hill*, which was brought to theatres by much of the same team that was responsible for *Four Weddings and a Funeral*. This new Working Title production displaced *Four Weddings and a Funeral* as the biggest British hit in the history of cinema, with earnings equalling $363 million worldwide.[46] As it became exemplary of modern romantic comedies in mainstream culture, the film was also received well by critics. CNN reviewer Paul Clinton said, "*Notting Hill* stands alone as another funny and heartwarming story about love against all odds."[55] Reactions to Grant's Golden Globe-nominated performance were varied, with Salon.com's Stephanie Zacharek criticising that, "Grant's performance stands as an emblem of what's wrong with *Notting Hill*. What's maddening about Grant is that he just never cuts the crap. He's become one of those actors who's all shambling self-caricature, from his twinkly crow's feet to the time-lapsed half century it takes him to actually get one of his lines out."[56] The film provided both its stars a chance to satirise the woes of international notoriety, most noted of which was Grant's turn as a faux-journalist who sits through a dull press junket with, what the *New York Times* called, "a delightfully funny deadpan."[57] Grant also released his second production output, a fish-out-of-water mob comedy *Mickey Blue Eyes*, that year. It was dismissed by critics, performed modestly at the box office, and garnered its actor-producer mixed reviews for his starring role. Roger Ebert thought, "Hugh Grant is wrong for the role [and] strikes one wrong note and then another,"[58] whereas Kenneth Turan, writing in the *Los Angeles Times*, said, "If he'd been on the Titanic, fewer lives would have been lost. If he'd accompanied Robert Scott to the South Pole, the explorer would have lived to be 100. That's how good Hugh Grant is at rescuing doomed ventures."[59]

While promoting Woody Allen's *Small Time Crooks* on NBC's *The Today Show* in 2000, Grant told host Matt Lauer, "It's my millennium of bastards".[60] In 2000, Grant also joined the Supervisory Board of IM Internationalmedia AG, the powerful Munich-based film and media company.[61]

Small Time Crooks starred Grant, in the words of film critic Andrew Sarris, as "a petty, petulant, faux-Pygmalion art dealer, David, [who] is one of the sleaziest and most unsympathetic characters Mr. Allen has ever created."[62] In a role devoid of his comic attributes, the *New York Times* wrote: "Mr. Grant deftly imbues his character with exactly a perfect blend of charm and nasty calculation."[63] A year later, his turn as a charming but womanising book publisher Daniel Cleaver in *Bridget Jones's Diary* (2001) was proclaimed by *Variety* to be "as sly an overthrow of a star's polished posh – and nice – poster image as any comic turn in memory".[64] The film, adapted from Helen Fielding's novel of the same name, was an international hit, earning $281 million worldwide.[46] Grant was, according to the *Washington Post*, fitting as "a cruel, manipulative cad, hiding behind the male god's countenance that he knows all too well".[65]

Grant's "immaculate comic performance" (BBC) as the trust-funded womaniser, Will Freeman, in the film adaptation of Nick Hornby's best-selling novel *About a Boy* received raves from critics.[66] Almost universally praised, with an Academy Award-nominated screenplay, *About a Boy* (2002) was determined by the *Washington Post* to be "that rare romantic comedy that dares to choose messiness over closure, prickly independence over fetishised coupledom, and honesty over typical Hollywood endings."[67] *Rolling Stone* wrote, "The acid comedy of Grant's performance carries the film [and he] gives this pleasing heartbreaker the touch of gravity it needs,"[68] while Roger Ebert observed that "the Cary Grant department is understaffed, and Hugh Grant shows here that he is more than a star, he is a resource."[69] Released a day after the blockbuster *Star Wars Episode II: Attack of the Clones*, *About a Boy* was a more modest box office grosser than other successful Grant films, making all of $129 million globally.[46] The film earned Grant his third Golden-Globe nomination, while the London Film Critics Circle named Grant its Best British Actor and *GQ* honoured him as one of the magazine's men of the year 2002.[70] "His performance can only be described as revelatory," wrote critic Ann Hornaday, adding that "Grant lends the shoals layer upon layer of desire, terror, ambivalence and self-awareness."[67] *The New York Observer* concluded: "[The film] gets most of its laughs from the evolved expertise of Hugh Grant in playing characters that audiences enjoy seeing taken down a peg or two as a punishment for philandering and womanising and simply being too handsome for words-and with an English accent besides. In the end, the film comes over as a messy delight, thanks to the skill, generosity and good-sport, punching-bag panache of Mr. Grant's performance."[71] *About a Boy* also marked a notable change in Grant's boyish look. Now 41, he had lost weight and also abandoned his trademark floppy hair. *Entertainment Weekly*'s Owen Gleiberman took note of Grant's maturation in his review, saying he looked noticeably older and that it "looked good on him."[72] He added that Grant's "pillowy cheeks are flatter and a bit drawn, and the eyes that used to peer with 'love me' cuteness now betray a shark's casual cunning. Everything about him is leaner and spikier (including his hair, which has been shorn and moussed into a Eurochic bed-head mess), but it's not just his surface that's more virile; the nervousness is gone, too. Hugh Grant has grown up, holding on to his lightness and witty cynicism but losing the stuttering sherry-club mannerisms that were once his signature. In doing so, he has blossomed into the rare actor who can play a silver-tongued sleaze with a hidden inner decency."[72]

Grant was also paired with Sandra Bullock in Warner Bros.'s *Two Weeks Notice*, which made $199 million internationally but was judged poorly by professional reviewers.[46] *The Village Voice* concluded that Grant's creation of a spoiled billionaire fronting a real estate business was "little more than a Britishism machine."[73]

Two Weeks Notice was followed by the 2003 ensemble comedy, *Love Actually*, headlined by Grant as the British Prime Minister. A Christmas release by Working Title Films, the film was promoted as "the ultimate romantic comedy" and accumulated $246 million at the international box office.[46] It marked the directorial debut of Richard Curtis, who told the *New York Times* that Grant adamantly tempered the characterisation of the role to make his character more authoritative and less haplessly charming than earlier Curtis incarnations.[74] Roger Ebert claimed that "Grant has flowered into an absolutely splendid romantic comedian" and has "so much self-confidence that he plays the British prime minister as if he took the role to be a good sport."[75] Film critic Rex Reed, on the contrary, called Grant's performance "an oversexed bachelor spin on Tony Blair" as the star "flirted with himself in the paroxysm of self-love that has become his acting style."[76]

A speech delivered by Grant in *Love Actually* – where he extols the virtues of Great Britain and refuses to cave to the pressure of its longstanding ally, the United States – was etched in the transatlantic memory as a satirical, wishful statement on the concurrent Bush-Blair relationship.[77] Blair responded by saying, "I know there's a bit of us that would like me to do a Hugh Grant in *Love Actually* and tell America where to get off. But the difference between a good film and real life is that in real life there's the next day, the next year, the next lifetime to contemplate the ruinous consequences of easy applause."[78]

In 2004, Grant reprised his role as Daniel Cleaver for a small part in *Bridget Jones: The Edge of Reason*, which, like its predecessor, made more than $262 million commercially.[46] Gone from the screen for two years, Grant next reteamed with Paul Weitz (*About a Boy*) for the black comedy *American Dreamz* (2006). Grant starred as the acerbic host of an *American Idol*-like reality show where, according to Caryn James of the *New York Times*, "nothing is real ... except the black hole at the centre of the host's heart, as Mr. Grant takes Mr. Cowell's villainous act to its limit."[79] *American Dreamz* failed financially but Grant was generously praised. He played his self-aggrandising character, an amalgam of Simon Cowell and Ryan Seacrest, with smarmy self-loathing. *The Boston Globe* proposed that this "just may be the great comic role that has always eluded Hugh Grant,"[80] and critic Carina Chocano said, "He is twice as enjoyable as the preening bad guy as he was as the bumbling good guy."[81]

Grant in Brussels, October 2008

In 2007, Grant starred opposite Drew Barrymore in a parody of pop culture and the music industry called *Music and Lyrics*. The Associated Press described it as "a weird little hybrid of a romantic comedy that's simultaneously too fluffy and not whimsical enough."[82] Though he neither listens to music nor owns any CDs,[24] Grant learned to sing, play the piano, dance (a few mannered steps) and studied the mannerisms of prominent musicians to prepare for his role as a has-been pop singer, based loosely on Andrew Ridgeley.[9] *The Star-Ledger* dismissed the performance, writing that "paper dolls have more depth."[83] The film, with its revenues totalling $145 million, allowed Grant to mock disposable pop stardom and fleeting celebrity through its washed-up lead character. According to the *San Francisco Chronicle*, "Grant strikes precisely the right note with regard to Alex's career: He's too intelligent not to be a little embarrassed, but he's far too brazen to feel anything like shame."[84] In 2009, Grant starred opposite Sarah Jessica Parker in the romantic comedy *Did You Hear About the Morgans?*, which was a commercial as well as a critical failure.[85]

Work ethic

Grant is well known for having a very strong work ethic. He has called being a successful actor a mistake and has repeatedly talked of his hope that film stardom would just be "a phase" in his life, lasting no more than ten years.[45] He pins his lack of interest in acting on two different thoughts: first, that he drifted into the job as a temporary joke at age 23 and finds it an immature way for a grown man to spend his time;[86] and secondly, because he believes to have already given the one remarkable comic performance he had hoped to create on screen.[87] A self-confessed "committed and passionate" perfectionist on a film set,[11] Grant has constantly opted to describe himself as a reluctant actor, who chooses to be neutral about his career and works mostly with friends from previous collaborations.[6][88] Richard Curtis, a frequent collaborator, revealed that Grant is not fluid about the filmmaking process and tends to be unrelaxed while filming because he does not feel as though he's in the director's hands and prefers instead to take responsibility for giving a definitive performance.[9] Grant is noted by co-workers for demanding endless takes until he achieves the desired shot according to his own standard.[89][90]

A 2007 *Vogue* profile of Grant referred to him as a man with a "professionally misanthropic mystique."[9] The observation followed published facts such as that Grant conducts his interviews alone (without any publicists),[91] and has derided focus groups, market research and overriding emphasis on the opening weekend.[92] Grant decided to let go of his agent in 2006, ending a 10-year relationship with CAA.[93] Besides proudly proclaiming in interviews to have never listened to external views on his career, he stated that he does not require the hand-holding an agent provides.[9] A few months before firing his agent, he said, "They've known for years that I have total control. I've never taken any advice on anything."[87]

He has stuck to the genre of comedy, especially the romantic comedy, for almost all of his mainstream film career. He also never ventures to play characters who are not British. While some film critics, such as Roger Ebert, have defended the limited variety of his performances, others have dismissed him as a one-trick pony. Eric Fellner, co-owner of Working Title Films and a long-time collaborator of Grant, said, "His range hasn't been fully tested, but each performance is unique."[94] A majority of Grant's popular films in the 1990s followed a similar plot that captured an optimistic bachelor experiencing a series of embarrassing incidents to find true love, often with an American woman. In earlier films, Grant was adept at plugging into the stereotype of a repressed Englishman for humorous effects, allowing him to gently satirise his characters as he summed them up and played against the type simultaneously.[41] These performances were sometimes deemed overbearing, in the words of *Washington Post*'s Rita Kempley, due to his "comic overreactions—the mugging, the stuttering, the fluttering eyelids." She added: "He's got more tics than Benny Hill."[95] Grant's penchant for conveying his characters' feelings with mannerisms, rather than direct emotions, has been one of the foremost objections raised against his acting style. Stephen Hunter of the *Washington Post* once stated that, to be effective as a comic performer, he must get "his jiving and shucking under control."[96] Film historian David Thomson wrote in *The New Biographical Dictionary of Film* about how it is merely "itchy mannerisms" that Grant equates with screen acting.[97]

Grant's screen persona of later films, in the new millennium, gradually developed into a cynical, self-loathing cad.[98] Claudia Puig of *USA Today* celebrated this transformation with the observation that finally "gone [were] the self-conscious 'Aren't I adorable' mannerisms that seemed endearing at the start of [Grant's] film career but have grown cloying in more recent movies."[99] Using his facial contortions and an affected stammer for varied comic purposes,[100] According to Carina Chocano, amongst film critics, the two tropes most commonly associated with Grant are that he reinvented his screen persona in *Bridget Jones's Diary* and *About a Boy* and dreads the possibility of becoming a parody of himself.[101]

His preference for levity over dramatic range has been a controversial topic in establishment circles, prompting him to say:

> I've never been tempted to do the part where I cry or get AIDS or save some people from a concentration camp just to get good reviews. I genuinely believe that comedy acting, light comedy acting, is as hard as, if not harder than serious acting, and it genuinely doesn't bother me that all the prizes and the good reviews automatically by knee-jerk reaction go to the deepest, darkest, most serious performances and parts. It makes me laugh.[87]

However, in 2012, Grant played several non-comedic cameo roles in the epic drama film *Cloud Atlas*, an experience he has spoken positively of. He plays six characters in the film, all of which he said are "incredibly evil". Of his decision to appear in the film and of how difficult it was for him to play one of the more violent characters in the movie, he said:

> I do a lot of killing and raping [in the film]... But it was a laugh. I thought before I read it that I'd turn it down, which I normally do, but I was interested in meeting [*Cloud Atlas* co-directors] the Wachowskis because I have always admired them enormously. And they are so charming and fascinating.... I slightly called my own bluff. In one of the parts I am a cannibal, about 2,000 years in the future, and I thought, "I can do that. It's easy." And then I am suddenly standing in a cannibal skirt on a mountaintop in Germany and they are saying, "You know, hungry! We must have that flesh-eating, like a leopard who is so hungry," and I am thinking, "I can't do that! Just give me a witty line!"[102]

In the media

Grant has repeatedly spoken about his boredom with playing the celebrity in the press[103] and is known in popular media for his guarded privacy.[104] About the culture of celebrity, he told *Vogue*, "My theory is that it's like bodybuilders who inject testosterone, which means that their own powers to generate testosterone shut down forever. The fake esteem you get from being in the public eye feels like self-worth, but actually your own powers to produce it shut down. The stuff that really counts is your own. And that's, I think, why people go bonkers."[9] On probing of his personal life, he has remained incredibly steadfast in "offering a dead bat to any question he feels is not general enough."[105] Meanwhile, acquaintances portray him as a complicated man with an anarchic and sharp constitution.[9][41] "There is at least as much of Hugh that is charismatic, intellectual, and whose tongue," according to Mike Newell, "is maybe too clever for its own good as there is of him that's gorgeous and kind of woolly and flubsy."[106] Filmmaker Paul Weitz, calling Grant funny, observed that "he perceives flaws in himself and other people, and then he cares about their humanity nonetheless."[107] British newspapers regularly refer to him as grumpy.[108][109][110][111][112]

Libel lawsuits

In 1996, Grant won substantial damages from News (UK) Ltd over what his lawyers called a "highly defamatory" article published in January 1995. The company's now-defunct newspaper, *Today*, had falsely claimed that Grant verbally abused a young extra with a "foul-mouthed tongue lashing" on the set of *The Englishman Who Went Up a Hill But Came Down a Mountain.*[113]

On 27 April 2007, Grant accepted undisclosed damages from the Associated Newspapers over claims made about his relationships with his former girlfriends in three separate tabloid articles, which were published in the *Daily Mail* and *The Mail on Sunday* on 18, 21 and 24 February. His lawyer stated that all of the articles' "allegations and factual assertions are false."[114] Grant said, in a written statement, that he took the action because: "I was tired of the *Daily Mail* and *Mail on Sunday* papers publishing almost entirely fictional articles about my private life for their own financial gain." He went on to take the opportunity to stress, "I'm also hoping that this statement in court might remind people that the so-called 'close friends' or 'close sources' on which these stories claim to be based almost never exist."[115]

Legal troubles

On 27 June 1995, Grant was arrested in an L.A. Vice police operation not far from Sunset Boulevard for misdemeanour lewd conduct in a public place with Hollywood prostitute Divine Brown.[116] He pleaded no contest and was fined $1,180, placed on two years' summary probation, and was ordered to complete an AIDS education program.[117][118]

Hugh Grant mugshot, 1995

The arrest occurred about two weeks before the release of Grant's first major studio film, *Nine Months*, which he was scheduled to promote on several American television shows. *The Tonight Show with Jay Leno* had him booked for the same week and, as recalled in former employee Don Sweeney's memoirs, "despite his arrest, Hugh Grant kept his appointment to appear on Jay's show."[119] The interview was a career-making hit for Leno (who asked Grant, "What the hell were you thinking?") and Grant was singled out for not making excuses for the incident.[120][121] He famously said:

❝ I think you know in life what's a good thing to do and what's a bad thing, and I did a bad thing. And there you have it.[122] ❞

On *Larry King Live*, Grant declined the host Larry King's repeated invitations to probe his psyche, saying that psychoanalysis was "more of an American syndrome" and he himself was "a bit old fashioned."[123] He told the host: "I don't have excuses."[124] Grant was appreciated for "his refreshing honesty" as he "faced the music and handled it with tongue [in] cheek."[125]

In April 2007, Grant was arrested on allegations of assault made by paparazzo Ian Whittaker.[126] Grant made no official statement and did not comment on the incident.[127] Charges were dropped on 1 June by the Crown Prosecution Service on the grounds of "insufficient evidence."[128]

Phone hacking exposé

In April 2011 Grant published an article in the *New Statesman* entitled "The Bugger, Bugged"[129] about a conversation (following an earlier encounter) with Paul McMullan, former journalist and paparazzo for *News of the World*. In unguarded comments which were secretly taped by Grant, McMullan alleged that editors at the *Daily Mail* and *News of the World*, particularly Andy Coulson, had ordered journalists to engage in illegal phone tapping and had done so with the full knowledge of senior British politicians. McMullan also said that every British Prime Minister from Margaret Thatcher onwards had cultivated a close relationship with Rupert Murdoch and his senior executives. He stressed the friendship between David Cameron and Rebekah Brooks (née Wade), agreeing when asked that both of them must have been aware of illegal phone tapping, and asserting that Cameron's inaction could be explained by self-interest:

> "Cameron is very much in debt to Rebekah Wade for helping him not quite win the election ... So that was my submission to parliament – that Cameron's either a liar or an idiot."[129]

When asked by Grant whether Cameron had encouraged the Metropolitan Police to "drag their feet" on investigating illegal phone tapping by Murdoch's journalists, McMullan agreed that this had happened, but also stated that the police themselves had taken bribes from tabloid journalists, so had a motive to comply:

> "20 per cent of the Met has taken backhanders from tabloid hacks. So why would they want to open up that can of worms?... And what's wrong with that, anyway? It doesn't hurt anyone particularly."[129]

Grant's article attracted considerable interest, due to both the revelatory content of the taped conversation, and the novelty of Grant himself "turning the tables" on a tabloid journalist.[130]

Whilst the allegations regarding the *News of the World* continued to receive coverage in the broadsheets and similar media (Grant appeared for example on BBC Radio 4) it was only with the revelation that the voicemail of the by then murdered Millie Dowler had been hacked, and evidence for her murder enquiry had been deleted, that the coverage turned from media interest to widespread public (and eventually political) outrage. Grant became something of a spokesman against Murdoch's News Corporation, culminating in a bravura performance on BBC television's *Question Time* in July 2011.[131]

On 27 June Grant spoke about the media scandal in UK and media ownership at the new media forum 27 in the European parliament after he met Neelie Kroes and MEPs to discuss EU action to end media monopolies.

Personal life

In 1987, while playing Lord Byron in a Spanish production called *Remando Al Viento* (1988), Grant met actress Elizabeth Hurley, who was cast in a supporting role as Byron's former lover Claire Clairmont.[45] Grant started dating the aspiring model while shooting and their relationship was subsequently the subject of much media attention. In 1995, Hugh Grant was arrested for "lewd conduct" with a prostitute in Hollywood. At the time, he'd been with Elizabeth Hurley since 1987. After 13 years together, the two made "a mutual and amicable decision" to split in May 2000.[132] Rumoured to have been briefly dating former pantomime actress from the Midlands, Michaela Westbury, from 2003 up until 2004 when he then began dating Jemima Khan under the intense scrutiny of British tabloids.[9] Three years later, in February 2007, Grant's publicist announced that the couple had "decided to split amicably".[133] The spokesman added, "Hugh has nothing but positive things to say about Jemima".

Grant during the second round of Alfred Dunhill Links Championship, October 2007

Grant is godfather to Hurley's son Damian.[134] In November 2011, it was announced that Grant had become a father to a baby girl, Tabitha, earlier that autumn.[131] The identity of the mother, with whom Grant had a "fleeting affair" according to his publicist, was not at first announced; however, it was later revealed to be a Chinese woman, Tinglan Hong.[135][136] The publicist went on to say that "while this was not planned, Hugh could not be happier or more supportive. He and the mother have discussed everything and are on very friendly terms."[137] In an interview on *The Ellen DeGeneres Show* in April 2012, Grant revealed that his daughter's Chinese name is Xiao Xi, meaning "happy surprise".[138]

Grant has claimed that Hong has been "badly treated" by the media, saying that press intrusion prevented him from attending the birth of his daughter in September 2011. Grant said, "I was at one of the party conferences, about to give a speech, and was pacing about on the end of the phone. I shouldn't have gone to the hospital at all, because it brought all this attention down on the mother's head. But I couldn't really resist it, so I went on the second day". Hong later obtained an injunction which allowed Hugh Grant to visit her and baby Tabitha in peace.[131]

A famous "golfing addict",[139] Grant is a scratch golfer and is a regular at pro-am tournaments with membership at the Sunningdale Golf Club. He is also frequently pictured by the paparazzi at the famed Scottish golf courses in St Andrews, Kingsbarns and Carnoustie.[140] Highly competitive,[141] he reportedly plays with a lot of money at stake.[142] As a young boy, he played rugby union on his school's first XV team at centre and played football as an avid fan of Fulham F.C.. He is also a fan of Scottish side Rangers F.C.[143] thanks to his grandfather who was Scottish. He continued to play in a Sunday-morning football league in south-west London after college and remains an "impassioned Fulham supporter."[27] Grant's other interests include snooker[144] and tennis.[145]

In 2011, the BBC apologised after Grant made a remark about gay rugby players when he was invited into the commentary box during coverage of an England V Scotland game at Twickenham Stadium. Talking about playing rugby during his school days, Grant said: "I discovered it hurt less if you tackled hard than if you tackled like a queen."[146]

Charity work

Grant is a Patron of The DIPEx Charity,[147] founded by Ann McPherson, a charity that publishes the websites Healthtalkonline [148] and Youthhealthtalk [149]; and a Patron of the Fynvola Foundation, named after his late mother, a charity which provides nursing and care for older learning-disabled people.[150] He is also a supporter of Marie Curie Cancer Care, whose Great Daffodil Appeal he promoted in March 2008.[151]

References

[1] "Transcript of Afternoon Hearing 21 November 2011" (http://www.levesoninquiry.org.uk/wp-content/uploads/2011/11/Transcript-of-Afternoon-Hearing-21-November-2011.pdf). The Leveson Inquiry. . Retrieved 13 December 2012.

[2] D'Alessandro, Anthony (16 December 2002). "Englishman who grossed B.O.". Variety.

[3] Sharon Knolle and Liza Foreman (16 December 2002). "Scribe's alter ego evolves on celluloid". Variety: p. A8.

[4] Knolle, Sharon (16 December 2002). "Prince Charming". Variety: p. A1.

[5] "Rotten Tomatoes: Hugh Grant" (http://www.rottentomatoes.com/celebrity/hugh_grant/). IGN Entertainment. . Retrieved 25 September 2007.

[6] Kehr, Dave (17 May 2002). "For Hugh Grant, Natural Does It" (http://query.nytimes.com/gst/fullpage.html?res=9507EED91139F934A25756C0A9649C8B63). The New York Times: p. 13. . Retrieved 11 September 2007.

[7] Hodges, Jeremy (22 April 2002). "About a very private girl". Daily Mail.

[8] "British screen legends: Hugh Grant" (http://news.bbc.co.uk/1/hi/entertainment/film/2780369.stm). BBC. 21 February 2003. . Retrieved 28 September 2007.

[9] MacSweeney, Eve (1 February 2007). "Reluctant Romeo". Vogue: pp. 232–37. ISSN 00428000.

[10] Parker, Eloise (3 February 2007). "Why Grant's so grumpy". Daily Post: p. 13.

[11] "Bridget Jones's Diary: Interview With Hugh Grant" (http://www.cinema.com/articles/332/bridget-joness-diary-interview-with-hugh-grant.phtml). cinema.com. . Retrieved 10 October 2007.

[12] "Deaths England and Wales 1984–2006" (http://www.findmypast.co.uk/BirthsMarriagesDeaths.jsp). Findmypast.co.uk. . Retrieved 21 November 2011.

[13] Gilchrist, Jim (17 August 2005). "Stars dig up surprises with their ancestors" (http://news.scotsman.com/genealogy/Stars-dig-up-surprises-with.2652717.jp). The Scotsman. . Retrieved 10 September 2007.

[14] "Grants of Glenmoriston" (http://www.electricscotland.com/webclans/dtog/grant2.html). ElectricScotland.com. . Retrieved 28 September 2007.

[15] Hugh's Family Tree (http://www.ancestry24.co.za/Content/Website/Profiles/HughGrant.aspx)

[16] Hodgson, Richard. "Ancestors of a 21st century British family" (http://wc.rootsweb.ancestry.com/cgi-bin/igm.cgi?op=PED&db=ancestorsearch&id=I371). MyFamily.com,Inc.. . Retrieved 10 September 2007.

[17] Cobain, Ian (4 June 2000). "Survivors of 'sacrificed' division still feel bitter" (http://home.clara.net/clinchy/51st.htm). The Sunday Telegraph. .

[18] Ritchie, John (24 January 2001). "'Upstage Guy? I should be so lucky" (http://www.telegraph.co.uk/arts/main.jhtml?xml=/arts/2001/01/24/tlritc24.xml). The Daily Telegraph (London). . Retrieved 10 September 2007.

[19] Nikkhah, Roya (9 October 2006). "Hugh Grant's (early) life in pictures" (http://www.telegraph.co.uk/news/1528474/Hugh-Grant's-(early)-life-in-pictures.html). The Daily Telegraph (London). . Retrieved 10 September 2007.

[20] Presenter: James Lipton (12 May 2002). "Inside the Actors Studio: Hugh Grant" (http://www.bravotv.com/Inside_the_Actors_Studio). Inside the Actors Studio. Season 8. Episode 813. Bravo. .

[21] "James Grant – 30 Years of Watercolours" (http://www.jmlondon.com/pages/artistexhibitions/26311.html). jmlondon.com. . Retrieved 18 October 2007.

[22] Richard Boullemier (21 July 2007). "Chris bids farewell" (http://www.richmondandtwickenhamtimes.co.uk/news/1561135.0/). Richmond & Twickenham Times. . Retrieved 11 September 2007.

[23] WENN (13 July 2001). "Hugh Loses His Mother" (http://www.cinema.com/news/item/4604/hugh-loses-his-mother.phtml). cinema.com. . Retrieved 11 September 2007.

[24] "Grant's Views". Variety: p. A2. 16 December 2002.

[25] Zaslow, Jeffrey (23 May 1999). "Charming sex symbol? Handsome bumbler? Male chauvinist?" (http://www.usaweekend.com/99_issues/990523/990523talk.html). USA Weekend. . Retrieved 10 September 2007.

[26] Norbert B. Laufenberg (2005). Entertainment Celebrities. Trafford Publishing. p. 271.

[27] Philip, Robert (30 March 2003). "Fulham and golf top bill in Grant's off-screen life" (http://www.telegraph.co.uk/sport/2398868/Fulham-and-golf-top-bill-in-Grant's-off-screen-life.html). The Daily Telegraph (London). . Retrieved 14 September 2007.

[28] "Hugh Grant amongst past pupils bidding farewell to Chris Hammond" (http://chiswickw4.com/default.asp?section=info&spage=common/conschools95.htm). ChiswickW4.com. 11 July 2007. . Retrieved 11 September 2007.

[29] Presenter: James Lipton (12 May 2002). "Inside the Actors Studio: Hugh Grant" (http://www.bravotv.com/Inside_the_Actors_Studio). Inside the Actors Studio. Season 8. Episode 813. Bravo. .

[30] "Hugh Knew?" (http://hughgrant.free.fr/Interviews/people0502.html). *People*. May 2002. . Retrieved 3 October 2007.

[31] http://www.ouff.co.uk

[32] "Previous Judges: Hugh Grant" (http://www.costabookawards.com/awards/previous_judges.aspx). Costa Book Awards. . Retrieved 10 September 2007.

[33] Driscoll, Margarette (13 October 2002). "Interview: Margarette Driscoll meets Anna Chancellor" (http://www.timesonline.co.uk/tol/news/article1170104.ece?token=null&offset=0). *The Sunday Times* (London). . Retrieved 10 September 2007.

[34] Johnston, Damon (9 June 2002). "A not so rosy Hugh reveals his flaws". *Sunday Telegraph*: p. 99.

[35] Zep. "Biography for Peter Kosminsky" (http://www.imdb.com/name/nm0467225/bio). IMDb. . Retrieved 10 September 2007.

[36] http://www.latymer-upper.org/scholarships-1.html

[37] Marchbank (30 May 1999). "Hugh's a rude boy". *Sunday Mail*: p. 74.

[38] British Council (11 September 2005). "Hugh Grant Fulham FC (England)" (http://www.wanguoqunxing.com/cms4/modules.php?name=Content&pa=showpage&pid=50). ClubFootball-Fan Channel. . Retrieved 10 September 2007.

[39] Presenters: Valerie Pringle and Dan Matheson (6 September 1999). "British Filmmaker Divides Time Between Producing and Acting". *Canada AM*. CTV Television, Inc..

[40] WENN (10 May 2002). "Hugh Grant Wistful For Radio Days" (http://www.imdb.com/news/wenn/2002-05-10#celeb8). IMDB. . Retrieved 11 September 2007.

[41] Arnold, Gary (14 May 1995). "'Charming, witty guy' puts his mark on summer films". *The Washington Times*: p. D3.

[42] Sturgis, John (11 March 1998). "Pub Theatre that launched host of stars fights final curtain call". *Evening Standard*: p. 17.

[43] Lang, Chris (24 August 1998). "Personal Profile: Just the Job". *Evening Standard*: p. 4.

[44] Brown, Joe (15 April 1994). "Bitter Moon". *Washington Post*.

[45] David, Kamp (1 May 2003). "Runaway bachelor". *Vanity Fair*: p. 170. ISSN 07338899.

[46] "Hugh Grant" (http://www.boxofficemojo.com/people/chart/?id=hughgrant.htm). Box Office Mojo. . Retrieved 11 September 2007.

[47] Chris Jones (3 June 2005). "Faces of the week: Richard Curtis" (http://news.bbc.co.uk/2/hi/uk_news/magazine/4606743.stm). BBC. . Retrieved 11 September 2007.

[48] Marx, Andy (8 July 1994). "Grant inks two-year deal at Castle Rock". *Variety*.

[49] Presenter: Jane Clayson (16 May 2002). "Hugh Grant discusses his new film 'About a Boy'". *The Early Show*. CBS.

[50] "Hugh Grant and ex- may close movie company" (http://www.accessmylibrary.com/coms2/summary_0286-7194114_ITM). UPI. 19 November 2004. . Retrieved 30 September 2007.

[51] Howe, Desson (14 July 1995). "Movie Reviews:Nine Months" (http://www.washingtonpost.com/wp-srv/style/longterm/movies/videos/ninemonthspg13howe_c02245.htm). *The Washington Post*. . Retrieved 29 September 2007

[52] Maslin, Janet (21 July 1995). "Film Review:A Look at Hugh Grant Before His Big Success" (http://web.archive.org/web/20080101194838/http://movies.nytimes.com/movie/review?res=990CE3DD1530F932A15754C0A963958260). *The New York Times*. Archived from the original (http://movies.nytimes.com/movie/review?res=990CE3DD1530F932A15754C0A963958260) on 1 January 2008. . Retrieved 29 September 2007

[53] Ebert, Robert (25 September 1995). "Movie Reviews:An Awfully Big Adventure" (http://rogerebert.suntimes.com/apps/pbcs.dll/article?AID=/19950922/REVIEWS/509220301/1023). *Chicago Sun-Times*. . Retrieved 29 September 2007

[54] Guthmann, Edwards (21 July 1995). "This Grant `Adventure' An Awfully Chilly One" (http://www.sfgate.com/cgi-bin/article.cgi?f=/c/a/1995/07/21/DD64380.DTL). *San Francisco Chronicle*. . Retrieved 29 September 2007

[55] Paul Clinton (27 May 1999). "Review: Julia, Hugh a perfect match for 'Notting Hill'" (http://www.cnn.com/SHOWBIZ/Movies/9905/27/review.notting.hill/). CNN. . Retrieved 21 May 2007.

[56] Zacharek, Stephanie (28 May 1999). "Film Review:Notting Hill" (http://www.salon.com/ent/movies/review/1999/05/28/notting/index.html). Salon.com. . Retrieved 29 September 2007

[57] Maslin, Janet (28 May 1999). "Film Review:Looking for a Book And Finding a Man" (http://web.archive.org/web/20071230191915/http://movies.nytimes.com/movie/review?res=9D00E3DB1F31F93BA15756C0A96F958260). *The New York Times*. Archived from the original (http://movies.nytimes.com/movie/review?res=9D00E3DB1F31F93BA15756C0A96F958260) on 30 December 2007. . Retrieved 29 September 2007

[58] Ebert, Robert (20 August 1999). "Movie Reviews:Mickey Blue Eyes" (http://rogerebert.suntimes.com/apps/pbcs.dll/article?AID=/19990820/REVIEWS/908200303/1023). *Chicago Sun-Times*. . Retrieved 29 September 2007

[59] Turan, Kenneth (20 August 1999). "Movie Review: Mickey Blue Eyes" (http://web.archive.org/web/20060420064457/http://www.calendarlive.com/movies/reviews/cl-movie990819-5,0,299920.story). *Los Angeles Times*. Archived from the original (http://www.calendarlive.com/movies/reviews/cl-movie990819-5,0,299920.story) on 20 April 2006. . Retrieved 29 September 2007

[60] Presenter: Matt Lauer (17 May 2000). "Hugh Grant discusses his new film, 'Small Time Crooks'". *The Today Show*. NBC.

[61] "Hugh Grant joins board of IM Internationalmedia AG" (http://www.prnewswire.co.uk/cgi/news/release?id=50370). PR Newswire Europe Limited. 8 May 2000. . Retrieved 20 September 2007.

[62] Sarris, Andrew (28 May 2000). "With Woody's Cookie Caper, Some Careers Could Cool Off" (http://www.observer.com/node/42991). *The New York Observer* (New York Observer). . Retrieved 29 September 2007

[63] Holden, Stephen (20 May 2000). "Film Review: Just Take the Money and Run? Nah, She Wants Class and Culcha" (http://movies.nytimes.com/movie/review?res=9C00E0DD143AF93AA25756C0A9669C8B63). *The New York Times*. . Retrieved 29 September 2007

[64] Robey, Tim (16 December 2002). "Auds Prefer Grant Unattached". *Variety*: pp. A2–A4.

[65] Hunter, Stephen (13 April 2001). "Chaos and Cads" (http://www.washingtonpost.com/wp-srv/entertainment/movies/reviews/ bridgetjonessdiaryhunter.htm). *The Washington Post.* . Retrieved 29 September 2007

[66] Dawson, Tom (22 April 2002). "Film Review: About a Boy (2002)" (http://www.bbc.co.uk/films/2002/03/22/ about_a_boy_2002_review.shtml). *BBC* (BBC). . Retrieved 29 September 2007

[67] Hornaday, Ann (17 May 2002). "'About a Boy': A Rake's Amusingly Slow Progress" (http://www.washingtonpost.com/wp-dyn/content/ article/2002/05/17/AR2005033116336.html). *The Washington Post*: p. C01. . Retrieved 29 September 2007

[68] Peter, Travers (6 June 2002). "Reviews: About A Boy" (http://www.rollingstone.com/reviews/movie/5947699/review/5947700/ about_a_boy). *Rolling Stone* (Rolling Stone Australia). . Retrieved 29 September 2007

[69] Ebert, Roger (17 May 2002). "Movie Reviews: About A Boy" (http://rogerebert.suntimes.com/apps/pbcs.dll/article?AID=/20020517/ REVIEWS/205170301/1023). *Chicago Sun-Times.* . Retrieved 29 September 2007

[70] "*Hugh Grant* Film Actor, Comedy". *GQ*: p. 325. November 2002.

[71] Sarris, Andrew (26 May 2002). "Old Dog Loves New Trick, A Ploy for Seducing Singletons" (http://www.observer.com/node/46050). *The New York Observer* (New York Observer). . Retrieved 29 September 2007

[72] Gleiberman, Owen (15 May 2002). "Review: About A Boy" (http://www.ew.com/ew/article/0,,237958,00.html). *Entertainment Weekly.* . Retrieved 7 December 2012

[73] Park, Ed (25 December 2002). "Working Weak" (http://web.archive.org/web/20071210115738/http://www.villagevoice.com/film/ 0252,park,40780,20.html). *The Village Voice.* Archived from the original (http://www.villagevoice.com/film/0252,park,40780,20.html) on 10 December 2007. . Retrieved 29 September 2007

[74] Lyall, Sara (3 November 2003). "Four Comedies and a Collaboration" (http://query.nytimes.com/gst/fullpage. html?res=9C06EFD71F31F931A35752C1A9659C8B63). *The New York Times.* . Retrieved 30 March 2008.

[75] Ebert, Roger (7 November 2003). "Movie Reviews: Love Actually" (http://rogerebert.suntimes.com/apps/pbcs.dll/article?AID=/ 20031107/REVIEWS/311070304/1023). *Chicago Sun-Times.* . Retrieved 29 September 2007

[76] Reed, Rex (9 November 2003). "Lovesick Brits Ooze Treacle" (http://www.observer.com/node/48296). *The New York Observer* (New York Observer). . Retrieved 29 September 2007

[77] Hugh Grant (actor) and Thornton, Billy Bob (actor) (2003). *Love Actually: Prime Minister confronts U.S. President* (http://youtube.com/ watch?v=PDiqDIWKSuw) (Motion picture). Universal Pictures. . Retrieved 17 October 2007.

[78] "Blair lambasts 'fringe fanatics'" (http://news.bbc.co.uk/1/hi/uk_politics/4287906.stm). BBC. 27 September 2005. . Retrieved 3 October 2007.

[79] James, Caryn (26 April 2006). "Pop Beats Politics in the Race For Laughs" (http://query.nytimes.com/gst/fullpage. html?res=9F01E2D8123FF935A15757C0A9609C8B63). *The New York Times.* . Retrieved 29 September 2007

[80] Burr, Ty (21 April 2006). "American Dreamz Movie Review" (http://www.boston.com/movies/display?display=movie&id=8601). *Boston Globe.* . Retrieved 29 September 2007

[81] Chocano, Carina (21 April 2006). "Movie Review: 'American Dreamz'" (http://web.archive.org/web/20071024032044/http://www. calendarlive.com/movies/chocano/cl-et-americandreamz21apr21,0,5775553.story). *Los Angeles Times.* Archived from the original (http:// www.calendarlive.com/movies/chocano/cl-et-americandreamz21apr21,0,5775553.story) on 24 October 2007. . Retrieved 29 September 2007

[82] Lemire, Christy (13 February 2007). "Review: 'Music and Lyrics' an Odd Combo" (http://www.sfgate.com/cgi-bin/article.cgi?f=/n/a/ 2007/02/12/entertainment/e143605S25.DTL). *San Francisco Chronicle.* Associated Press. . Retrieved 29 September 2007

[83] Whitty, Stephen. "Film Review: Music and Lyrics". *The Star-Ledger*

[84] LaSalle, Mike (14 February 2007). "When cute couple write pop songs, they may find love" (http://www.sfgate.com/cgi-bin/article. cgi?file=/c/a/2007/02/14/DDG8SO3FGI1.DTL&type=movies). *San Francisco Chronicle.* . Retrieved 29 September 2007

[85] "Did You Hear About the Morgans? (2009)" (http://boxofficemojo.com/movies/?id=grantparker09.htm). Box Office Mojo. . Retrieved 28 January 2010.

[86] Presenter: Seamus O'Regan (10 January 2003). "Romantic Comedy Film Stars Hugh Grant and Sandra Bullock". *Canada AM.* CTV Television, Inc..

[87] "American Dreamz: Hugh Grant Question and Answer" (http://www.cinema.com/articles/4029/ american-dreamz-hugh-grant-question-and-answer.phtml). cinema.com. . Retrieved 10 September 2007.

[88] Thompson, Bob (27 January 2007). "Shrug, actually: "Hugh Said, Drew Said,"". *National Post* (Canada): p. TO30.

[89] Foreman, Liza (16 December 2002). "Curtis, Grant team for boffo B.O.". *Variety*: pp. A8.

[90] Presenter: Scott Simon (8 November 2003). "Richard Curtis discusses his new film, 'Love Actually'". *Weekend Edition Saturday.* NPR.

[91] Klein, Joshua (18 August 1999). "Interview: Hugh Grant" (http://www.avclub.com/content/node/22971). *The Onion (AV Club).* . Retrieved 12 September 2007.

[92] Lyman, Rick (20 August 1999). "Sweating Out The Numbers" (http://query.nytimes.com/gst/fullpage. html?res=9A06E2DC1438F933A1575BC0A96F958260). *The New York Times*: p. 23. . Retrieved 11 September 2007.

[93] Fleming, Michael (30 November 2006). "Grant has alone time". *Variety*: p. 4.

[94] Marre, Oliver (29 April 2007). "I want to be alone. Oh really?". *The Observer.*

[95] Kempley, Rita (12 July 1995). "'Nine Months'" (http://www.washingtonpost.com/wp-srv/style/longterm/movies/videos/ ninemonthspg13kempley_c021e6.htm). *The Washington Post.* . Retrieved 29 September 2007

[96] Hunter, Stephen (14 February 2007). "'Music and Lyrics': Work Is What Makes Life Hum" (http://www.washingtonpost.com/wp-dyn/content/article/2007/02/13/AR2007021301081.html). *The Washington Post.* . Retrieved 29 September 2007

[97] David Thomson *A New Biographical Dictionary of Film*, London: Little Brown, 2002, p.352. Published in New York by Knopf.

[98] Dargis, Manohla (21 April 2006). "Paul Weitz's 'American Dreamz': An 'Idol' Clone With a Presidential Aura" (http://movies.nytimes.com/2006/04/21/movies/21drea.html). *The New York Times.* . Retrieved 29 September 2007

[99] Puig, Claudia (16 May 2002). "'About a Boy' has singular charm" (http://www.usatoday.com/life/movies/2002/2002-05-17-boy-review.htm). *USA Today.* . Retrieved 29 September 2007

[100] Hodgman, John (12 November 2006). "How to Be Funny" (http://www.nytimes.com/2006/11/12/magazine/12hodgman.html?_r=1&oref=slogin). *The New York Times.* . Retrieved 29 September 2007.

[101] Chocano, Carina (14 February 2007). "A reluctant leading man" (http://www.latimes.com/entertainment/news/movies/cl-et-hugh14feb14,1,7879541.story?coll=la-promo-entnews&ctrack=1&cset=true). *Los Angeles Times.* . Retrieved 11 September 2007.

[102] De Semlyen, Phil (15 February 2012). "Exclusive: Hugh Grant Talks Cloud Atlas" (http://www.empireonline.com/news/story.asp?NID=33147). *Empire.* . Retrieved 2012-11-02.

[103] Kung, Michelle (11 February 2007). "Fashioning Hugh into a proper pop star" (http://www.boston.com/ae/movies/articles/2007/02/11/fashioning_hugh_into_a_proper_pop_star/). *The Boston Globe*: p. 13. . Retrieved 11 September 2007.

[104] "Hugh Grant pays a moving tribute to his mother at charity dinner1" (http://www.hellomagazine.com/celebrities/2008/06/08/hugh-gala-mum-speech/). *Hello!.* 8 June 2008. . Retrieved 12 June 2008.

[105] Masterson, Lawrie (23 April 2006). "Taken for granted". *Sunday Tasmanian*: p. A06.

[106] Svetkey, Benjamin (30 December 1994). "Cover Story: 7 HUGH GRANT" (http://www.ew.com/ew/article/0,,305086,00.html). *Entertainment Weekly.* . Retrieved 21 September 2007.

[107] Ginsberg, Merle (April 2002). "True Hugh" (http://web.archive.org/web/20071231055629/http://www.style.com/w/feat_story/032102/full_page.html). *W.* Archived from the original (http://www.style.com/w/feat_story/032102/full_page.html) on 31 December 2007. . Retrieved 21 October 2007.

[108] Malone, Carole (14 November 2004). "Hugh big soft nellie" (http://findarticles.com/p/articles/mi_qn4161/is_20041114/ai_n12909433). *Sunday Mirror*. p. 31. . Retrieved 19 September 2007.

[109] Baracaia, Alexa (10 November 2004). "Hugh loses his cool". *Evening Standard*: p. 9.

[110] Carroll, Sue (7 February 2007). "Who do you think you are, Mr. Grunt?" (http://www.mirror.co.uk/news/columnists/sue-carroll/2007/02/07/who-do-you-think-you-are-mr-grunt-89520-18586631/). *Daily Mirror*: p. 13. . Retrieved 21 September 2007.

[111] "Hugh's that grump?". *Daily Record*: p. 19. 6 February 2007.

[112] Turner, Janice (29 January 2005). "In this girls' world, boys are deviants" (http://www.timesonline.co.uk/tol/comment/columnists/janice_turner/article507846.ece). *Times Online* (London). . Retrieved 19 September 2007.

[113] Howard, Stephen (4 June 1996). "Actor Hugh wins substantial libel award". Press Association.

[114] "Hugh Grant accepts libel damages" (http://news.bbc.co.uk/2/hi/entertainment/6598937.stm). BBC. 27 April 2007. . Retrieved 24 February 2007.

[115] Tryhorn, Chris (27 April 2007). "Associated pays Grant damages" (http://www.guardian.co.uk/media/2007/apr/27/associatednewspapers.pressandpublishing). *The Guardian* (London). . Retrieved 17 February 2007.

[116] Wilson, Jeff (27 June 1995). "Suave, Charm and Good Looks: Why Would Hugh Grant Pay for Sex?". Associated Press.

[117] Moyes, Jojo (12 July 1995). "Grant pays for his 'lewd conduct'". *The Independent*: p. 1.

[118] "British actor pleads no contest to lewd conduct". *Deutsche Presse-Agentur.* 12 July 1995.

[119] Sweeney, Don (June 2006). "Tonight Show Hits the Road". *Backstage at the Tonight Show: From Johnny Carson to Jay Leno.* Maryland, USA: Taylor Trade Publishing. p. 210.

[120] Lowry, Brian (12 July 1995). "Hugh-man interest lifts 'Leno' rating". *Variety*: p. 5.

[121] Kitty Bean Yancey, Jeannie Williams (11 July 1995). "Grant confesses: No excuse for escapade". *USA Today*: p. 1D.

[122] "Nine Months star Hugh Grant runs talk show gauntlet" (http://www.cnn.com/SHOWBIZ/HughGrant/). CNN. 11 July 1995. . Retrieved 24 February 2007.

[123] "Hugh Grant Declines Interviewer's Invitation to Probe His Psyche". Associated Press. 12 July 1995.

[124] Interviewer: Larry King (12 July 1995). "Hugh Grant Talks About His Arrest". *Larry King Live*. CNN.

[125] "Hugh Grant finds "honesty" best policy" (http://www.cnn.com/SHOWBIZ/HughGrant/). CNN. 17 July 1995. . Retrieved 24 February 2007.

[126] "Hugh Grant arrested over 'attack'" (http://news.bbc.co.uk/2/hi/entertainment/6595297.stm). BBC. 26 April 2007. . Retrieved 1 October 2007.

[127] "Hugh Grant arrested over "baked beans attack"" (http://www.reuters.com/article/entertainmentNews/idUSL2652442420070426). Reuters. 26 April 2007. . Retrieved 26 April 2007.

[128] "No assault charges for Hugh Grant" (http://news.bbc.co.uk/2/hi/entertainment/6714025.stm). BBC. 1 June 2007. . Retrieved 3 October 2007.

[129] Hugh Grant (12 April 2011). "The bugger, bugged" (http://www.newstatesman.com/newspapers/2011/04/phone-yeah-cameron-murdoch). *New Statesman.* .

[130] "From Stephen Fry to Hugh Grant: The rise of the celebrity activist" (http://www.guardian.co.uk/theguardian/2011/apr/16/celebrity-activists-hugh-grant). *The Guardian.* 16 April 2011. .

[131] "Hugh Grant's best role yet – scourge of News International" (http://www.guardian.co.uk/commentisfree/2011/jul/08/ hugh-grant-news-international-rupert-murdoch). *The Guardian*. 8 July 2011. .

[132] "Hugh Grant and Elizabeth Hurley announce split" (http://nl.newsbank.com/nl-search/we/Archives?p_product=APAB& p_theme=apab&p_action=search&p_maxdocs=200&s_dispstring=Hugh Grant and Elizabeth Hurley announce split& p_field_advanced-0=&p_text_advanced-0=("Hugh Grant" and "Elizabeth Hurley announce split")&xcal_numdocs=20&p_perpage=10& p_sort=YMD_date:D&xcal_useweights=no). Associated Press. 23 May 2000. . Retrieved 17 February 2007.

[133] "Hugh Grant splits with girlfriend Jemima Khan" (http://uk.reuters.com/article/domesticNews/idUKN1629135520070216). Reuters. 16 February 2007. . Retrieved 24 February 2007.

[134] "Liz Hurley's son finally permitted to watch godfather Hugh Grant's movie" (http://in.news.yahoo.com/ liz-hurleys-son-finally-permitted-watch-godfather-hugh-132513227.html). Yahoo news. . Retrieved 21 April 2012.

[135] "A fleeting affair with girl 19 years his junior, now Hugh's a daddy" (http://www.dailymail.co.uk/tvshowbiz/article-2056360/ Hugh-Grant-baby-Tinglan-Hong-Actor-father-1st-time.html). *Daily Mail*. 2 November 2011. . Retrieved 21 November 2011.

[136] "Hugh Grant's supplemental witness statement to the Leveson inquiry" (http://www.guardian.co.uk/media/2011/nov/23/ hugh-grant-leveson-inquiry-supplemental-statement). *The Guardian*. 23 November 2011. . Retrieved 23 November 2011.

[137] "Hugh Grant Welcomes a Daughter" (http://www.people.com/people/article/0,,20541724,00.html). *People*. 1 November 2011. . Retrieved 1 November 2011.

[138] "Hugh Grant on being a dad" (http://www.youtube.com/watch?v=RDQv5SZU5eM). *The Ellen DeGeneres Show*. 2012-04-26. .

[139] "British Pair to star in a Hollywood classic" (http://wc.rootsweb.ancestry.com/cgi-bin/igm.cgi?op=PED&db=ancestorsearch& id=I371). St Andrews Links. 2001. . Retrieved 10 September 2007.

[140] Mclean, Sally (27 August 2002). "Par-fect day suits Hugh". *Daily Record*: p. 15.

[141] Riddell, Don (8 December 2006). "Why golf is no joke for Hugh Grant" (http://www.cnn.com/2006/SHOWBIZ/Movies/11/02/golf. grant/index.html). CNN. . Retrieved 17 September 2007.

[142] "Hugh Beauty: I love playing Golf for cash". *The Sunday Mail*: p. 15. 5 January 2003.

[143] "100,000 Rangers fans set to head south as Manchester lifts booze ban" (http://www.dailyrecord.co.uk/news/scottish-news/2008/05/ 10/100k-rangers-fans-set-to-head-south-as-manchester-lifts-booze-ban-86908-20412871/). Dailyrecord.co.uk. . Retrieved 21 November 2011.

[144] Forsyth, Jenny (14 April 2002). "About a Boy star's lessons on set". *The Sunday Mirror*. p. 38.

[145] "Up Close and Personal". *Variety*: pp. A10–12. 16 December 2002.

[146] http://www.pinknews.co.uk/2011/03/14/bbc-apologises-for-hugh-grants-gay-rugby-comment/

[147] "Healthtalkonline "About us"" (http://www.healthtalkonline.org/Overview/ThePeople). *Healthtalkonline main website*. .

[148] http://www.healthtalkonline.org

[149] http://www.youthhealthtalk.org

[150] "Fynvola Foundation" (http://www.fynvola.org.uk). Fynvola Foundation. .

[151] "The Great Daffodil Appeal" (http://www.mariecurie.org.uk/aboutus/news/news_archive/news_archive_2008/ hugh_grant_radio_advert.htm). Marie Curie Cancer Care. . Retrieved 7 March 2008.

External links

- Hugh Grant (http://www.imdb.com/name/nm424/) at the Internet Movie Database
- Hugh Grant (http://movies.yahoo.com/movie/contributor/1800019156) at Yahoo! Movies
- Hugh Grant (http://www.allrovi.com/name/p28225) at AllRovi
- Hugh Grant (http://www.screenonline.org.uk/people/id/481336) at the British Film Institute's Screenonline
- Hugh Grant (http://www.charlierose.com/guest/view/1745) on *Charlie Rose*
- Hugh Grant (http://www.guardian.co.uk/film/hughgrant) collected news and commentary at *The Guardian*
- Hugh Grant (http://topics.nytimes.com/top/reference/timestopics/people/g/hugh_grant/index.html) collected news and commentary at *The New York Times*, and in NYT Movies (http://movies.nytimes.com/ person/28225/Hugh-Grant)
- Works by or about Hugh Grant (http://worldcat.org/identities/lccn-no96-14456) in libraries (WorldCat catalog)

Hungry Hill (film)

Hungry Hill	
Directed by	Brian Desmond Hurst
Produced by	William Sistrom
Starring	Margaret Lockwood Dennis Price Cecil Parker Dermot Walsh Michael Denison Jean Simmons
Music by	John Greenwood, played by the London Symphony Orchestra, directed by Muir Mathieson

Hungry Hill is a 1947 British film directed by Brian Desmond Hurst and starring Margaret Lockwood, Dennis Price and Cecil Parker with a screenplay by Terence Young and Daphne du Maurier, from the novel by Daphne du Maurier.

A feud is waged between two families in Ireland - the Brodricks and the Donovans - over the sinking of a copper mine in Hungry Hill by *Copper John* Brodrick. The feud has repercussions down the generations.

Cast

- Margaret Lockwood as Fanny Rosa
- Dennis Price as Greyhound John Brodrick
- Cecil Parker as Copper John Brodrick
- Michael Denison as Henry Brodrick
- F.J. McCormick as Old Tim
- Arthur Sinclair as Morty Donovan
- Jean Simmons as Jane Brodrick
- Eileen Crowe as Bridget
- Eileen Herlie as Katherine
- Barbara Waring as Barbara Brodrick
- Michael Golden as Sam Donovan
- Siobhán McKenna as Kate Donovan
- Dan O'Herlihy as Harry Brodrick
- Henry Mollison as Dr. Armstrong
- Dermot Walsh as Wild Johnnie Brodrick

External links

- *Hungry Hill (film)* [1] at the Internet Movie Database

References

[1] http://www.imdb.com/title/tt0039479/

Mysteries of the Bible

Mysteries of the Bible	
Narrated by	Jean Simmons Richard Kiley
Country of origin	United States
No. of seasons	5
No. of episodes	45
Production	
Running time	45 minutes
Broadcast	
Original channel	A&E
Original run	March 25, 1994 – June 13, 1998

Mysteries of the Bible is an hour-long television series that was originally broadcast by A&E from March 25, 1994 until June 13, 1998 and aired reruns until 2002. The series was about biblical mysteries and was produced by FilmRoos. The Discovery Channel and BBC also released a series of the same name in 2003.[1][2] National Geographic produced a series with this title in 2006.[3]

List of Episodes

Title	Original Airdate	Chapters/ Acts	Interviews	NOTES
# 1 "Moses at Mt. Sinai"	original air date 25 March 1994[4]			
# 2 "Jesus at the Galilee"	original air date 1 April 1994[5]			
# 3 "Joshua at the Wall of Jericho"	original air date 8 April 1994[6]			
# 4 "Cities of Evil: Sodom and Gomorrah"	original air date 15 April 1994[7]			
# 5 "Masada—The Last Fortress"	original air date 22 April 1994[8]			
# 6 "Jesus: Holy Child"	original air date 29 April 1994[9]	**1.** One Birth: Two Stories **2.** The Puzzle Of Bethelehem **3.** The Magi And The Star **4.** The Virgin Birth **5.** A Story Of Christmas	Interviews with John Dominic Crossan, Ronald F. Hock, Dr. Michael L. Cook, John Mosley	

# 7 "A Violent God"	original air date 6 May 1994[10]			
# 8 "Noah and the Flood"	original air date 13 May 1994[11]			
# 9 "Scarlet Women of the Bible"	original air date 20 May 1994[12]	1. Eve: Innocence And Knowledge 2. Delilah: Seduction And Betrayal 3. Jezebel: Foreign Gods 4. A Painted Face 5. Salome: A Dance And A Murder	Interviews with Dr. Tamara Eskenazi, Dr. Jo Ann Hackett, Dr. David Gunn, Dr. Claudia Camp, Dr. Susan Niditch, Dr. Daniel Smith-Christopher, Dr. John Wilson, Dr. William G. Dever, Rabbi David Wolpe	
# 10 "Jerusalem: Holy Deadly City"	original air date 27 May 1994[13]			

Season 2

Title	Original Airdate	Chapters/ Acts	Interviews	NOTES
# 1 "King David: Poet Warrior"	original air date 16 September 1994[14]	1. God's Chosen King 2. Dead Run 3. A United Kingdom 4. Fall From Grace 5. Pretender To The Throne	Interviews with Walter Zanger, Dr. Avraham Biran, Rabbi David Wolpe, Dr. P. Kyle McCarter Jr., Daniel Smith-Christopher, Dr. Baruch Halpern, Dr. William G. Dever, Rabbi Aron Tendler	
# 2 "Abraham: One Man, One God"	original air date 6 January 1995[15]	1. War of the Idols 2. A Journey of Faith 3. The Covenant 4. A Father's Sacrifice 5. Tombs of the Patriarchs	Interviews with Rabbi David Wolpe, Walter Zanger, Dr. Nahum Sarna, Dr. Marc Z. Brettler, William G. Dever, and Dr. Wadad Kadi	
# 3 "Apocalypse: The Puzzle of Revelation"	original air date 13 January 1995[16]	1. Doomsday Scenario 2. The Four Horsemen of the Apocalypse 3. The End of the World 4. Armageddon 5. The Place of Battles		
# 4 "Archenemy: The Philistines"	original air date 27 January 1995[17]	1. A Savage People 2. A Mysterious People 3. Enemy And Neighbor 4. Fight To the Finish 5. A Mysterious Disappearance	Interviews with Walter Zanger, Dr. Trude Dothan, Barry M. Gitlen, Robert Stieglitz, Seymour Gitin, Daniel Smith-Christopher	
# 5 "Queen Esther: Far Away and Long Ago"	original air date 10 March 1995[18]	1. The Winds & The Exiles 2. At the Crossroads 3. Exits and Entrances 4. God Behind the Scenes 5. Prejudice and Genocide	Interviews with	
# 6 "Prophets: Soul Catchers"	original air date 17 March 1995[19]	1.Thus Saith The Lord 2.Channels Of God 3.It Is Written 4.Holy City, Holy Men 5.Silence	Interviews with David L. Lieber, Walter Zanger, Herbert B. Huffmon, Katheryn Pfisterer, Katherine Doob Sakenfeld, Joseph Blekinsopp, Walter Bruggemann	
# 7 "The Execution of Jesus"	original air date 14 April 1995[20]	1. Into Jerusalem 2. Miracles And Betrayal 3. Condemned To Die 4. The Crucifixtion 5. The Promise	Father Donald Senior, Father John P. Meier, John Dominic Crossan, Bart D. Ehrman, Donald Hagner, Adela Yarbro Collins, Michael L. Cook, John McCray	

Season 3

Title	Original Airdate	Chapters/ Acts	Interviews	NOTES
# "Joseph: Master of Dreams"	original air date 9 September 1995[21]	1. Destiny 2. Coat of Many Colors 3. Seduction 4. A Pharaoh Dreams 5. Long Lost Brother	Interviews with Rabbi David Wolpe, Donald Redford, James K. Hoffmeier, Daniel Smith-Christopher, William G. Dever, Nahum M. Sarna	
# "Herod the Great"	original air date 15 December 1995[22]	1. An Uneasy King 2. Trail of Blood 3. Grand Obsession 4. Jewel By The Sea 5. The End of Violence	Interviews with Dr. Kenneth G. Holum, Dr. Lawrence H. Schiffman, Dr. Shaye Cohen, Walter Zanger, and Dr. Peter Richardson.	
# "The Bible's Greatest Secrets"	original air date 4 January 1996[23]	1. Quest In The Holy land 2. New Ideas, New Science 3. The Warrior Archeologist 4. Into The Past 5. Bones, Stones, And Computer Chips	Interviews with Walter Zanger, Eric M. Myers, Hershel Shanks, Amnon Ben-Tor, Carol Myers, Oleg Grabar, William G. Dever	
# "The Last Revolt"	original air date 7 January 1996[24]	1. Roots of Revolution 2. Jerusalem: A City Divided 3. A Questionable Source 4. Prologue To Destruction 5. Fall of the Temple	Interviews with Walter Zanger, Lawrence Schiffman, Peter Richardson, Dr. Shaye Cohen, Richard A. Horsely, Mordecai Aviam, David L. Barr, John Dominic Crossan	
# "Angels and Devils"	original air date 18 January 1996[25]			
# "Life and Death Of the Holy Temple"[26]	original air date 25 January 1996[27]	1. The Holy Of Holies 2. The Ark Of The Covenant	Interviews with Rabbi Aron B Tendler, Rabbi David Wolpe, Graham Hancock, Baruch A. Levine	
# "Who Wrote the Bible? Part 1 of 2"	original air date 25 February 1996[28]		Interviews with Lawrence Schiffman, Rabbi David Wolpe, Aron Tendler, Jerry Falwell	
# "Who Wrote the Bible? Part 2 of 2"	original air date 25 February 1996[29]			
# "Heaven and Hell"	original air date 6 April 1996[30]			
# "The Lost Years of Jesus"	original air date 25 May 1996[31]	1. Quest For Jesus 2. Into India 3. England And The Holy Grail 4. Discovery In The Wilderness 5. Revolt In Palestine	Interviews with Michael L. Cook, Paul Park, Robert Eisenman, William Bramley, Elizabeth McNamer, Holger Kersten, Yatindra Bnatnagar	

Season 4

Title	Original Airdate	Chapters/ Acts	Interviews	NOTES
#1 "Job: The Devil's Test"	original air date 12 September 1996[32]		Interviews with Carole Fontaine,	
#2 "Jacob's Ladder"	original air date 26 September 1996[33]	1. Destiny and Deception 2. Angels 3. Forbidden Marriage 4. Wrestling With God 5. The Ten Lost Tribes	Interviews with Rabbi David Wolpe, Carole Fontaine, Douglas Stuart, Walter Zanger, Dr. Lawrence H. Schiffman, and Daniel Smith-Christopher.	
#3 "Biblical Angels"	original air date 14 November 1996[34]	1. Divine Spirits 2. Angels In Exile 3. The Apocalypse 4. Celestial Guardians 5. Earthly Spirits	Interviews with Roy-Charles Coulombe, Carol A. Newsom, Lawrence H. Schiffman, Rabbi David Wolpe, Isaac Canales, Michael Allen	
#4 "The Last Supper"	original air date 21 November 1996[35]	1. Journey To Jerusalem 2. A Deadly Premonition 3. The Passover Seder 4. The Betrayal 5. Holy Communion	Interviews with Karen Torjesen, Bart Ehrman, John Dominic Crossan, Lawrence Schiffman, Donald Senior	
#5 "Love and Sex in the Hebrew Bible"	original air date 12 December 1996[36]	1. Be Fruitful and Multiply 2. Sex and Marriage 3. Forbidden Sex 4. Affairs of State 5. Erotica		
#6 "Cain and Abel: A Murder Mystery"	original air date 8 March 1997[37]	1.Blood Brothers 2.The Motive 3.The Crime 4.The Fugitive 5.My Brother's Keeper	Interviews with Rabbi David Wolpe, Carole Fontaine, Douglas Stuart, Ronald S. Hendel, Nahum M. Sarna	
#7 "The Story of Creation"	original air date 6 April 1997[38]	1. In The Beginning 2. On The Seventh Day 3. Adam's Rib 4. Paradise Lost 5. Birth of the Universe	Interviews with Rabbi David Wolpe, Carole Fontaine, Nahum M. Sarna, Robert C. Newman, Douglas Stuart	
#8 "Paul the Apostle"	original air date 13 April 1997[39]	1. Road To Damascus 2. The Hidden Years 3. The Mysteries Of Tarsus 4. New Clues, Ancient World 5. The Enignma Of The End	Interviews with Robert M. Price, Rev Robert Morris, Wayne Meeks, Susan Alcock, Paul Maier	
#9 "King Solomon"	original air date 20 April 1997[40]	1. The Gift of Wisdom 2. A Child Divided In Two 3. Power Corrupts 4. Queen of Sheba 5. Night of Passion	Interviews with Carole Fontaine, Rabbi David Wolpe, Barbara Koltuv, Rabbi Aron B. Tendler, Daniel Smith-Christopher, Stuart Lasine, Carol Meyers	
#10 "Mary of Nazareth"	original air date 11 May 1997[41]	1. A Prayer Answered 2. Chosen By God 3. Jesus Is Born 4. A Mysterious Role 5. Visions of the Holy Mother	Interviews with Carole Fontaine, Beverly R. Gaventa, Paul L. Maier, Gloria Blanchfield Thomas.	
#11 "The 10 Commandments"	original air date 8 June 1997[42]	1. Chosen People 2. The Golden Calf 3. Wilderness of the Spirit 4. Crime and Punishment 5. Tablets of the Covenant	Interviews with Rabbi David Wolpe, Carole Fontaine, Stephen Breck Reid, Father Thomas P. Rausch, Pamela Scalise	

Season 5

Title	Original Airdate	Chapters/ Acts	Interviews	NOTES
# "Messiah"	original air date 10 August 1997[43]			
# "Old Testament Heroines"	original air date 1 November 1997[44]			
# "Judas: The Ultimate Betrayal"	original air date 6 December 1997[45]	1. The Man Who Walked With Jesus 2. Final Pilgrimage 3. Woe To The Man 4. The Fateful Kiss 5. Father, Forgive Them	Interviews with Ruth tucker, John Dominic Crossan, Hyam Maccoby, William Klassen	
# "Maccabees: Revolution and Redemption"	original air date 20 December 1997[46]	1. A Tyrannical Empire 2. A Leader Arises 3. War! 4. Rededication 5. Miracle	Interviews with David Baron, Erich Gruen, Robert Eisenman, Lawrence Schiffman, Anthony Saladrini	
# "John the Baptist"	original air date 7 March 1998[47]	1. Miraculous Birth 2. Out of the Wilderness 3. Herald of the Messiah 4. Arrest and Conviction 5. The Dance of Salome	Interviews with John Dominic Crossan, Isaac J. Canales, Father Thomas P. Rausch, Robert Eisenman PHD, James D. Tabor.	
# "Magic and Miracles in the Old Testament"	original air date 7 June 1998[48]	1. Let My People Go! 2. The Miraculous Journey 3. The Witch of Endor 4. Miracle Vs. Magic 5. The Everlasting Miracle	Interviews with Byron G. Curtis, Rabbi David Wolpe, Yair Zakovitch, Kenneth A. Kitchen, Hans Goedicke	
# "Samson and Delilah"	original air date 13 June 1998[49]		Interviews with Rabbi David Wolpe,	

Note that there may be more episodes.

Discovery Series

- *The Exodus Revealed*
- *Helena*
- *The Secret of the Dead Sea Scrolls*
- *Jesus and the Shroud of Turin*
- *Heaven, Our Eternal Home*
- *The Gates of Jerusalem*

References

[1] BBC Press Release (http://www.bbc.co.uk/pressoffice/bbcworldwide/worldwidestories/pressreleases/2003/08_august/mipcom.shtml)

[2] Imdb page of BBC 2003 series "Mysteries of the Bible" (http://www.imdb.com/title/tt1291913/)

[3] Imdb page of National Geographic 2006 series "Mysteries of the Bible" (http://www.imdb.com/title/tt1036227/)

[4] http://television.aol.com/episode/mysteries-of-the-bible-moses-at-mt-sinai/ancient-mysteries-with-leonard-nimoy/10933314

[5] http://television.aol.com/episode/mysteries-of-the-bible-jesus-in-the-galilee/ancient-mysteries-with-leonard-nimoy/10933315

[6] http://television.aol.com/episode/mysteries-of-the-bible-joshua-at-the-walls-of-jericho/ancient-mysteries-with-leonard-nimoy/10933316

[7] http://television.aol.com/episode/mysteries-of-the-bible-cities-of-evil-sodom-and-gomorrah/ancient-mysteries-with-leonard-nimoy/10933317

[8] http://television.aol.com/episode/mysteries-of-the-bible-masada-the-last-fortress/ancient-mysteries-with-leonard-nimoy/10933318

[9] http://television.aol.com/episode/mysteries-of-the-bible-jesus-holy-child/ancient-mysteries-with-leonard-nimoy/10933319

[10] http://television.aol.com/episode/mysteries-of-the-bible-a-violent-god/ancient-mysteries-with-leonard-nimoy/10933320

[11] http://television.aol.com/episode/mysteries-of-the-bible-noahs-lost-ark/ancient-mysteries-with-leonard-nimoy/10933321

[12] http://television.aol.com/episode/mysteries-of-the-bible-scarlet-women-of-the-bible/ancient-mysteries-with-leonard-nimoy/10933322

[13] http://television.aol.com/episode/mysteries-of-the-bible-jerusalem-holy-deadly-city/ancient-mysteries-with-leonard-nimoy/10933323

[14] http://television.aol.com/episode/mysteries-of-the-bible-king-david-poet-warrior/ancient-mysteries-with-leonard-nimoy/10933331

[15] http://television.aol.com/episode/mysteries-of-the-bible-abraham-one-man-one-god/ancient-mysteries-with-leonard-nimoy/10933334

[16] http://television.aol.com/episode/mysteries-of-the-bible-apocalypse-the-puzzle-of-revelation/ancient-mysteries-with-leonard-nimoy/320574

[17] http://television.aol.com/episode/mysteries-of-the-bible-archenemy-the-philistines/ancient-mysteries-with-leonard-nimoy/10933335

[18] http://television.aol.com/episode/mysteries-of-the-bible-queen-esther-far-away-and-long-ago/ancient-mysteries-with-leonard-nimoy/10933336

[19] http://television.aol.com/episode/mysteries-of-the-bible-prophets-soul-catchers/ancient-mysteries-with-leonard-nimoy/10933337

[20] http://television.aol.com/episode/mysteries-of-the-bible-the-execution-of-jesus/ancient-mysteries-with-leonard-nimoy/10933338

[21] http://television.aol.com/episode/mysteries-of-the-bible-joseph-master-of-dreams/ancient-mysteries-with-leonard-nimoy/10933345

[22] http://television.aol.com/episode/mysteries-of-the-bible-herod-the-great/ancient-mysteries-with-leonard-nimoy/10933348

[23] http://television.aol.com/episode/the-bibles-greatest-secrets/ancient-mysteries-with-leonard-nimoy/560060

[24] http://www.tvguide.com/tvshows/mysteries-bible/episodes/197463

[25] http://television.aol.com/episode/mysteries-of-the-bible-angels-and-devils/ancient-mysteries-with-leonard-nimoy/10933357

[26] http://www.amazon.com/dp/B000F48C0Q

[27] http://www.amazon.com/dp/B000LJ4RZY

[28] http://www.amazon.com/dp/B000LG7UQK

[29] http://www.amazon.com/dp/B000GK4EPQ

[30] http://television.aol.com/episode/mysteries-of-the-bible-heaven-and-hell/ancient-mysteries-with-leonard-nimoy/10933359

[31] http://www.amazon.com/dp/B000LG6NU4

[32] http://www.amazon.com/dp/B000LG75XI

[33] http://www.amazon.com/dp/B000QSM1B2

[34] http://www.fancast.com/tv/Mysteries-of-the-Bible/10379/episodes/Biblical-Angels/201067

[35] http://www.fancast.com/tv/Mysteries-of-the-Bible/10379/episodes/The-Last-Supper/201068

[36] http://www.fancast.com/tv/Mysteries-of-the-Bible/10379/episodes/Love-and-Sex-in-the-Hebrew-Bible/201072

[37] http://www.amazon.com/dp/B000GJ02U8

[38] http://www.fancast.com/tv/Mysteries-of-the-Bible/10379/episodes/Story-of-Creation/201078

[39] http://www.fancast.com/tv/Mysteries-of-the-Bible/10379/episodes/Paul-the-Apostle/201079

[40] http://www.fancast.com/tv/Mysteries-of-the-Bible/10379/episodes/King-Solomon/201080

[41] http://www.fancast.com/tv/Mysteries-of-the-Bible/10379/episodes/Mary-of-Nazareth/201081

[42] http://www.fancast.com/tv/Mysteries-of-the-Bible/10379/episodes/The-Ten-Commandments/201083

[43] http://www.fancast.com/tv/Mysteries-of-the-Bible/10379/episodes/Messiah/201085

[44] http://www.fancast.com/tv/Mysteries-of-the-Bible/10379/episodes/Old-Testament-Heroines/201087

[45] http://www.fancast.com/tv/Mysteries-of-the-Bible/10379/episodes/Judas%3A-The-Ultimate-Betrayal/201089

[46] http://www.fancast.com/tv/Mysteries-of-the-Bible/10379/episodes/The-Maccabees%3A-Revolution-and-Redemption/201090

[47] http://www.fancast.com/tv/Mysteries-of-the-Bible/10379/episodes/John-the-Baptist/201093

[48] http://www.fancast.com/tv/Mysteries-of-the-Bible/10379/episodes/Magic-and-Miracles-of-the-Old-Testament/201094

[49] http://www.fancast.com/tv/Mysteries-of-the-Bible/10379/episodes/Samson-and-Delilah/201095

External links

- Internet Movie Database: *Mysteries of the Bible* (http://www.imdb.com/title/tt0106077/)
- A&E Store (http://store.aetv.com/html/product/index.jhtml?id=76897)
- Discovery Store (http://shopping.discovery.com/Mysteries-of-the-Bible-DVD-Set.shtml)
- Variety Magazine review of *Mysteries of the Bible: Abraham: One Man, One God* (http://www.variety.com/review/VE1117903547.html?categoryid=31&cs=1), Alan Rich, January 6, 1995
- Amazon Episode page (http://www.amazon.com/dp/B000GIPKWY)

National Board of Review Award for Best Actress

The **National Board of Review of Motion Pictures Award for Best (Lead) Actress** is one of the annual film awards given by the National Board of Review of Motion Pictures.

Winners

1940s

Year	Winner	Film	Role
1945	**Joan Crawford**	*Mildred Pierce*	Mildred Pierce Beragon
1946	**Anna Magnani**	*Rome, Open City*	Pina
1947	**Celia Johnson**	*This Happy Breed*	Ethel Gibbons
1948	**Olivia de Havilland**	*The Snake Pit*	Virginia Stuart Cunningham
1949	not awarded		

1950s

Year	Winner	Film	Role
1950	**Gloria Swanson**	*Sunset Boulevard*	Norma Desmond
1951	**Jan Sterling**	*Ace in the Hole*	Lorraine Minosa
1952	**Shirley Booth**	*Come Back, Little Sheba*	Lola Delaney
1953	**Jean Simmons**	*The Actress*	Ruth Gordon Jones
		The Robe	Diana
		Young Bess	Princess Elizabeth
1954	**Grace Kelly**	*The Country Girl*	Georgie Elgin
		Dial M for Murder	Margot Mary Wendice
		Rear Window	Lisa Carol Fremont
1955	**Anna Magnani**	*The Rose Tattoo*	Serafina Delle Rose
1956	**Dorothy McGuire**	*Friendly Persuasion*	Eliza Birdwell
1957	**Joanne Woodward**	*No Down Payment*	Leola Boone
		The Three Faces of Eve	Eve White / Eve Black / Jane
1958	**Ingrid Bergman**	*The Inn of the Sixth Happiness*	Gladys Aylward
1959	**Simone Signoret**	*Room at the Top*	Alice Aisgill

1960s

Year	Winner	Film	Role
1960	**Greer Garson**	*Sunrise at Campobello*	Eleanor Roosevelt
1961	**Geraldine Page**	*Summer and Smoke*	Alma Winemiller
1962	**Anne Bancroft**	*The Miracle Worker*	Anne Sullivan
1963	**Patricia Neal**	*Hud*	Alma Brown
1964	**Kim Stanley**	*Séance on a Wet Afternoon*	Myra Savage
1965	**Julie Christie**	*Darling*	Diana Scott
		Doctor Zhivago	Lara Antipova
1966	**Elizabeth Taylor**	*Who's Afraid of Virginia Woolf?*	Martha
1967	**Edith Evans**	*The Whisperers*	Maggie Ross
1968	**Liv Ullmann**	*Hour of the Wolf (Vargtimmen)*	Alma Borg
		Shame (Skammen)	Eva Rosenberg
1969	**Geraldine Page**	*Trilogy*	Sook

1970s

Year	Winner	Film	Role
1970	**Glenda Jackson**	*Women in Love*	Gudrun Brangwen
1971	**Irene Papas**	*The Trojan Women*	Helen
1972	**Cicely Tyson**	*Sounder*	Rebecca Morgan
1973	**Liv Ullmann**	*The New Land (Nybyggarna)*	Kristina
1974	**Gena Rowlands**	*A Woman Under the Influence*	Mabel Longhetti
1975	**Isabelle Adjani**	*The Story of Adele H. (L'histoire d'Adèle H.)*	Adèle Hugo/Adèle Lewry
1976	**Liv Ullmann**	*Face to Face (Ansikte mot ansikte)*	Jenny Isaksson
1977	**Anne Bancroft**	*The Turning Point*	Emma Jacklin
1978	**Ingrid Bergman**	*Autumn Sonata (Höstsonaten)*	Charlotte Andergast
1979	**Sally Field**	*Norma Rae*	Norma Rae Webster

1980s

Year	Winner	Film	Role
1980	**Sissy Spacek**	*Coal Miner's Daughter*	Loretta Lynn
1981	**Glenda Jackson**	*Stevie*	Stevie Smith
1982	**Meryl Streep**	*Sophie's Choice*	Sophie Zawistowski
1983	**Shirley MacLaine**	*Terms of Endearment*	Aurora Greenway
1984	**Peggy Ashcroft**	*A Passage to India*	Mrs. Moore
1985	**Whoopi Goldberg**	*The Color Purple*	Celie Johnson
1986	**Kathleen Turner**	*Peggy Sue Got Married*	Peggy Sue
1987	**Lillian Gish**	*The Whales of August*	Sarah Webber
	Holly Hunter	*Broadcast News*	Jane Craig

| 1988 | **Jodie Foster** | *The Accused* | Sarah Tobias |
| 1989 | **Michelle Pfeiffer** | *The Fabulous Baker Boys* | Susie Diamond |

1990s

Year	Winner	Film	Role
1990	**Mia Farrow**	*Alice*	Alice Tate Smith
1991	**Geena Davis**	*Thelma & Louise*	Thelma Dickinson
	Susan Sarandon		Louise Sawyer
1992	**Emma Thompson**	*Howards End*	Margaret Schlegel
1993	**Holly Hunter**	*The Piano*	Ada McGrath
1994	**Miranda Richardson**	*Tom & Viv*	Vivienne Haigh-Wood
1995	**Emma Thompson**	*Sense and Sensibility*	Elinor Dashwood
		Carrington	Dora Carrington
1996	**Frances McDormand**	*Fargo*	Marge Gunderson
1997	**Helena Bonham Carter**	*The Wings of the Dove*	Kate Croy
1998	**Fernanda Montenegro**	*Central Station (Central do Brasil)*	Dora
1999	**Janet McTeer**	*Tumbleweeds*	Mary Jo Walker

2000s

Year	Winner	Film	Role
2000	**Julia Roberts**	*Erin Brockovich*	Erin Brockovich
2001	**Halle Berry**	*Monster's Ball*	Leticia Musgrove
2002	**Julianne Moore**	*Far from Heaven*	Cathy Whitaker
2003	**Diane Keaton**	*Something's Gotta Give*	Erica Barry
2004	**Annette Bening**	*Being Julia*	Julia Lambert
2005	**Felicity Huffman**	*Transamerica*	Stanley Schupak/Bree Osbourne
2006	**Helen Mirren**	*The Queen*	Queen Elizabeth II
2007	**Julie Christie**	*Away from Her*	Fiona Anderson
2008	**Anne Hathaway**	*Rachel Getting Married*	Kym
2009	**Carey Mulligan**	*An Education*	Jenny

2010s

Year	Winner	Film	Role
2010	**Lesley Manville**	*Another Year*	Mary
2011	**Tilda Swinton**	*We Need to Talk about Kevin*	Eva Khatchadourian
2012	**Jessica Chastain**	*Zero Dark Thirty*	Maya

New Milford, Connecticut

New Milford, Connecticut	
— Town —	

Flag   Seal

Motto: "Gateway To Litchfield County"[1]

Location in Litchfield County, Connecticut

Coordinates: 41°35′N 73°24′W	
Country	United States
State	Connecticut
NECTA	Danbury
Region	Housatonic Valley
Settled	1707
Incorporated	1712
Government	
• **Type**	Mayor-council
• **Mayor**	Patricia A. Murphy
Area	
• **Total**	63.7 sq mi (165.0 km^2)
• **Land**	61.6 sq mi (159.5 km^2)
• **Water**	2.1 sq mi (5.5 km^2)
Elevation	282 ft (86 m)
Population (2005)[2]	
• **Total**	28,667

• Density	465/sq mi (180/km^2)
Time zone	Eastern (UTC-5)
• Summer (DST)	Eastern (UTC-4)
ZIP code	06755, 06776
Area code(s)	860
FIPS code	09-52630
GNIS feature ID	0213474
Website	Town of New Milford Connecticut [3]

New Milford is a town in southern Litchfield County, Connecticut, United States 14 miles (23 km) north of Danbury, on the Housatonic River. It is the largest town in the state in terms of land area at nearly 62 square miles (161 km^2). The population was 28,671 according to the Census Bureau's 2006 estimates.[2] The town center is also listed as a census-designated place (CDP).

New Milford is home to the Canterbury School, a well-known Roman Catholic boarding school. The school's Chapel of Our Lady features the Jose M. Ferrer Memorial Carillon. The house that inspired the 1946 novel and 1948 film, *Mr. Blandings Builds His Dream House*, still stands in the Merryall section of town.

History

Colonial times

In 1707, John Noble Sr., previously of Westfield, Massachusetts and his eight-year-old daughter Sarah Noble were the first Anglo-American settlers. (A public school was later named after Sarah Noble.) They were soon joined by others who had also bought land there.[4]

On October 17, 1711, twelve families (including about 70 people) petitioned the General Assembly to create the town, together with the associated privilege of levying a tax to support a minister. With the legislature's approval, the town was organized the next year. The residents soon secured Daniel Boardman to preach and he was ordained as the minister of the Congregational Church [5] on November 21, 1716.[4][6]

American Revolution

Roger Sherman lived in New Milford before moving to New Haven in 1761.[4] He later became a member of the Continental Congress and signed both the Declaration of Independence and U.S. Constitution. The lot of his former house is the site of the present Town Hall.

During the American Revolution, the 7th Connecticut Regiment (also known as 19th Continental Regiment) was raised in town on September 16, 1776. The regiment, and the New Milford men in it, would see action in the Battle of Brandywine, Battle of Germantown and the Battle of Monmouth. In total, the town "sent 285 men to fight in the War out of a total population of 2,776."[4]

The Boardman family

- David Sherman Boardman (1786–1864), was the youngest child of Deacon Sherman and Sarah (Bostwick) Boardman. He became a lawyer in town and later chief judge in Litchfield County Court. He served as judge of probate for the district of New Milford in 1805, and held the place by successive annual appointments for sixteen years. He was elected Representative to the General Assembly eight times.

- Elijah Boardman (1760–1823) was a U.S. Senator representing Connecticut. Born in New Milford, he was educated by private tutors, and served in the American Revolutionary War.

- William Whiting Boardman (1794–1871), a U.S. Representative born in town, was the son of Elijah Boardman. He was a Connecticut state senator in the fourth district, 1830–32, a member of the Connecticut State House of Representatives, 1836–39, 1845, and 1849–51; Speaker of the Connecticut State House of Representatives, 1836, 1839, and 1845; US Representative from Connecticut's second district, 1840-43. He died in New Haven, Connecticut, and is interred at Grove Street Cemetery in New Milford.

Elijah Boardman, 1789, painted by Ralph Earl

19th and 20th centuries

In the second half of the 19th century, many new industries came to town. The Water Witch Engine Company, local telephone and electricity companies, and newspapers were all founded. Factories in town made buttons, paint and varnish, hats, furniture, pottery, lime, dairy products and pasteboard, among other goods. Tobacco became the major crop in the area, and tobacco warehouses sprang up to handle its storage and processing before sales.[4]

In 1942 Buck's Rock Camp was founded off of Bucks Rock Road, and has remained in operation ever since.

The population of New Milford was 4,804 in 1900; by 1910, the population had grown to 5,010. As of 2002, the town had a population of approximately 28,000.

21st century

The town has constructed a 1,000,000 gallon sewer plant expansion on West Street, sewer pump station on Boardman Road, reconstruction of the Rte. 67/ Grove Street Intersection, and ambulance facility on Scovill Street.

The town has additionally added a skate park at Young's Field (2006), reconstructed the Tennis and Basketball Courts at Young's Field (2010), reconstructed the Basketball Court at Williamson Park in Gaylordsville (2010), and several streetscape projects were completed by the Department of Public Works (DPW) with Grant money on Church Street, Whittlesey Avenue and the west side of East Street (2009/2010). Candlewoof Dog Park is completed on Pickett District Road. A bocce ball court was constructed at the Senior Center by Boy Scout Troop 66 (2012).

Geography

New Milford is located on the northeastern shore of Lake Candlewood. The Aspetuck River, Still River and Housatonic River flow through the town.

According to the United States Census Bureau, the town has a total area of 63.7 square miles (165 km^2), making it the largest town in Connecticut. 61.6 square miles (160 km^2) of it is land and 2.1 square miles (5.4 km^2) of it (3.31%) is water. The CDP corresponding to the town center has a total area of 3.4 square miles (8.8 km^2). 3.4 square miles (8.8 km^2) of it is land and 0.04 square miles (0.1 km^2) of it (0.88%) is water.

Principal communities

- Gaylordsville (06755)
- Boardman Bridge
- Lower Merryall
- Merwinsville
- New Milford Center
- Northville
- Park Lane
- Still River
- Upper Merryall
- Lanesville

Public library, built in 1897-1898, as it appeared c. 1905

- Downtown
- SouthSide

Demographics

As of the census[7] of 2000, there were 27,121 people, 10,018 households, and 7,273 families residing in the town. The population density was 440.4 people per square mile (170.0/km²). There were 10,710 housing units at an average density of 173.9 per square mile (67.1/km²). The racial makeup of the town was 94.33% White, 1.41% Black or African American, 0.15% Native American, 1.91% Asian, 0.03% Pacific Islander, 0.68% from other races, and 1.50% from two or more races. Hispanic or Latino of any race were 2.77% of the population.

There were 10,018 households out of which 38.0% had children under the age of 18 living with them, 60.0% were married couples living together, 9.0% had a female householder with no husband present, and 27.4% were non-families. 21.3% of all households were made up of individuals and 6.4% had someone living alone who was 65 years of age or older. The average household size was 2.68 and the average family size was 3.15.

In the town the population was spread out with 27.4% under the age of 18, 5.8% from 18 to 24, 33.1% from 25 to 44, 24.2% from 45 to 64, and 9.5% who were 65 years of age or older. The median age was 37 years. For every 100 females there were 97.0 males. For every 100 females age 18 and over, there were 93.8 males.

The median income for a household in the town was $65,354, and the median income for a family was $75,775. Males had a median income of $50,523 versus $34,089 for females. The per capita income for the town was $29,630. About 2.1% of families and 3.3% of the population were below the poverty line, including 2.7% of those under age 18 and 5.5% of those age 65 or over.

Town center

As of the census[2] of 2000, there were 6,633 people, 2,756 households, and 1,603 families residing in the town center CDP. The population density was 1,955.7 inhabitants per square mile (755.5/km²). There were 2,872 housing units at an average density of 846.8 per square mile (327.1/km²). The racial makeup of the CDP was 93.19% White, 1.82% Black or African American, 0.27% Native American, 2.11% Asian, 0.02% Pacific Islander, 0.84% from other races, and 1.75% from two or more races. Hispanic or Latino of any race were 3.09% of the population.

There were 2,756 households out of which 30.9% had children under the age of 18 living with them, 42.4% were married couples living together, 11.4% had a female householder with no husband present, and 41.8% were non-families. 33.2% of all households were made up of individuals and 9.4% had someone living alone who was 65 years of age or older. The average household size was 2.37 and the average family size was 3.07.

In the CDP the population was spread out with 24.4% under the age of 18, 8.2% from 18 to 24, 35.9% from 25 to 44, 20.3% from 45 to 64, and 11.2% who were 65 years of age or older. The median age was 35 years. For every 100 females there were 93.8 males. For every 100 females age 18 and over, there were 88.5 males.

The median income for a household in the CDP was $48,186, and the median income for a family was $58,367. Males had a median income of $38,571 versus $26,833 for females. The per capita income for the CDP was $22,912. About 3.7% of families and 6.3% of the population were below the poverty line, including 8.7% of those under age 18 and 6.7% of those age 65 or over.

Transportation

As a suburb of Danbury, New Milford is served by fixed-bus routes of the Housatonic Area Regional Transit. The main highways of the town are Route 7 and Route 202. There is a proposal to electrify and extend the Danbury Branch of the Metro-North Railroad north of Danbury to New Milford.[8]

The long-awaited completion of Super 7 happened in November 2009. The realignment of Grove Street and Prospect Hill Road (Rte. 67) was completed in the Fall of 2010. The Department of Public Works (DPW) awarded Stimulus ARRA Project 95-249 Grove Street (south of Anderson Ave) and Boardman Road (west of O+G Quarry). This was completed in the fall of 2010.

Schools

Elementary:

- Northville Elementary School,
- Hill & Plain Elementary School,
- John Pettibone Elementary School

Intermediate:

- Sarah Noble Intermediate School

Middle:

- Schaghticoke Middle School

High:

- New Milford High School

Private:

- Canterbury School
- Faith Preparatory

Sports

GMS Rowing Center, May 28, 2012

New Milford is home to the GMS Rowing Center.[9] Founded in 2003, it manages a US Rowing Training Center Program. It has a highly successful Middle and High School (Junior) Program which competes at Youth National Championships, Junior National Team Trials, The "Royal Canadian Henley" and has sent rowers to the Junior World Rowing Championships.[10] In 2011 GMS also had rowers representing the USA at the Under 23 World Championships in Amsterdam, The Netherlands and at the World Rowing Championships at Bled, Slovenia.[11]

Population

Historical population of New Milford[12]	
1756	1,137
1774	2,776
1782	3,015
1790	3,167
1800	3,221
1810	3,537
1820	3,830
1830	3,979
1840	3,974
1850	4,058
1860	3,535
1870	3,586
1880	3,907
1890	3,917
1900	4,804
1910	5,010
1920	4,781
1930	4,700
1940	5,559
1950	5,799
1960	8,318
1970	14,601
1980	19,420
1990	23,629

2000	27,121
2006	28,671 (Estimate)

National Register of Historic Sites

- Boardman's Bridge — Boardman Road at Housatonic River, northwest of New Milford (added June 13, 1976)
- Carl F. Schoverling Tobacco Warehouse — 1 Wellsville Avenue (added May 12, 1982)
- E. A. Wildman & Co. Tobacco Warehouse — 34 Bridge Street (added November 20, 1988)
- Hine-Buckingham Farms — 44, 46, and 48 Upland Road, 78, 81 Crossman Road (added June 7, 2004)
- Housatonic Railroad Station — Railroad Street (added April 1, 1984)
- J. S. Halpine Tobacco Warehouse — West and Mill Streets (added 1982)
- John Glover Noble House (added September 29, 1977)
- Lover's Leap Bridge — south of New Milford on Pumpkin Hill Road (added June 13, 1976)
- Merritt Beach & Son Building — 30 Bridge Street (added May 28, 1992)
- Merryall Union Evangelical Society Chapel — Chapel Hill Road (added July 5, 1986)
- New Milford Center Historic District — Bennitt and Elm Streets, Center Cemetery, East, South Main, Mill, and Railroad Streets (added July 13, 1986)
- United Bank Building — 19-21 Main Street (added May 12, 1982)

Notable people

- Léonie Fuller Adams, poetry consultant to Library of Congress (now titled poet laureate)
- Elizabeth Bentley, spy
- Bill Blass, fashion designer
- David Sherman Boardman, lawyer, judge and politician
- Elijah Boardman, US senator
- William Whiting Boardman, US congressman
- Kenny Coolbeth, motorcycling champion
- Bob Costas, sportscaster
- Fortunato Depero, painter, writer, sculptor and graphic designer
- Diane von Furstenberg, fashion designer, who plans to be buried at her 100-acre (0.4 km^2) farm in town[13]
- Florence Eldridge, stage and screen actress
- Peter Gallagher, film, stage and TV actor
- Lillian Hellman, playwright
- Skitch Henderson, pianist, composer and conductor
- Ian Hunter, English singer-songwriter
- Keith Kane, guitarist and founding member of Vertical Horizon[14]
- Henry Kissinger, diplomat and secretary of state
- Eartha Kitt, singer and actress
- Columbia Lancaster, congressman
- Fredric March, film and stage actor
- Florence Maybrick, murderer
- Christopher Meloni, film and television actor
- Hap Moran, football player
- William H. Noble, congressman
- M. Scott Peck, psychiatrist and self-help author
- Joan Rivers, comedian and writer

- Adam Shankman, movie director
- Roger Sherman, signer of Declaration of Independence and Constitution
- Jean Simmons, film, stage and television actress
- Solmous Wakeley, pioneer Wisconsin legislator
- Joseph J. Went, general
- Horace Wheaton, congressman
- Theodore White, political author of the 1960s–1970s
- Edward, legendary vagabond and traveler

Movies filmed in New Milford

The following movies with their actual or expected year of release have been filmed in New Milford:[15]

- *The Case of the Cosmic Comic* (1976)
- *The Brass Ring* (1983) (TV)
- *BlackMale* (2000)
- *Mr. Deeds* (2002)
- *Zero Day* (2003)
- *Psychoanalysis Changed My Life* (2003)
- *The Ballad of Jack and Rose* (2005)
- *Seepage!* (2005)
- *Retribution* (2006)
- *The Six Wives of Henry LeFay* (2007)
- *The Private Lives of Pippa Lee* (2009)
- *25/8* renamed to *My Soul to Take* (2009)
- *Halloween II (2009 film)* (2009)
- *All Good Things* (2010)

References

[1] "Town of New Milford Connecticut" (http://www.newmilford.org/). New Milford, Connecticut. . Retrieved September 22, 2012.

[2] U.S. Census Bureau Population Estimates (http://www.census.gov/popest/cities/files/SUB-EST2005_9.csv)

[3] http://www.newmilford.org/

[4] "New Milford History" (http://www.nmhistorical.org/learningzone/index.htm), *Learning Zone* section, Historical Society of New Milford Website, accessed August 2, 2006

[5] http://www.nmchurch.org/

[6] "History" (http://www.nmchurch.org/history.htm), New Milford Congregational Church, accessed 23 Dec 2010

[7] "American FactFinder" (http://factfinder.census.gov). United States Census Bureau. . Retrieved 2008-01-31.

[8] "New Milford Town Web Site *12/27/2007: Rail Study*" (http://www.newmilford.org/controls//eventview.aspx?MODE=SINGLE& ID=135). . Retrieved 2008-03-04.

[9] http://www.newmilford-chamber.com/_Sports_and_Fitness.html

[10] http://www.usrowing.org/Pressbox/AthleteBios/ElizabethYoungling.aspx

[11] http://www.usrowing.org/Pressbox/AthleteBios/2011SeniorTeamBios.aspx

[12] http://www.sots.ct.gov/RegisterManual/SectionVII/SecVIITOC.htm

[13] Carlson, Wendy, "Did I Mention The Graves Out Back?" (http://www.nytimes.com/2010/04/18/realestate/18posting. html?pagewanted=print), news article, *The New York Times*, page 1 of the "Real Estate" section, April 18, 2010, retrieved same day

[14] Catlin, Roger (2001-02-01). "Vertical Horizon Reaches For Stars: From Acoustic To Metal, Band Finally Hits It Big" (http://articles. courant.com/2001-02-01/features/0102011910_1_vertical-horizon-matt-scannell-new-rock-bands). *Hartford Courant*. . Retrieved 2011-07-17.

[15] (http://us.imdb.com/List?endings=on&&locations=New+Milford,+Connecticut,+USA) "Internet Movie DataBase" Web site, "New Milford, Connecticut" Web page, accessed August 2, 2006

External links

- Town of New Milford Connecticut (http://www.newmilford.org/) Portal style website, Government, Business, Library, Recreation and more
- Town of New Milford Public Works (http://www.newmilford.org/content/57/193/default.aspx/)
- New Milford Public Library (http://www.biblio.org/newmilford/)
- New Milford Historical Society (http://www.nmhistorical.org/)
- New Milford School District (http://www.newmilfordps.org/)
- New Milford Chamber of Commerce (http://www.newmilford-chamber.com/)
- New Milford First Congregational Church (http://www.nmchurch.org)
- New Milford Tricentennial Celebration in 2007 (http://www.newmilford300.org/)
- Northwest Connecticut Convention & Visitors Bureau (http://www.litchfieldhills.com/app/index.jsp)
- New Milford Land Use Regulations (http://ahhowland.com/resources/Litchfield_County/new_milford_ct/new_milford_ct_regulations.html)
- Online reprint of "History of the Towns of New Milford and Bridgewater, Connecticut, 1703-1882" by Samuel Orcutt (http://archive.org/details/historytownsnew00orcugoog)
- City-Data.com (http://www.city-data.com/city/New-Milford-Connecticut.html) Comprehensive Statistical Data and more about Milford

North and South (TV miniseries)

North and South	
Complete Collection DVD cover	
Genre	Historical drama
Creator	David L. Wolper
Produced by	Paul Freeman
Starring	James Read Patrick Swayze Lesley-Anne Down Wendy Kilbourne Terri Garber Genie Francis and others
Country	United States
Original channel	TVA
Release date	Book I: November 3, 1985 Book II: May 4, 1986 Book III: February 27, 1994
Running time	90 minutes/episode
No. of episodes	Book I: 6 Book II: 6 Book III: 3

North and South is the title of three American television miniseries broadcast on the ABC network in 1985, 1986, and 1994. Set before, during, and immediately after the American Civil War, they are based on the 1980s trilogy of novels *North and South* by John Jakes.[1] The 1985 first installment, *North and South*, remains the seventh-highest rated miniseries in TV history.[2][3][4] *North and South: Book II* (1986) was met with similar success, while 1994's *Heaven and Hell: North and South Book III* was poorly received by both critics and audiences.[5][6]

The saga tells the story of the enduring friendship between Orry Main of South Carolina (Patrick Swayze) and George Hazard of Pennsylvania (James Read), who become best friends while attending the United States Military Academy at West Point but later find themselves and their families on opposite sides of the war.[1] The slave-owning Mains are rural planters, while the Hazards, who resided in a small Northern mill town, live by manufacturing and industry, their differences reflecting the divisions between North and South that eventually led to the Civil War.[7]

Cast

The initial 1985 miniseries cast Patrick Swayze as Orry Main and James Read as George Hazard, with Lesley-Anne Down as Orry's love interest Madeline and Wendy Kilbourne as George's future wife Constance.[8] Kirstie Alley played George's outspoken abolitionist sister Virgilia, with Genie Francis as Orry's "good" sister Brett and Terri Garber as his selfish and wicked sister Ashton, as well as Philip Casnoff as Elkanah Bent, George and Orry's nemesis.[8] All of these actors returned for the 1986 sequel, joined by Parker Stevenson as Billy Hazard, George's brother and Brett's paramour.[9]

North and South (1985) also featured many well-known actors as guest stars, including Elizabeth Taylor as bordello proprietor Madam Conti, David Carradine as the sadistic Justin LaMotte, Hal Holbrook as Abraham Lincoln, Gene Kelly as Bent's father Senator Charles Edwards, Robert Mitchum as Colonel Patrick Flynn, M.D., Johnny Cash as abolitionist John Brown, Jean Simmons as Orry's mother Clarissa Main, Mitchell Ryan as Orry's father Tillet Main, Jonathan Frakes as George's older brother Stanley Hazard, Robert Guillaume as abolitionist Frederick Douglass, Morgan Fairchild as Burdetta Halloran, David Ogden Stiers as Congressman Sam Greene, and Olivia Cole as Madeline's devoted but doomed servant Maum Sally.[8] John Jakes' wife Rachel also made an appearance in Episode 6 as Lincoln's wife Mary. *North and South: Book II* (1986) saw the return of Carradine as LaMotte, Holbrook as Lincoln, and Stiers as Congressman Greene, as well as new guests Lloyd Bridges as Jefferson Davis, Anthony Zerbe as Ulysses S. Grant, Nancy Marchand as Dorothea Dix, Jimmy Stewart as Miles Colbert, Wayne Newton as Captain Thomas Turner, and William Schallert as Robert E. Lee,[9] with Linda Evans as Rose Sinclair and Olivia de Havilland as Mrs. Neal. 1994's *Heaven and Hell* featured Peter O'Toole as "louche actor" Sam Trump[10] and Billy Dee Williams as Francis Cardozo.

Filming of the miniseries resulted in four marriages amongst the cast and crew. James Read and Wendy Kilbourne fell in love while shooting scenes where their characters, George Hazard and Constance Flynn Hazard, fell in love. They were married in 1988 and now have two children. Jonathan Frakes and Genie Francis, who had previously played opposite each other on the failed NBC soap *Bare Essence*, eventually married in 1988. Lesley-Anne Down married assistant cameraman Don E. FauntLeRoy in 1986. When they met during filming of Book 1, both were married to someone else, but eventually obtained divorces.[11] Terri Garber married *North and South* cameraman Chris Hager in 1985. The couple divorced four years later, and have a daughter named Molly.

Character	North and South 1985	North and South: Book II 1986	Heaven and Hell: North and South Book III 1994
Orry Main	Patrick Swayze	Patrick Swayze	Patrick Swayze (Archive/Uncredited)
George Hazard	James Read	James Read	James Read
Madeline Fabray LaMotte Main	Lesley-Anne Down	Lesley-Anne Down	Lesley-Anne Down
Constance Flynn Hazard	Wendy Kilbourne	Wendy Kilbourne	Wendy Kilbourne
Virgilia Hazard Grady	Kirstie Alley	Kirstie Alley	
Ashton Main Huntoon Fenway / Young Ashton / Young Ashton	Terri Garber / Temi Epstein (Ep. 1) / Stephanie Jolluck (Ep. 2)	Terri Garber	Terri Garber
Brett Main Hazard / Young Brett / Young Brett	Genie Francis / Nikki Creswell (Ep. 1) / Melissa Manley (Ep. 2)	Genie Francis	Genie Francis
Elkanah Bent	Philip Casnoff	Philip Casnoff	Philip Casnoff
Charles Main	Lewis Smith	Lewis Smith	Kyle Chandler
Billy Hazard / Young Billy	John Stockwell / Cary Guffey (Ep. 1)	Parker Stevenson	
Stanley Hazard	Jonathan Frakes	Jonathan Frakes	Jonathan Frakes
Isabel Truscott Hazard	Wendy Fulton	Mary Crosby	Deborah Rush
Justin LaMotte	David Carradine	David Carradine	
Clarissa Gault Main	Jean Simmons	Jean Simmons	
Maude Hazard	Inga Swenson	Inga Swenson	
Burdetta Halloran	Morgan Fairchild	Morgan Fairchild	
Congressman Sam Greene	David Ogden Stiers	David Ogden Stiers	
James Huntoon	Jim Metzler	Jim Metzler	
Salem Jones	Tony Frank	Tony Frank	

Priam	David Harris	David Harris	
Semiramis	Erica Gimpel	Erica Gimpel	
Cuffey	Forest Whitaker	Forest Whitaker	
Ned Fisk	Andrew Stahl	Andrew Stahl	
Maum Sally	Olivia Cole		
Madam Conti	Elizabeth Taylor		
Garrison Grady	Georg Stanford Brown		
Tillet Main	Mitchell Ryan		
Ironworker	Ray Spruell		
Barman	Ronnie Stutes		
Augusta Barclay		Kate McNeil	
Rafe Baudeen		Lee Horsley	
Miles Colbert		Jimmy Stewart	
Mrs. Neal		Olivia de Havilland	
Rose Sinclair		Linda Evans	
Captain Thomas Turner		Wayne Newton	
Colonel Hiram Berdan		Kurtwood Smith	
Ezra		Beau Billingslea	
Lt. Stephen Kent		Whip Hubley	
Hope Hazard		Jennifer and Michele Steffin	Mary Elizabeth McCae
Sam Trump			Peter O'Toole
Adolphus			Rip Torn
Cooper Main			Robert Wagner
Judith Stafford Main			Cathy Lee Crosby
Gus Main			Cameron Finley
Running Wolf			Ted Thin Elk
Gettys			Cliff De Young
Jack Quinlan			Woody Watson
Isaac			Stan Shaw
Jane			Sharon Washington
Historical figures			
Person	**Book I** **1985**	**Book II** **1986**	**Book III** **1994**
Abraham Lincoln	Hal Holbrook	Hal Holbrook	
Mary Todd Lincoln	Rachel Jakes *(uncredited)*		
Ulysses S. Grant	Mark Moses	Anthony Zerbe	Rutherford Cravens
Frederick Douglass	Robert Guillaume		
John Brown	Johnny Cash		
George B. McClellan	Chris Douridas		
George Pickett	Cody W. Hampton		

Tom "Stonewall" Jackson	William Preston Daly		
Jefferson Davis		Lloyd Bridges	
Robert E. Lee		William Schallert	
Dorothea Dix		Nancy Marchand	
Francis Cardozo			Billy Dee Williams
Major Anderson	James Rebhorn		

Crew

North and South (1985) was directed by Richard T. Heffron, from a script adaptation by Patricia Green, Douglas Heyes, Paul F. Edwards, and Kathleen A. Shelley. It was produced by David L. Wolper, Paul Freeman, Rob Harland, and Chuck McLain, with music by Bill Conti and Stevan Larner as cinematographer. Wolper also produced 1986's *North and South: Book II* with his son Mark Wolper, as well as Stephanie Austin and Robert Papazian. Conti returned as composer, with Kevin Connor directing, Jacques R. Marquette as cinematographer, and a script by Heyes and Richard Fielder. *Heaven and Hell: North and South Book III* (1994) was directed by Larry Peerce from a script by Suzanne Clauser. Hal Galli produced the miniseries, with music by David Bell and Don E. FauntLeRoy as cinematographer.

Plot

Book I: *North and South*

- **Episode 1** (summer 1842 - summer 1844) - Young Southerner Orry Main, the only son of a wealthy South Carolina plantation owner, goes to West Point. During the journey, he meets and falls in love with beautiful New Orleans French-Creole Madeline Fabray. In New York City, Orry meets Northerner George Hazard, the second son of a wealthy Pennsylvania steel-factory owner, who is also on his way to West Point. They soon become close friends. At the Academy, they meet the amoral egomaniac Elkanah Bent, a fellow cadet from Georgia. Bent is a handsome, smooth-talking man who hides his evil, twisted nature beneath his charm and good looks. He takes an instant dislike to Orry and George and uses his status as their drillmaster to constantly harass them. Orry keeps writing letters to Madeline, although it seems that she has not been responding. After a two-year absence, the men return home for a summer leave. George's abolitionist sister, Virgilia, immediately takes a dislike to Orry as he keeps slaves. While at home, Orry is devastated to learn that Madeline is getting married to his cruel neighbor, plantation owner Justin LaMotte. Orry has an argument with his father over the hiring of the brutal and sadistic Salem Jones as the plantation overseer. Orry stops Jones from using a bullwhip to "punish" a slave. After Orry sees Madeline get married, they find out that Madeline's father has been hiding Orry's letters so that she would marry Justin.
- **Episode 2** (autumn 1844 - spring 1848) - Bent continues his cruelty towards George, Orry, and their friends. The men, with some help from other cadets, make Bent a fool and he is forced to leave the Academy. When Bent learns of George and Orry's involvement, he promises them he will have revenge. George and Orry graduate from West Point. They leave to fight in the Mexican War. During the Battle of Churubusco, Bent, who has used his political connections to obtain a superior rank, orders George and Orry to lead a suicidal charge against the Mexican forces. Both men survive, but Orry is shot in his left leg and is permanently crippled. Meanwhile, George meets Constance Flynn, the Irish Catholic daughter of an Army surgeon, and falls in love. They plan to marry. Orry turns to drink to drown his sorrows. With the Mexican War over, George quits the army, finds Bent, and beats him up. George tells Bent that, if he ever harms Orry or him again, George will kill Bent. Traumatized by his injuries, Orry temporarily becomes a recluse. When Madeline helps Priam, one of Orry's slaves, escape, one of the other slaves gets whipped for helping Priam.

- **Episode 3** (spring 1848 - summer 1854) Orry and Madeline become secret lovers. George gets married to Constance and Orry is his best man. Orry's father dies and Orry inherits the family plantation. His first act is to fire the brutal Salem Jones as overseer. Jones vows revenge. Orry's cousin Charles, who does not have good relations with the Main family, is challenged to a pistol duel in a dispute over a woman. Orry helps Charles to survive the duel and they become friends. The Mains visit the Hazards in Pennsylvania. Orry's sister Ashton courts George's brother Billy. Billy and Charles are going to attend West Point together, just as Orry and George did. Orry and George begin a partnership cotton mill at Orry's plantation in South Carolina; they do so on George's condition that Orry not use slave labor in the mill. Virgilia is furious that her family has allowed slaveowners into their house and tries to humiliate them, angering the rest of her family.

- **Episode 4** (summer 1854 - autumn 1856) - The Hazards visit the Mains in South Carolina. Billy discovers how vain and wicked Ashton can be and falls in love with Ashton's younger sister Brett. George's sister Virgilia helps one of the local slaves escape and gets into trouble. While dying, Madeline's father tells her that her mother's grandmother was black. Billy and Charles graduate from West Point, and both families attend the graduation. Ashton sleeps with many of Billy's friends and gets pregnant. She asks Madeline for help, and Madeline takes her to a local midwife who performs a secret abortion. When Madeline lies to Justin about where she was while she was helping Ashton, he beats Madeline, locks her in a spare bedroom and leaves her to starve and kills Maum Sally.

- **Episode 5** (spring 1857 - November 1860) - Madeline is drugged by Justin and disappears from society, even seeming to forget her love for Orry. Ashton marries James Huntoon, an ambitious but easily-manipulated South Carolina politician. Orry visits George, but they have a serious argument over the issue of slavery. Orry does not want Brett to marry Billy because of the growing tensions between the North and South. Virgilia marries the slave she helped escape from the Main plantation in South Carolina. They both join abolitionist leader John Brown. In 1859 Brown makes his famous raid on Harpers Ferry, Virginia, to arm and free the slaves there. The U.S. Army stops the raid, Virgilia's husband is killed, Priam is wounded, and Brown is captured. Virgilia escapes, but is more bitter than ever towards Southerners. Abraham Lincoln is elected President; several Southern states make plans to secede from the U.S. and establish themselves as a separate nation.

- **Episode 6** (November 6, 1860 - April 1861) - Having argued with Orry and fled to Ashton's house in Charleston, Brett meets Billy who is stationed at Fort Sumter. George visits Orry and the two apologize to each other. Orry gives Brett permission to marry Billy. South Carolina secedes from the Union, infuriating Orry. Brett and Billy get married. Ashton schemes to have Billy killed, partly out of jealously, and partly because Billy is now a "Yankee" enemy. She fails, thanks to the drugged Madeline, who overhears Ashton and Justin's scheme and informs Orry. Orry is enraged at Ashton and tells her that she is no longer a member of the Main family. Madeline leaves Justin and takes refuge with Orry at his family's plantation. Now off the drugs, Madeline plans to divorce Justin and marry Orry. Orry goes to the Hazard's mansion near Philadelphia to give George his part of their cotton mill money. When he arrives, Orry discovers that George and Constance have a baby girl named Hope. Virgilia finds out that Orry is present and tries to have him killed by forming a lynch mob which threatens the Hazard estate; the mob's leaders demand that George give them the "rebel traitor", there is little doubt that they intend to kill Orry. George and Orry face down the mob with shotguns and Orry boards a train to return to South Carolina. The two friends part, unsure if they will ever see each other again. The Civil War begins.

Book II: *Love and War*

- **Episode 1** (June 1861 - July 21, 1861) - Orry and Charles, now officers in the Confederate Army, leave the Main family plantation for the war in Virginia. Orry, despite having been against secession, becomes a general and military aide to Confederate President Jefferson Davis in the Confederate capital of Richmond. Meanwhile, George and Billy are in Washington, D.C., where they are officers in the U.S. Army. Billy joins the U.S. Sharpshooters regiment, while George becomes a military aide to U.S. President Abraham Lincoln. Charles, a Confederate cavalry officer, meets Augusta Barclay, a Virginia belle who smuggles medicine for the southern soldiers. Virgilia wants to work as a nurse at a Washington, D.C. military hospital and asks fellow abolitionist Congressman Sam Greene for help. Orry's cruel and manipulative sister Ashton meets her match in Elkanah Bent, who sees the Civil War as a great way to get rich by smuggling forbidden luxury goods through the U.S. Navy blockade of the South. Bent and Ashton quickly become lovers, while Ashton's politician husband, James Huntoon, is unaware of his wife's adultery. With Orry and Charles gone to war, Justin kidnaps Madeline from the Main family plantation and burns the cotton barn; Orry's mother is injured trying to stop the fire. The First Battle of Bull Run takes place with George and Constance getting caught up in the panicked aftermath as they reluctantly watch from a distance. The South is the winner.

- **Episode 2** (July 1861 - summer 1862) - Hearing about her mother's injury, Brett and one of the Main household servants, Semiramis, make the dangerous trip from Washington, D.C. to the Main plantation in South Carolina. Along the way, Semiramis is captured by Union soldiers, but rescued by Brett. Orry leaves Richmond and returns to South Carolina as well; he finds Madeline at Justin's plantation and kills Justin in a fight. Orry and Madeline finally get married. Orry discovers Bent's illegal smuggling enterprise and stops it by capturing Bent's blockade runners, arresting his men, and destroying most of his merchandise. Bent and Ashton vow revenge. Meanwhile in Pennsylvania, George's older brother Stanley takes over the family's steel factories. His greedy wife Isabel talks him into profiteering from the war by using cheap, low-grade iron to make cannons for the U.S. Army; the cannons often explode and kill Northern soldiers. They forge George's name on the documents, in case the cannons are traced back to Hazard Iron.

- **Episode 3** (September 17, 1862 - spring 1864) - At the bloody battle of Antietam, Charles and Billy nearly kill each other, but each allows the other to escape. Charles's friend Ambrose is killed in the battle by one of the poor-quality cannons made by Hazard Iron. Afterwards, President Abraham Lincoln's Emancipation Proclamation frees the slaves in the rebel Southern states. Most of the slaves leave the Main plantation in South Carolina, but a few remain. Ashton visits her family's plantation, supposedly to see her recovering mother and sister Brett, but in reality to carry out Bent's revenge against Orry. Ashton tells Madeline that she knows that Madeline's mother was a high-priced black prostitute in New Orleans, and that, unless Madeline leaves Orry with no explanation, she will reveal this secret and "ruin" Orry's public reputation. Madeline flees to Charleston where she is befriended by a suave gambler and begins working for the city's poor and orphans who are suffering from the war. Meanwhile, Bent — who has become increasingly psychotic and unstable — begins planning to assassinate Confederate President Jefferson Davis and become the dictator of the South. Billy, sick of not having seen his wife Brett for nearly two years, goes AWOL from the U.S. Army and makes his way to South Carolina, where he and Brett spend some time together. Ashton discovers Billy's presence and goes to tell the local authorities, but Billy is saved when Brett threatens her sister with a pitchfork long enough for Billy to escape.

- **Episode 4** (May 1864 - late autumn 1864) - When Billy returns to his regiment, his commanding officer threatens to court-martial and execute him if he ever leaves again. Billy is also placed in harm's way by being put in charge of the regiment's skirmishers. George is captured in a raid by Southern forces and taken to the dreaded Libby Prison in Richmond, where he is tortured by the prison's ruthless commandant. Orry is shot and taken to the hospital where Virgilia works; despite her hatred of Southerners, she helps him recover and allows him to escape. Later, Virgilia is accused of allowing a wounded Southern soldier to die and is fired from the hospital. Desperate for money and work, she goes to Congressman Greene for help. He gives her money in exchange for sex. Charles saves Augusta from being raped by Northern soldiers at her farm in Virginia, and the two become lovers.

- **Episode 5** (December 1864 - February 1865) - The war has turned against the South. Orry and Charles save George from Libby Prison, kill the commandant in a fight, and allow George to return to the North. Madeline helps starving people in Charleston. Returning home, George learns of his brother and sister-in-law's illegal business schemes to use cheap iron to build cannon. He forces Stanley and Isabel to admit guilt. Bent tries to kill Madeline in Charleston, but she is rescued by her gambler friend, who saves Madeline but is fatally shot by Bent. Orry learns of Bent's plan to overthrow the Confederate government from Ashton's husband James Huntoon, who Bent enlisted to help him. In a final fight, Orry and Huntoon attack Bent's hideout near Richmond. Bent is (apparently) killed when the ammunition he was hiding in a barn explodes. Ashton confesses to Orry that she helped Bent drive Madeline away, and Orry tells Huntoon that he never wants to see his sister again. Ashton asks Huntoon to forgive her, but he tells her that it is too late.

- **Episode 6** (March 1865 - April 1865) - The fighting ends with a Northern victory. Orry and George lead troops against each other in the last major battle at Petersburg; Orry is wounded. Confederate General Robert E. Lee surrenders his army to U.S. Army General Ulysses Grant. Virgilia kills Congressman Greene after he refuses to help her anymore, and is sentenced to death by hanging. She and George have a tearful farewell before her execution. George learns that Orry is wounded and searches for him, finally finding him in a Union hospital. Their reunion is spoiled when both learn that President Lincoln has been shot. George helps Orry find Madeline, who reveals that Orry is now the father of their son. Charles goes to Augusta's farm and finds that she has died giving birth to his child, a son. He goes to Charleston and gets his child from Augusta's uncle's wife. Salem Jones, the cruel and brutal former overseer of the Main plantation, joins with one of the Main's former slaves, Cuffey, to plan an attack on the Main plantation. Their plan is to loot and steal everything from the mansion, kill the Main family, and burn the mansion. With the war over, Billy quits the army and reunites with Brett at her family's plantation. Orry, Madeline, their baby, and George all set out for the Main plantation. Salem Jones leads several former slaves in his attack on the plantation; they burn the mansion before being killed or driven off by Charles, Billy, and Ezra, a former slave who is engaged to marry Brett's slave Semiramis. Orry, George, and Madeline arrive, with the former two helping to fend off the last of the attackers. Orry's mother is killed in the attack by Cuffey while trying to prevent Semiramis' rape, but Cuffey is shot dead by Charles, while Salem Jones is similarly dispatched when he tries to rape Brett. Orry and George pledge to renew their family's friendship, and George agrees to help Orry rebuild his plantation home by reopening the cotton mill and letting Orry take the profits.

Book III: *Heaven and Hell*

- **Episode 1** (summer 1865 - autumn 1865) - Elkanah Bent, having survived the explosion of his hidden ammunition depot near Richmond, becomes obsessed with getting "final revenge" on Orry and George, whom he blames for his failures in life. He begins his revenge by going to Richmond and murdering Orry Main with a single stab wound. Furious, Ashton tries unsuccessfully to kill Bent; she then moves to the Old West to start a new life. Heartbroken at Orry's death, Madeline tries to rebuild the Main family mansion at Mont Royal and helps local freed slaves, to the disapproval of most of her white neighbors. After learning of Orry's death, George goes to Mont Royal and helps Madeline. Charles Main, now a corporal in the U.S. Cavalry in the Old West, meets and romances Willa Parker. Ashton begins working as a prostitute in Santa Fe; her goal is to earn enough money to buy Mont Royal. Carrying out the next part of his plan of revenge, Bent goes to the Hazard mansion near Philadelphia and murders George's wife Constance.

- **Episode 2** (autumn 1865 - spring 1866) - Devastated by news of his wife's murder, George begins searching for Bent to exact justice. Cooper Main, Orry's older brother, becomes a member of the Ku Klux Klan and begins working to undermine his sister-in-law Madeline's efforts to help local blacks. Isabel, George's greedy sister-in-law, wants to buy Mont Royal and evict the Main family. Charles continues to work as a cavalryman in the Old West, and continues to romance Willa. Realizing that she cannot stand against Cooper and Isabel alone, Madeline asks George for help. Charles helps to form a unit of buffalo soldiers. Cavalrymen massacre a Cheyenne village.

- **Episode 3** (spring 1866 - spring/summer 1866) - George arrives at Mont Royal to help Madeline, and they fall in love. Carrying out the final part of his revenge, Bent kidnaps Charles and Augusta's son Gus. When George learns of this, he goes West and finds Charles. Together the two men rescue Gus, hunt down Bent, and hang him. The hanging ends the personal "war" between Bent and the Main and Hazard families. When Ashton finally gets home, she weeps when she sees that Mont Royal has been burned. George and Charles return to Mont Royal to help Madeline and the freed slaves defeat the Ku Klux Klan. Cooper takes Madeline during the fight, and George rides after to save her. When Cooper is told by Gettys to kill both Madeline and George, he refuses. Gettys shoots Cooper, who kills Gettys before he dies. Charles says his goodbyes before returning to Willa and Gus, while George and Madeline plan for their future together.

Awards and nominations

The *North and South* miniseries were nominated (N) and awarded (W) with many different awards around the world, among which the most significant are :

Year	Award	N/W	Category/People
1986	Golden Globes	N	David Carradine for *Best Performance by an Actor in a Supporting Role in a Series, Mini-Series or Motion Picture Made for TV* (N&S1)
1986	Golden Globes	N	Lesley-Anne Down for *Best Performance by an Actress in a Supporting Role in a Series, Mini-Series or Motion Picture Made for TV* (N&S1)
1986	Emmy	W	many people for *Outstanding Achievement in Costuming for a Miniseries or a Special* (N&S1, ep.4)
1986	Emmy	N	Virginia Darcy for *Outstanding Achievement in Hairstyling for a Miniseries or a Special* (N&S1, ep.1)
1986	Emmy	N	many people for *Outstanding Achievement in Makeup for a Miniseries or a Special* (N&S1, ep.6)
1986	Emmy	N	Bill Conti for *Outstanding Achievement in Music Composition for a Miniseries or a Special (Dramatic Underscore)* (N&S1, ep.1)
1986	Emmy	N	Stevan Larner for *Outstanding Cinematography for a Miniseries or a Special* (N&S1, ep.6)
1986	Emmy	N	many people for *Outstanding Editing for a Miniseries or a Special - Single Camera Production* (N&S1, ep.4)
1986	Emmy	N	many people for *Outstanding Sound Editing for a Miniseries or a Special* (N&S1, ep.2)
1986	Emmy	N	many people for *Outstanding Achievement in Hairstyling for a Miniseries or a Special* (N&S2, ep.1)
1986	Emmy	N	Robert Fletcher for *Outstanding Costume Design for a Miniseries or a Special* (N&S2, ep.1)
1986	Emmy	N	many people for *Outstanding Sound Editing for a Miniseries or a Special* (N&S2, ep.6)
1995	ASC Award	N	Don E. FauntLeRoy for *Outstanding Achievement in Cinematography in Mini-Series* (N&S3, ep.3)

Media

VHS and DVD releases

North and South Books I and II were released on NTSC VHS in the United States. Book III was never released on VHS in the United States. Books I, II and III were released on PAL VHS in Europe.

All three Books were released on Region 1 DVD in October 2004. This release also included a bonus featurette with John Jakes and David Wolper talking about the books and the miniseries; James Read, Lesley-Anne Down, and Patrick Swayze discussing their characters; general thoughts of other cast and crew members; plus information about the historical background and trials of its reconstruction for the miniseries.

The Region 2 DVD release contained only Books I and II at first, but eventually Book III also became available, with the bonus featurette included. All volumes were sold as separate boxes, but later on they were also available in one box.

Soundtrack

A soundtrack CD published by Varèse Sarabande in 1985 (VCD47250) contains tracks from the music scores of two Bill Conti films, *North and South* and *The Right Stuff*. It includes the following tracks from *North and South*:[12]

1. Main Title 3:45
2. Southern Life 1:38
3. Love In The Chapel 4:04
4. A Close Call 2:00
5. Returning Home 2:13
6. Last Embrace 2:57
7. Final Meeting 2:28

The Varèse Sarabande Soundtrack Club released the entire score to *North and South* (1985) in a four-CD box set on February 25, 2008.[13] The tracks in this set are the original recordings used in the production of the series. The entire score to *North and South: Book II* (1986) was released on October 3, 2008 and includes three CDs.[14]

References

[1] *Editorial Review:* North and South *(1982)* (http://books.google.com/books?id=WHohAQAAIAAJ&dq=isbn:0151669988& ei=PsFCS_KYH5zElASGtYiuAQ&cd=1). Kirkus Reviews (c) VNU Business Media, Inc.. 1982. . Retrieved January 5, 2010.

[2] Bennett, Mark (August 8, 2007). "John Jakes' journey to *New York Times* bestseller list included boyhood years in Terre Haute" (http://www.tribstar.com/archivesearch/local_story_220164949.html). *Tribune-Star*. TribStar.com. . Retrieved January 7, 2010.

[3] Thompson, Bill (March 18, 2002). "Bestselling novelist penning saga of fictional Charleston family" (http://www.depauw.edu/news/index.asp?id=11968). *The Post and Courier*. Excerpted at DePauw.edu. . Retrieved January 7, 2010.

[4] Jones, Mary Ellen (November 30, 1996). "The People's Author: The Life of John Jakes" (http://books.google.com/books?id=2pzmvCXfuoAC&pg=PA3&lpg=PA3&dq=highest+rated+miniseries+jakes&source=bl&ots=wMhwmYz79n& sig=gnjdl2g_URPhmDLhAGaKOBqpgvI&hl=en&ei=1VlFS9SuFZKuNtCCle0C&sa=X&oi=book_result&ct=result&resnum=1& ved=0CAcQ6AEwADgK#v=onepage&q=&f=false). *John Jakes: A Critical Companion*. Greenwood Press. p. 3. ISBN 0-313-29530-1. . Retrieved January 7, 2010.

[5] http://www.reviewgraveyard.com/2008_reviews/dvd/08-10-20_north-south3.htm

[6] DVD Verdict http://www.dvdverdict.com/reviews/northandsouth.php

[7] O'Connor, John J. (November 1, 1985). "TV Weekend; *North and South*, A Mini-series" (http://www.nytimes.com/1985/11/01/arts/tv-weekend-north-and-south-a-mini-series.html). *The New York Times* (NYTimes.com). . Retrieved January 7, 2010.

[8] Leonard, John (November 4, 1985). *Slavs, Slaves, and Shoulders (Review:* North and South*)* (http://books.google.com/books?id=7McBAAAAMBAJ&pg=PA58&dq=teri+garber&ei=cgtES5OsL6WSkATHtsHJBw&client=firefox-a&cd=10#v=onepage& q=&f=false). pp. 58–61. . Retrieved January 7, 2010.

[9] Leonard, John (May 5, 1986). *The Blue, The Gray, and the Déshabille (Review:* North and South: Book II*)* (http://books.google.com/books?id=DucCAAAAMBAJ&pg=PA85&dq=teri+garber&ei=cgtES5OsL6WSkATHtsHJBw&client=firefox-a&cd=9#v=onepage&q=& f=false). p. 85. . Retrieved January 7, 2010.

[10] O'Connell, Patricia (February 25, 1994). *Review: John Jakes'* Heaven and Hell: North and South Part 3 (http://www.variety.com/review/VE1117902409.html?categoryid=32&cs=1). Variety.com (http://books.google.com/books?id=PS1g1rnX7rsC&pg=RA11-PA23& dq=teri+garber&lr=&ei=Vw1ES-u4FpPslQT5xJTGBw&client=firefox-a&cd=45#v=onepage&q=&f=false). . Retrieved January 7, 2010.

[11] Allis, Tim (February 28, 1994). "The Spoils of War" (http://www.people.com/people/archive/article/0,,20107588,00.html). *People magazine*. Vol. 41, No. 8. . Retrieved January 16, 2010.

[12] It may be noted that the VCD47250 tracks are re-recordings, as the CD notes state that the tracks were recorded November 25, 1985, which was after *North and South* had originally aired.

[13] http://www.varesesarabande.com/details.asp?pid=VCL%2D0208%2D1072

[14] http://www.varesesarabande.com/details.asp?pid=VCL%2D0908%2D1082

External links

- *North & South* (http://www.imdb.com/title/tt0088583/) at the Internet Movie Database (1985)
- *North and South* (http://www.allrovi.com/movies/movie/v35639) at AllRovi
- *North and South* (http://www.tv.com/shows/north-and-south-1985/) at TV.com
- *North & South, Book II* (http://www.imdb.com/title/tt0090490/) at the Internet Movie Database (1986)
- *Heaven & Hell: North & South, Book III* (http://www.imdb.com/title/tt0108823/) at the Internet Movie Database (1994)
- Official DVD Homepage (http://warnervideo.com/northsouth/home.html)

Norte y Sur (serie de televisión)

Ophelia

Ophelia	
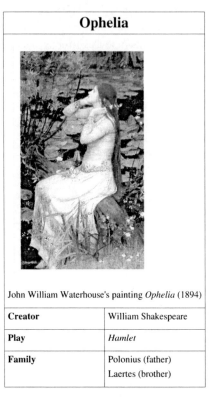 John William Waterhouse's painting *Ophelia* (1894)	
Creator	William Shakespeare
Play	*Hamlet*
Family	Polonius (father) Laertes (brother)

Ophelia is a fictional character in the play *Hamlet* by William Shakespeare. She is a young noblewoman of Denmark, the daughter of Polonius, sister of Laertes, and potential wife of Prince Hamlet. As one of the few female characters in the play, she is used as a contrasting plot device to Hamlet's mother, Gertrude.

Plot

In Ophelia's first speaking appearance in the play,[1] she is seen with her brother, Laertes, who is leaving for France. Laertes warns her that Hamlet, the heir to the throne of Denmark, does not have the freedom to marry whomever he wants. Ophelia's father, Polonius, enters while Laertes is leaving, and also forbids Ophelia to pursue Hamlet, whom he fears is not earnest about her.

In Ophelia's next appearance,[2] she tells Polonius that Hamlet rushed into her room with his clothing askew, and with a "hellish" expression on his face, and only stared at her and nodded three times, without speaking to her. Based on what Ophelia tells him, about Hamlet acting in such a "mad" way, Polonius concludes that he was wrong to forbid Ophelia to see Hamlet, and that Hamlet must be mad because of lovesickness for Ophelia. Polonius immediately decides to go to Claudius (the new King of Denmark, and also Hamlet's uncle and stepfather) about the situation. Polonius later suggests[3] to Claudius that they hide behind an arras to overhear Hamlet speaking to Ophelia when Hamlet thinks the conversation is private. Since Polonius is now sure that Hamlet is lovesick for Ophelia, he thinks Hamlet will express love for Ophelia. Claudius agrees to try the eavesdropping plan later.

The plan leads to what is commonly called the 'Nunnery Scene'.[4] Polonius instructs Ophelia to stand in the lobby of the castle while he and Claudius hide. Hamlet enters the room, in a different world from the others, and recites his "To be, or not to be" soliloquy. Hamlet approaches Ophelia and talks to her. He tells her "get thee to a nunnery." Hamlet becomes angry, realizes he has gone too far, and says "I say we will have no more marriages", and exits. Ophelia is left bewildered and heartbroken, sure that Hamlet is insane. After Hamlet storms out, Ophelia makes her

"O, what a noble mind is here o'erthrown" soliloquy.

Ophelia by John Everett Millais (1852) is part of the Tate Gallery collection. His painting influenced the image in Kenneth Branagh's *Hamlet*

The next time Ophelia appears is at the 'Mousetrap Play'[5] which Hamlet has arranged to try to prove that Claudius killed King Hamlet. Hamlet sits with Ophelia and makes sexually suggestive remarks, also saying that woman's love is brief.

Later that night, after the play, Hamlet kills Polonius [6] during a private meeting between Hamlet and his mother, Queen Gertrude. At Ophelia's next appearance,[7] after her father's death, she has gone mad, due to what the other characters interpret as grief for her father. She talks in riddles and rhymes, sings some "mad" and bawdy songs about death and a maiden losing her virginity. After bidding everyone a "good night", she exits.

The final time Ophelia appears in the play is after Laertes comes to the castle to challenge Claudius over the death of his father, Polonius. Ophelia sings more songs and hands out flowers, citing their symbolic meanings although interpretations of the meanings differ. The only herb that Shakespeare gives Ophelia herself is rue; "... there's rue for you, and here's some for me; we may call it herb of grace o'Sundays; O, you must wear your rue with a difference". Rue is well known for its symbolic meaning of regret, but the herb is also highly poisonous and has powerful abortive properties.[8]

In Act 4 Scene 7, Queen Gertrude, in her monologue (*There is a willow grows aslant the brook*), reports that Ophelia had climbed into a willow tree, and then a branch broke and dropped Ophelia into the brook, where she drowned. Gertrude says that Ophelia appeared "incapable of her own distress". Gertrude's announcement of Ophelia's death has been praised as one of the most poetic death announcements in literature.[9]

We later see a sexton at the graveyard insisting Ophelia must have killed herself.[10] Laertes is outraged by what

Ophelia by Alexandre Cabanel

the cleric says, and replies that Ophelia will be an angel in heaven when the cleric "lie[s] howling" in hell.

At Ophelia's funeral, Queen Gertrude sprinkles flowers on Ophelia's grave ("sweets to the sweet,") and says she wished Ophelia could have been Hamlet's wife. Laertes then jumps into Ophelia's grave excavation, asking for the burial to wait until he has held her in his arms one last time and proclaims how much he loved her. Hamlet, nearby, then challenges Laertes and claims that he loved Ophelia more than "forty thousand" brothers could. After her funeral scene, Ophelia is no longer mentioned.

Portrayal

While it is known that Richard Burbage played Hamlet in Shakespeare's time, there is no evidence of who played Ophelia; since there were no professional actresses on the public stage in Elizabethan England, we may be certain that she was played by a boy.[11]

The early modern stage in England had an established set of emblematic conventions for the representation of female madness: dishevelled hair worn down, dressed in white, bedecked with wild flowers, Ophelia's state of mind would have been immediately 'readable' to her first audiences.[12] "Colour was a major source of stage symbolism", Andrew Gurr explains, so the contrast between Hamlet's "nighted colour" (1.2.68) and "customary suits of solemn black" (1.2.78) and Ophelia's "virginal and vacant white" would have conveyed specific and gendered associations.[13] Her action of offering wild flowers to the court suggests, Showalter argues, a symbolic deflowering, while even the manner of her 'doubtful death', by drowning, carries associations with the feminine (Laertes refers to his tears on hearing the news as "the woman").

Mary Catherine Bolton
(afterwards Lady Thurlow)
(1790-1830) as Ophelia in 1813,
opposite John Philip Kemble's
Hamlet

Gender structured, too, the early modern understanding of the distinction between Hamlet's madness and Ophelia's: melancholy was understood as a male disease of the intellect, while Ophelia would have been understood as suffering from erotomania, a malady conceived in biological and emotional terms.[14] This discourse of female madness influenced Ophelia's representation on stage from the 1660s, when the appearance of actresses in the English theatres first began to introduce "new meanings and subversive tensions" into the role: "the most celebrated of the actresses who played Ophelia were those whom rumor credited with disappointments in love."[15] Showalter relates a theatrical anecdote that vividly captures this sense of overlap between a performer's identity and the role she plays:

Soprano Mignon Nevada as Ophelia in an
operatic adaptation of *Hamlet*, circa 1910.

"The greatest triumph was reserved for Susan Mountfort, a former actress at Lincoln's Inn Fields who had gone mad after her lover's betrayal. One night in 1720 she escaped from her keeper, rushed to the theater, and just as the Ophelia of the evening was to enter for her mad scene, "sprang forward in her place ... with wild eyes and wavering motion." As a contemporary reported, "she was in truth *Ophelia herself*, to the amazement of the performers as well as of the audience—nature having made this last effort, her vital powers failed her and she died soon after."[16]

During the 18th century, the conventions of Augustan drama encouraged far less intense, more sentimentalized and decorous depictions of Ophelia's madness and sexuality. From Mrs Lessingham in 1772 to Mary Bolton, playing opposite John Kemble in 1813, the familiar iconography of the role replaced its passionate embodiment. Sarah Siddons played Ophelia's madness with "stately and classical dignity" in 1785.[17]

Since that time, Ophelia has been a frequent subject in artwork, often in a Romantic or Classical style, as the images on this page show.

Many great actresses have played Ophelia on stage over the years. In the 19th century she was portrayed by Helen Faucit, Dora Jordan, Frances Abington, and Peg Woffington, who won her first real fame by playing the role.[18] Theatre manager Tate Wilkinson declared that next to Susannah Maria Cibber, Elizabeth Satchell (of the famous Kemble family) was the best Ophelia he ever saw.[19]

Ophelia has been portrayed on screen since the days of early silent films. Dorothy Foster played Ophelia opposite Charles Raymond's Hamlet in the 1912 film *Hamlet*. Jean Simmons played Ophelia opposite Laurence Olivier's Oscar-winning Hamlet performance in 1948; Simmons was also nominated for the Academy Award for Best Supporting Actress. More recently, Ophelia has been portrayed by Marianne Faithfull (1969), Helena Bonham Carter (1990), Kate Winslet (1996), Julia Stiles (2000) and Gugu Mbatha-Raw (2009). Themes associated with Ophelia have led to movies such as *Ophelia Learns to Swim* (2000), and *Dying Like Ophelia* (2002).[20]

In many theatre and film adaptations she is portrayed barefoot in the mad scenes, including Kozintsev's 1964 version, Zeffirelli's 1990 film, 1996 and 2000 versions.

Psychologist Mary Pipher attributed the name of her 1994 book *Reviving Ophelia* to Shakespeare's Ophelia. In her book, Pipher examines the troubled lives of the modern American adolescent girls. Through her extensive clinical work with troubled young women, Pipher takes a closer look at the competing influences that lead adolescent girls in a negative direction. For example, Pipher attributes the competing pressure from parents, peers, and the media for girls to reach an unachievable ideal. Girls are expected to meet goals while still holding on to their sanity. These pressures are further complicated when young women undergo physical changes out of their control, like the biological developmental changes in puberty. Shakespeare's Ophelia was thought to be going through erotomania; however, Ophelia and Pipher's patients display many of the same characteristics. Pipher believes the Ophelia of Shakespeare's era was entirely misunderstood, much like her patients. In order to understand the complex mind of an adolescent, one must look at the woman from a holistic perspective in order to gain a greater understanding of her outlook on life.

Lisa Klein's 2006 novel, *Ophelia*, uses her as the main protagonist. As opposed to her portrayal in the play, Ophelia uses madness as a cover, much like Hamlet does. Hamlet secretly marries her, though she is unaware of his own ruse of insanity. She eventually fakes her own death to escape the Danish court and preserve her life and that of her unborn baby, leaving to a convent in France. While there, she studies herbal remedies and takes on a task of being a medical worker for the sisters.

Footnotes

[1] *Hamlet*, Act 1, Scene 3
[2] *Hamlet*, Act 2, Scene 1
[3] *Hamlet*, Act 2, Scene 2
[4] *Hamlet*, Act 3, Scene 1
[5] *Hamlet*, Act 3, Scene 2
[6] *Hamlet*, Act 3, Scene 4
[7] *Hamlet*, Act 4, Scene 5
[8] http://www.sisterzeus.com/ERC_Rutin.html
[9] For one example of praise see "The Works of Shakespeare," in 11 volumes (Hamlet in volume 10,) edited by Henry N. Hudson, published by James Munroe and Company, 1856: "This exquisite passage is deservedly celebrated. Nothing could better illustrate the Poet's power to make the description of a thing better than the thing itself, by giving us his eyes to see it with."
[10] *Hamlet*, Act 5, Scene 1
[11] Taylor (2002, 4); Banham (1998, 141); Hattaway asserts that "Richard Burbage [...] played Hieronimo and also Richard III but then was the first Hamlet, Lear, and Othello" (1982, 91); Peter Thomson argues that the identity of Hamlet as Burbage is built into the dramaturgy of several moments of the play: "we will profoundly misjudge the position if we do not recognize that, whilst this is Weiner Hamlet talking *about* the groundlings, it is also Burbage talking *to* the groundlings" (1983, 24); see also Thomson (1983, 110) on the first player's beard. A researcher at the British Library feels able to assert only that Burbage "probably" played Hamlet; see its page on *Hamlet* (http://www.bl.uk/treasures/shakespeare/playhamlet.html).
[12] Showalter (1985, 80-81). In Shakespeare's *King John* (1595/6), the action of act three, scene four turns on the semiotic values of hair worn up or down and disheveled: Constance enters "*distracted, with her hair about her ears*" (17); "Lady, you utter madness, and not sorrow",

Pandolf rebukes her (43), yet she insists that "I am not mad; this hair I tear is mine" (45); she is repeatedly bid to "bind up your hairs"; she obeys, then subsequently unbinds it again, insisting "I will not keep this form upon my head / When there is such disorder in my wit" (101-102).(

[13] Gurr (1992, 193) and Showalter (1985, 80-81).

[14] Showalter (1985, 80-81).

[15] Showalter (1985, 80, 81).

[16] Showalter (1985, 81-82).

[17] Showalter (1985, 82).

[18] William Cullen Bryant & Evert A. Duyckinck (eds.), The Complete Works of Shakespeare, 1888

[19] *Some aspects of provincial drama in the eighteenth century*Frederick T. Wood English Studies, Volume 14, Issue 1 - 6 1932 (p. 73)

[20] Internet Movie Database, imdb.com

References

- Banham, Martin, ed. 1998. *The Cambridge Guide to Theatre*. Cambridge: Cambridge University Press. ISBN 0-521-43437-8.
- Charney, Maurice. 2000. *Shakespeare on Love & Lust*. New York: Columbia University Press. ISBN 0-231-10429-4.
- Gurr, Andrew. 1992. *The Shakespearean Stage 1574-1642*. Third ed. Cambridge: Cambridge University Press. ISBN 0-521-42240-X.
- Hattaway, Michael. 1982. *Elizabethan Popular Theatre: Plays in Performance*. Theatre Production ser. London and Boston: Routledge and Kegan Paul. ISBN 0-7100-9052-8.
- Thomson, Peter. 1983. *Shakespeare's Theatre*. Theatre Production ser. London and Boston: Routledge and Kegan Paul. ISBN 0-7100-9480-9.
- Wells, Stanley, and Sarah Stanton, eds. 2002. *The Cambridge Companion to Shakespeare on Stage*. Cambridge Companions to Literature ser. Cambridge: Cambridge University Press. ISBN 0-521-79711-X.

External links

- 'Shakespeare's Ophelia?' (http://www.independent.co.uk/arts-entertainment/theatre-dance/news/did-a-little-girl-picking-marigolds-inspire-shakespeares-ophelia-2294347.html), Rob Sharp, *The Independent*, 8 June 2011
- 'Five Truths' (http://www.vam.ac.uk/content/articles/f/five-truths/), directed by Katie Mitchell created for the Victoria and Albert Museum, 12 July 2011

Primetime Emmy Award for Outstanding Supporting Actress in a Miniseries or a Movie

Primetime Emmy Award for Outstanding Supporting Actress in a Miniseries or a Movie	
Awarded for	Outstanding Supporting Actress in a Miniseries or a Movie
Presented by	Academy of Television Arts & Sciences
Country	United States
Currently held by	Jessica Lange, *American Horror Story* (2012)
Official website	http://www.emmys.com/

This is a list of the winners of the Primetime Emmy Award for **Outstanding Supporting Actress – a Miniseries or Movie**.

Award winners

1970s

- **1978: Blanche Baker - *Holocaust* as Anna Weiss**
- **1979: Esther Rolle – *Summer of My German Soldier* as Ruth**

1980s

- **1980: Mare Winningham – *Amber Waves* as Marlene Burkhardt**
  - Eileen Heckart - *F.D.R.: The Last Year* as Eleanor Roosevelt
  - Patricia Neal - *All Quiet on the Western Front* as Mrs. Baumer
  - Carrie Nye - *Moviola: The Scarlett O'Hara War* as Tallulah Bankhead
- **1981: Jane Alexander – *Playing for Time* as Alma Rose**
  - Colleen Dewhurst - *The Women's Room* as Val
  - Patty Duke - *The Women's Room* as Lily
  - Shirley Knight - *Playing for Time* as Frau Lagerfuhrerin Maria Mandel
  - Piper Laurie - *The Bunker* as Magda Goebbels
- **1982: Penny Fuller – *The Elephant Man* as Mrs. Kendal**
  - Claire Bloom - *Brideshead Revisited* as Lady Marchmain
  - Judy Davis - *A Woman Called Golda* as Golda Myerson/Meir
  - Vicki Lawrence - *Eunice* as Thelma "Mama" Harper
  - Rita Moreno - *Portrait of a Showgirl* as Rosella DeLeon
- **1983: Jean Simmons – *The Thorn Birds* as Fee Cleary**
  - Judith Anderson - *Kennedy Center Tonight: Medea* as Nurse
  - Polly Bergen - *The Winds of War* as Rhoda Henry
  - Bette Davis - *Little Gloria... Happy at Last* as Alice Gwynnne Vanderbilt
  - Piper Laurie - *The Thorn Birds* as Anne Mueller

- **1985: Kim Stanley – *Cat on a Hot Tin Roof* as Big Mama**
  - Penny Fuller - *Cat on a Hot Tin Roof* as Mae
  - Ann Jillian - *Ellis Island* as Nellie Byfield
  - Deborah Kerr - *A Woman of Substance* as Emma Harte
  - Alfre Woodard - *Words by Heart* as Claudie Sills
- **1986: Colleen Dewhurst – *Between Two Women* as Barbara Petherton**
  - Phyllis Frelich - *Love is Never Silent* as Janice Ryder
  - Dorothy McGuire - *Amos* as Hester Farrell
  - Vanessa Redgrave - *Peter the Great* as Tsarevna Sophia
  - Sylvia Sidney - *An Early Frost* as Beatrice McKenna
- **1987: Piper Laurie – *Promise* as Annie Gilbert**
  - Claudette Colbert - *The Two Mrs. Grenvilles* as Alice Grenville
  - Olivia de Havilland - *Anastasia: The Mystery of Anna* as Dowager Empress Maria
  - Christine Lahti - *Amerika* as Althea Milford
  - Elizabeth Wilson - *Nutcracker: Money, Madness and Murder* as Berenice Bradshaw
- **1988: Jane Seymour – *Onassis: The Richest Man in the World* as Maria Callas**
  - Stockard Channing - *Echoes in the Darkness* as Susan Reinert
  - Ruby Dee - *Gore Vidal's Lincoln* as Elizabeth Keckley
  - Julie Harris - *The Woman He Loved* as Alice
  - Lisa Jacobs - *The Attic: The Hiding of Anne Frank* as Anne Frank

- **1984: Roxana Zal – *Something About Amelia* as Amelia Bennett**
  - Beverly D'Angelo - *A Streetcar Named Desire* as Stella DuBois Kowalski
  - Patty Duke - *George Washington* as Martha Washington
  - Cloris Leachman - *Ernie Kovacs: Between the Laughter* as Mary Kovacs
  - Tuesday Weld - *The Winter of Our Discontent* as Margie Young-Hunt

- **1989: Colleen Dewhurst – *Those She Left Behind* as Margaret Page**
  - Peggy Ashcroft - *A Perfect Spy* as Miss Duber
  - Polly Bergen - *War and Remembrance* as Rhoda Henry
  - Glenne Headly - *Lonesome Dove* as Elmira Johnson
  - Paula Kelly - *The Women of Brewster Place* as Theresa

1990s

- **1990: Eva Marie Saint – *People Like Us* as Lil Van Degan Altemus**
  - Stockard Channing - *Perfect Witness* as Liz Sapperstein
  - Colleen Dewhurst - *Lantern Hill* as Elizabeth
  - Swoosie Kurtz - *The Image* as Joanne Winstow-Darvish
  - Irene Worth - *The Shell Seekers* as Dolly Keeling

- **1991: Ruby Dee – *Decoration Day* as Rowena**
  - Olympia Dukakis - *Lucky Day* as Katherine Campbell
  - Vanessa Redgrave - *Young Catherine* as Empress Elizabeth
  - Doris Roberts - *The Sunset Gang* as Mimi Finklestein
  - Elaine Stritch - *An Inconvenient Woman* as Rose

- **1992: Amanda Plummer – *Miss Rose White* as Lusia**
  - Anne Bancroft - *Broadway Bound* as Kate Jerome
  - Bibi Besch - *Doing Time on Maple Drive* as Lisa Carter
  - Penny Fuller - *Miss Rose White* as Miss Kate Ryan
  - Maureen Stapleton - *Miss Rose White* as Tanta Perla

- **1993: Mary Tyler Moore – *Stolen Babies* as Georgia Tann**
  - Ann-Margret - *Alex Haley's Queen* as Sally Jackson
  - Lee Grant - *Citizen Cohn* as Dora Cohn
  - Peggy McCay - *Woman on the Run: The Lawrencia Bembenek Story* as Virginia Bembenek
  - Joan Plowright - *Stalin* as Olga

- **1994: Cicely Tyson – *Oldest Living Confederate Widow Tells All* as Castalia**
  - Anne Bancroft - *Oldest Living Confederate Widow Tells All* as Lucy Marsden (age 99 - 100)
  - Swoosie Kurtz - *And the Band Played On* as Mrs. Johnstone
  - Lee Purcell - *Secret Sins of the Father* as Ann Theilman
  - Lily Tomlin - *And the Band Played On* as Dr. Selma Dritz

- **1995: Judy Davis – *Serving in Silence: The Margarethe Cammermeyer Story* as Diane**

- **1995: Shirley Knight – *Indictment: The McMartin Trial* as Peggy Buckey**
  - Sonia Braga - *The Burning Season* as Regina de Catrvalho
  - Sissy Spacek - *The Good Old Boys* as Spring Renfro
  - Sada Thompson - *Indictment: The McMartin Trial* as Virginia McMartin

- **1996: Greta Scacchi – *Rasputin* as Tsarina Alexandra**
  - Kathy Bates - *The Late Shift* as Helen Kushnick
  - Diana Scarwid - *Truman* as Bess Truman
  - Mare Winningham - *The Boys Next Door* as Sheila
  - Alfre Woodard - *Gulliver's Travels* as Queen of Brobdingnag

- **1997: Diana Rigg – *Rebecca* as Mrs. Danvers**
  - Kirstie Alley - *The Last Don* as Rose Marie Clericuzio
  - Bridget Fonda - *In the Gloaming* as Anne
  - Glenne Headly - *Bastard Out of Carolina* as Aunt Ruth
  - Frances McDormand - *Hidden in America* as Gus

- **1998: Mare Winningham – *George Wallace* as Lurleen Wallace**
  - Helena Bonham Carter - *Merlin* as Morgan le Fay
  - Julie Harris - *Ellen Foster* as Leonora Nelson
  - Judith Ivey - *What the Deaf Man Heard* as Lucille
  - Angelina Jolie - *George Wallace* as Cornelia Wallace

- **1999: Anne Bancroft – *Deep in My Heart* as Gerry Eileen Cummins**
  - Jacqueline Bisset - *Joan of Arc* as Isabelle d'Arc
  - Olympia Dukakis - *Joan of Arc* as Mother Babette
  - Bebe Neuwirth - *Dash and Lilly* as Dorothy Parker
  - Cicely Tyson - *A Lesson Before Dying* as Tante Lou
  - Dianne Wiest - *The Simple Life of Noah Dearborn* as Sarah McClellan

2000s

- **2000: Vanessa Redgrave – *If These Walls Could Talk 2* as Edith Tree**
  - Kathy Bates – *Annie* as Agatha Hannigan
  - Elizabeth Franz – *Death of a Salesman* as Linda Loman
  - Melanie Griffith – *RKO 281* as Marion Davies
  - Maggie Smith – *David Copperfield* as Betsey Trotwood
- **2001: Tammy Blanchard – *Life with Judy Garland: Me and My Shadows* as young Judy Garland**
  - Anne Bancroft – *Haven* as Mama Gruber
  - Brenda Blethyn – *Anne Frank: The Whole Story* as Auguste Van Pels
  - Holly Hunter – *Things You Can Tell Just by Looking at Her* as Rebecca Waynon
  - Audra McDonald – *Wit* as Susie Monahan
- **2002: Stockard Channing – *The Matthew Shepard Story* as Judy Shepard**
  - Joan Allen – *The Mists of Avalon* as Morgause
  - Anjelica Huston – *The Mists of Avalon* as Viviane
  - Diana Rigg – *Victoria and Albert* as Baroness Lehzen
  - Sissy Spacek – *Last Call* as Zelda Fitzgerald
- **2003: Gena Rowlands – *Hysterical Blindness* as Virginia Miller**
  - Kathy Baker – *Door to Door* as Gladys Sullivan
  - Anne Bancroft – *The Roman Spring of Mrs. Stone* as Contessa
  - Juliette Lewis – *Hysterical Blindness* as Beth Tocyznski
  - Helen Mirren – *Door to Door* as Mrs. Porter
- **2004: Mary-Louise Parker – *Angels in America* as Harper Pitt**
  - Julie Andrews – *Eloise at Christmastime* as Nanny
  - Anne Heche – *Gracie's Choice* as Rowena Larson
  - Anjelica Huston – *Iron Jawed Angels* as Carrie Chapman Catt
  - Angela Lansbury – *The Blackwater Lightship* as Dora

- **2005: Jane Alexander – *Warm Springs* as Sara Delano Roosevelt**
  - Kathy Bates – *Warm Springs* as Helena Mahoney
  - Camryn Manheim – *Elvis* as Gladys Presley
  - Charlize Theron – *The Life and Death of Peter Sellers* as Britt Ekland
  - Joanne Woodward – *Empire Falls* as Francine Whiting
- **2006: Kelly Macdonald – *The Girl in the Café* as Gina**
  - Ellen Burstyn – *Mrs. Harris* as Former Tarnower Steady
  - Shirley Jones – *Hidden Places* as Aunt Batty
  - Cloris Leachman – *Mrs. Harris* as Pearl Schwartz
  - Alfre Woodard – *The Water Is Wide* as Mrs. Brown
- **2007: Judy Davis – *The Starter Wife* as Joan McAllister**
  - Toni Collette – *Tsunami: The Aftermath* as Kathy Graham
  - Samantha Morton – *Longford* as Myra Hindley
  - Anna Paquin – *Bury My Heart at Wounded Knee* as Elaine Goodale
  - Greta Scacchi – *Broken Trail* as Mrs. Nola Johns
- **2008: Eileen Atkins – *Cranford* as Deborah Jenkyns**
  - Laura Dern – *Recount* as Katherine Harris
  - Ashley Jensen – *Extras: The Extra Special Series Finale* as Maggie Jacobs
  - Audra McDonald – *A Raisin in the Sun* as Ruth Younger
  - Alfre Woodard – *Pictures of Hollis Woods* as Edna Reilly
- **2009: Shohreh Aghdashloo – *House of Saddam* as Sajida Khairallah Talfah**
  - Marcia Gay Harden – *The Courageous Heart of Irena Sendler* as Janina Krzyżanowska
  - Janet McTeer – *Into the Storm* as Clementine Churchill
  - Jeanne Tripplehorn – *Grey Gardens* as Jacqueline Kennedy Onassis
  - Cicely Tyson – *Relative Stranger* as Pearl

2010s

Year	Actor	Program	Role	Network
2009-2010 (62nd)	**Julia Ormond**	***Temple Grandin***	**Eustacia Grandin**	**HBO**
	Kathy Bates	*Alice*	The Queen of Hearts	Syfy
	Catherine O'Hara	*Temple Grandin*	Aunt Ann	HBO
	Susan Sarandon	*You Don't Know Jack*	Janet Good	HBO
	Brenda Vaccaro	*You Don't Know Jack*	Margo Janus	HBO
2010-2011 (63rd)	**Maggie Smith**	***Downton Abbey***	**Violet Crawley, Dowager Countess of Grantham**	**PBS**
	Eileen Atkins	*Upstairs, Downstairs*	Maud, Lady Holland	PBS
	Melissa Leo	*Mildred Pierce*	Lucy Gessler	HBO
	Mare Winningham	*Mildred Pierce*	Ida Corwin	HBO
	Evan Rachel Wood	*Mildred Pierce*	Veda Pierce	HBO

2011-2012 (64th)	Jessica Lange	*American Horror Story*	Constance Langdon	FX
	Frances Conroy	*American Horror Story*	Moira O'Hara	FX
	Judy Davis	*Page Eight*	Jill Tankard	PBS
	Sarah Paulson	*Game Change*	Nicolle Wallace	HBO
	Mare Winningham	*Hatfields & McCoys*	Sally McCoy	History

Most wins

2 wins

- Jane Alexander
- Judy Davis
- Colleen Dewhurst
- Mare Winningham

Multiple nominations

2 nominations

- Eileen Atkins
- Polly Bergen
- Ruby Dee
- Olympia Dukakis
- Patty Duke
- Julie Harris
- Glenne Headly
- Anjelica Huston
- Shirley Knight
- Swoosie Kurtz
- Cloris Leachman
- Audra McDonald
- Diana Rigg
- Greta Scacchi
- Maggie Smith
- Jane Alexander
- Sissy Spacek

3 nominations

- Stockard Channing
- Penny Fuller
- Piper Laurie
- Vanessa Redgrave
- Cicely Tyson

4 nominations

- Kathy Bates
- Judy Davis
- Colleen Dewhurst
- Alfre Woodard

5 nominations

- Anne Bancroft
- Mare Winningham

Stewart Granger

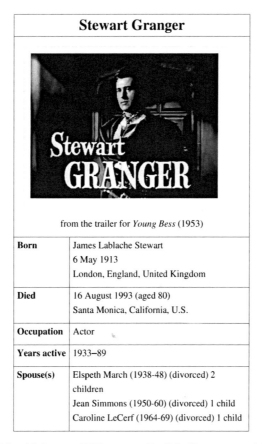

Stewart Granger	
from the trailer for *Young Bess* (1953)	
Born	James Lablache Stewart 6 May 1913 London, England, United Kingdom
Died	16 August 1993 (aged 80) Santa Monica, California, U.S.
Occupation	Actor
Years active	1933–89
Spouse(s)	Elspeth March (1938-48) (divorced) 2 children Jean Simmons (1950-60) (divorced) 1 child Caroline LeCerf (1964-69) (divorced) 1 child

Stewart Granger (6 May 1913 – 16 August 1993) was an English film actor, mainly associated with heroic and romantic leading roles. He was a popular leading man from the 1940s to the early 1960s rising to fame through his appearances in the Gainsborough melodramas.

Early life

He was born **James Lablache Stewart** in Old Brompton Road, west London, the only son of Major James Stewart, OBE and his wife Frederica Eliza (née Lablache). Granger was educated at Epsom College and the Webber Douglas Academy of Dramatic Art. He was the great-great grandson of the opera singer Luigi Lablache and the grandson of the actor Luigi Lablache. When he became an actor, he was advised to change his name in order to avoid being confused with the American actor James Stewart. (Granger[1] was his Scottish grandmother's maiden name.) Off-screen friends and colleagues continued to call him Jimmy for the rest of his life, but to the general public he became Stewart Granger.

Career

In 1933, he made his film debut as an extra. It was at this time he met Michael Wilding and they remained friends until Wilding's death in 1979. Years of theatre work followed, initially at Hull Repertory Theatre and then, after a pay dispute, at Birmingham Repertory Theatre. Here he met Elspeth March, a leading actress with the company, who became his first wife.

At the outbreak of war, Granger enlisted in the Gordon Highlanders, then transferred to the Black Watch with the rank of second lieutenant.[2] But Granger suffered from stomach ulcers - he was invalided out of the army in 1942.[3]

Early Stardom

His first starring film role was in the Gainsborough Pictures period melodrama *The Man in Grey* (1943), a film that helped to make him a huge star in Britain. A string of popular but critically dismissed films followed, including *The Magic Bow* in which Granger played Niccolò Paganini and *Madonna of the Seven Moons* (1945) which the critic Leslie Halliwell called "novelettish balderdash killed stone dead by stilted production". An exception was *Saraband for Dead Lovers* (1948), an Ealing Studios production. The screenplay was by John Dighton and Alexander Mackendrick, who would later direct *The Ladykillers* (1955) and *Sweet Smell of Success*. Granger was cast as the outsider, the handsome gambler who is perceived as 'not quite the ticket' by the established order, the Hanoverian court where the action is mostly set. Granger stated that this was one of few films of his of which he was proud.

In 1949 Granger was reported as earning around £30,000 a year.[4]

That year Granger made *Adam and Evelyne*, starring with Jean Simmons. The story, about a much older man and a teenager whom he gradually realises is no longer a child but a young woman with mature emotions and sexuality had obvious parallels to Granger's and Simmons's own lives. Granger had first met the very young Jean Simmons when they both worked on Gabriel Pascal's *Caesar and Cleopatra* (1945). Three years on, Simmons had transformed from a promising newcomer into a star - and a very attractive young woman. They married the following year in a bizarre wedding ceremony organised by Howard Hughes - one of his private aircraft flew the couple to Tucson, Arizona, where they were married, mainly among strangers, with actor Michael Wilding as Granger's best man.[5]

After Granger's stage production of Leo Tolstoy's *The Power of Darkness* (a venture he had intended to provide a vehicle for him to star with Jean Simmons) had been very poorly received when it opened in London at the Lyric Theatre on 25 April 1949, the disappointment, added to dissatisfaction with the Rank Organisation, led his thoughts to turn to Hollywood.

One of his last roles was in the 1989-90 Broadway production of *The Circle* by W. Somerset Maugham, opposite Glynis Johns and Rex Harrison in Harrison's final role.[6] The production actually opened at Duke University for a three-week run, followed by performances in Baltimore and Boston before opening 14 November 1989 on Broadway. [7] [8]

Hollywood

In 1949, Granger made the move; MGM was looking for someone to play H. Rider Haggard's hero Allan Quatermain in a film version of *King Solomon's Mines*. On the basis of the huge success of this film, released in 1950, he was offered a seven-year contract by MGM. Following two less successful assignments, *Soldiers Three* and *The Light Touch*, in 1952, he starred in *Scaramouche* in the role of Andre Moreau, the bastard son of a French nobleman, a part Ramón Novarro had played in the 1923 version of Rafael Sabatini's novel. Soon after this came the remake of *The Prisoner of Zenda* (1952), for which his theatrical voice, stature (6'3"; 191 cm) and dignified profile made him a natural.

In 1952 he and Jean Simmons sued Howard Hughes for $250,000 damages arising from an alleged breach of contract.[9][10] The case settled out of court.[11]

In *Moonfleet* (1955), Granger was cast as an adventurer, Jeremy Fox, in the Dorset of 1757, a man who rules a gang of cut-throat smugglers with an iron fist until he is softened by a 10-year-old boy who worships him and who believes only the best of him. The film was directed by Fritz Lang and produced by John Houseman, a former associate of Orson Welles. *Footsteps in the Fog* was the third and final film Granger and Jean Simmons made together - Simmons played a Cockney housemaid who finds that her adventurer employer (Granger) has poisoned his rich wife in order to inherit her wealth. *Bhowani Junction* (1956), was adapted from a John Masters novel about colonial India on the verge of obtaining independence. Ava Gardner played an Anglo-Indian (mixed race) woman caught between the two worlds of the British and the Indians, and Granger the British officer with whom (in a change from the novel) she ultimately fell in love. His films *The Little Hut* (1957), a coy sex comedy, and *Gun Glory* (1957), a Western story of redemption, both bombed.[12] *North to Alaska* with John Wayne, 'a brawling comedy western', was the last Hollywood film Granger made.

Granger had become a successful cattle rancher but he left Hollywood in the wake of the break up of his second marriage.

International career

In Germany, Granger acted in the role of Old Surehand in three Western films adapted from novels by German author Karl May, with French actor Pierre Brice (playing the fictional Indian chief Winnetou), in *Unter Geiern* (*Frontier Hellcat*) (1964), *Der Ölprinz* (*Rampage at Apache Wells*) (1965) and *Old Surehand* (*Flaming Frontier*) (1965). He was united with Pierre Brice and Lex Barker, also a hero of Karl May films, in *Gern hab' ich die Frauen gekillt* (*Killer's Carnival*) (1966). In the German Edgar Wallace film series of the 1960s, he was seen in *The Trygon Factor* (1966). He lated estimated he made more than $1 1/2 million in the 1960s but lost all of it.[13]

He subsequently replaced actor Lee J. Cobb, Charles Bickford and John McIntire on NBC's *The Virginian* as the new owner of the Shiloh ranch on prime-time TV for its ninth year (1971).[14]

Retirement

In the 1970s Granger retired from acting and went to live in southern Spain, where he invested in real estate. He returned to acting in 1981 with the publication of his autobiography, claiming he was bored.[15] Granger spent the last decade of his life appearing in TV shows and on the stage. He even starred in a German soap-opera called *Das Erbe der Guldenburgs* (*The Guldenburg Heritage*) (1987).

Personal life

He was married three times:

* Elspeth March (1938–1948); two children, Jamie and Lindsay
* Jean Simmons (1950–1960), (with whom he had starred in *Adam and Evelyne*, *Young Bess* and *Footsteps in the Fog*); one daughter, Tracy
* Caroline LeCerf (1964–1969); one daughter, Samantha

Stewart Granger claimed in his autobiography[16] that Deborah Kerr had approached him romantically in the back of his chauffeur-driven car at the time he was making *Caesar and Cleopatra*. Although married to Elspeth March, he states that he and Kerr went on to have an affair.[17] Deborah Kerr disputed this claim, commenting, "He should be so lucky."

In 1956, Granger became a naturalised citizen of the United States.

He died in Santa Monica, California from prostate cancer at the age of 80.

Appraisal

In 1970, Granger said "Stewart Granger was quite a successful film star, but I don't think he was an actor's actor."[18]

Among the films Granger was announced to star in but ended up being made with other actors included *Ivanhoe* (1951), *Mogambo* (1953), *The King's Thief* (1955) and *Man of the West* (1958).[19]

Filmography

• *A Southern Maid* (1933)	• *Moonfleet* (1955)
• *Give Her a Ring* (1934)	• *Footsteps in the Fog* (1956)
• *Over the Garden Wall* (1934)	• *The Last Hunt* (1956)
• *I Spy* (1934)	• *Bhowani Junction* (1956)
• *Under Secret Orders* (1937)	• *The Little Hut* (1957)
• *So This Is London* (1939)	• *Gun Glory* (1957)
• *Convoy* (1940)	• *The Whole Truth* (1958),
• *Secret Mission* (1942), with James Mason	• *Harry Black* (1958)
• *Thursday's Child* (1943)	• *North to Alaska* (1960)
• *The Man in Grey* (1943)	• *The Secret Partner* (1961)
• *The Lamp Still Burns* (1943)	• *Marcia o Crepa (The Legion's Last Patrol/Commando (1964 film))* (1962)
• *Love Story* (1944)	• *Sodom and Gomorrah* (1962)
• *Madonna of the Seven Moons* (1945)	• *Swordsman of Siena* (1962)
• *Fanny by Gaslight* (1944)	• *The Shortest Day* (1963), comedic spoof of *The Longest Day*
• *Madonna of the Seven Moons* (1945)	• *The Secret Invasion* (1964)
• *Waterloo Road* (1945)	• *Among Vultures* (1964)
• *Caesar and Cleopatra* (1945)	• *The Crooked Road* (1965)
• *Caravan* (1946)	• *Das Geheimnis der drei Dschunken* (1965)
• *The Magic Bow* (1946)	• *Der Ölprinz* (1965)
• *Captain Boycott* (1947)	• *Flaming Frontier* (1965)
• *Blanche Fury* (1948)	• *Killer's Carnival* (1966)
• *Saraband for Dead Lovers* (1948)	• *Target for Killing* (1966)
• *Woman Hater* (1948)	• *The Trygon Factor* (1966)
• *Adam and Evelyne* (1949)	• *Requiem for a Secret Agent* (1966)
• *King Solomon's Mines* (1950)	• *The Last Safari* (1967)
• *Soldiers Three* (1951)	• *Any Second Now* (1969) (TV)
• *The Wild North* (1952)	• *The Virginian* (1970-71) (TV series)
• *The Light Touch* (1952)	• *The Hound of the Baskervilles* (1972) (TV) as Sherlock Holmes
• *Scaramouche* (1952)	• *The Wild Geese* (1978)
• *The Prisoner of Zenda* (1952)	• *Murder, She Wrote* TV episode Paint Me a Murder (1985)
• *Salome* (1953)	• *Hell Hunters* (1986)
• *Young Bess* (1953)	• *Fine Gold* (1989)
• *All the Brothers Were Valiant* (1953)	• *Gabriel's Fire* (1991) - episode
• *Beau Brummell* (1954)	
• *Green Fire* (1954)	

Box office ranking

At the peak of his career, exhibitors voted Granger among the top stars at the box office:

- 1945 - 9th biggest star in Britain (2nd most popular British star)[20]
- 1946 - 6th biggest star in Britain (3rd most popular British star)[21]
- 1947 - 5th most popular British star in Britain[22]
- 1948 - 5th most popular British star in Britain.[23]
- 1949 - 7th most popular British star in Britain.[24]
- 1952 - 19th most popular star in the US [25]
- 1953 - 21st most popular star in the US and 8th most popular in Britain

Unmade Films

- *The Donnybrook Fighter* (1952)[26]
- *Robinson Crusoe* (early 1950s)[27]
- *Highland Fling* (1957)[28]
- *Ever the Twain* (1958)[29]

Select Theatre Credits

- *The Sun Never Sets* - Drury Lane Theatre, London, 1938
- *Serena Blandish* - 1938 - with Vivien Leigh
- *Autumn* - with Flora Robson
- *House in the Square*
- *To Dream Again*
- *Rebecca*
- *The Circle* - 1989 - with Rex Harrison and Glynis Johns

References

[1] Name for a farm bailiff. Anglo-Norman French: *grainger*, Old French: *grangier*. From Late Latin *granicarius*, a derivative of *granica* 'granary'.

[2] In the 1985 Murder, She Wrote episode, "Paint Me a Murder", Granger wore a blazer with a metal-embroidered Black Watch breast pocket badge.

[3] Shiach, Don: *Stewart Granger: Last of the Swashbucklers* (chapter 1). Aurum Press, 2005

[4] "THE STARRY WAY." (http://nla.gov.au/nla.news-article49687775). *The Courier-Mail (Brisbane, Qld. : 1933 - 1954)* (Brisbane, Qld.: National Library of Australia): p. 2. 9 April 1949. . Retrieved 4 August 2012.

[5] Shiach 2005

[6] Rich, Frank (1989-11-21). "Review/Theater; Rex Harrison Back on Broadway" (http://www.nytimes.com/1989/11/21/theater/review-theater-rex-harrison-back-on-broadway.html). *The New York Times*. . Retrieved 2009-05-12.

[7] "Coming Full `Circle`" (http://articles.chicagotribune.com/1989-06-29/features/8902130507_1_james-m-nederlander-night-music-edible-art). *Chicago Tribune*. 1989-06-29. . Retrieved 2012-06-17.

[8] Treadwell, David (1989-12-15). "COLUMN ONE : Culture in the South Rises Again" (http://articles.latimes.com/1989-12-15/news/mn-178_1_glory-days/2). *The Los Angeles Times*. . Retrieved 2012-06-17.

[9] Howard Hughes May Take Stand in Trial This Week: RKO Executive's Appearance Moved Up in Suit by Jean Simmons and Stewart Granger Los Angeles Times (1923-Current File) [Los Angeles, Calif] 3 July 1952: 16.

[10] Actor Granger, RKO Studios Trade Shenanigan Charges: Rival Tax Claims Made in $250,000 Suit for Damages Los Angeles Times (1923-Current File) [Los Angeles, Calif] 18 June 1952: A1.

[11] HUGHES, FILM ACTORS SETTLE COURT BATTLE Special to THE NEW YORK TIMES.. New York Times (1923-Current file) [New York, N.Y] 18 July 1952: 10.

[12] Shiach 2005 p.183

[13] Stewart Granger plans his return--as actor, not star Chicago Tribune (1963-Current file) [Chicago, Ill] 26 Nov 1981: e10

[14] GRANGER comes to SHILOH Smith, Cecil. Los Angeles Times (1923-Current File) [Los Angeles, Calif] 30 Aug 1970: k31b.

[15] Stewart Granger plans his return--as actor, not star Chicago Tribune (1963-Current file) [Chicago, Ill] 26 Nov 1981: e10

[16] Granger, Stewart. *Sparks Fly Upward*, Putnam; 1st American edition (1981), ISBN 0-399-12674-0

[17] "Stewart Granger" (http://www.leninimports.com/stewart_granger.html#partone). . Retrieved 2007-11-19.

[18] Stewart Granger, 80, Star in Swashbuckler Roles By WILLIAM GRIMES. New York Times (1923-Current file) [New York, N.Y] 18 Aug 1993: D18.

[19] METRO CONSIDERS CAST FOR 'IVANHOE': JEAN SIMMONS MAY GET ROLE OF ROWENA--STEWART GRANGER WILL PLAY THE TITLE PART OF LOCAL ORIGIN By THOMAS F. BRADY Special to THE NEW YORK TIMES.. New York Times (1923-Current file) [New York, N.Y] 27 Dec 1950: 39.

[20] 'Bloomer Girl' to Play Instead of Jolson Opus, *Los Angeles Times* (1923-Current File) [Los Angeles, Calif] 23 Mar 1946: A5.

[21] "FILM WORLD." (http://nla.gov.au/nla.news-article46266039). *The West Australian (Perth, WA : 1879 - 1954)* (Perth, WA: National Library of Australia): p. 20 Edition: SECOND EDITION.. 28 February 1947. . Retrieved 11 July 2012.

[22] 'Bing's Lucky Number: Pa Crosby Dons 4th B.O. Crown', *The Washington Post* (1923-1954) [Washington, D.C] 3 Jan 1948: 12.

[23] 'BRITTEN'S "RAPE OF LUCRETIA": NEW YORK DIVIDED', *The Manchester Guardian* (1901-1959) [Manchester (UK)] 31 Dec 1948: 8.

[24] "Bob Hope Takes Lead from Bing In Popularity." (http://nla.gov.au/nla.news-article2759831). *The Canberra Times (ACT : 1926 - 1954)* (ACT: National Library of Australia): p. 2. 31 December 1949. . Retrieved 24 April 2012.

[25] "Martin And Lewis Top U.S. Film Poll." (http://nla.gov.au/nla.news-article18296500). *The Sydney Morning Herald (NSW : 1842 - 1954)* (NSW: National Library of Australia): p. 3. 27 December 1952. . Retrieved 25 April 2012.

[26] Looking at Hollywood: Stewart Granger Will Play Role of an Irish Pugilist Hopper, Hedda. Chicago Daily Tribune (1923-1963) [Chicago, Ill] 30 Oct 1952: c4.

[27] 'Young Bess' Gets Green Light for July Start; Veterans Set for Roles Schallert, Edwin. Los Angeles Times (1923-Current File) [Los Angeles, Calif] 19 Apr 1952: 7.

[28] Granger Will Star in 'Highland Fling' Hopper, Hedda. Los Angeles Times (1923-Current File) [Los Angeles, Calif] 26 Jan 1957: B2.

[29] Comedy Slated to Star Simmons and Granger; Student Wins Top Part Schallert, Edwin. Los Angeles Times (1923-Current File) [Los Angeles, Calif] 27 Feb 1957: C9.

External links

- Stewart Granger (http://www.imdb.com/name/nm0001289/) at the Internet Movie Database
- Stewart Granger (http://www.ibdb.com/person.asp?ID=42809) at the Internet Broadway Database
- Stewart Granger (http://www.screenonline.org.uk/people/id/447683) at the British Film Institute's Screenonline
- Britmovie.co.uk (http://www.britmovie.co.uk/actors/Stewart-Granger)
- Photographs and literature (http://film.virtual-history.com/person.php?personid=440)
- (http://www.bbc.co.uk/archive/hollywood/10267.shtml) BBC interview with Gloria Hunniford
- Stewart Granger (http://www.findagrave.com/cgi-bin/fg.cgi?page=gr&GRid=8122) at Find a Grave

The Blue Lagoon (1949 film)

For the 1980 film, see The Blue Lagoon (1980 film)

The Blue Lagoon	
Lobby card	
Directed by	Frank Launder
Produced by	Sidney Gilliat Frank Launder
Written by	**Novel:** Henry De Vere Stacpoole **Screenplay:** John Baines Michael Hogan Frank Launder
Starring	Jean Simmons Donald Houston Noel Purcell James Hayter Cyril Cusack
Music by	Clifton Parker
Cinematography	Geoffrey Unsworth
Editing by	Thelma Connell
Distributed by	General Film Distributors (UK) Universal Pictures (USA)
Release date(s)	1 October 1949
Running time	101 minutes
Country	United Kingdom
Language	English

The Blue Lagoon is a 1949 British romance and adventure film produced and directed by Frank Launder, starring Jean Simmons and Donald Houston. The screenplay was adapted by John Baines, Michael Hogan and Frank Launder from the novel *The Blue Lagoon* by Henry De Vere Stacpoole. The original music score was composed by Clifton Parker and the cinematography was by Geoffrey Unsworth.

The film tells the story of two young children shipwrecked on a tropical island paradise in the South Pacific. Emotional feelings and physical changes arise as they grow to maturity and fall in love. The film has major thematic similarities to the Biblical story of Adam and Eve.

Plot

In the Victorian period, Emmeline Foster and Michael Reynolds, two British children, are the survivors of a shipwreck in the South Pacific. After days afloat, they are marooned on a lush tropical island in the company of kindly old sailor Paddy Button. Eventually, Paddy dies in a drunken binge, leaving Emmeline and Michael, now attractively grown up, all alone with each other. Together, they survive solely on their resourcefulness, and the bounty of their remote paradise.

Years pass and both Emmeline and Michael become tanned, athletic and nubile young adults. Eventually, their relationship, more along the lines of brother and sister in their youth, blossoms into love, and then passion. Emmeline and Michael have their baby boy, and they live together as common-law husband and wife, content in their solitude. But their marriage is threatened by the arrival of two evil traders, who force the child to dive for pearls at gunpoint, before killing each other off.

Emmeline is reminded of the outside world and wants to leave the island. She fears for the child if she and Michael should die, and begins to think of his future. Michael finally succumbs to her pleading and they pack a small boat and leave the island. But becalmed in the middle of the ocean, they succumb to exposure. They are found by a British ship, but the film leaves their fate ambiguous.

Cast

Actor	Role
Jean Simmons	Emmeline Foster
Donald Houston	Michael Reynolds
Susan Stranks	Emmeline (younger)
Peter Rudolph Jones	Michael (younger)
Noel Purcell	Paddy Button
James Hayter	Dr. Murdock
Cyril Cusack	James Carter
Nora Nicholson	Mrs. Stannard
Maurice Denham	Ship's Captain
Philip Stainton	Mr. Ansty
Patrick Barr	Second Mate
Lyn Evans	Trotter
Russell Waters	Craggs
John Boxer	Nick Corbett
Bill Raymond	Marsden

Background and production

* The film was a remake of a black and white silent film shot in the United Kingdom in 1923, not long after the publication of the Henry De Vere Stacpoole novel on which it was based. The 1923 version was directed by W. Bowden and Dick Cruickshanks, starring Molly Adair and Dick Cruickshanks.
* Donald Houston was selected over 5,000 applicants, 100 of whom were screen tested.[1]
* The evil traders were invented for this film and were not part of the novel.
* The film was shot on location in Fiji, Yasawa Islands,[2] and at Pinewood Studios, Iver Heath, Buckinghamshire, England.

Reception

The film was the seventh most popular movie at the British box office in 1949.[3]

Other versions and sequel

- The film was remade in 1980 starring Brooke Shields and Christopher Atkins. The updated version of *The Blue Lagoon*, directed by Randal Kleiser, was much closer to the spirit of Henry DeVere Stacpoole's original novel for it included nudity and sexual content, although not as much as the book.
- The updated version was followed in 1991 by the sequel *Return to the Blue Lagoon*, starring Milla Jovovich and Brian Krause. The sequel bears a strong similarity to the 1980 film, also directed by Randal Kleiser. It bears very little resemblance to Stacpoole's sequel, *The Garden of God*. The pearl-greedy traders do not appear in Stacpoole's original novel. However, in Stacpoole's third book, *The Gates of Morning*, a pair of sailors attack the people of a nearby island for pearls after seeing a woman wearing a double pearl hair ornament, as Emmeline does in the 1949 film.

References

[1] "FLIM FLASH CABLE." (http://nla.gov.au/nla.news-article59458734). *Sunday Times (Perth, WA : 1902 - 1954)* (Perth, WA: National Library of Australia): p. 12 Supplement: The Sunday Times MAGAZINE. 21 December 1947. . Retrieved 7 July 2012.

[2] *Jean Simmons Goes Native*, cover story , *Illustrated* magazine 15 January 1949

[3] "TOPS AT HOME." (http://nla.gov.au/nla.news-article49700937). *The Courier-Mail (Brisbane, Qld. : 1933 - 1954)* (Brisbane, Qld.: National Library of Australia): p. 4. 31 December 1949. . Retrieved 24 April 2012.

External links

- *The Blue Lagoon (1949)* (http://www.imdb.com/title/tt0041190/) at the Internet Movie Database
- *The Blue Lagoon (1949)* (http://tcmdb.com/title/title.jsp?stid=69220) at the TCM Movie Database
- *The Blue Lagoon (1949)* (http://www.allrovi.com/movies/movie/v85509) at AllRovi

The Clouded Yellow

The Clouded Yellow	
Directed by	Ralph Thomas
Produced by	Betty E. Box
Written by	Janet Green
Starring	Trevor Howard Jean Simmons Sonia Dresdel
Music by	Benjamin Frankel
Distributed by	Rank Film Distributors
Release date(s)	1951
Country	United Kingdom
Language	English

The Clouded Yellow is a 1951 British mystery film directed by Ralph Thomas and produced by Betty E. Box for Carillon Films.

Plot synopsis

After leaving the British Secret Service, David Somers (played by Trevor Howard) finds work cataloging butterflies at the country house of Nicholas and Jess Fenton. (The "clouded yellow" of the title is a rare species of butterfly.) After the murder of a local gamekeeper, suspicion (wrongfully) falls on their niece, Sophie Malraux (Jean Simmons). Somers helps Sophie to escape arrest and they go on the run together, Somers using his secret-service skills and contacts to evade the police. After a cross-country chase they arrive at Liverpool with the intention of leaving the country by ship. The true identity of the murderer is revealed in a climax on a warehouse roof.

Newcastle upon Tyne

A significant proportion of the action in the middle of the film was shot on location in Newcastle upon Tyne, featuring scenes on the quayside, the area around the Castle Keep and the Central Station, and the suburb of Jesmond.

Liverpool

Some scenes were filmed in Liverpool's China Town, Toxteth, Liverpool Docks and on the Liverpool Overhead Railway. The railway closed in 1956 and was subsequently dismantled.

Cast

- Trevor Howard as David Somers
- Jean Simmons as Sophie Malraux
- Sonia Dresdel as Jess Fenton
- Barry Jones as Nicholas Fenton
- Kenneth More as Willy Shepley
- Geoffrey Keen as Police Inspector

- André Morell as Secret Service Chief
- Michael Brennan as Police Superintendent
- Gerard Heinz as Dr. Karl Cesare
- Lily Kann as Minna Cesare
- Eric Pohlmann as Taxidermist
- Richard Wattis as Employment Agent
- Sandra Dorne as Kyra

External links

- *The Clouded Yellow* [1] at the Internet Movie Database
- The Clouded Yellow review at www.VideoVista.net [2]

References

[1] http://www.imdb.com/title/tt0042333/
[2] http://www.videovista.net/reviews/oct08/cloudy.html

The Dain Curse

The Dain Curse	
1st edition cover	
Author(s)	Dashiell Hammett
Country	United States
Language	English
Genre(s)	Mystery, Crime, Novel
Publisher	Knopf (first edition)
Publication date	1929
Media type	Print (Hardcover & Paperback)
ISBN	NA
Preceded by	*Red Harvest*
Followed by	*The Maltese Falcon*

The Dain Curse is a novel written by Dashiell Hammett and published in 1929. Before its publication in book form, it was serialized in *Black Mask*.[1]

Plot summary

The detective known only as The Continental Op investigates a theft of diamonds from the Leggett family of San Francisco. The plot involves a supposed curse on the Dain family, said to inflict sudden and violent deaths upon those in their vicinity. Edgar Leggett's wife is a Dain, as is his daughter Gabrielle Leggett.

The detective untangles a web of robberies, lies and murder. It is discovered that young Gabrielle Leggett is also involved in a mysterious religious cult and is addicted to drugs.

Gabrielle escapes from the cult and marries her fiancé, but bloodshed continues to follow them. The Continental Op protects Gabrielle, and helps her recover from her morphine addiction. He finally discovers the reason behind all the mysterious, violent events surrounding Gabrielle and the Dains.

The novel is structured in three parts, each concerning different mysteries, Part One: "The Dains", Part Two: "The Temple" and Part Three: 'Quesada".

Characters in *The Dain Curse*

- The Continental Op – Private Detective (called in the miniseries "Hamilton Nash")
- Madison Andrews – Leggett's attorney
- Claude Baker – Witnessed Gabrielle driving away in Quesada
- Mrs. Begg – The Leggetts' previous servant
- Eric Carter – Collinson's alias in Quesada
- Ralph Coleman – Member of Temple of the Holy Grail cult
- Eric Collinson – Gabrielle's fiancé, employed at Spear, Camp and Duffy
- Hubert Collinson – Eric's father
- Laurence Collinson – Eric's older brother
- Dick Cotton – Quesada marshal
- Alice Dain – Mrs. Leggett's maiden name

- Lily Dain – Alice's sister, Gabrielle's mother
- Warren Daley – The Leggetts' neighbor
- Debro – "Carters'" nearest neighbor in Quesada
- Sheriff Feeney – In Quesada
- Mrs. Fink – Employee at Temple of the Holy Grail
- Tom Fink – Special effects man at Temple of the Holy Grail
- Owen Fitzstephan – A writer and friend of Nash
- Dick Foley – Continental detective
- Big-foot Gerber – Cigar store owner
- Aaronia Haldorn – Joseph's wife
- Joseph Haldorn – Head of Temple of the Holy Grail cult
- Manuel Haldorn – Joseph and Aaronia's son
- Watt Halstead – Of Halstead and Beauchamp, a jeweler
- Mr. & Mrs. Harper – Gabrielle's mysterious friends
- Minnie Hershey – The Leggett's servant
- Jacques Labaud – Mayenne/Leggett's fellow convict/escapee
- Gabrielle Leggett – daughter of Edgar Leggett
- Edgar Leggett – Gabrielle's father, scientist
- Mrs. Leggett, née Alice Dain
- Mickey Linehan – Continental operative
- Walter Martin – Mayenne/Leggett's alias
- Al Mason – Continental operative
- Maurice Pierre de Mayenne – Edgar Legett's real name
- Mary Nunez – "Carters'" servant
- O'Gar – Homicide detail detective-sergeant, SFPD (San Francisco Police Department)
- Mrs. Priestly – The Leggetts' neighbor
- Pat Reddy – O'Gar's partner, SFPD
- Dr. Riese – Doctor responding to finding of Leggett's body, Gabrielle's doctor
- Mrs. Livingston Rodman – Member of Temple of the Holy Grail cult
- Ben Rolly – Quesada deputy sheriff
- Harry Ruppert – Upton's employee
- Rhino Tingley – Minnie's boyfriend
- Louis Upton – Private detective from New York
- Vernon – Quesada district attorney
- Harve Whidden – Saw Gabrielle and a man driving away in Quesada

TV mini-series adaptation

The novel was adapted into a CBS television miniseries in 1978 by director E.W. Swackhamer and producer Martin Poll,[2] which starred James Coburn, Hector Elizondo, Jean Simmons, Jason Miller, Nancy Addison (as Gabriella), and in a brief part, a pre-*Star Trek* Brent Spiner. It received three Emmy Award nominations (one for the director). The script (by Robert W. Lenski) won the 1978 Edgar Award for Best Television Feature or Miniseries. An edited version of the series was released on VHS in the 1990s; a complete, full-length, two-disc DVD edition is now available.

References

[1] Phillips, Gene D. (2011). *Out of the Shadows: Expanding the Canon of Classic Film Noir* (http://books.google.com/books?id=FkaiKgWJtdYC&pg=PA227), p. 227. Scarecrow Press, Inc.

[2] "Martin Poll dies at 89, Producer drew Oscar nom for 'The Lion in Winter'" (http://www.variety.com/article/VR1118052696?refCatId=13). *Variety Magazine*. 2012-04-16. . Retrieved 2012-04-24.

External links

- Audio files of book (http://www.archive.org/details/TheDainCurse)
- *The Dain Curse* (TV mini-series) (http://www.imdb.com/title/tt0076999/) at the Internet Movie Database

The Dawning

The Dawning	
DVD cover	
Directed by	Robert Knights
Produced by	Sarah Lawson
Written by	Jennifer Johnston (novel) Bernard MacLaverty
Starring	Anthony Hopkins Rebecca Pidgeon Hugh Grant Trevor Howard Jean Simmons Adrian Dunbar
Music by	Simon May
Cinematography	Adrian Biddle
Editing by	Max Lemon
Distributed by	TVS Television The Vista Organisation Ltd.
Running time	97 minutes
Country	United Kingdom
Language	English

The Dawning is a 1988 British film, based on Jennifer Johnston's novel, *The Old Jest* which depicts the Irish War of Independence through the eyes of the Anglo-Irish landlord class. It starred Anthony Hopkins, Hugh Grant, Jean Simmons, Trevor Howard, and Rebecca Pidgeon, and was produced by Sarah Lawson, through her company Lawson Productions.

Plot

The film opens with Angus Barrie (Anthony Hopkins), an Irish Republican Army member, walking through hills, and coming to rest on a beach, where there is a little hut. Meanwhile, Nancy Gulliver (Rebecca Pidgeon) having just left school, burns all her books in happiness. It is her birthday, and her aunt (Jean Simmons) has invited over Harry (Hugh Grant), with whom she's desperately in love, to tea. However, during the course of the film, as a result of Harry's behaviour with another girl and the way he treats Nancy, she realises that her love for Harry was nothing more than childish infatuation.

One day, Nancy goes down to the beach, and notices that her hut has been slept in. She leaves a note requesting that it be left alone. Soon after, she is on the beach reading, when Barrie comes up to her. Over the course of the film, the two develop a relationship, despite her not really knowing and understanding his job: he is one of the first people that became part of a group named the IRA, and is on the run from the government. Nevertheless, she grows fond of Barrie, and dubs him "Cassius" ("because you have a mean and hungry look!")

After Cassius asks her to pass on a message to a colleague, several constables of the Royal Irish Constabulary are gunned down at a horse race show. Later that day, the R.I.C. comes to see Nancy, and ask her if she knows where Cassius is. The police officers' suspicion is aroused when Nancy's grandfather (played by Trevor Howard) says he saw her talking to a man on the beach. She denies any knowledge. When they leave, she runs to the cottage on the beach where Cassius was staying to tell him to flee, only to find that he has already packed. As they walk out, a light shines on them: the RIC has found him. He is gunned down, much to Nancy's distress. The film ends with Nancy back at home, considerably older and wiser than when the film started.

Cast

- Anthony Hopkins as Cassius a.k.a. Angus Barrie
- Rebecca Pidgeon as Nancy Gulliver
- Jean Simmons as Aunt Mary
- Trevor Howard as Grandfather
- Tara MacGowran as Maeve
- Hugh Grant as Harry
- Nicholas Fitzsimons as Slain Soldier
- Ronnie Masterson as Bridie
- John Rogan as Mr. Carroll
- Joan O'Hara as Maurya
- Charmian May as Celia Brabazon
- Ann Way as George Brabazon
- Mark O'Regan as Joe Mulhare
- Brendan Laird as Tommy Roche
- Adrian Dunbar as Capt. Rankin
- Geoffrey Greenhill as Cpl. Tweedie

Production

The Dawning was filmed in Ireland in the mid-1980s, largely on location in Ireland. The beach scenes were filmed extensively at Goat Island, a small cove on the Irish coast, close to the county boundary between Cork and Waterford. Some "Big House" exteriors were shot at Woodbine Hill in the same district. Incidentally, it was Rebecca Pidgeon's first feature film, and Trevor Howard's final film; he died shortly after production ended, and the film was dedicated to him. (Howard had made an earlier IRA film in 1946, the classic *I See a Dark Stranger*.) It was also Jean Simmons' first feature film for nearly ten years. Despite having contributed largely to the production, Bernard MacLaverty was uncredited as a screenwriter. The film was shown at the AFI/Los Angeles International Film Festival (New British Cinema - BritFest 2), the Cannes Film Festival (for market purposes), and at the Montreal World Film Festival (in competition, where it was successful, winning two prizes).[1][2] Actors Anthony Hopkins and Hugh Grant reunited five years later in 8 Academy Award-nominated film *The Remains of the Day*.

Critical reception

The Dawning was received largely positively by the critics, will a five star review from Time Out, describing the film as "solidly crafted ... its main strength lies in the performances" and mentioning that Rebecca Pidgeon had given a "remarkable debut".[3] China Daily noted that Hopkins had played his character "wonderfully".[4]

Awards and nominations

- Montréal World Film Festival (1988)
  - won Jury Prize *Robert Knights*[5][6]
  - won Prize of the Ecumenical Jury - Special Mention - *Robert Knights*[5][7]
- Austin Texas International Film Festival (1988)
  - Won best picture award

References

[1] The Dawning - *Variety* details (http://www.variety.com/profiles/Film/main/111541/The Dawning.html?dataSet=1)

[2] *The Dawning* trivia at Movies.com (http://movies.go.com/moviescommunity/tidbits?movieid=808673)

[3] Time Out Review (http://www.timeout.com/film/reviews/65010/the-dawning.html)

[4] DVD reviews (http://app1.chinadaily.com.cn/star/2004/0115/wh-event.html)

[5] IMDb - Awards and Nominations (http://www.imdb.com/title/tt0094955/awards)

[6] <Montreal Film Festival Official Website - Archives (http://www.ffm-montreal.org/palmares/en_1988.html)

[7] <Montreal Film Festival Official Website - Archives (http://www.ffm-montreal.org/palmares/en_1988.html)

External links

- *The Dawning* (http://www.imdb.com/title/tt0094955/) at the Internet Movie Database

The Drumhead

"The Drumhead"	
***Star Trek: The Next Generation* episode**	
Picard, before Satie's Inquisition	
Episode no.	Season 4 Episode 21
Directed by	Jonathan Frakes
Written by	Jeri Taylor
Featured music	Ron Jones
Cinematography by	Marvin Rush
Production code	195
Original air date	April 29, 1991
Guest actors	
• Bruce French - Sabin Genestra	
• Spencer Garrett - Simon Tarses	
• Henry Woronicz - J'Dan	
• Earl Billings - Thomas Henry	
• Jean Simmons - Admiral Norah Satie	
• Ann Shea - Nellen Tore	

"**The Drumhead**" is the 95th episode of the science fiction television series *Star Trek: The Next Generation*, the 21st episode of the fourth season. It was directed by cast member Jonathan Frakes[1] ("Commander William T. Riker").

An explosion aboard the *Enterprise* brings a Starfleet Admiral out of retirement to investigate the possibilities of sabotage, espionage and treason aboard the Federation flagship.

Plot

When an explosion within the dilithium chamber of the Federation starship *Enterprise*'s engine room, appears to be the work of sabotage, Starfleet Command dispatches retired Rear Admiral Norah Satie to lead an investigation to uncover the cause.

Satie discovers that J'Dan, a Klingon exchange officer, had been using modified hypospray syringes to encode information into amino acid sequences for secret transport. J'Dan is forced to admit his collaboration with the Romulans but attests he did not sabotage the chamber. Satie and Picard expand their investigation to interview crewmen who associated with J'Dan. One of the interviewees is medical technician Simon Tarses who claims that his only relationship with J'Dan was to administer injections necessary to treat a rare disease, but Satie's Betazoid aide senses that Tarses is concealing something. Meanwhile, Geordi and Data determine that the hatch failed due to simple fatigue, not sabotage.[2] Picard considers the matter closed, but Satie pushes to complete her investigation of Tarses. During a second interview with Tarses, this time in front of an audience, Satie's aide falsely accuses Tarses of using a compound found in Sickbay to sabotage the hatch. He then accuses Tarses of falsifying his academy entrance application and that he is in fact one quarter Romulan, not one quarter Vulcan as he claims. Tarses, shaken, invokes his rights under the Seventh Guarantee of the Federation Constitution and refuses to answer the accusation on the grounds that his answer may serve to incriminate him.

Satie uses this discovery as a pretext to expand her investigations. Picard objects, but Satie reveals that she has been in constant contact with Starfleet Command and that all future hearings will be open and that Admiral Thomas Henry of Starfleet Security will attend. Though Picard resolves to prevent her from conducting a witchhunt, he finds himself summoned to be interviewed before the tribunal. Satie uses the hearing to accuse Picard of numerous transgressions of the Prime Directive and other Starfleet orders. When Worf stands to defend Picard's actions, Satie turns on him, pointing out Picard's poor judgment in having a Chief of Security who is the son of a traitor. Picard recalls a quote from Satie's father: "With the first link, the chain is forged. The first speech censured, the first thought forbidden, the first freedom denied, chains us all irrevocably."[3] Satie is infuriated. She accuses Picard of being a Romulan collaborator who plans to destroy the Federation from within and claims "I've brought down bigger men than you, Picard!" Satie's fanatacism proves to be her undoing as Admiral Henry leaves the room and calls an end to the investigation.

Worf and Picard reflect on Satie's disgrace and Worf expresses regret for assisting her in her investigation. Picard points out that Satie appeared to serve a noble cause while in fact subverting the principles of the Federation. He concludes that the price of their freedom is eternal vigilance.

Notes

- Guest star Jean Simmons, a noted longtime Trekker,[4] portrays retired Rear Admiral Norah Satie, a special investigator who visits the Federation starship *Enterprise*.
- Michael Dorn said this was one of his two favorite episodes, the other being "The Offspring".[5]
- "The Drumhead" was the last *Star Trek* episode to be scored by Ron Jones, who was fired shortly after its completion by producers Rick Berman and Peter Lauritson as "Ron's stuff was getting big and somewhat flamboyant" and the producers "decided to move on and try other composers".[6]

DVD

This episode is featured on the *Star Trek: The Next Generation* - Jean-Luc Picard Collection DVD set for Region 1 only. It is the fourth of seven episodes featured on disc 1 of the two-disc set.

References

[1] "The Drumhead" (http://www.imdb.com/title/tt0708793/). *IMDB*. . Retrieved December 28, 2012.

[2] Zack Handlen (January 20, 2011). "Qpid/The Drumhead" (http://www.avclub.com/articles/qpidthe-drumhead,50266/). *AV Club*. . Retrieved December 28, 2012.

[3] "The Greatest Star Trek Quotes" (http://jpetrie.myweb.uga.edu/startrek.html). *John Petrie*. . Retrieved December 28, 2012.

[4] "Simmons, Jean" (http://www.startrek.com/database_article/simmons). *StarTrek.com*. . Retrieved December 28, 2012.

[5] "ST:TNG: Final Unity: Michael Dorn Interview" (http://gaming.trekcore.com/finalunity/dorninterview.html). TrekCore.com. . Retrieved March 12, 2008.

[6] "Rick Berman Answers Your Questions - Part 1" (http://www.startrek.com/article/rick-berman-answers-your-questions-part-1). StarTrek.com. March 1, 2011. . Retrieved April 6, 2011.

- Star Trek The Next Generation DVD set, volume 4, disc 6, selection 1.

External links

- "The Drumhead" (http://www.imdb.com/title/tt0708793/) at the Internet Movie Database
- "The Drumhead" (http://www.tv.com/shows/star-trek-the-next-generation/the-drumhead-19081/) at TV.com
- "The Drumhead" (http://en.wikipedia.org/wiki/Memoryalpha:the_drumhead) at Memory Alpha (a Star Trek wiki)
- "The Drumhead" (http://www.startrek.com/startrek/view/library/episodes/TNG/detail/68496.html) at StarTrek.com

The Egyptian (film)

The Egyptian	
Theatrical release poster	
Directed by	Michael Curtiz
Produced by	Darryl F. Zanuck
Written by	Philip Dunne Casey Robinson Mika Waltari (novel)
Starring	Jean Simmons Victor Mature Gene Tierney Michael Wilding Edmund Purdom Bella Darvi Peter Ustinov Tommy Rettig
Music by	Bernard Herrmann Alfred Newman
Cinematography	Leon Shamroy
Editing by	Barbara McLean
Distributed by	20th Century Fox
Release date(s)	24 August 1954
Running time	139 minutes
Country	United States
Language	English
Budget	$3.9 million[1]
Box office	$4.25 million (US rentals)[2][3]

The Egyptian is an American 1954 epic film made in CinemaScope by 20th Century Fox, directed by Michael Curtiz and produced by Darryl F. Zanuck. It is based on Mika Waltari's novel of the same name and the screenplay was adapted by Philip Dunne and Casey Robinson. Leading roles were played by Edmund Purdom, Jean Simmons, Peter Ustinov and Michael Wilding. Cinematographer Leon Shamroy was nominated for an Academy Award in 1955.

Plot

The Egyptian tells the story of Sinuhe, a struggling physician in 18th dynasty Egypt (14th Century BC.) who is thrown by chance into contact with the pharaoh Akhnaton. He rises to and falls from great prosperity, wanders the world, and becomes increasingly drawn towards a new religion spreading throughout Egypt. His companions throughout are his lover, a shy tavern maid named Merit, and his corrupt but likable servant Kaptah.

While out lion hunting with his sturdy friend Horemheb, Sinuhe discovers Egypt's newly ascendant pharaoh Akhnaton, who has sought the solitude of the desert in the midst of a religious epiphany. While praying the ruler is stricken with an epileptic seizure, with which Sinhue is able to help him. The grateful Akhnaton makes his savior court physician and gives Horemheb a post in the Royal Guard, a career previously denied to him by low birth. His new eminence gives Sinuhe an inside look at Akhnaton's reign, which is made extraordinary by the ruler's devotion to a new religion that he feels has been divinely revealed to him. This faith rejects Egypt's traditional gods in favor of monotheistic worship of the sun, referred to as the Aten. Akhnaton intends to promote Aten-worship throughout Egypt, which earns him the hatred of the country's corrupt and politically active traditional priesthood.

Life in court does not prove to be good for Sinuhe; it drags him away from his previous ambition of helping the poor, and is the means of his falling obsessively in love with a courtesan named Nefer. He squanders all of his and his parents' property in order to buy her gifts, only to have her reject him nonetheless. Returning dejectedly home, Sinuhe learns that his parents have committed suicide over his shameful behavior. He has their bodies embalmed so that they can pass on to the afterlife, and, having no way to pay for the service, works off his debts in the embalming house.

Lacking a tomb in which to put his parents' mummies, Sinuhe buries them in the sand amid the lavish funerary complexes of the Valley of the Kings. Merit finds him there and warns him that Akhnaton has condemned him to death; one of the pharaoh's daughters fell ill and died while Sinuhe was working as an embalmer, and the tragedy is being blamed on his desertion of the court. Merit urges Sinuhe to flee Egypt and rebuild his career elsewhere, and the two of them share one night of passion before he takes ship out of the country.

For the next ten years Sinuhe and Kaptah wander the known world, where their superior Egyptian medical training gives them an excellent reputation as healers. Sinuhe finally saves enough money from his fees to return home; he buys his way back into the favor of the court with a precious piece of military intelligence he learned abroad, informing Horemheb (now commander of the Egyptian army) that the barbarian Hittites plan to attack the country with superior iron weapons.

Akhnaton is in any case ready to forgive Sinuhe, according to his religion's doctrine of mercy and pacifism. These qualities have made Aten-worship extremely popular amid the common people, including Merit with whom Sinuhe is reunited. He finds that she bore him a son named Thoth (a result of their night together many years ago), who shares his father's interest in medicine.

Meanwhile the priests of the old gods have been fomenting hate crimes against the Aten's devotees, and now urge Sinuhe to help them kill Akhnaton and put Horemheb on the throne instead. The physician is privately given extra inducement by the princess Baketamun; she reveals that he is actually the son of the previous pharaoh by a concubine, discarded at birth because of the jealousy of the old queen and raised by foster parents. The princess now suggests that Sinuhe could poison both Akhnaton and Horemheb and rule Egypt himself (with her at his side).

Sinuhe is still reluctant to perform this evil deed until the Egyptian army mounts a full attack on worshipers of the Aten. Kaptah manages to smuggle Thoth out the country, but Merit is killed while seeking refuge at the new god's altar. In his grief Sinuhe blames Akhnaton for the whole mess and administers poison to him at their next meeting. The pharaoh realizes what has been done, but accepts his fate. He still believes his faith was true, but that he has understood it imperfectly; future generations will be able to spread the same faith better than he.

Sinuhe allows Horemheb to become pharaoh, but the warlord is still indignant that his old friend had considered murdering him. He banishes Sinuhe to the shores of the Red Sea; the physician grows old in solitude, still inspired by the glimpse of another world he has been afforded through Akhnaton.

The film concludes with a caption reading, "These things happened thirteen centuries before the birth of Jesus Christ".

Cast

- Jean Simmons as Merit
- Victor Mature as Horemheb
- Gene Tierney as Baketamon
- Michael Wilding as Akhnaton
- Bella Darvi as Nefer
- Peter Ustinov as Kaptah
- Edmund Purdom as Sinuhe
- Judith Evelyn as Taia
- Henry Daniell as Mekere
- John Carradine as Grave robber
- Carl Benton Reid as Senmut
- Tommy Rettig as Thoth
- Anitra Stevens as Queen Nefertiti
- Peter Reynolds as Sinuhe, age 10

Production

The script was based on the Waltari novel of the same name. It is elaborated in the book, but not the film, that Sinuhe was named by his mother from The Story of Sinuhe, which does include references to Aten but was written many centuries before the 18th dynasty. The use of the "Cross of Life" ankh to represent Akhnaton's "new" religion reflects a popular and esoteric belief in the 1950s that monotheistic Atenism was a sort of proto-Christianity. While the ankh has no known connection to the modern cross,[4] the principal symbol of Aten was not an ankh but a solar disk emitting rays, though the rays usually ended with a hand holding out an ankh to the worshipers. The sun-disk is seen only twice; when we first meet Akhnaton in the desert, he has painted it on a rock, and Sinuhe says "Look! He worships the face of the sun." It appears again as part of the wall painting above Akhnaton's throne. With that said, the ankh was used in the original novel. Likewise, Akhnaton's dying revelation that God is much more than the face of the sun is actually found among his best-known writings.[5]

Some of the sets, costumes, and props from this film were bought and re-used by Cecil B. DeMille for *The Ten Commandments*. As the events in that story take place seventy years after those in *The Egyptian*, this re-use creates an unintended sense of continuity. The commentary track on the *Ten Commandments* DVD points out many of these re-uses. Only three actors, Mimi Gibson, Michael Ansara and John Carradine, and a handful of extras, appeared in both pictures. The Prince Aly Khan was a consultant during filming, he was engaged to Gene Tierney. Marlon Brando was to star as Sinuhe, but did not like the script and dropped out at the last minute. Farley Granger was the next choice and considered the role, but then decided he was not interested after having just moved to New York. Dirk Bogarde was then offered the role but also turned it down. Finally it was handed to a young up and coming contract actor Edmund Purdom.

Marilyn Monroe coveted the role of Nefer, only to discover that it was earmarked for the protegee (mistress) of producer Darryl F. Zanuck, Bella Darvi. This would be the second of only three American films featuring Darvi, who returned to Europe and later committed suicide.

Music

Owing to the short time available in post-production, the composing duties on the film score were divided between two of 20th Century-Fox's best-known composers: Alfred Newman and Bernard Herrmann.

Newman would later conduct the score in a re-recording for release on Decca Records. Musician John Morgan undertook a "restoration and reconstruction" of the score for a recording conducted by William T. Stromberg in 1998, on Marco Polo Records. The performance of the score recorded for the film was released by Film Score Monthly in 2001.

References

[1] Aubrey Solomon, *Twentieth Century Fox: A Corporate and Financial History*, Scarecrow Press, 1989 p248

[2] Aubrey Solomon, Twentieth Century Fox: A Corporate and Financial History, Scarecrow Press, 1989 p225

[3] 'The Top Box-Office Hits of 1954', *Variety Weekly*, January 5, 1955

[4] Taylor Ellison, The Ancient Ankh (http://www.touregypt.net/featurestories/ankh.htm), part of the Tour Egypt background material, website found 2009-01-03.

[5] The Worship of Aten (http://www.touregypt.net/atenwor.htm), part of the Tour Egypt background material, webpage found 2009-01-03.

External links

- *The Egyptian* (http://www.imdb.com/title/tt0046949/) at the Internet Movie Database
- *The Egyptian* (http://www.allrovi.com/movies/movie/v15390) at AllRovi
- *The Egyptian* (http://tcmdb.com/title/title.jsp?stid=73930) at the TCM Movie Database
- Complete listing of recordings of the film score (http://www.soundtrackcollector.com/catalog/soundtrackdetail.php?movieid=1574\)

The Grass Is Greener

The Grass Is Greener	
Directed by	Stanley Donen
Produced by	Stanley Donen James H. Ware
Written by	Hugh Williams Margaret Vyner
Starring	Cary Grant Deborah Kerr Robert Mitchum Jean Simmons
Music by	Noël Coward
Cinematography	Christopher Challis
Editing by	James Clark
Distributed by	Universal
Release date(s)	December 23, 1960
Running time	104 min.
Language	English
Box office	$6 million (US)[1]

The Grass Is Greener is a 1960 comedy film featuring an ensemble cast consisting of screen veterans Cary Grant, Deborah Kerr, Robert Mitchum, and Jean Simmons, directed by Stanley Donen. The film was adapted by Hugh Williams and Margaret Vyner from the play of the same name which they had written and found success with in London's West End.

Plot

The Earl and Countess of Rhyall (Cary Grant and Deborah Kerr) are facing financial troubles and are therefore forced to permit guided tours of their stately home.

A suave, somewhat obnoxious American oil tycoon, Charles Delacro (Robert Mitchum), barges into the lady of the manor's private quarters, either deliberately or by mistake. He introduces himself, explaining the family name was originally "Delacroix" but his grandfather tired of Americans pronouncing the "X" in the name.

Delacro's attentions to the Countess turn her head. Rather than behave jealously, the Earl invites the American to come visit, along with an equally grating ex-girlfriend of Lord Rhyall's, the American heiress Hattie Durant (Jean Simmons).

A love triangle (or quadrangle) soon develops, kicking off a tale of love, jealousy and other strong emotions that eventually leads the gentlemen to a duel with pistols.

Cast

- Cary Grant *as* Victor, Earl of Rhyall
- Deborah Kerr *as* Hilary, Countess of Rhyall
- Robert Mitchum *as* Charles Delacro
- Jean Simmons *as* Hattie Durant
- Moray Watson *as* Trevor Sellers, the Butler

Set design

British interior decorator Felix Harbord served as the film's special consultant for settings.

Reception

While the film was a moderate success at the U.K. box office, it fared much worse in the United States. Reviews of the film were mostly lukewarm. Despite its initial failure, the film has since developed a following and has been a staple of American cable television. At the time of its release, Jean Simmons's performance as a madcap heiress earned some praise and a Laurel Award nomination.

References

[1] "The Grass is Greener - Box Office Data" (http://www.the-numbers.com/movies/1960/0GRGR.php). The Numbers. . Retrieved 14 November 2011.

External links

- *The Grass Is Greener* (http://www.imdb.com/title/tt0053877/) at the Internet Movie Database

The Happy Ending

The Happy Ending	
Theatrical release poster	
Directed by	Richard Brooks
Produced by	Richard Brooks
Written by	Richard Brooks
Starring	Jean Simmons John Forsythe Shirley Jones Lloyd Bridges Teresa Wright Dick Shawn Nanette Fabray Bobby Darin Tina Louise Kathy Fields Karen Steele
Music by	Michel Legrand
Cinematography	Conrad L. Hall
Editing by	George Grenville
Distributed by	United Artists

The Happy Ending is a 1969 film written and directed by Richard Brooks, which tells the story of a repressed housewife who longs for liberation from her husband and daughter. It stars Jean Simmons (who received an Oscar nomination), John Forsythe, Shirley Jones, Lloyd Bridges and Teresa Wright.

Synopsis

1953: Through the course of a Colorado autumn and winter, Mary Spencer (Simmons) and Fred Wilson (Forsythe) lead an idyllic existence. Mary drops out of college (with 6 months to go) to marry Fred. Their perfect wedding mirrors the happy endings of the films Mary loves.

1969: It is the Wilsons' 16th wedding anniversary. On his way to work, Fred, a successful tax consultant, tells their maid Agnes (Nanette Fabray) that he has found vodka hidden in Mary's wardrobe and asks Agnes to keep an eye on his wife. Mary sets out for the beauty parlour. At an airline office, however, Mary buys a one-way ticket to Nassau, Bahamas.

On the flight she recalls the horrors of last year's anniversary party, when Fred had drunkenly flirted with a blond divorcee, and she had taken refuge in the bottle and a rerun of *Casablanca*. At a stop-over, she calls home and learns this year's anniversary party has been a different sort of disaster. Her daughter Marge (Kathy Fields) is scared by Mary's call—it reminds her of the time she had found her mother unconscious after an overdose.

En route to Nassau, Mary meets Flo (Jones), an old college friend she has not seen since 1953. While Mary settled down to married life, Flo has been the mistress of a series of married men. She is on her way to Nassau to meet her latest beau, Sam (Bridges). Mary tells her she has had to get away from Fred, so Flo promises to look after her.

In the Bahamas, Mary enjoys the sun and long, empty stretches of beach. At a casino, she meets Franco (Bobby Darin), a hustler from Los Angeles who is down on his luck. Franco mistakenly assumes that Mary is wealthy. He affects an Italian accent and tells Mary he is a journalist who writes about film stars. She agrees to go to "his" boat, but Franco quickly loses interest when it transpires Mary is not wealthy, confessing his scam.

Walking by the ocean, Mary recalls the occasion of her suicide attempt—she had returned from having a face lift to learn that Fred was in Reno with a girl. Marge had found her and rushed her mother to hospital. After that, Mary resumed drinking, recklessly spent a lot of money, and crashed her car while driving drunk.

In the present, Sam proposes to Flo, who accepts. Mary flies back home. Agnes helps her move into rooms she has rented away from Fred and Marge. She takes a job and enrolls in night classes at the university. It is here that Fred finds her, one evening. "What went wrong?" he asks. "All our friends are married, and they're happy."

Production

The film was rated 'M' certificate, and has a running time of 117 minutes.

Music for the film was composed and conducted by Michel Legrand, the song lyrics by Alan and Marilyn Bergman, sung by Michael Dees and Bill Eaton. The film was nominated for Academy Awards for Best Actress in a Leading Role, (Jean Simmons) and Best Music, Song (Michel Legrand, Alan Bergman and Marilyn Bergman, for "What Are You Doing the Rest of Your Life?"). The song was one of the eight pieces of music chosen by Jean Simmons when she appeared on the BBC radio programme *Desert Island Discs* on 9 August 1975.[1]

References

[1] *Desert Island Discs*, "Castaway: Jean Simmons" (http://www.bbc.co.uk/radio4/features/desert-island-discs/castaway/ a3d7f7f4#p009n6cw)

External links

- *The Happy Ending* (http://www.imdb.com/title/tt0064405/) at the Internet Movie Database

The Robe (film)

The Robe	
Original CinemaScope poster	
Directed by	Henry Koster
Produced by	Frank Ross
Screenplay by	• Gina Kaus • Albert Maltz • Philip Dunne
Based on	*The Robe* by Lloyd C. Douglas
Starring	• Richard Burton • Jean Simmons • Victor Mature • Michael Rennie
Music by	Alfred Newman
Cinematography	Leon Shamroy
Editing by	Barbara McLean
Distributed by	20th Century Fox
Release date(s)	• September 16, 1953
Running time	135 minutes
Country	United States
Language	English
Budget	$4.1 million[1]
Box office	$36 million (United States)[2]

The Robe is a 1953 American Biblical epic film that tells the story of a Roman military tribune who commands the unit that crucifies Jesus. The film was made by 20th Century Fox and is notable for being the first film released in the widescreen process CinemaScope.

The picture was directed by Henry Koster and produced by Frank Ross. The screenplay was adapted by Gina Kaus, Albert Maltz, and Philip Dunne from the Lloyd C. Douglas novel of the same name. The music score was composed by Alfred Newman and the cinematography was by Leon Shamroy.

The first widescreen movie in more than two decades stars Richard Burton, Jean Simmons, Victor Mature and Michael Rennie, with Dean Jagger, Jay Robinson, Richard Boone, and Jeff Morrow. The film used the same lenses as John Wayne's 1930 70 mm Grandeur widescreen Western epic for Fox, Raoul Walsh's *The Big Trail*.

The Robe had one sequel, *Demetrius and the Gladiators*.

The reason Lloyd Douglas wrote the novel *The Robe* was to answer the question: what happened to the Roman soldier who won Jesus' robe through a dice game?

Plot

The action takes place in Ancient Rome, Judaea, Capri, and Galilee in a time period stretching from 32 A.D. to 38 A.D.[3]

Marcellus Gallio (Richard Burton), son of an important Roman senator (Torin Thatcher) and himself a military tribune begins the film in a prologue that introduces the viewer to the might and scope of the Roman empire. He is notorious as a ladies' man, but he is captivated by the reappearance of a childhood sweetheart Diana (Jean Simmons), ward of the Emperor Tiberius (Ernest Thesiger) and Empress Julia (Rosalind Ivan), in Caligula's pavilion. As Caligula is the grandnephew and heir to Tiberius, Diana is unofficially promised in marriage to him as Empress Julia thinks Diana would be good for him.

When Caligula comes to the marketplace with military fanfare to take part in the slave auction, Marcellus makes the mistake of bidding against him for a defiant Greek slave Demetrius (Victor Mature) – and winning. Caligula feels he had been made a fool of in front of Diana, while Marcellus feels that he had wronged Demetrius by stopping him earlier when he had escaped from his slaveholders. Angrily Caligula leaves with Diana and the rest of his military escort and issues orders for Marcellus to receive a military transfer to Jerusalem in Palestine.

Marcellus has Demetrius released, and he orders him to go on his own to the Gallio home. At the Gallio home, Cornelia and Lucia, Marcellus's mother and sister, are informed by Diana about the situation at the marketplace. Lucia remarks that Marcellus is still in love with Diana. Marcellus is surprised to find Demetrius waiting for him when he gets home. Unofficially Marcellus had freed Demetrius, but Demetrius feels honor bound to compensate Marcellus by being his servant.

Demetrius accompanies Marcellus to Palestine, but before the galley sails, Diana comes to see Marcellus, pledging her love for him and her intention to intercede on his behalf with Tiberius. Marcellus declares his love for Diana and asks her to make the emperor promise not to give her in marriage to Caligula.

Marcellus rides into Jerusalem with the centurion Paulus (Jeff Morrow) on the same day as Jesus' triumphal entry on Palm Sunday. Jesus confronts Demetrius as he rides into Jerusalem, silently calling him with his eyes to be his follower. When Demetrius later finds out what the Romans have in store for Jesus, he tries to warn him about the intentions of the Romans to arrest him. However, Jesus has already been arrested, as Demetrius finds out from a chance meeting with Judas.

Jesus is arrested and condemned by Pontius Pilate (Richard Boone), the procurator, who sends for Marcellus to take charge of the detail of Roman soldiers assigned to crucify him. As Pilate finishes washing his hands, he tells Marcellus that he is being recalled to Italy by the emperor and tells Marcellus of the duty he must perform before he leaves. As Marcellus leaves, Pilate pines about the past night and asks for water so that he can wash his hands again.

Marcellus and the other soldiers cast lots for Jesus' robe, and Marcellus wins. On the way back into Jerusalem, Marcellus compels Demetrius to throw the robe over him as the two of them are caught in the rain. It is then that Marcellus begins to feel remorse for the crucifixion of Jesus. When the robe is on him he has a painful seizure, and he orders Demetrius to take it off him. When Demetrius does so he has had enough: he curses Marcellus and the Roman Empire and runs away.

Marcellus now behaves like a madman haunted by nightmares of the crucifixion. What sets him off is any reference to being "out there" on Calvary. He cries out fitfully, "Were you out there?!" He does this in the presence of Tiberius himself when he reports to him on Capri. Tiberius is portrayed as a benevolent elder statesman, who wants to help Marcellus, so, at the prompting of his soothsayer Dodinius (Francis Pierlot) and Marcellus's own enthusiasm, he gives him an imperial commission to find and destroy the robe while gathering a list of names of Jesus' followers. At Diana's request, Tiberius leaves her free to marry Marcellus even though Tiberius believes him to be mad.

After leaving Capri, Marcellus is next seen sometime later with a Syrian guide Abidor (Leon Askin) outside the village of Cana. He is posing as a cloth merchant going about buying up homespun cloth. To further his investigation Marcellus pays exorbitant prices for any kind of cloth, even rags.

Justus, a weaver in Cana (Dean Jagger), reprimands his fellow Christians for accepting such unfair prices as being contrary to the teachings of Jesus and his fellow Christians give back the excess amounts voluntarily. Seeing Justus as a lead in his investigations Marcellus seeks to ingratiate himself with Justus by giving his young grandson Jonathan (Nicolas Koster), whose club foot had been healed by Jesus, one of his pack donkeys. Marcellus also wanders in on a public performance by the paralytic Miriam as she sings a song of Jesus' resurrection.

When Marcellus returns to his camp he is confronted by a greedy Abidor, who wants to turn in Justus and the others to Pilate, who has ordered the arrest of Jesus' followers. Abidor, who is obsessed with making money, threatens to tell the people of Cana that Marcellus crucified Jesus, which drives Marcellus to beat Abidor and send him away violently.

The next day Marcellus is furious with Jonathan for giving his donkey to his physically challenged friend David, because he did not yet understand the teachings of Jesus. Miriam, who is sitting nearby kindly confronts Marcellus, and urges him to see Peter (Michael Rennie), who has come to Cana with a Greek companion. Marcellus guesses that this is Demetrius and goes off to Shalum's Inn to confront him.

Marcellus finds Demetrius alone, and demands that he get the robe and destroy it. Demetrius gives the robe to Marcellus, who refuses to touch it, and Demetrius tells him that if he wants it destroyed, he will have to destroy it himself. Marcellus picks the robe up with his sword, and as he becomes frozen with fear, the robe slides down the sword onto him. He is terrified, but this time, as the robe touches him, he finds that the pain he has been carrying since the robe first touched him vanishes and that he is no longer afraid. He feels the true power of the robe and of the one who wore it. In that moment, Marcellus believes in Jesus Christ, is relieved from the madness of his guilt, and becomes a Christian.

The two men go outside and Justus calls the villagers together and begins to introduce Peter. Justus tells the gathered crowd that, on the night of Jesus' arrest, only Peter stood by Jesus. Peter tries to correct Justus but Justus tells Peter that his turn to speak will come and continues. Suddenly, Justus is pierced by an arrow and falls. The assembly turns to see Paulus and a large detachment of Roman soldiers, with the gloating Abidor lurking among them. Several other villagers are killed before Marcellus intervenes, ordering them to stop. Paulus informs him that his orders are no longer valid; Tiberias is dead and Caligula is emperor. Marcellus informs Paulus that an imperial commission is valid even after a Roman emperor dies. Paulus tells Marcellus to make him obey via a sword duel. Marcellus asks Paulus if he will keeps his word to withdraw the troops if Marcellus wins the duel. Paulus says that if Marcellus wins, the troops are his because Paulus will be dead. Marcellus accepts the challenge to a duel. After a prolonged struggle Marcellus prevails. Rather than killing Paulus, as is expected of him, Marcellus hurls his sword into a tree. He challenges Paulus to give the order to his soldiers to withdraw. Paulus, recognizing the mercy extended to him by Marcellus, salutes Marcellus and orders the soldiers to leave.

Peter invites Marcellus to join him and Demetrius as missionaries. Marcellus hesitates, and when Peter tells him that he denied Jesus three times on the night he was arrested, Marcellus confesses his role in Jesus' death. Peter points out to him that Jesus forgave him from the cross in the dramatic words showcased before, "Father, forgive them for they know not what they do" (Luke 23:34a). Marcellus then pledges his life to Jesus and agrees to go with them. Their missionary journey takes them through Antioch, Ephesus, Corinth, and then to Rome, but they must proceed "undercover" with their base in the catacombs because the Emperor Caligula has proscribed them.

In Rome, Caligula summons Diana from her retreat at the Gallio home to tell her that Marcellus has become a traitor to Rome by being a Christian. He takes her to the guard room where a captured Demetrius is being tortured. Diana runs out of the palace to Marcipor (David Leonard), the Gallio family slave, who is a secret Christian. Diana guesses that Marcipor is a Christian and has seen Marcellus, and she gets him to take her to Marcellus.

Marcellus and Diana are reunited, and Marcellus tells her the story of the robe and his own conversion but Diana only thinks the story of Jesus, justice, and love is a nice story but that the world doesn't work that way. Diana gives Marcellus information on where Demetrius is in the imperial palace, and Marcellus and his fellow Christians manage to rescue him. They are almost too late as Demetrius is near death, but Peter comes to the Gallio home where

Demetrius has been taken and heals him. Caligula scolds his Roman soldiers for letting the prisoner get away and issues orders to bring Marcellus to him alive to stand trial by the end of the day or they will all be sent to the galleys.

A physician friend of Senator Gallio, Marius (Thomas Browne Henry), is called in to help Demetrius, but is unable to heal him. Marius states that science has limits. Marcellus prays to God and Peter then knocks on the door and ask to be alone with Demetrius. Peter lays his hand on Demetrius and heals him. Marius, a proud man, is resentful of Peter's ability to heal Demetrius and leaves with the purpose of betraying Marcellus to Caligula. Marcellus tells his father, Senator Gallio, that he wants to return and tell his father more about Christianity; however, his father says this will be the last time they see each other because he feels his son has betrayed Rome by becoming a Christian and, therefore, he no longer has a son. Marcellus promises Diana that he will send for her tomorrow and kisses Diana as he leaves.

Marcellus flees with Demetrius but, when they are pursued by soldiers, Marcellus gives himself up so that Demetrius can escape. He is captured and put on trial. Diana visits Marcellus in prison on the night before his trial and requests he not defy Caligula. Marcellus tells Diana of Miriam, the crippled girl who found herself fortunate to be lame; of the poor, young boy Jonathan, to whom Marcellus gave the fine donkey and he then selflessly gave it away to another boy without a second thought; and how other Christians do not deny Christ to save their skin. Diana wants to believe but does not feel she can if Marcellus dies. If he dies now, Diana tells him, that she feels his death would be for nothing and that she needs Marcellus.

Caligula makes Diana sit next to him for Marcellus' trial. He then tells the crowd of Senators and Roman nobles that there is a secret party of seditionists called "Christians" and how their actions are comparable to the traitor Spartacus. He then tells them that one of their own, Marcellus, has joined these "conspirators" and thus is being tried by all of them for treason. Marcellus informs the crowd that it is true that he is a Christian; however, he denies the charge that Christians are plotting against the state. When Caligula says that Christians believe Jesus is a king, Marcellus tells everyone that Jesus is a king but that His Kingdom is not of this world and Jesus seeks to reign in the hearts and mind in the name of justice and charity. Caligula asks about the robe that Marcellus is holding and Marcellus tries to show Caligula his opportunity to accept Christ. Marcellus tries to hand the robe to Caligula but Caligula refuses to touch it as he considers it to be "bewitched". He orders one of his soldiers to take the robe and destroy it, but Diana asks to keep it instead.

Marcellus informs Caligula that, if Rome turns to the ways of justice and charity, then Rome will be saved; however, if Rome stayed on its present course, then it would be destroyed. To the crowd, this sounds treasonous and Caligula condemns Marcellus to death by the wish of the members of the audience based on what they've heard. Caligula, in an effort to show mercy to Marcellus, tells him to renew his allegiance to Rome and renounce his faith in Jesus Christ. Marcellus kneels to Caligula to renew his pledge to Rome, a pledge he states that he has never broken, but then stands and states that he cannot renounce his belief in Jesus. Marcellus tells Caligula that Jesus is his King and Caligula's King and that Jesus is the Son of God. Diana then accepts Christ, and seeks to join Marcellus, the man she considers to be her husband, in His Kingdom. When Caligula tells Diana that there are no charges against her, she provides a reason for her to be charged with the same crime as Marcellus by telling the audience how evil an emperor Caligula is. Caligula screams out as she states her condemnation of his rules and then condemns Diana to die alongside Marcellus.

As Diana and Marcellus are marched out of the emperor's court, Marcellus is acknowledged by his repentent father and Diana hands the robe to Marcipor. Diana and Marcellus pause to smile at each other as they peacefully walk out of the courtroom to meet their earthly fate. A chorus of "Hallelujah" plays and clouds are in the background behind Diana and Marcellus as the film ends.

Historical inaccuracies

Despite the careful attention to Roman history and culture displayed in the film, there are some inaccuracies: the emperor Tiberius' wife Julia, who had been banished from Rome by her father Augustus years before Tiberius acceded to the imperial throne, was already dead.

Cast

- Richard Burton as Marcellus Gallio
- Jean Simmons as Diana
- Victor Mature as Demetrius
- Michael Rennie as Peter
- Jay Robinson as Caligula
- Dean Jagger as Justus
- Torin Thatcher as Sen. Gallio
- Sally Corner as Cornelia Gallio
- Pamela Robinson as Lucia Gallio
- Richard Boone as Pontius Pilate
- Betta St. John as Miriam
- Jeff Morrow as Paulus
- Ernest Thesiger as Tiberius
- Rosalind Ivan as Empress Julia the Elder
- Dawn Addams as Junia
- Leon Askin as Abidor
- Helen Beverley as Rebecca
- Frank Pulaski as Quintus
- David Leonard as Marcipor
- Michael Ansara as Judas
- Jay Novello as Tiro
- Donald C. Klune as Jesus of Nazareth
- Cameron Mitchell as the voice of Jesus

Background and production

The Robe was originally announced for filming by RKO in the 1940s, and was set to be directed by Mervyn LeRoy,[4] but the rights were eventually sold to Twentieth Century Fox for a reported $100,000.[5]

Jeff Chandler was originally announced for the role of Demetrius.[6]

The film was advertised as "the modern miracle you see without glasses", a dig at the 3D movies of the day. Since many theaters of the day were not equipped to show a CinemaScope film, two versions of *The Robe* were made: one in the standard screen ratio of the day, the other in the widescreen process. Setups and some dialogue differ between the versions.

The film was usually shown on television using the standard 1.33:1 aspect ratio version that fills a standard television screen rather than the CinemaScope version. American Movie Classics may have been the first to offer telecasts of the widescreen version. Recent DVDs and Blu-ray Discs of the film, however, present the film in the original widescreen format, as well as the multitrack stereophonic soundtrack. The 2009 DVD and Blu-ray Disc releases contain a special feature that compares selected scenes between the Cinemascope version and the standard version.

When the original soundtrack album was issued on LP by Decca Records, it used a remix for only monaural sound rather than the stereo sound that was originally recorded. MCA, which acquired the rights to the American Decca recordings, issued an electronic stereo version of the mono tape. RCA Victor included a suite from the film, recorded in Dolby surround sound, in its album *Captain from Castile*, which honored longtime Fox musical director Alfred Newman (composer of the *The Robe*'s musical score); Charles Gerhardt conducted London's National Philharmonic Chorus. In 2003, Varèse Sarabande released a two-CD set of the original stereophonic recording on their club label. The 2009 DVD and Blu-ray Disc releases contain isolated stereophonic score tracks.

Reception

The film earned estimated rentals of $17.5 million in North America during its initial theatrical release.[7]

The film had one sequel, *Demetrius and the Gladiators* (1954), which featured Victor Mature in the title-role, making *The Robe* the only Biblical epic with a sequel.

Awards and nominations

- The film won Academy Awards for Best Art Direction – Set Decoration, Color (Lyle Wheeler, George Davis, Walter M. Scott, Paul S. Fox), and Best Costume Design, Color (Charles Le Maire).[8] It was nominated for Best Actor in a Leading Role (Richard Burton), Best Cinematography, Color, and Best Picture.
- The film also won the Golden Globe Award for Best Picture.

First telecast

The film was first telecast by ABC-TV on Easter weekend in 1967, at the relatively early hour of 7:00 P.M., E.S.T, to allow for family viewing. In a highly unusual move, the film was shown with only one commercial break – a luxury not even granted to the then-annual telecasts of *The Wizard of Oz*.[9]

References

[1] Aubrey Solomon, *Twentieth Century Fox: A Corporate and Financial History*, Scarecrow Press, 1989 p248

[2] The Robe (http://www.boxofficemojo.com/movies/?id=robe.htm). Box Office Mojo. Retrieved January 20, 2010.

[3] The beginning date is given as the 18th year of Tiberius, and the ending date is a year after the historical year of the accession of Caligula (Jay Robinson) as Roman emperor. Diana tells Caligula that she had not heard from Marcellus for almost a year when Marcellus was in Cana of Galilee. At that time Marcellus was told by Paulus that Caligula was then the emperor.

[4] "Religion: Celluloid Revival" (http://www.time.com/time/magazine/article/0,9171,778109,00.html?promoid=googlep). *Time*. April 24, 1944. . Retrieved May 25, 2010.

[5] "STAGE AND SCREEN." (http://nla.gov.au/nla.news-article48276393). *The Advertiser (Adelaide, SA : 1931 - 1954)* (Adelaide, SA: National Library of Australia): p. 7. 1 August 1953. . Retrieved 12 July 2012.

[6] Jeff Chandler Likely for Demetrius; 'Highest Mountain' New Purchase Schallert, Edwin. Los Angeles Times (1923-Current File) [Los Angeles, Calif] 01 Aug 1952: B7.

[7] "All Time Domestic Champs", *Variety*, 6 January 1960 p 34

[8] "NY Times: The Robe" (http://movies.nytimes.com/movie/41635/The-Robe/details). *NY Times*. . Retrieved 2008-12-21.

[9] "Television: Mar. 24, 1967" (http://www.time.com/time/magazine/article/0,9171,836861,00.html). *Time*. March 24, 1967. . Retrieved May 25, 2010.

External links

- *The Robe* (http://www.afi.com/members/catalog/DetailView.aspx?s=&Movie=50996) at the American Film Institute Catalog
- *The Robe* (http://www.imdb.com/title/tt0046247/) at the Internet Movie Database

The Thorn Birds

The Thorn Birds	
1st edition	
Author(s)	Colleen McCullough
Country	Australia
Language	English
Genre(s)	Family saga
Publisher	Harper & Row
Publication date	April 1977
Media type	Print (Hardback & Paperback)
Pages	692
ISBN	ISBN 0-06-012956-5 (first edition, hardback)
OCLC Number	2886288 [1]
Dewey Decimal	823
LC Classification	PR9619.3.M32 T5 1977

The Thorn Birds is a 1977 best-selling novel by Colleen McCullough, an Australian author.

In 1983 it was adapted as a TV mini-series that, during its television run 27–30 March, became the United States' second highest rated mini-series of all time behind *Roots*; both series were produced by television veteran David L. Wolper.

The mini-series starred Richard Chamberlain, Rachel Ward, Barbara Stanwyck, Christopher Plummer, Bryan Brown, Mare Winningham, Philip Anglim, and Jean Simmons. It was directed by Daryl Duke.

Set primarily on Drogheda, a fictional sheep station in the Australian outback, the story focuses on the Cleary family and spans the years 1915 to 1969.

In 2003, the novel was listed at number 64 on the BBC's survey The Big Read.[2]

Plot

The epic begins with Meghann "Meggie" Cleary, a four-year-old girl living in New Zealand in the early twentieth century, the only daughter of Paddy, an Irish farm labourer, and Fee, his harassed but aristocratic wife. Although Meggie is a beautiful child with curly red-gold hair, she receives little coddling and must struggle to hold her own against her numerous older brothers. Of these brothers, her favourite is the eldest, Frank, a rebellious young man who is unwillingly preparing himself for the blacksmith's trade. He is much shorter than his brothers, but very strong; also, unlike the other Clearys, he has black hair and eyes.

Paddy is poor, but has a wealthy sister, Mary Carson, who lives in Australia on an enormous sheep station called Drogheda. One day, Paddy receives a letter from Mary offering him a job on her estate. He accepts, and the whole family moves to the Outback.

Here Meggie meets Ralph de Bricassart, a young, capable, and ambitious priest who, as punishment for insulting a bishop, has been relegated to a remote parish in the town of Gillanbone, near Drogheda. Ralph has befriended Mary, hoping a hefty enough bequest from her to the Catholic Church might liberate him from his exile. Ralph is strikingly handsome; "a beautiful man"; and Mary, who does not bother to conceal her desire for him, often goes to great lengths to see if he can be induced to break his vows. Ralph blandly shrugs off these attentions and continues his visits. Meanwhile, he cares for all the Clearys and soon learns to cherish beautiful but forlorn little Meggie. Meggie, in return, makes Ralph the centre of her life.

Frank's relationship with his father, Paddy, has never been peaceful. The two vie for Fee's attention, and Frank resents the many pregnancies Paddy makes her endure. One day, after Fee, now in her forties, reveals she is again pregnant, the two men quarrel violently and Paddy blurts out the truth about Frank: he is not Paddy's son. Long ago, Fee had been the adored only daughter of a prominent citizen. Then she had an affair with a married politician, and the result, Frank, was already eighteen months old when her mortified father married her off to Paddy. Because he resembles her lost love, Fee has always loved Frank more than her other children. To the sorrow of Meggie and Fee, when Frank learns that Paddy is not his father, he runs away to become a boxer. Fee later gives birth to twin boys, James and Patrick (Jims and Patsy), but shows little interest in them. Shortly afterward, Meggie's beloved little brother, Hal, dies.

With Frank gone and Hal dead, Meggie clings to Ralph more than ever. This goes largely unnoticed because Ralph has now been her mentor for several years; however, as she ripens into womanhood, some begin to question their close relationship, including Ralph and Meggie themselves. Mary Carson has also noticed their changing relationship, and from motives of jealousy mingled with Machiavellian cruelty, she devises a plan to separate Ralph from Meggie by tempting him with his heart's desire: a high place in the Church hierarchy. Although her will of record leaves the bulk of her estate to Paddy, she quietly writes a new one, making the Roman Catholic Church the main beneficiary and Ralph the executor.

In the new will, the true magnitude of Mary's wealth is finally revealed. Drogheda is not the centre of her fortune as Ralph and Paddy have long believed but is merely a hobby, a diversion from her true financial interests. Mary's wealth is derived from a vast multi-national financial empire worth over thirteen million Pounds (about A$200 million in modern terms). The sheer size of Mary's bequest will virtually guarantee Ralph's rapid rise in the church. She also makes sure that after she dies only Ralph, at first, will know of the new will — forcing him to choose between Meggie and his own ambition. She also provides for her disinherited brother, promising him and all his grandchildren a home on Drogheda as long as any of them live.

At Mary's seventy-second birthday party, Ralph goes to great lengths to avoid Meggie, now seventeen and dressed in a beautiful rose-pink evening gown; later, he explains that others might not see his attention as innocent. Mary dies in the night. Ralph duly learns of the new will. He sees at once the subtle genius of Mary's plan and, although he weeps and calls her "a disgusting old spider" he takes the new will to her lawyer without delay. The lawyer, scandalised, urges Ralph to destroy the will, but to no avail. The bequest of thirteen million pounds works its expected magic, and Ralph soon leaves to begin his rapid advance in the Church.

Before he leaves, Meggie confesses her love for him; after the birthday party, Ralph finds her crying in the family cemetery and they share a passionate kiss, but Ralph refuses her because of his duties as a priest and begs Meggie to find someone to love and marry.

The Clearys learn that Frank has been convicted of murder after killing someone in a fight. He spends three decades in prison.

Paddy and his son Stuart are killed; Paddy dies in a lightning fire, and Stu is killed by a wild boar shortly after finding his father's body. Meanwhile, Ralph, unaware of Paddy and Stu's deaths, is on his way to Drogheda and suffers minor injuries when his plane bogs in the mud. As Meggie tends his wounds, she tries to seduce him and is rebuffed. Ralph remains at Drogheda only long enough to conduct the funerals.

Three years later, a new ranch worker named Luke O'Neill begins to court Meggie. Although his motives are more mercenary than romantic, she marries him because he looks a little bit like Ralph, but mainly because he is not Catholic and wants little to do with religion-her own way of getting back at Ralph. She soon realises her mistake. After a brief honeymoon, Luke, a skinflint who regards women as sex objects and prefers the company of men, finds Meggie a live-in job with a kindly couple, the Muellers, and leaves to join a gang of itinerant sugarcane cutters in

North Queensland. Before he leaves, he appropriates all Meggie's savings and arranges to have her wages paid directly to him. He tells her he is saving money to buy a homestead; however, he quickly becomes obsessed with the competitive toil of cane-cutting and has no real intention of giving it up. Hoping to change Luke's ambition and settle him down, Meggie deliberately thwarts his usual contraception and bears Luke a red-haired daughter, Justine. The new baby, however, makes little impression on Luke.

Father Ralph visits Meggie during her difficult labour; he has come to say goodbye, as he is leaving Australia for Rome. He sees Meggie's unhappiness for himself, and pities her. Justine proves to be a fractious baby, so the Muellers send Meggie to an isolated island resort for a rest. Father Ralph returns to Australia, learns of Meggie's whereabouts from Anne Mueller, and joins her for several days. There, at last, the lovers consummate their passion, and Ralph realises that despite his ambition to be the perfect priest, his desire for Meggie makes him a man like other men. Father Ralph returns to the Church, and Meggie, pregnant with Ralph's child, decides to separate from Luke. She tells Luke what she really thinks of him, and returns to Drogheda, leaving him to his cane-cutting.

Back home, she gives birth to a beautiful boy whom she names Dane. Fee, who has had experience in such matters, notices Dane's resemblance to Ralph as soon as he is born. The relationship between Meggie and Fee takes a turn for the better. Justine grows into an independent, keenly intelligent girl who loves her brother dearly; however, she has little use for anyone else, and calmly rebuffs Meggie's overtures of motherly affection.

None of Meggie's other surviving brothers ever marry, and Drogheda gradually becomes a place filled with old people.

Ralph visits Drogheda after a long absence and meets Dane for the first time; and although he finds himself strangely drawn to the boy, he fails to recognize that they are father and son. Dane grows up and decides, to Meggie's dismay, to become a priest. Fee tells Meggie that what she stole from God, she must now give back. Justine, meanwhile, decides to become an actress and leaves Australia to seek her dream in England. Ralph, now a Cardinal, becomes a mentor to Dane, but still blinds himself to the fact that the young man is his own son. Dane is also unaware of their true relationship. Ralph takes great care of him, and because of their resemblance people mistake them for uncle and nephew. Ralph and Dane encourage the rumour. Justine and her brother remain close, although he is often shocked at her sexual adventures and free-wheeling lifestyle. She befriends Rainer Hartheim, a German politician who is a great friend of both Dane and Ralph's - unbeknown to her, he falls deeply in love with her. Their friendship becomes the most important in her life, and is on the verge of becoming something more when tragedy strikes.

Dane, who has just become a priest, is vacationing in Greece. While there, he goes swimming one day and dies while rescuing two women from a dangerous current. Meggie reveals before Dane's funeral that Dane is Ralph's son. Ralph dies in Meggie's arms after the funeral.

Justine breaks off all communications with Rainer and falls into a depressed, hum-drum existence. Eventually, they renew their acquaintance on strictly platonic terms, until Rainer visits Drogheda alone in order to urge Meggie to help him pursue Justine's hand in marriage.

Justine, now the sole surviving grandchild of Fee and Paddy Cleary, finally accepts her true feelings for Rainer. They marry, but have no plans to live on Drogheda.

The book's title refers to a mythical bird that searches for thorn trees from the day it is hatched. When it finds the perfect thorn, it impales itself, and sings the most beautiful song ever heard as it dies.

List of characters

- **Meghann "Meggie" Cleary** — The central character, the only daughter in a large family of sons. The novel takes her from early childhood to old age.
- **Father Ralph de Bricassart** — Meggie's true love, a handsome Irish Catholic priest.
- **Padraic "Paddy" Cleary** — Meggie's father, a kind and simple labouring Irishman.
- **Fiona "Fee" Armstrong Cleary** — Paddy's wife and Meggie's mother, an aristocratic woman who has come down in the world.
- **Francis "Frank" Armstrong Cleary** — Meggie's eldest brother, Fee's illegitimate first son. A favourite with Meggie and Fee both.
- **Mary Elizabeth Cleary Carson** — Paddy's immensely wealthy older sister; Father Ralph's benefactor; owner of Drogheda.
- **Luke O'Neill** — Meggie's husband during an unhappy three-year marriage; father of Justine.
- **Dane O'Neill** — Son of Meggie and Ralph, Meggie's pride and joy, drowned in Greece at the age of twenty-six.
- **Justine O'Neill** — Daughter of Meggie and Luke, an intelligent, independent girl. At the end, she is the only surviving grandchild of Paddy and Fee Cleary.
- **Luddie and Anne Mueller** — Meggie's employers during her marriage to Luke. They become lifelong friends.
- **Bob, Jack, and Hughie Cleary** — Meggie's older brothers. They all resemble Paddy and live out their days, unmarried, on Drogheda.
- **Stuart "Stu" Cleary** — A quiet, kindly boy who resembles his mother and is closest to Meggie in age.
- **Harold "Hal" Cleary** — Meggie's cherished baby brother. He dies when he's four years old.
- **James and Patrick "Jims and Patsy" Cleary** — Twin boys, Meggie's youngest brothers.
- **Rainer "Rain" Moerling Hartheim** — Friend of Ralph and eventually Dane. Member of the West German Parliament and eventual husband of Justine.
- **Archbishop (later Cardinal) Vittorio di Contini-Verchese** — Ralph's mentor, friend to Rainer and Dane.

Influences on popular culture

In *The Sopranos* episode "College", Carmela Soprano and her priest, Father Phil Intintola, watch *The Remains of the Day* on Tony Soprano's stolen DVD player and skirt dangerously close to forsaking Phil's priestly and Carmela's marital vows, while Tony, Meadow, and AJ spend the night elsewhere. The next morning, Tony expresses suspicion after learning that Father Phil has spent the night, to which Carmela sarcastically responds, "Do I look like the friggin' thornbird over here?"

In the television show *Reba* there is an episode in which the character Barbra Jean has a crush on her reverend, whom she refers to as "Reverend Yummy-Pants". She sends him a copy of The Thorn Birds as a hint.

References

[1] http://worldcat.org/oclc/2886288
[2] "BBC - The Big Read" (http://www.bbc.co.uk/arts/bigread/top100_2.shtml). BBC. April 2003, Retrieved 13 November 2012

The Thorn Birds on ABC, 1983, TV Show (http:// www. tvguide. com/ tvshows/ thorn-birds/ cast/ 205014), tvguide.com

External links

- Photos of the first edition of The Thorn Birds (http://www.mansionbooks.com/BookDetail.php?bk=268)

The Thorn Birds (TV miniseries)

The Thorn Birds	
Directed by	Daryl Duke
Written by	Carmen Culver Lee Stanley Colleen McCullough (novel)
Starring	Richard Chamberlain Rachel Ward Barbara Stanwyck Christopher Plummer Jean Simmons Bryan Brown Philip Anglim Richard Kiley
Music by	Henry Mancini
Cinematography	Bill Butler
Editing by	Robert F. Shugrue David Saxon Carroll Timothy O'Meara
Country	United States
Language	English
Original channel	ABC
Release date	
Running time	467 minutes

The Thorn Birds is a television mini-series broadcast on ABC between 27 and 30 March 1983. It starred Richard Chamberlain, Rachel Ward, Barbara Stanwyck, Christopher Plummer, Richard Kiley, Bryan Brown, Mare Winningham, Philip Anglim and Jean Simmons. It was directed by Daryl Duke and based on a novel by Colleen McCullough.

Set primarily on Drogheda, a fictional sheep station in the Australian outback, the story focuses on three generations of the Cleary Family and spans the years 1920 to 1962.

Deviations from the novel

The novel begins in New Zealand on December 8, 1915, Meggie Cleary's fourth birthday. The miniseries begins in Australia five years later.

Three of Paddy and Fiona's children, Hughie and twins Jims and Patsy, are left out of the miniseries. In the miniseries, Meggie and Stuart visit Frank in prison, where Frank eventually dies. In the novel, Ralph acts as a go-between and no one in the Cleary family sees Frank until he is released from prison after 30 years.

In the novel, Meggie is totally ignorant of sexual matters until her wedding and has her own childish idea of how babies are made, which is revealed in her dialogue with Ralph. In the corresponding dialogue in the film, she is at least aware that animals copulate. Jastin visits Greece with Dane in the miniseries, while in the novel she stays in London.

Ralph dies while sitting in a chair with Meggie's head in his lap, recalling the legend of the thorn bird, not in Meggie's arms as in the novel, and not immediately after Dane's funeral.

Cast

Actor	Role
Richard Chamberlain	Ralph de Bricassart
Rachel Ward	Meggie Cleary (as an adult)
Sydney Penny	Meggie Cleary (as a child)
Barbara Stanwyck	Mary Carson
Richard Kiley	Paddy Cleary
Jean Simmons	Fee Cleary
Bryan Brown	Luke O'Neill
Mare Winningham	Justine O'Neill
Philip Anglim	Dane O'Neill
Ken Howard	Rainer Hartheim
John Friedrich	Frank Cleary
Dwier Brown	Stuart Cleary (as an adult)
Vidal Peterson	Stuart Cleary (as a child)
Piper Laurie	Anne Mueller
Earl Holliman	Luddie Mueller
Christopher Plummer	Archbishop Vittorio di Contini-Verchese
Brett Cullen	Bob Cleary
Stephen W. Burns	Jack Cleary
Barry Corbin	Pete
Holly Palance	Miss Carmichael
John de Lancie	Alastair MacQueen
Allyn Ann McLerie	Mrs. Smith
Richard Venture	Harry Gough
Stephanie Faracy	Judy
Antoinette Bower	Sarah MacQueen

Filming

- Although the mini-series is set in Australia it was filmed in the United States. The outback scenes were filmed in southern California and the Queensland scenes were filmed on the Hawaiian island of Kauai. The *Drogheda* main house was a set built on the Big Sky Ranch in Simi Valley, California.

- The mountainous terrain of the southern California "outback" filming location does not resemble western New South Wales, which is predominantly level to gently rolling.

- The mini-series included "the most dangerous bus in Australia". Since filming took place in the US an American bus was used. In Australia, where there is right-hand drive, it would set down its passengers in the middle of the road.

- In the miniseries, *Drogheda*, Mary Carson's sheep station, is said to have been named after the Irish town of Drogheda, by a former resident of that town. However, its name is mispronounced by all characters as "Drog-ee-da". In fact, the g should be silent and the e short. A former resident would pronounce it as

Draw-hed-ah or Dro-hed-ah (with a soft o as in "drop").

- A "midquel" was produced in 1996, by CBS entitled *The Thorn Birds: The Missing Years*, which tells the story of the 19 years unaccounted for in the original miniseries

- New York Jets offensive tackle D'Brickashaw Ferguson was named after the character Ralph de Bricassart.

- Rachel Ward, who was born in 1957, plays the mother of a daughter played by 1959 born actress Mare Winningham, and a son played by 1953 born actor Philip Anglim.

- Rachel Ward met her husband Bryan Brown on the set while filming the series. Brown plays Luke O'Neill who marries Ward's character, Meggie Cleary.

- Actor Bryan Brown, was actually the only Australian born cast member hired in a major role. This is not too unusual since although the series takes place in Australia, Luke O'Neill and Meggie's children were the only major characters who were Australian born. Father Ralph, Mary Carson, and Paddy Cleary were all Irish born. Fee and most of the Cleary children were born in New Zealand.

- During casting, actress Jane Seymour was considered for the role of Meggie Cleary and the role of Mary Carson was originally offered to Audrey Hepburn.

- The serial has had great success in France. The French title is "Les oiseaux se cachent pour mourir" (The birds hide to die). The series is still regularly repeated on TV channels.

Emmy Awards

The Mini-series was nominated in 16 categories at the Primetime Emmy Awards in 1983, 7 of which were for acting. The winning actors were:

- Outstanding Lead Actress in a Limited Series or a Special- Barbara Stanwyck.
- Outstanding Supporting Actor in a Limited Series or a Special- Richard Kiley.
- Outstanding Supporting Actress in a Limited Series or a Special- Jean Simmons.

Also nominated for their roles:

- Outstanding Lead Actor in a Limited Series or a Special- Richard Chamberlain.
- Outstanding Supporting Actor in a Limited Series or a Special- Bryan Brown.
- Outstanding Supporting Actor in a Limited Series or a Special- Christopher Plummer.
- Outstanding Supporting Actress in a Limited Series or a Special- Piper Laurie.

Competing against these actors were Roger Rees and David Threlfall for their performances in the television version of the Royal Shakespeare Company's *The Life and Adventures of Nicholas Nickleby*, which beat out both *The Thorn Birds* and *The Winds of War* for Best Miniseries.

External links

- Encyclopedia of Television [1]
- *The Thorn Birds* [2] at the Internet Movie Database

References

[1] http://www.museum.tv/archives/etv/T/htmlT/thornbirds/thornbirds.htm
[2] http://www.imdb.com/title/tt0085101/

The Woman in the Hall

The Woman in the Hall	
Directed by	Jack Lee
Produced by	Ian Dalrymple
Written by	Ian Dalrymple (screenplay) G. B. Stern (novel and screenplay)) Jack Lee (screenplay)
Starring	Ursula Jeans Jean Simmons Cecil Parker
Music by	Temple Abady
Release date(s)	28 October 1947
Running time	93 minutes

The Woman in the Hall is a 1947 British drama film, directed by Jack Lee, with a screenplay by Jack Lee, Ian Dalrymple and Gladys Bronwyn Stern, from Stern's novel. It was released in 1947. "A studio bound melodrama, it seems atypical of Lee's later films, but the struggles of an individual to achieve a goal and through that struggle develop into a better person was a recurrent theme." The film features the screen debut of future television star Susan Hampshire.

Plot

Lorna Blake, (Ursula Jeans) is a widow with two daughters. She augments her slender income by using her children to extort money - visiting the houses of the rich to tell a pathetic story and beg for help. And Lorna makes a rich capture when Sir Halmar Bernard, (Cecil Parker), proposes to her. She tells him that she has only one daughter, Molly (Jill Freud, credited as Jill Raymond). When her other daughter, Jay (Jean Simmons), is arrested for forging a cheque, she refuses to help her.

Cast

- Ursula Jeans as Lorna Blake
- Jean Simmons as Jay
- Cecil Parker as Sir Halmar

External links

- *The Woman in the Hall* [1] at the Internet Movie Database
- Jack Lee [2] at the British Film Institute's Screenonline

References

[1] http://www.imdb.com/title/tt0039999/

[2] http://www.screenonline.org.uk/people/id/513342

They Do It with Mirrors

They Do It with Mirrors	
Dust-jacket illustration of the US (true first) edition. See *Publication history* (below) for UK first edition jacket image.	
Author(s)	Agatha Christie
Cover artist	Not known
Country	United States
Language	English
Genre(s)	Crime novel
Publisher	Dodd, Mead and Company
Publication date	1952
Media type	Print (Hardback & Paperback)
Pages	187 pp (first edition, hardback)
ISBN	NA
Preceded by	*Mrs McGinty's Dead*
Followed by	*A Daughter's a Daughter*

They Do It With Mirrors is a work of detective fiction by Agatha Christie and first published in the US by Dodd, Mead and Company in 1952 under the title of ***Murder with Mirrors***[1][2] and in UK by the Collins Crime Club on 17 November that year[3] under Christie's original title. The US edition retailed at $2.50 [2] and the UK edition at ten shillings and sixpence (10/6).[3] The book features her detective Miss Marple.

Plot summary

As the story opens, Jane Marple is paying a visit to her old friend Ruth Van Rydock. Miss Marple, Ruth, and Ruth's sister Carrie Louise were all friends together at the same school in Italy when they were girls. Ruth is worried that something is very wrong at Stonygates, the Victorian mansion where Carrie Louise lives with her husband Lewis Serrocold. She can't explain any real reason for these worries, but she fears that Carrie Louise may be in danger of some kind. Ruth asks Miss Marple to visit her and find out what is going on.

Carrie Louise is delighted to have Jane Marple for a visit at Stonygates. The old Victorian mansion, though owned outright by Carrie Louise, has been converted into a home for delinquent boys which is run by Carrie Louise's husband, Lewis Serrocold. Lewis Serrocold is actually Carrie Louise's third husband; she was also once widowed and once divorced. Carrie Louise has always been attracted to men who had their minds on noble causes. Her first husband, Mr. Gulbrandsen, was a great philanthropist, and Mr. Serrocold is devoted to the idea of reforming juvenile delinquents and teaching them how to contribute to society. The boys are involved in theatrical productions and many other activities around the estate during the day, but at night they are confined to their own quarters. The family has the central block of the house to themselves.

The family includes many people who are connected to each other only through Carrie Louise. Mildred Strete is the only blood relative of Carrie Louise who is resident at Stonygates. She is Carrie Louise's daughter by her first marriage. Carrie Louise also had an adopted daughter, Pippa, who died after giving birth to her own daughter, Gina. Now an adult, Gina is married to an American named Walter Hudd and has recently returned to Stonygates. Juliet Bellever (nicknamed Jolly), a longtime companion, caretaker, and friend of Carrie Louise is also a permanent fixture at the mansion. Stephen and Alex Restarick, Carrie Louise's stepsons from her second marriage, are also frequent visitors.

Also frequently present at Stonygates is Lewis Serrocold's assistant, Edgar Lawson. Edgar is an awkward young man whom the others dismiss as pompous and half-mad. He seems to suffer from both a persecution complex and delusions of grandeur. On several occasions he confides to others that he is the illegitimate son of a great man, and claims that powerful enemies are conspiring to keep him from his rightful position.

Christian Gulbrandsen, a member of the Stonygates Board of Trustees and the son of Carrie Louise's first husband from his previous marriage, arrives unexpectedly to see Lewis Serrocold. Everyone assumes he is there on business, but no one is sure exactly why. After dinner, Mr. Gulbrandsen retires to the guest room to type a letter. Miss Marple and the others gather in the Great Hall. A fuse blows out, and Walter goes to repair it.

Edgar Lawson bursts into the darkened room, screaming that Lewis Serrocold is his real father. Edgar and Mr. Serrocold go into the study and Edgar locks the door behind him. Everyone in the Great Hall listens intently as Edgar screams accusations at Mr. Serrocold, then they hear multiple gunshots. When the door is finally opened, they are surprised but relieved to see that Mr. Serrocold is alive and well, Edgar in tears, and several bullet holes in the walls.

Yet there has been a murder at Stonygates that night after all. When Juliet Bellever goes to check on Christian Gulbrandsen, she finds him dead. He was shot while working at his typewriter, and the letter he was writing is gone. Lewis Serrocold later reveals to the police that he took the letter to keep his wife from learning its contents. He explains that he and Mr. Gulbrandsen were both concerned that Carrie Louise's recent poor health was due to deliberate poisoning.

At that point, Alex Restarick, Stephen's brother(Carrie Louise's stepsons from her second marriage), arrives. He becomes the most likely suspect since the police who come to investigate find an unaccounted period of time between his arrival in the car and his appearance in the Great Hall.

Alex Restarick's remarks about stage scenery lead Miss Marple to reflect on all kinds of stage illusion, such as conjurers who perform magic by using mirrors and stage sets and assistants who are in on the trick. When Alex and a boy who claimed to have seen something on the night of the murder are both killed, Miss Marple realizes who has been behind the plotting at Stonygates: Lewis Serrocold. The attempted poisoning of Carrie Louise never happened; it was an explanation hastily concocted by Serrocold to explain Christian Gulbrandsen's sudden appearance at Stonygates and his secretive conference with Mr. Serrocold. In fact, Gulbrandsen had discovered that Mr. Serrocold was embezzling from the Gulbrandsen Trust, and Serrocold and his unstable accomplice, Edgar Lawson, killed him to silence him. The murder was accomplished via illusion and misdirection, as Alex Restarick and Miss Marple both eventually realized: "behind the scenes" of the interior of the house, which everyone had been focused on, there was a terrace by which someone could exit the study and re-enter the house to commit murder without being seen by the rest of the residents. This was what Mr. Serrocold had done, while Lawson, using his acting talents and different voices, had continued both sides of the loud argument by himself.

When confronted by the police, Edgar Lawson panics and flees the house, jumping into an old boat in an attempt to cross a lake on the property. The boat is rotted though, and as it begins to sink, Lewis Serrocold jumps into the lake to rescue his accomplice. Both men are caught in the reeds that line the lake, and drown before police are able to rescue them, bringing an end to the case.

Literary significance and reception

Maurice Richardson of *The Observer* of 30 November 1952 summed up thus: "First half is lively and the trick alibi for the murder of the stepson neat enough; there is a marked decline in sprightliness later on, but half a shot is better than no dope."[4]

Robert Barnard: "Unusual (and not entirely convincing) setting of delinquent's home, full of untrustworthy adolescents and untrustworthy do-gooders. Christie not entirely at home, perhaps because she believes (in Miss Marple's words) that 'young people with a good heredity, and brought up wisely in a good home...they are really...the sort of people a country *needs*.' Otherwise highly traditional, with houseplans, Marsh-y inquisitions, and second and third murders done most perfunctorily. Definite signs of decline."[5]

Film, TV or theatrical adaptations

The novel's first adaptation was as *Murder with Mirrors* in 1985 for television with Sir John Mills as Lewis Serrocold, Bette Davis as Carrie Louise, Tim Roth as Edgar Lawson and Helen Hayes as Miss Marple.

It was adapted again for the BBC series *Miss Marple* starring Joan Hickson as Miss Marple, Jean Simmons as Carrie-Louise Serrocold, Joss Ackland as Lewis Serrocold and Faith Brook as Ruth van Rydock; first broadcast on 29 December 1991. The film was basically faithful to the novel, with the exception that Alex survives the attack on his life.

It was adapted for the fourth season of *Marple*, starring Julia McKenzie as Miss Marple, Penelope Wilton as Carrie Louise Serrocold, Brian Cox as Lewis Serrocold, and Joan Collins as Ruth Van Rydock. It was broadcast on 1 January 2010.

Some elements of the plot were also incorporated into the 1964 film *Murder Ahoy!*, which starred Margaret Rutherford as Miss Marple, along with a token tribute to *The Mousetrap*. Instead of a sprawling Victorian estate, the delinquent boys are housed on board a retired ship called the Battledore, and they go ashore periodically to commit mischief under the direction of their criminal mastermind. Apart from these elements, however, this film is not based on any of Christie's works.

Publication history

- 1952, Dodd Mead and Company (New York), 1952, Hardback, 187 pp
- 1952, Collins Crime Club (London), 17 November 1952, Hardback, 192 pp
- 1954, Pocket Books (New York), Paperback, 165 pp
- 1956, Fontana Books (Imprint of HarperCollins), Paperback, 187 pp
- 1966, Ulverscroft Large-print Edition, Hardcover, 224 pp
- 1969, Greenway edition of collected works (William Collins), Hardcover, 223 pp
- 1970, Greenway edition of collected works (Dodd Mead), Hardcover, 223 pp
- 1974, Pan Books, Paperback, 187 pp
- 2005, Marple Facsimile edition (Facsimile of 1952 UK first edition), 7 November 2005, Hardcover, ISBN 0-00-720847-2

A condensed version of the novel was first published in the US in *Cosmopolitan* magazine in the issue for April 1952 (Volume 132, Number 4) under the title *Murder With Mirrors* with illustrations by Joe Bowler.

In the UK the novel was first serialised in the weekly magazine *John Bull* in six abridged instalments from 26 April (Volume 91, Number 2391) to 31 May 1952 (Volume 91, Number 2396) with illustrations by George Ditton.[6]

International titles

- Czech: *Smysluplná vražda* (A Meaningful Murder)
- German: *Fata Morgana* (Fata Morgana)

References

[1] John Cooper and B.A. Pyke. *Detective Fiction - the collector's guide*: Second Edition (Pages 82 and 87) Scholar Press. 1994. ISBN 0-85967-991-8

[2] American Tribute to Agatha Christie (http://home.insightbb.com/~jsmarcum/agatha45.htm)

[3] Chris Peers, Ralph Spurrier and Jamie Sturgeon. *Collins Crime Club – A checklist of First Editions*. Dragonby Press (Second Edition) March 1999 (Page 15)

[4] *The Observer* 30 November 1952 (Page 9)

[5] Barnard, Robert. *A Talent to Deceive – an appreciation of Agatha Christie* - Revised edition (Page 207). Fontana Books, 1990. ISBN 0-00-637474-3

[6] Holdings at the British Library (Newspapers - Colindale). Shelfmark: NPL LON LD116.

External links

- *They Do It With Mirrors* (http://www.agathachristie.com/story-explorer/stories/they-do-it-with-mirrors-1/) at the official Agatha Christie website
- *Murder with Mirrors (1985)* (http://www.imdb.com/title/tt0089640/) at the Internet Movie Database
- *They Do It with Mirrors (1991)* (http://www.imdb.com/title/tt0103078/) at the Internet Movie Database
- *Marple: They Do It with Mirrors (2009)* (http://www.imdb.com/title/tt1297403/) at the Internet Movie Database

This Could Be the Night (film)

This Could Be the Night	
VHS Cover	
Directed by	Robert Wise
Produced by	Joe Pasternak
Written by	**Short Story:** Cornelia Baird Gross **Screenplay:** Isobel Lennart
Starring	Jean Simmons Paul Douglas
Cinematography	Russell Harlan
Editing by	George Boemler
Distributed by	Metro-Goldwyn-Mayer
Release date(s)	May 14, 1957
Running time	104 minutes
Country	United States
Language	English

This Could Be the Night is a 1957 MGM comedy-drama film directed by Robert Wise. The movie is based on the short stories by Cornelia Baird Gross and stars Jean Simmons and Paul Douglas. Actor Anthony Franciosa made his debut in this film.

Plot

Anne Leeds is a school teacher with only four weeks of experience. She takes a part-time job as a secretary to an ex-bootlegger and horse playing gambler by the name of Rocco. He's a Broadway nightclub owner with a heart of gold who eventually falls in love with Anne. However, he knows he's too old for her, so keeps his feelings to himself.

Eventually, Anne finds that she "thinks" she's in love with his younger partner Tony Armotti, a typical playboy type who is afraid to fall in love because it might mean marriage. Tony lives in a walkup apartment above the nightclub, where he often entertains beautiful women. The stairs to the apartment are on the alley behind the club.

The entire nightclub loves Anne but Tony resents her because he wants to take care of her and protect her. Eventually after confronting Tony, Anne quits because Tony tells her he does not love her and never will. After she quits the entire nightclub patronizes Tony over whether Anne quit or was fired; So he goes to where she is currently working and after helping her escape when police raid the gambling den, convinces her to take back the job she quit from. The movie ends with Ivy singing This Could Be the Night.

Cast

- Jean Simmons – *Anne Leeds*
- Paul Douglas – *Rocco*
- Anthony Franciosa – *Tony Armotti*
- Julie Wilson – *Ivy Corlane*
- Neile Adams – *Patsy St. Clair*
- Joan Blondell – *Crystal St. Clair*
- J. Carrol Naish – *Leon*
- Rafael Campos – *Hussein Mohammed*
- Zasu Pitts – *Mrs. Katie Shea*
- Tom Helmore – *Stowe Devlin*
- Murvyn Vye – *Waxie London*
- Vaughn Taylor – *Ziggy Dawit*
- Frank Ferguson – *Mr. Shea*
- Chuck Berry – *Cameo appearance*
- June Blair – *Chorus Girl*
- Bess Flowers – *Nightclub Extra*

External links

- *This Could Be the Night* [1] at the Internet Movie Database

References

[1] http://www.imdb.com/title/tt0051074/

This Earth Is Mine (1959 film)

This Earth Is Mine	
Directed by	Henry King
Written by	Alice Tisdale Hobart (novel) Casey Robinson (screenplay)
Starring	Rock Hudson Jean Simmons Claude Rains Dorothy McGuire
Distributed by	Universal International Pictures
Release date(s)	June 26, 1959
Running time	124 minutes
Country	United States
Language	English
Box office	$3.4 million (est. US/ Canada rentals)[1]

This Earth Is Mine is a 1959 American drama film directed by Henry King and starring Rock Hudson and Jean Simmons. The film portrays the lives and loves of the Rambeau family, a California winemaking dynasty trying to survive during Prohibition in the United States.

Summary

Elizabeth (Jean Simmons), an English cousin of the Rambeau family, arrives in California in 1931 for a casual visit with her aunt and uncle, only to find her future pre-determined with a pre-arranged marriage to Andre Swann, a young cousin of another branch of the family. Another cousin, John Rambeau (Rock Hudson), disagrees with those plans, informs Elizabeth that she's being married off to consolidate the family's wine holdings, hints at other dark secrets of the Rambeau family, and casually romances her. Elizabeth is conflicted over the entire series of events.

The patriarch of the family, Phillipe (Claude Rains), wanting to keep the winemaking heritage of his family pure, refuses to deal with bootleggers eager for a ready-made supply of alcohol. John, however, is not so righteous, and arranges deals with Chicago gangsters for the valley's wine supply. Violence, gunplay, and wildfires ensue. Elizabeth is caught in the middle, between Andre, the gentle man she is to marry (but who wants to be a priest) and John, the passionate man ready to make a deal with the devil to survive. And John may already have started a family of his own, fathering an illegitimate child with a vinyard worker—and the woman's husband is not one to go along with the whole sordid mess. Months, and years, of lies, blackmail and conflict follow, ending with the romantic union of John and Elizabeth, and their commitment to the Rambeau winemaking heritage.

Plot

In 1931, Lon Rambeau sends his daughter Elizabeth Rambeau away from London to Napa Valley, California to visit Lon's father Philippe Rambeau and Phillipe's sister Martha Fairon, owners of vast vineyards and a grand estate. Philippe and Martha welcome Elizabeth lavishly, then reveal the real reason for the celebration of her arrival: her betrothal, unknown to Elizabeth, between her and her cousin, Andre Swann. John Rambeau, obviously disliked by matriarch Martha, arrives at the party, flirts with Elizabeth and leads her out into the vineyards, where he mischievously reveals Rambeau family secrets: Philippe uses marriage to tighten the family hold on the valley; Phillipe's sister Martha and daughter Charlotte (John's mother) had been married off to local landowners in order to increase the vineyard holdings — Phillipe now wants to marry off grand-daughter Elizabeth to Andre in order to absorb the Stag's Leap Winery (also, Andre had wanted to become a priest, but was not allowed to do so, and had been forced to join the family business).

Continuing his explanation, John points out his house nearby, where his invalid mother Charlotte now lives, and says that he now knows that Martha's husband (John's uncle, Francis Fairon) is his real father, even though everyone claims that Charlotte's late husband had been the biological father to both John and his sister Monica. John then takes the speechless Elizabeth into his arms and kisses her, but she pulls away and runs into the house.

The next day, John gets into an argument with Philippe by insisting that they ignore Prohibition laws and sell their grapes (and wine) to bootleggers. Philippe, who loves John, insists on remaining lawful, explaining once again how he will continue to cultivate and study wines until the time comes to sell them legally. John volunteers to show Elizabeth around the winery, bitterly pointing out the vast stores of wine going to waste. When he asks her about her past and tries to kiss her again, she once again pulls away. As they wander the estate, one of the female workers, Buz Dietrick, flirts with John. Back at the house, Martha spirits Elizabeth away to a lunch with Andre, who is quite comfortable with the idea of an arranged marriage.

Meeting with the local association of grape growers, John tells them that he will make them rich by selling their grapes to a syndicate in Chicago. Some of the traditional growers insist on gaining Philippe's approval first. Ignoring them, John leaves for Chicago to meet with the syndicate — soon after, thugs arrive in the Napa Valley and force the growers to sign contracts.

When John returns to Napa months later, the growers, now grown rich from John's arrangement with the Chicago syndicate, welcome him warmly. John meets the growers at a nightclub, where he finds Buz sitting with her boyfriend, Luigi Griffanti. They all watch Elizabeth and Andre (still not married) dance. John once again romances Elizabeth, who, hoping to dissuade his interest, reveals to him that her father had sent her away from England because she had been involved in a torrid love affair with a cruel man, and she now desires a safe marriage with Andre. A jealous John accuses her of "prostituting" herself for real estate, and she slaps him. John then turns to Buz for comfort, convincing her to leave Luigi and drive off with him. Later, Andre drives Elizabeth home, where he confesses that he is growing to love her. Inside, Martha, aware of Elizabeth's ambivalent feelings over John, confronts her about her past, urging her to marry Andre before he realizes he is getting "damaged goods."

John returns home and tells his mother he will leave the next day for Chicago. The next day Elizabeth, having had a change of heart, races off to see John before his train leaves — she finds him at the station and tells him she loves him. Thrilled, John insists that she wait for his return.

A few months later, a pregnant Buz shows up at the estate to inform Phillipe that the baby is John's — Buz and her father blackmail Philippe. Elizabeth, nearby, hears all, and collapses with grief. Martha directs Buz to tell Luigi the baby is his. Buz and Luigi soon marry, but she fights with both him and his mother when they want to name the baby Cesare, and she wants to name the baby ... John.

Months pass. Martha tries to convince an impatient Andre to wait for Elizabeth to set a wedding date. When John finally returns to Napa Valley, Elizabeth is up in the mountain orchard with Philippe, listening to him explain that this is sacred ground to him, as it was his first plot of land, and his beloved wife is buried here. At the estate, Martha greets John coldly and warns him that he must now conduct business through her, because Philippe is ill. After successfully persuading Martha that they can make millions by selling the Rambeau grapes to the Chicago syndicate, John drives to the mountain orchard. There, Philippe, horrified by John's shady dealings, commands him to leave, as does Elizabeth, who tells him she knows the truth about Buz's baby. Protesting that he can prove that Buz has lied, John races away, accidentally throwing a lit cigarette into the parched fields, starting a blaze. By the time the fire is noticed, it is too late, and the out-of-control wildfire destroys most of the mountain orchard.

Unaware of the fire, John rushes to Buz's house, where mother-in-law Griffanti, upon hearing John's name, figures out that John is her grandson's actual father. As Buz agrees that she will tell Elizabeth that the baby is not John's, Luigi, at his mother's urging, attacks John in a jealous rage. John manages to get away, but Luigi pulls out a gun and shoots him.

At the hospital, John is diagnosed with temporary partial paralysis — when Elizabeth visits to beg his forgiveness, he turns away from her bitterly. Soon, he is able to walk with crutches, and returns home, where he tells his uncle Francis and mother Charlotte that he knows about their affair, which resulted in his birth. John takes the blame for the orchard fire — in return, he forgives the two of them for their deceit, and asks for their forgiveness in exchange.

Months later, Philippe dies, and matriarch Martha gathers the family together for the reading of the will. To Martha's shock and dismay, Philippe has divided the estate equally between his children and grandchildren — he also leaves the mountain orchard to John, the valley vineyards to the still-unmarried Elizabeth, and nothing to Martha. Although Martha is greatly pained by what she sees as an injustice, both she and her husband Francis realize that now she will finally be more interested in her husband and her marriage, instead of the family business.

Within a few weeks, John has restored his mountain orchard to health. One day, Elizabeth joins him with a gift: a grape vine cutting from her valley vineyard. They graft the valley cutting onto a mountain vine, talk about the melding of "valley sweetness" with "mountain strength", and, finally, fall into each other's arms, declaring their love for each other.

Production

The screenplay for the film, based on the novel *The Cup and the Sword* by American novelist Alice Tisdale Hobart was written by Casey Robinson, best known for writing most of Bette Davis' best films. Director Henry King had been successfully directing Hollywood films since the 1920s — this film was one of his last. Film composer Hugo Friedhofer (who had won an Oscar for Best Music for 1946's *The Best Years of Our Lives*) wrote the music; three-time Oscar-winner Winton C. Hoch was the cinematographer.

Production company was Vintage Productions, in partnership with Universal–International Pictures. Production dates for the film were September 2, 1958 through early November, 1958. The production was filmed in Technicolor, with monoaural sound. Napa Valley locations used for filming were:

• Beaulieu Vineyard
• Beringer Vineyards
• Cella Vineyards
• Charles Krug Vineyards
• Christian Brothers Vineyards
• Inglenook Winery
• Italian Swiss Colony Vineyards
• Louis M. Martini Vineyards
• Mayacamas Vineyards
• Paul Masson Mountain Winery
• Schramsberg Vineyards
• Sebastiani Vineyards
• Stags' Leap Winery (name actually mentioned as part of the plot)
• Sucram Ranch

Local residents of the Napa Valley were used as extras in some scenes,[2] and the stars were taught proper vineyard procedures by locals — a difficulty for left-handed Rock Hudson, for whom a left-handed teacher had to be found to demonstrate the proper way to attach a bud from one plant to the root of another,[3] a scene important to the plot at the end of the film.

The New York opening of the film was June 26, 1959; the Los Angeles opening was July 8, 1959.

Cast

Credited roles

- Rock Hudson played John Rambeau
- Jean Simmons played Elizabeth Rambeau
- Dorothy McGuire played Martha Fairon
- Claude Rains played Philippe Rambeau
- Kent Smith played Francis Fairon
- Anna Lee played Charlotte Rambeau
- Ken Scott played Luigi Griffanti
- Augusta Merighi played Mrs. Griffanti
- Francis Bethencourt played Andre Swann
- Stacy Graham played Monica
- Peter Chong played Chu
- Geraldine Wall played Maria
- Alberto Morin played Petucci
- Penny Santon played Mrs. Petucci
- Jack Mather played Dietrich
- Ben Astar played Yakowitz
- Dan White played Judge Gruber
- Lawrence Ung played David, the Chauffeur
- Robert Aiken played Tim Rambeau (as Ford Dunhill)
- Cynthia Chenault played Buz Dietrick (as Cindy Robbins)
- Don Cornell played Singer of Title Song (voice)

Uncredited roles

- Lionel Ames played Nate Forster
- Jean Blake played Suzanne
- Olga Borget played Bit Part
- Gino DeAgustino played The Porter
- Adonis De Milo played Mamoulian
- George DeNormand played Ronald Fairon
- Paul King played Bit Part
- Karyn Kupcinet played Clarissa Smith
- Alexander Lockwood played Dr. Regis
- Torben Meyer played Hugo
- Thomas Murray played Bit Part
- Emma Palmese played Bit Part
- Emory Parnell played Berke
- Josephine Parra played Juanita
- Janelle Richards played Cousin
- Ethel Sway played Bit Part
- Philip Tonge played Dr. Albert Stone
- Cecil Weston played Rambeau friend

Critical reception

The film was not well-received:

- VARIETY (January 1, 1959): *This film is almost completely lacking in dramatic cohesion. It is verbose and contradictory, and its complex plot relationships from Alice Tisdale Hobart's novel, "The Cup and the Sword" begin with confusion and end in tedium.*[4]
- New York Times (June 27, 1959): *In describing the intramural trials and tribulations besetting a wealthy clan of California vineyard owners, under the title "This Earth Is Mine," Universal-International has come up with an ambitious family saga as handsome as it is hollow. ... It opened yesterday at the Roxy, where the grapes stole the show.*[5]

... although the winemaking community appears to have enjoyed it:

- *The film gives simple-to-understand descriptions of both the winemaking process and how to taste and appreciate wine. It's bad melodrama, but it's first class Napa Valley history.*[6]

References

[1] "1959: Probable Domestic Take", *Variety*, 6 January 1960 p 34

[2] Online archive of (http://napavalleyregister.com/lifestyles/real-napa/article_43598b32-5b19-11df-90f6-001cc4c002e0.html) Brennan, Nancy S. (May 9, 2010) "DEAD MEN & WOMEN DO TELL TALES: The keys to a rich life" article in Napa Valley Register

[3] Chip bud grafting / This Earth is mine (http://pinanapavalley.blogspot.com/2008/12/chip-bud-grafting-this-earth-is-mine.html) (December 11, 2008) webpage of the Piña Napa Valley (http://pinanapavalley.blogspot.com/) website

[4] "This Earth Is Mine" (review by Film Staff), VARIETY Magazine, (January 1, 1959) (http://www.variety.com/review/VE1117795653.html?categoryid=31&cs=1&p=0) in Online VARIETY article archive

[5] "This Earth Is Mine" (Movie Review) New York Times (June 27, 1959) (http://movies.nytimes.com/movie/review?res=9C07E6D71E3CE63BBC4F51DFB0668382649EDE) in the online New York Times article archive

[6] Movies of the Vine — Nine Films about Wine (http://eastcoastwineries.blogspot.com/2009/07/movies-of-vine-eight-films-about-wine.html) (July 3, 2009) webpage (with an "This Earth Is Mine" movie poster) on the East Coast Wineries (http://eastcoastwineries.blogspot.com/) website

External links

- *This Earth Is Mine* (http://www.imdb.com/title/tt0053355/) at the Internet Movie Database
- *This Earth Is Mine* (http://tcmdb.com/title/title.jsp?stid=92953) at the TCM Movie Database

Turner Classic Movies

Turner Classic Movies	
Launched	April 14, 1994
Owned by	Turner Broadcasting System (Time Warner)
Picture format	480i (SDTV) 1080i (HDTV)
Country	United States
Broadcast area	Nationwide (also available in Canada with substitutions; international versions in Spain, Asia, Latin America, U.K. and Ireland)
Headquarters	Atlanta, Georgia, United States
Sister channel(s)	TBS, TNT, Cartoon Network, Boomerang, CNN, HLN, TruTV (United States) TCM 2 (UK & Ireland)
Website	TCM.com [1]
Availability	
Satellite	
DirecTV	Channel 256 (SD/HD) Channel 1256 (VOD)
Dish Network	Channel 132 (SD/HD)
DSTV	Channel 109
Tata Sky (India)	Channel 357
n	Channel 44
Cable	
UPC Poland	Channel 487
IPTV	
AT&T U-verse	Channel 790 (SD) Channel 1790 (HD)
Verizon FiOS	Channel 230
Bell Fibe TV (Canada)	Channel 292

Turner Classic Movies (TCM) is an American movie-oriented cable television channel, owned by the Turner Broadcasting System, a subsidiary of Time Warner, featuring commercial-free classic movies, mostly from the Turner Entertainment film library, which comprises the pre-May 1986 MGM, RKO and pre-1950 Warner Bros. films. TCM is headquartered at the Techwood Campus in Atlanta, Georgia, in Midtown.

About TCM

Turner Classic Movies is essentially commercial-free, advertising only TCM products, promos for specific films scheduled to air on the channel in primetime, typically using the film's original movie trailer. It also airs promos for special programming and featurettes about classic film actors and actresses in between features. TCM's content has also remained mostly uncut and uncolorized (depending upon the original content of movies, particularly movies rated by the MPAA after 1968). Because of the uncut and commercial-free nature of the channel, TCM is formatted similarly to a premium channel; as such, viewers might find that certain films, particularly those made from the 1960s onward, may feature nudity, sexual content, violence and strong profanity; the channel also features premium channel-style ratings bumpers seconds before a film starts.

From time to time, the channel shows restored versions of films, particularly old silent films with newly commissioned musical soundtracks. TCM is also a major backer of WGBH's Descriptive Video Service program, and many of the films aired on the network have visual description for the blind and visually impaired, which are accessible through the SAP option through a television or cable/satellite receiver.

As a result, viewers interested in tracing the career development of actresses like Barbara Stanwyck or Greta Garbo or actors like Cary Grant or Humphrey Bogart have the unique opportunity to see most of the feature films made during their careers, from beginning to end. Unlike AMC and Fox Movie Channel, Turner Classic Movies presents many of its features in their original screen aspect ratio (widescreen or full screen) whenever possible. TCM also regularly presents widescreen presentations of films not available in the format on any home video release. In 2008, TCM was given a Peabody Award for excellence in broadcasting.[2]

History

Eight years before the launch of TCM, Ted Turner had acquired Metro-Goldwyn-Mayer, but shortly after sold the studio while retaining the library for itself. The vast library of Turner Entertainment would serve as the base program upon its launch; Turner Classic Movies officially debuted on April 14, 1994 at 6 p.m. ET with Ted Turner ceremonially launching the channel in New York City's Times Square district.[3][4] The date was chosen for its significance as "the exact centennial anniversary of the first public movie showing in New York City." The very first movie ever screened on TCM was the 1939 classic epic *Gone with the Wind*, exactly what its sister station, TNT, had aired as its debut program six years before.

At the time of its launch, TCM was available to only approximately one million cable subscribers;[5] the channel served as a competitor of AMC (at the time, called American Movie Classics), which had a virtually identical format to TCM as both cable channels ran mostly pre-1970 films; though by 2002, AMC had reformatted itself to feature films from all eras, leaving TCM as the only cable movie channel devoted entirely to classic films.

Before the creation of TCM, quite a few titles from its vast library of movies were broadcast – with commercial interruptions – on Turner's TNT channel, along with Turner's controversial colorized versions of black-and-white classics such as *The Maltese Falcon*. When TCM was created in 1994, however, colorization did not carry over to the new channel. As Gary R. Edgerton wrote in the winter 2000 issue of *The Journal of Popular Film and Television*, TCM immediately advertised itself in April 1994 "with the promise: 'uninterrupted, uncolorized and commercial-free!' Attitudes had evidently come full circle. Colorization was now unfashionable and unprofitable — even for Ted Turner and his colleagues at TBS."

In 1996, the Turner Broadcasting System merged with Time Warner. Not only did this put TCM and Warner Bros. under the same corporate umbrella, but it also gave TCM access to the post-1949 Warner Bros. library (which itself includes other acquired properties such as the Lorimar, Saul Zaentz, and National General Pictures libraries); incidentally, TCM had already been running some of Warner's film titles through a licensing agreement with the studio made prior to the launch of the channel.[6]

In 2000, TCM launched the annual Young Composers Film Competition [7], inviting aspiring composers to participate in a judged competition. Grand prize has been the opportunity to score a restored, feature-length silent film, mentored by a well-known composer, with subsequent premiere of the new work on the TCM channel. As of 2006, films which have been rescored include *Camille* (1921) with Rudolph Valentino, two Lon Chaney films, *Ace of Hearts* (1921) and *Laugh, Clown, Laugh* (1928), and Greta Garbo's *The Temptress* (1926).

More recently, TCM has collaborated in boxed set DVD releases of previously unreleased films by noted actors, directors, or studios. The sets often include bonus discs including documentaries and shorts from the TCM library. In April 2010, TCM held the first TCM Classic Film Festival, at the Grauman's Chinese Theater and the Grauman's Egyptian Theater in Hollywood. Hosted by Robert Osborne, the four-day long annual festival celebrated Hollywood and its movies, and featured celebrity appearances, special events and screenings of around 50 classic movies including several newly restored by the Film Foundation, an organization devoted to preserving Hollywood's classic film legacy.[8] Upon completion of the festival, TCM announced that they would hold a second festival in 2011.[9]

From July to December 2011, Osborne was on medical leave; guest hosts presented each night's films.[10]

Programming

TCM's vast library of films spans several decades of cinema and includes thousands of film titles. TCM's programming season runs from February until the following March of each year when a retrospective of Oscar-winning and Oscar-nominated movies is shown, called *31 Days of Oscar*. Gaps between features are filled with theatrically released movie trailers and classic short subjects (from series such as *The Passing Parade*, *Crime Does Not Pay*, *Pete Smith Specialties*, Robert Benchley, etc.) under the banner name *TCM Extras* (formerly *One Reel Wonders*). In 2007, some of the short films featured on TCM began appearing on TCM's website. In part to allow these interstitials, Turner Classic Movies airs its feature films at the top or bottom to the hour, or at one-quarter past or before the hour, instead of in varying time slots. The network also airs original content, mostly documentaries about classic movie personalities and particularly notable films.

Movie library

Besides MGM, United Artists[11] and Warner Bros. releases, TCM also shows films under license from Universal Studios, Paramount Pictures, 20th Century Fox, Walt Disney Productions, Columbia Pictures, StudioCanal and Janus Films. Most pre-1950 Paramount releases are owned by EMKA, Ltd./NBCUniversal Television Distribution, while Paramount (currently owned by Viacom) holds on to most of its post-1949 releases, which are handled for television by Trifecta Entertainment & Media. Columbia's output is owned by Sony through Sony Pictures Television, the films of 20th Century Fox (owned by the News Corporation), are handled for television by 20th Television, and Walt Disney Productions (owned by The Walt Disney Company) has their output handled for television by Disney-ABC Domestic Television. TCM occasionally shows some classic films from 20th Century Fox,[12] Paramount Pictures,[13] Universal Studios, Columbia Pictures and Toho Company Ltd., but they are licensed individually.

Although a vast majority of the movies shown on Turner Classic Movies are from the 1930s through 1960s, some are more contemporary; it is not uncommon for TCM to air films released in the 1970s, 1980s or (nowadays) the 1990s and the early 2000s.

Hosted and special programming

Most feature movies shown in prime time (8 p.m.-2:30 a.m. Eastern Time) are presented by film historian Robert Osborne, who has been with the network since its launch in 1994. Osborne is occasionally joined by guest programmers responsible for choosing that evening's films; examples of such programmers during 2012 include Jules Feiffer, Anthony Bourdain, Debra Winger, Ellen Barkin, Spike Lee, Regis Philbin, and Jim Lehrer.[14] Recently, movies shown during the daytime on weekends feature host Ben Mankiewicz, Herman J. Mankiewicz's grandson and great-nephew of Joseph L. Mankiewicz. Mankiewicz also hosted the network's *Cartoon Alley* series featuring classic animation, which aired on Saturday mornings between 2004 and 2007.

The Essentials is a weekly program on Saturdays, spotlighting a specific movie and containing a special introduction and post-movie discussion; the spotlight movie is often replayed the following Sunday at 6 p.m. ET. The current hosts are Osborne and Drew Barrymore. Each August, TCM suspends its regular schedule for a special "month of stars", featuring entire days devoted to a single star, offering movies and specials pertaining to the star of the day; however, Turner Classic Movies airs a "Star of the Month" year-round, except during special programming, in which every Wednesday during each month starting at 8 p.m. ET the majority of (if not all) feature films from a classic film star are shown during primetime and the late night/early morning hours. A star's birthday is also an occasion for a one-day or one-evening festival showing several of that artist's best, earliest, or least-known pictures.

"Silent Sunday Nights", airing Sunday nights, features silent films from the United States and abroad, usually in the latest restored version and often with new music scores; "Silent Sunday Nights" is occasionally pre-empted for other special programming. Following the "Silent Sunday Nights" feature(s), "TCM Imports" airing on Sunday nights around 2 a.m. ET, is a weekly presentation that features foreign films; "TCM Imports" previously ran on Saturdays until the early 2000s. TCM also features a monthly program block called the "TCM Guest Programmer", in which once a month the channel features a selection of films that are favorites of that month's celebrity guest, in which the guest discusses the film with Robert Osborne (an offshoot of this block featuring TCM employees was done throughout the month of February 2011). In addition, TCM occasionally commemorates a recent death of a classic film star by running a 24-hour marathon of their signature film work in their honor.

In December 1998, TCM debuted "TCM Remembers", which is a tribute to recently deceased notable film personalities (actors, producers, composers, directors, writers, cinematographers, etc.) airing occasionally during promo breaks between films. The segments appear in two forms: individual tributes and a longer end-of-year compilation. Following the recent death of an especially famous film personality (usually an actor or director), the segment will feature a montage of select shots of the deceased's work. During the second half of each December, a longer, more inclusive "TCM Remembers" interstitial is run honoring most or all of the noted film personalities who died during the last year. The soundtracks for these clipreels are introspective melodies by indie artists such as Badly Drawn Boy (2007) or Steve Earle (2009).[15] Very often, when a well-known actor, producer, or director dies, the network will devote an entire day's schedule to showing movies associated with the individual, airing within days following the person's death.

In October 2006, the network premiered *TCM Underground*, a Friday late-night series hosted by rocker/filmmaker Rob Zombie, which features a number of cult films personally selected by Zombie. Films in the series include *Plan 9 from Outer Space* (1959), *Sisters* (1973), *Night of the Living Dead* (1968), *Bride of the Monster* (1955), *Faster, Pussycat! Kill! Kill!* (1965), and *Electra Glide in Blue* (1973). Rob Zombie no longer hosts "TCM Underground", and the presentation no longer has a host.

In the summer of 2007, the network began airing "Funday Night at the Movies", hosted by voice-over actor Tom Kenny (best known as the voice of SpongeBob SquarePants). This series of programming, which lasted throughout the summer, brought classic films such as *The Wizard of Oz* (1939), *Sounder* (1972), *Bringing Up Baby* (1938), *Singin' in the Rain* (1952), *Mr. Smith Goes to Washington* (1939), *The Adventures of Robin Hood* (1938), and *20,000 Leagues Under the Sea* (1954) to a whole new generation of children and their families.

For the summer of 2008, TCM launched "Essentials Jr.", a youth-oriented version of its *The Essentials* weekly series hosted by actors Abigail Breslin and Chris O'Donnell, which included such family-themed films as *National Velvet* (1944), *The Courtship of Eddie's Father* (1963), *Meet Me in St. Louis* (1944), *Captains Courageous* (1937), and *Yours, Mine and Ours* (1968), as well as more eclectic selections as *Sherlock Jr.* (1924), *The Music Box* (1932), *Harvey* (1950), *20 Million Miles to Earth* (1957), *Mutiny on the Bounty* (1935), *On the Town* (1949), and *The Man Who Knew Too Much* (1956). In 2009, John Lithgow became the host of "The Essentials Jr." All featured programming has their own distinctive feature presentation open for the particular scheduled presentation. Bill Hader serves as host of the 2011 season of *Essentials, Jr.*

An occasional month-long series, *Race and Hollywood*, showcases films by and about people of non-white races, featuring discussions of how these pictures influenced white people's image of said races, as well as how people of those races viewed themselves. Previous installments have included "Asian Images on Film" (2008),[16] "Native American Images on Film" (2010),[17] "Black Images on Film" in 2006[18] "Latino Images on Film" (2009)[19] and "Arab Images on Film" (2011).[20] The channel aired the film series *Screened Out* exploring gay images on film in 2007 and "Religion on Film" in 2005.

In 2011 TCM debuted a new television series entitled *AFI's Master Class: The Art of Collaboration.*[21][22]

TCM Remembers

TCM airs annual tributes to filmmakers and actors who have died in the past year, as well as individual tributes following the death of a major film star or director. The clipreels are produced by Sabotage Film Group, which specializes in music videos and promotional material.[23]

- TCM Remembers 1998: composer John Addison, Gene Autry, Binnie Barnes, Lloyd Bridges, Dane Clark, art director George Davis, John Derek, special effects visual Linwood G. Dunn, Alice Faye, Norman Fell, editor Gene Fowler, Jr., Douglas Fowley, Patricia Hayes, Valerie Hobson, Josephine Hutchinson, director Alan J. Pakula, Leonid Kinskey, director Akira Kurosawa, cinematographer Charles Lang, Phil Leeds, Jean Marais, E. G. Marshall, Roddy McDowall, Jeanette Nolan, Lucille Norman, Maidie Norman, Dick O'Neill, Maureen O'Sullivan, composer Gene Page, choreographer Jerome Robbins, Gene Raymond, Roy Rogers, Esther Rolle, Frank Sinatra, J. T. Walsh, Vincent Winter, O. Z. Whitehead, cinematographer Freddie Young and Robert Young.

- TCM Remembers 1999: Iron Eyes Cody, Betty Lou Gerson, Huntz Hall, Susan Strasberg, film critic Gene Siskel, Richard Kiley, director Stanley Kubrick, Garson Kanin, composer Ernest Gold, Ellen Corby, Charles "Buddy" Rogers, Rory Calhoun, Dirk Bogarde, Oliver Reed, DeForest Kelley, Bobs Watson, director Allan Carr, Sylvia Sidney, screenwriter Mario Puzo, screenwriter Norman Wexler, Ruth Roman, director Edward Dmytryk, director Charles Crichton, Victor Mature, editor Harold F. Kress, George C. Scott, Ian Bannen, Mabel King, Madeline Kahn and Desmond Llewelyn.

- TCM Remembers 2000: Douglas Fairbanks, Jr., Nancy Coleman, Rose Hobart, Muriel Evans, Steve Reeves, Gwen Verdon, Francis Lederer, Nan Leslie, director Don Weis, director Roger Vadim, Joan Marsh, Billy Barty, costume designer Bill Thomas, Max Showalter, Vittorio Gassman, Marie Windsor, Craig Stevens, David Tomlinson, Richard Farnsworth, director Claude Autant-Lara, film preserver James Card, Beah Richards, Julie London, Marceline Day, Nancy Marchand, Harold Nicholas, Nils Poppe, director Joseph H. Lewis, composer George Duning, director Lewis Allen, Ann Doran, Jean Peters, editor David Bretherlen, writer Curt Siodmak, screenwriter Ring Lardner, Jr., Alec Guinness, Loretta Young, Jason Robards, John Gielgud, Hedy Lamarr, Claire Trevor and Walter Matthau.

- TCM Remembers 2001: Anthony Quinn, Jack Lemmon, Rosemary DeCamp, Jacques Marin, Charlotte Coleman, Kathleen Freeman, Corinne Calvet, Ray Walston, Eleanor Summerfield, Jane Greer, David Graf, screenwriter Ken Hughes, Larry Tucker, cinematographer Henri Alekan, director Budd Boetticher, Herbert Ross, Wilkie Cooper, animator William Hanna, Paul Berry, Nancy Parsons, Tommy Hollis, Aaliyah, Eileen Heckart, Dale Earnhardt and George Harrison.

- TCM Remembers 2002: William Warfield, director George Sidney, Signe Hasso, Brad Dexter, producer Lew Wasserman, Ted Ashley, Lawrence Tierney, Leo McKern, Kim Hunter, John Agar, Jeff Corey, Dolores Gray, producer J. Lee Thompson, Eddie Bracken, Katy Jurado, animator Chuck Jones, Harold Russell, Eileen Heckart, Jack Kruschen, Buddy Lester, Adolph Green, director André de Toth, producer Richard Sylbert, Milton Berle, director Billy Wilder, director John Frankenheimer, Dudley Moore, Richard Harris, Rod Steiger and James Coburn.

- TCM Remembers 2003: Karen Morley, Penny Singleton, Donald O'Connor, David Hemmings, Art Carney, screenwriter David Newman, cinematographer Conrad Hall, director George Roy Hill, director Leni Riefenstahl, Kenneth Tobey, John Ritter, director Norman Panama, composer Michael Kamen, Martha Scott, Hume Cronyn, Buddy Hackett, Johnny Cash, Hope Lange, Richard Crenna, Sheb Wooley, Jack Elam, Gregory Hines, screenwriter George Axelrod, screenwriter Peter Stone, producer Philip Yordan, director Elia Kazan, Jeanne Crain, Horst Buchholz, Wendy Hiller, Bob Hope, screenwriter Daniel Taradash, Buddy Ebsen, director John Schlesinger, Robert Stack, Charles Bronson, Gregory Peck and Katharine Hepburn.

- TCM Remembers 2004: Irene Manning, Uta Hagen, Carl Anderson, Carrie Snodgress, Ray Charles, Paul Winfield, Alan King, Jan Sterling, Ron O'Neal, Bernard Punsly, Isabel Sanford, Ingrid Thulin, John Drew Barrymore, Virginia Grey, director Russ Meyer, producer Ray Stark, Peter Ustinov, Anna Lee, John Randolph, Frances Dee, Spalding Gray, Noble Willingham, Rodney Dangerfield, composers David Raksin, Jerry Goldsmith & Elmer Bernstein, Howard Keel, Ann Miller, Fay Wray, Tony Randall, Christopher Reeve, Ronald Reagan, Janet Leigh and Marlon Brando.

- TCM Remembers 2005: Sandra Dee, Virginia Mayo, John Vernon, cinematographer Tonino Delli Colli, Simone Simon, Eddie Albert, Marc Lawrence, playwright Arthur Miller, Ruth Hussey, Ossie Davis, screenwriter Gavin Lambert, Keith Andes, Geraldine Fitzgerald, screenwriter Evan Hunter, director Guy Green, Harold J. Stone, Pat Morita, producer Ismail Merchant, Sir John Mills, Richard Pryor, Kay Walsh, Teresa Wright, Suzanne Flon, art director John Box, Jocelyn Brando, screenwriter Ernest Lehman, composer Linda Martinez, director Morris Engel, Barbara Bel Geddes, director Robert Wise, June Haver, Brock Peters, Edward Bunker, Ruth Warrick, Lane Smith, Stanley DeSantis, Jean Parker, Sheree North and Anne Bancroft.

- TCM Remembers 2006: Marian Marsh, Elizabeth Allen, Jack Warden, Anthony Franciosa, Tamara Dobson, cinematographer Sven Nykvist, Red Buttons, Alida Valli, Mickey Spillane, director Gordon Parks, director Gillo Pontecorvo, Robert Donner, Darren McGavin, Mako Iwamatsu, Robert O. Cornthwaite, Richard Bright, producer Joseph Stefano, Barnard Hughes, Adrienne Shelly, Chris Penn, Vincent Schiavelli, Arthur Hill, art director Henry Bumstead, Jane Wyatt, Jack Wild, Paul Gleason, composer Malcolm Arnold, songwriter Betty Comden, director Vincent Sherman, Fayard Nicholas, Moira Shearer, Ken Richmond, writer Peter Benchley, Robert Earl Jones, Dennis Weaver, director Richard Fleischer, Don Knotts, Jack Palance, Peter Boyle, Maureen Stapleton, Bruno Kirby, director Robert Altman, June Allyson, Glenn Ford and Shelley Winters.

- TCM Remembers 2007: Solveig Dommartin, Ulrich Mühe, producer Carlo Ponti, Charles Lane, Miyoshi Umeki, Mala Powers, writer Peter Viertel, writer Norman Mailer, Barbara McNair, producer Sidney Sheldon, Ron Carey, cinematographer László Kovács, director Delbert Mann, writer A. I. Bezzerides, Bud Ekins, Deborah Kerr, Calvin Lockhart, Betty Hutton, Marcel Marceau, film critic Joel Siegel, Yvonne De Carlo, Bobby Mauch, Lois Maxwell, Barry Nelson, make-up artist William J. Tuttle, Alice Ghostley, Jack Williams, Gordon Scott, Laraine Day, Roscoe Lee Browne, Michel Serrault, writer Bernard Gordon, Richard Jeni, Kitty Carlisle Hart, director Bob Clark, director Richard Franklin, cinematographer Freddie Francis, Kerwin Mathews, Frankie Laine, Robert Goulet, Jack Valenti, director Michelangelo Antonioni, Jane Wyman and director Ingmar Bergman.

- TCM Remembers 2008: Richard Widmark, Edie Adams, Guillaume Depardieu, Robert DoQui, Charlton Heston, Cyd Charisse, George Carlin, Paul Scofield, Dick Martin, Sydney Pollack, special effects artist Stan Winston, Eva Dahlbeck, Michael Kidd, June Travis, producer Charles H. Joffe, Ken Ogata, screenwriter Irving Brecher, Roy Scheider, Brad Renfro, Paul Benedict, screenwriter John Michael Hayes, John Phillip Law, Michael Pate, Roberta Collins (later removed and replaced with Van Johnson), Isaac Hayes, director Joseph Pevney, screenwriter Arthur C. Clarke, Fred Crane, animator Ollie Johnson, director Michael Crichton, Evelyn Keyes, Breno Mello, Marpessa Dawn, Mel Ferrer, Jerry Reed, Heath Ledger, Robert J. Anderson, Suzanne Pleshette, director Anthony Minghella, Ben Chapman, Vampira, Hazel Court, Perry Lopez, Delmar Watson, Robert Arthur, director Kon Ichikawa, Joy Page, Bernie Mac, Forrest J Ackerman, Nina Foch, director Dino Risi, Dody Goodman, director Jules Dassin, screenwriter Abby Mann, Harvey Korman, Lois Nettleton, Estelle Reiner, Julie Ege, composer

Leonard Rosenman, Don LaFontaine, screenwriter Malvin Wald, director Jean Delannoy, Anita Page and Paul Newman.

- TCM Remembers 2009: Edmund Purdom, Natasha Richardson, Jody McCrea, Ricardo Montalbán, Al Martino, director Robert Mulligan, director Howard Zieff, Pamela Blake, Farrah Fawcett, producer Larry Gelbart, producer Charles H. Schneer, Edward Woodward, Jennifer Jones, Sam Bottoms, Patrick Swayze, Olga San Juan, Paul Burke, screenwriter Horton Foote, Sydney Chaplin, Susanna Foster, director Ken Annakin, cinematographer Jack Cardiff, Beverly Roberts, Kathleen Byron, Dorothy Coonan, producer Daniel Melnick, Jane Bryan, Ron Silver, David Carradine, Richard Todd, Gale Storm, Pat Hingle, Eartha Kitt, Lou Jacobi, Bea Arthur, composer Maurice Jarre, Dom DeLuise, Henry Gibson, screenwriter Budd Schulberg, Claude Berri, writer Dominick Dunne, Betsy Blair, James Whitmore, Joseph Wiseman, Patrick McGoohan, director John Hughes and Karl Malden.

- TCM Remembers 2010: director Arthur Penn, editor Dede Allen, Jean Simmons, director Roy Ward Baker, Lynn Redgrave, producer David Brown, editor Sally Menke, Harold Gould, director Dino De Laurentiis, Dennis Hopper, Jill Clayburgh, Robert Culp, James Mitchell, James MacArthur, Johnny Sheffield, Corey Haim, director Clive Donner, Kevin McCarthy, Cammie King, Eddie Fisher, director Éric Rohmer, John Forsythe, producer Irving Ravetch, art director Robert F. Boyle, Robert Ellenstein, producer Tom Mankiewicz, editor Suso Cecchi d'Amico, Fess Parker, Baby Marie Osborne, Lena Horne, Lionel Jeffries, Kathryn Grayson, Tony Curtis, Doris Eaton Travis, writer Joseph Stein, director Ronald Neame, Claude Chabrol, Gloria Stuart, June Havoc, Glenn Shadix, Peter Graves, Barbara Billingsley, Leslie Nielsen, director Blake Edwards, Zelda Rubinstein, cinematographer William A. Fraker, producer David L. Wolper, Meinhardt Raabe, director Irvin Kershner and Patricia Neal.

- TCM Remembers 2011: Farley Granger, Diane Cilento, Miriam Seegar, Anna Massey, Sybil Jason, screenwriter Jimmy Sangster, James Arness, Annie Girardot, Susannah York, William Campbell, Linda Christian, Jane Russell, Michael Sarrazin, Edith Fellows, Peter Falk, Pete Postlethwaite, Len Lesser, screenwriter Kevin Jarre, John Howard Davies, Paul Picerni, Betty Garrett, producer Gil Cates, Marilyn Nash, agent Sue Mengers, writer/designer Polly Platt, Hideko Takamine, Jeff Conaway, Edward Hardwicke, Tura Satana, Neva Patterson, cinematographer Gunnar Fischer, Mary Murphy, Dana Wynter, Elaine Stewart, Lena Nyman, Roberts Blossom, Jackie Cooper, Harry Morgan, Googie Withers, Barbara Kent, Cliff Robertson, Margaret Field, Anne Francis, Yvette Vickers, Paulette Dubost, Charles Napier, Maria Schneider, Norma Eberhardt, John Wood, director Sidney Lumet, composer John Barry, John Neville, Bill McKinney, Kenneth Mars, director Ken Russell, director Peter Yates, G. D. Spradlin, Leslie Brooks, Paul Massie, David Nelson, Jill Haworth, producer John Calley, screenwriter Arthur Laurents, Michael Gough and Elizabeth Taylor.

- TCM Remembers 2012: Andy Griffith, R. G. Armstrong, Alex Karras, director Theodoros Angelopoulos, Peter Breck, Keiko Tsushima, cinematographer Christopher Challis, director Tony Scott, Andy Williams, director Mel Stuart, Lupe Ontiveros, lyricist Hal David, Phyllis Diller, Phyllis Thaxter, visual effects producer Eileen Moran, Albert Freeman Jr., James Farentino, writer Ray Bradbury, screenwriter Frank Pierson, critic Andrew Sarris, Russell Means, screenwriter Tonino Guerra, Isuzu Yamada, Nicol Williamson, Ann Rutherford, Erland Josephson, Ben Gazzara, Susan Tyrrell, Whitney Houston, William Windom, production designer J. Michael Riva, Denise Darcel, screenwriter Frederica Sagor Maas, Turhan Bey, songwriter Robert Sherman, design director Stephen Frankfurt, illustrator Ralph McQuarrie, Tony Martin, Davy Jones, Levon Helm, composer Marvin Hamlisch, Jonathan Frid, Celeste Holm, cinematographer Bruce Surtees, director William Asher, Larry Hagman, writer Gore Vidal, Herbert Lom, swordmaster Bob Anderson, special effects artist Carlo Rambaldi, screenwriter Nora Ephron, Michael Clarke Duncan, director Chris Marker, producer Richard D. Zanuck and Ernest Borgnine.

TCM HD

In June 2009, Turner Classic Movies launched a high definition version of the channel, showing the same programming as its standard-definition channel. Initial programming was not in native high definition and was instead upconverted from standard definition, but benefited from the greater bandwidth allocated to the channel. Programs available on the high definition feed are broadcast in upconverted 1080i.

TCM Vault Collection

The Vault Collection consists of several different DVD lines of rare classic films that have been licensed, remastered, and released by Turner Classic Movies. These releases are the DVD debuts of all of the films featured in the collection. The initial batch of DVDs are pressed in limited quantities and subsequent batches are Made-On-Demand (MOD).

- *Universal Collection* – Films licensed by TCM from the Universal Studios vault.
- *The Lost RKO Collection* – RKO films from the 1930s.
- *TCM Archives* – A series of DVD boxsets released by Warner Home Video featuring Pre-Code and Silent Films which includes the Forbidden Hollywood series.
- *TCM Spotlight* – A series of DVD boxsets released by Warner Home Video featuring the popular Charlie Chan and stars such as Esther Williams, Errol Flynn, and Doris Day.

International versions

TCM is available in many other countries around the world. In Canada, Turner Classic Movies debuted in 2005 on the Shaw Cable system and Shaw Direct satellite service. Rogers Cable started offering TCM in December 2006 as a free preview channel for all digital customers, and added to the analogue package in February 2007. While the schedule for the Canadian channel is generally the same as the U.S. channel, some films are replaced for broadcast into Canada due to rights issues and other reasons. Other versions of TCM are available in Australia, France, Germany, the Netherlands, South Africa, Spain, Asia, Latin America, Scandinavia, the United Kingdom, Ireland and Poland. The UK version operates two channels, including a spinoff called TCM 2.

References

[1] http://www.tcm.com

[2] "Winners - 2000's" (http://www.peabody.uga.edu/winners/winners_2000s.php#2008). Grady College of Journalism and Mass Communication. 2008. . Retrieved 2012-03-16.

[3] Mitchell, Kim; Rod Granger. "Turner launches TCM" (http://www.highbeam.com/doc/1G1-15426709.html), *Multichannel News*, April 18, 1994. Retrieved February 28, 2011 from HighBeam Research.

[4] Lon Grahnke. "Classic Films Find New Cable Outlet In Turner Empire" (http://www.highbeam.com/doc/1P2-4223379.html), *Chicago Sun-Times*, April 10, 1994. Retrieved February 28, 2011 from HighBeam Research.

[5] Brown, Rich. "Few tickets for Turner Classic Movies" (http://www.highbeam.com/doc/1G1-15308051.html), *Broadcasting & Cable*, April 18, 1994. Retrieved February 28, 2011 from HighBeam Research.

[6] "Turner picks up Warner films" (http://www.highbeam.com/doc/1G1-14791509.html), *Broadcasting & Cable*, December 6, 1993. Retrieved February 28, 2011 from HighBeam Research:

[7] http://www.turnerclassicmovies-yfcc.com/

[8] Lumenick, Lou (November 5, 2009). "New TCM Film Festival goes head-to-head with Tribeca" (http://www.nypost.com/p/blogs/movies/item_3Wjf7vaaMrf7c6PHAaIJ3N). New York Post. . Retrieved 2012-03-16.

[9] "Turner Newsroom" (http://news.turner.com/article_display.cfm?article_id=5110). News.turner.com. .

[10] Lumenick, Lou (July 11, 2011). "Robert Osborne taking leave from TCM" (http://www.nypost.com/p/blogs/movies/robert_osborne_taking_leave_from_lQNj8sE5YfsOP9EA3nJ9TM). The New York Post. .

[11] Katz, Richard. "TCM purchases large MGM/UA film package" (http://www.highbeam.com/doc/1G1-16467574.html), *Multichannel News*, November 21, 1994. Retrieved February 28, 2011 from HighBeam Research.

[12] Dempsey, John. "TCM lands passel of pix from Fox" (http://www.highbeam.com/doc/1G1-121537050.html), *Daily Variety*, August 13, 2004. Retrieved February 28, 2011 from HighBeam Research.

[13] Brown, Rich. "Turner signs Paramount titles for $30M: new classic movie channel seeks additional packages to supplement MGM/RKO library" (http://www.highbeam.com/doc/1G1-13266775.html), *Broadcasting & Cable*, August 16, 1993. Retrieved February 28, 2011 from HighBeam Research.

[14] Bibel, Sara (February 22, 2012). "TCM Announces Guest Programmers for 2012, Including Jules Feiffer, Anthony Bourdain, Debra Winger, Ellen Barkin, Spike Lee, Regis Philbin and Jim Lehrer" (http://tvbythenumbers.zap2it.com/2012/02/22/ tcm-announces-guest-programmers-for-2012-including-jules-feiffer-anthony-bourdain-debra-winger-ellen-barkin-spike-lee-regis-philbin-and-jim-lehrer/ 121401/). *Press release*. . Retrieved 2012-03-16.

[15] TCM Remembers 2009 (http://www.tcm.com/mediaroom/video/282318/TCM-Remembers-2009-Movie-Promo-TCM-Original.html) at the TCM Website.

[16] Asian Images on Film (http://www.tcm.com/this-month/article/196827l0/ Race-Hollywood-Asian-Images-in-Film-Tuesdays-Thursdays-in-June-.html), article on TCM website.

[17] Native American Images on Film (http://www.tcm.com/this-month/article/296716l0/ Race-Hollywood-Native-American-Images-On-Film.html), article on TCM website.

[18] Black Images On Film (http://www.tcm.com/this-month/movie-news.html?id=133365& name=Race-Hollywood-Black-Images-on-Film), article on TCM website.

[19] Latino Images on Film (http://www.tcm.com/mediaroom/video/240408/Latino-Images-in-Film-TCM-Original-Latin-Non-Latin.html), Hispanic actors talk about casting.

[20] Arab Images on Film (http://www.tcm.com/this-month/article/411149l0/Arab-Images-on-Film.html), article on TCM website.

[21] David Hinckley (2011-11-14). "Steven Spielberg and John Williams tell stories by the score about 'Jaws' & 'E.T.' in 'AFI Master Class'" (http://www.nydailynews.com/entertainment/tv-movies/ steven-spielberg-john-williams-stories-score-jaws-amp-e-t-afi-master-class-article-1.977349#ixzz2Hyh7xTg2). *Daily News*. .

[22] J.C. Maçek III (2013-1-14). "'AFI Master Class': Zemeckis and Burgess Break It Down" (http://www.popmatters.com/pm/review/ 167227-afi-master-class-zemeckis-and-burgess-break-it-down/). *PopMatters*. .

[23] Sabotage Film Group website (http://sabotagefilmgroup.com/) displaying many TCM promos.

External links

- Official website (http://www.tcm.com)
- Official UK website (http://www.tcmuk.tv/)
- Turner Media Innovations (UK Sales house for TCM) (http://www.turnermediainnovations.com/)
- TCM Europe (http://www.tcmeurope.com/)
- TCM Movie Database (http://www.tcm.com/tcmdb/index.jsp) (TCMDb)
- Interviews with Robert Osborne about TCM's Classic Film Archive (http://www.cinemaretro.com/index.php?/ archives/ 1417-EXCLUSIVE-INTERVIEW-WITH-TURNER-MOVIE-CLASSICS-HOST-ROBERT-OSBORNE.html) by Cinema Retro

Uncle Silas

Uncle Silas	
First edition title page	
Author(s)	J. Sheridan Le Fanu
Country	England
Language	English
Genre(s)	Gothic mystery-thriller
Publisher	Dublin University Magazine (serialized) Richard Bentley (hardcover)
Publication date	1864
Media type	Printed

Uncle Silas is a Victorian Gothic mystery-thriller novel by the Irish writer J. Sheridan Le Fanu. It is notable as an early example of the locked room mystery subgenre. It is not a novel of the supernatural (despite a few creepily ambiguous touches), but does show a strong interest in the occult and in the ideas of Emanuel Swedenborg, a Swedish scientist, philosopher and Christian mystic.

Like many of Le Fanu's novels, it grew out of an earlier short story, "A Passage in the Secret History of an Irish Countess" (1839), which he also published as "The Murdered Cousin" in the 1851 collection *Ghost Stories and Tales of Mystery*. The setting of the original story was Irish; presumably it was changed to Derbyshire for the novel because this would appeal more to a British audience. It was first serialized in the *Dublin University Magazine* in 1864, under the title *Maud Ruthyn and Uncle Silas*, and appeared in December of the same year as a triple-decker novel from the London publisher Richard Bentley.[1]

Plot summary

The novel is a first person narrative told from the point of view of the teenaged Maud Ruthyn, an heiress living with her sombre, reclusive father Austyn Ruthyn in their mansion at Knowl. She gradually becomes aware of the existence of Silas Ruthyn, a black sheep uncle whom she has never met, who was once an infamous rake and gambler but is now apparently a fervently reformed Christian. Silas's past holds a dark mystery, which she gradually learns from her father and from her worldly, cheerful cousin Lady Monica: the suspicious suicide of a man to whom Silas owed an enormous gambling debt, which took place within a locked, apparently impenetrable room in Silas's mansion at Bartram-Haugh. Austyn is firmly convinced of his brother's innocence; Maud's attitude to Uncle Silas (whom we do not meet for the first 200 pages of the book) wavers repeatedly between trusting in her father's judgment, and growing fear and uncertainty.

In the first part of the novel, Maud's father hires a French governess, Madame de la Rougierre, as a companion for her. Madame de la Rougierre, however, turns out to be a sinister figure who has designs on Maud. (In a cutaway scene that breaks the first-person narrative, we learn that she is in league with Uncle Silas's good-for-nothing son Dudley.) She is eventually discovered by Maud in the act of burgling her father's desk; this is enough to ensure that she is dismissed.

Austyn Ruthyn obscurely asks Maud if she is willing to undergo some kind of "ordeal" to clear his brother Silas's and the family's name. She assents, and shortly thereafter her father dies. It turns out that he has added a codicil to his will: Maud is to stay with Uncle Silas until she comes of age. If she dies while in her minority, the estate will go to Silas. Despite the advice of her friends Lady Monica and Austyn's executor and fellow Swedenborgian, Dr. Bryerly, Maud consents to spend the next three and a half years of her life at Bartram-Haugh.

Life at Bartram-Haugh is initially strange but not unpleasant, despite ominous signs such as the uniformly unfriendly servants and a malevolent factotum of Silas's, the one-legged Dickon Hawkes. Silas himself is a sinister, soft-spoken old man who is openly contemptuous of his two children, the loutish Dudley and the untutored but friendly Milly (her rustic manners initially amaze Maud, but they become best friends). Silas is subject to mysterious catatonic fits which are attributed by his doctor to his massive opium consumption. Gradually, however, the trap closes around Maud: it is clear that Silas is attempting to coax or force her to marry Dudley. When that tactic fails, and as the time-limit of three-and-a-half years begins to shrink, a yet more sinister plot is hatched to ensure that Silas gains control of the Ruthyn estate.

Milly is sent away to a boarding school in France, and arrangements are made for Maud to join her after a period of three months. In the meantime, Madame de la Rougierre reappears in Silas's employ, over Maud's protests, and it is she who is charged with accompanying Maud first to London, and then on to Dover and across the channel. However, unbeknownst to Maud, who is asleep in the carriage for most of the journey, she has in fact been taken on a round trip to London and back. She is returned to Bartram-Haugh under cover of darkness, and although she soon discovers the trick, her demands for an explanation are ignored and she is locked into one of the mansion's many bedrooms. Madame de la Rougierre, however, having been kept ignorant of Silas' true intentions, unwittingly partakes of the drugged claret that was intended for Maud, and promptly falls asleep on the latter's bed. Late that night, Dudley scales the building and enters the unlit room through the window, which is set upon concealed hinges that allow it to be opened only from the outside. Maud, crouched and hidden in a corner, watches on in terror as Dudley takes a spiked hammer from his pocket and savagely attacks the figure lying on the bed. Madame de la Rougierre screams briefly and convulses, then lies still. Uncle Silas, who has been waiting outside the door, enters the room, allowing Maud to slip out undetected. With the help of Dickon Hawkes' daughter, whom Maud had befriended during her stay, she is swiftly conveyed by carriage to Lady Monica's estate, and away from Bartram-Haugh forever.

Silas is discovered in the morning lying dead of an opium overdose, while Dudley becomes a fugitive and is thought to be hiding in Australia. Maud is happily married to the charming and handsome Lord Ilbury and ends her recollections on a philosophical note:

> This world is a parable—the habitation of symbols—the phantoms of spiritual things immortal shown in material shape. May the blessed second-sight be mine—to recognise under these beautiful forms of earth the angels who wear them; for I am sure we may walk with them if we will, and hear them speak!

Allusions/references from other works

Uncle Silas remains Le Fanu's best-known and most popular novel. It was the source for Arthur Conan Doyle's *The Firm of Girdlestone*,[2] and remains a touchstone for contemporary mystery fiction. There are also strong connections between *Uncle Silas* and some of Wilkie Collins' better-known novels, especially *The Woman in White*; both writers, while recognisably within the Gothic tradition, depict heroines who are far more highly developed than the persecuted maidens of Ann Radcliffe and others.[3]

Film and television adaptations

A film version, also titled *Uncle Silas*, was made by Gainsborough Studios in 1947, directed by Charles Frank and starring Jean Simmons, Katina Paxinou and Derek Bond.[4] The heroine's given name was changed from Maud to Carolyn. It was re-titled *The Inheritance* in the United States, and the incestuous material was excised.

A feature length British television adaptation was made in 1968, for the Thames Television series *Mystery and Imagination*. Maud was played by Lucy Fleming, opposite Robert Eddison as Silas.[5]

Another adaptation, titled *The Dark Angel*, starring Peter O'Toole, was made for BBC Television in 1987.[6]

References

[1] McCormack, W. J. (1997). Sheridan Le Fanu. Gloucestershire: Sutton Publishing. ISBN 0-7509-1489-0.

[2] Cox, J. Randolph (1989). *Masters of Mystery and Detective Fiction: An Annotated Bibliography*. Pasadena, Calif.: Salem Press. p. 168. ISBN 0893566527.

[3] David Punter, 1996, "The Literature of Terror: A History of Gothic Fictions from 1765 to the Present Day", Vol. I, "The Gothic Tradition", pp. 203-6.

[4] "*Uncle Silas* (1947)" (http://www.imdb.com/title/tt0039492/). Internet Movie Database. .

[5] "*Mystery and Imagination - Uncle Silas* (1968)" (http://www.imdb.com/title/tt0304867/). Internet Movie Database. .

[6] "*The Dark Angel* (1987)" (http://www.imdb.com/title/tt0101659/). Internet Movie Database. .

External links

- Free unabridged audiobook by LibriVox.org: *Uncle Silas* (http://librivox.org/uncle-silas-by-j-sheridan-le-fanu/)

Uncle Silas (film)

Uncle Silas is a 1947 British drama film directed by Charles Frank and starring Jean Simmons, Katina Paxinou and Derrick De Marney.[1] It is an adaptation of the novel *Uncle Silas* in which a heiress is pursued by her uncle, who craves her money following her father's death.

Plot

Caroline Ruthyn is the teenage niece of the her elderly uncle Silas, a sickly and at one time unbalanced man who becomes her guardian on the death of her father. The fact that Silas is broke and greedy and young Caroline is the heir to her father's vast fortune is reason enough for Caroline to be wary, but her fears increase when she meets Silas's perverted son and when she discovers that her fearsome former governess, Madame de la Rougierre, is working with her uncle...

Cast

- Jean Simmons - Caroline Ruthyn
- Katina Paxinou - Madame de la Rougierre
- Derrick De Marney - Uncle Silas
- Derek Bond - Lord Richard Ilbury
- Sophie Stewart - Lady Monica Waring
- Esmond Knight - Doctor Bryerly
- Reginald Tate - Austin Ruthyn
- Manning Whiley - Dudley Ruthyn
- Marjorie Rhodes - Mrs Rusk

- John Laurie - Giles
- Frederick Burtwell - Branston
- George Curzon - Sleigh
- O. B. Clarence - Victor Clay
- Frederick Ranalow - Rigg
- Patricia Glyn - Mary Quince
- Robin Netscher - Tom

References

[1] http://ftvdb.bfi.org.uk/sift/title/55868

External links

- *Uncle Silas (film)* (http://www.imdb.com/title/tt0039492/) at the Internet Movie Database

Young Bess

Young Bess	
Lobby card	
Directed by	George Sidney
Produced by	Sidney Franklin
Written by	Jan Lustig Arthur Wimperis
Based on	Margaret Irwin (novel)
Starring	Jean Simmons Stewart Granger Deborah Kerr Charles Laughton
Music by	Miklós Rózsa
Cinematography	Charles Rosher
Editing by	Ralph E. Winters
Distributed by	Metro-Goldwyn-Mayer
Release date(s)	May 21, 1953
Running time	112 minutes
Country	United States
Language	English
Budget	$2,423,000[1]
Box office	$4,095,000[1]

Young Bess is a 1953 Technicolor biographical film made by Metro-Goldwyn-Mayer about the early life of Elizabeth I, from her turbulent childhood to the eve of her accession to the throne of England. The film starred Jean Simmons and Stewart Granger as Thomas Seymour, with Charles Laughton as Elizabeth's father, Henry VIII, a part he had played twenty years before in *The Private Life of Henry VIII*. The film was directed by George Sidney and produced by Sidney Franklin, from a screenplay by Jan Lustig and Arthur Wimperis based on the novel by Margaret Irwin (1944).

Plot

Following the execution of her mother, Anne Boleyn (Elaine Stewart), for infidelity, Elizabeth (Jean Simmons) is exiled to Hatfield House and declared illegitimate (thereby losing her place in line for the throne) by her father, King Henry VIII (Charles Laughton). She is accompanied by her loyal servants, Mr. Parry (Cecil Kellaway) and her governess Mrs. Ashley (Kay Walsh). Over the years, her position rises and falls on the whim of her father.

The child is periodically summoned back to London to become acquainted with Henry's latest spouse. When Henry marries his last wife, Catherine Parr (Deborah Kerr), the now-teenage Elizabeth finally rebels against her latest summons. However, the suave, handsome Lord Admiral Thomas Seymour (Stewart Granger) persuades her to change her mind, and Elizabeth and Catherine become good friends. Meanwhile, Henry is impressed and amused by the resolute defiance of his daughter (once again declared legitimate).

When Henry dies, Thomas's scheming brother Ned (Guy Rolfe) takes over as Lord Protector and guardian of King Edward VI (Rex Thompson) during his minority, overriding Henry's wish that Thomas raise the boy. Ned and Thomas do not like each other, and Ned's fear of his brother's ambition grows with each of Thomas's naval triumphs.

By now, Elizabeth realizes she is in love with Thomas. She refuses to believe Mrs. Ashley's warning that he loves someone else until she sees Thomas and Catherine embrace in secret. Ned had blocked Thomas from marrying into the royal family, but Elizabeth graciously persuades her brother to issue a royal decree sanctioning their marriage. As they live in the same household, Thomas grows too close to Elizabeth without even knowing it, until one day, Elizabeth kisses him and declares her love for him. She then wisely moves back to Hatfield.

Soon after, however, Catherine sickens and dies. Thomas comes to see Elizabeth. Ned has him arrested and charged with treason. He also accuses Elizabeth of plotting with Thomas to overthrow her brother. She goes to see Edward, but is too late to save Thomas from execution.

The film then shifts forward to 1558. Having survived the perils of her early life, and with Edward deceased and her elder sister Mary dying, Elizabeth is about to become Queen of England.

Cast

- Kay Walsh as Mrs. Ashley
- Guy Rolfe as Edward "Ned" Seymour
- Kathleen Byron as Anne Seymour, Ned's wife
- Cecil Kellaway as Mr. Parry
- Rex Thompson as Edward VI
- Robert Arthur as Barnaby, Thomas's page
- Leo G. Carroll as Mr. Mums, Elizabeth's tutor
- Norma Varden as Lady Tyrwhitt
- Alan Napier as Robert Tyrwhitt
- Noreen Corcoran as Bess as a child
- Ivan Triesault as Danish Envoy
- Elaine Stewart as Anne Boleyn
- Dawn Addams as Catherine Howard
- Doris Lloyd as Mother Jack
- Lumsden Hare as Archbishop Thomas Cranmer
- Lester Matthews as Sir William Paget
- Ann Tyrrell as Mary

Reception

According to MGM records, the film earned $1,645,000 in North America and $2,450,000 elsewhere, leading to a loss of $272,000.[1]

Awards

The film was nominated for two Academy Awards; for Best Costume Design and Best Art Direction (Cedric Gibbons, Urie McCleary, Edwin B. Willis, Jack D. Moore). [2]

References

[1] 'The Eddie Mannix Ledger', Margaret Herrick Library, Center for Motion Picture Study, Los Angeles

[2] "NY Times: Young Bess" (http://movies.nytimes.com/movie/118060/Young-Bess/details). *NY Times*. . Retrieved 2008-12-21.

External links

- *Young Bess* (http://www.imdb.com/title/tt0046564/) at the Internet Movie Database
- *Young Bess* (http://tcmdb.com/title/title.jsp?stid=519) at the TCM Movie Database
- *Young Bess* (http://www.allrovi.com/movies/movie/v1:118060) at AllRovi

Article Sources and Contributors

Jean Simmons *Source*: http://en.wikipedia.org/w/index.php?oldid=535417988 *Contributors*: Aardvarkzz, Abie the Fish Peddler, Adaobi, AdorableRuffian, Aesopos, AguireTS, All Hallow's Wraith, Ameliorate!, Angr, Angusmclellan, Anthony Winward, Astorknlam, Azucar, BSTemple, Baird, Bcsurvivor, Bender235, Billynomates009, Bongomatic, Brian Kurtz, Britte, Burkeanwhig, Buzzlightyear, Canadian Paul, CanisRufus, Cavarrone, Cburnett, Cecropia, Chadoz, Cheezyie, Chick Bowen, Chrism, Chzz, Ckatz, Clarityfiend, Collier626, Colonies Chris, Coughinink, Courcelles, Cst17, Cunningpal, D C McJonathan, D6, Daniaguilar, Deb, Deineka, Derek Ross, DickSummerfield, DonJay, Doulos Christos, Drpryr, Dutchy85, Emerson7, ErkinBatu, Eumolpo, Explicit, ExpressingYourself, F W Nietzsche, Freakachu, Freakmighty, Frecklefoot, GcSwRhIc, GeoffC51, Gibb0Yeo, Gimmetrow, Good Olfactory, Gracoo2, Henrymrx, Hjuk, Hydrargyrum, Ian Dunster, Ibbn, Irishguy, Irk, Itsfullofstars, JGG59, JGKlein, JHB, JackO'Lantern, JackofOz, Jeffman52001, Jim Michael, Jim1138, Johnwmc, Jooler, Joseph Spadaro, Josh Rumage, JustAGal, Jwillbur, Jzummak, Kameraad Pjotr, Ketiltrout, Khazar, Khazar2, Kintetsubuffalo, Ktexasrose, Kumioko (renamed), Kyle C Haight, LaVidaLoca, Lane, Leuliett, Levineps, Lkjhgfdsa 0, Lugnuts, MER-C, Manuel Trujillo Berges, Mark83, Marleau, MegX, Meredy, Michael C Price, Michael Drew, Mimihitam, Miracle Pen, Modal Jig, Moviefan, Necrothesp, NickelShoe, Nietzsche 2, Nightscream, Noirish, Nomdplume, Nues20, Ole.Holm, Orbicle, Owen, P.D., PPBlais, Pahuskahey, Pegship, Penelope001, PhantomS, Pharaway, Philip Cross, Pinkadelica, Quentin X, R'n'B, RJNeb2, Reedmalloy, RexNL, Richard Arthur Norton (1958-), Rjwilmsi, Rms125a@hotmail.com, Robina Fox, RogDel, Rossrs, Rrburke, RyanGerbil10, Salamurai, Sam Golden, Savolya, Sayerslle, Seanks, Seidenstud, Simon12, Skomorokh, SkyWalker, Spitfire, SteveCrook, Strongsauce, Tassedethe, Tesscass, The Thing That Should Not Be, Thefourdotelipsis, Thomas100000, Tim1965, Tinton5, Tkreuz, Tony00007, Unibond, VIPelle, VarietyPerson, Vary, Veganfishcake, Velpremus, Volatile, WFinch, WWGB, Weimar03, Whiteboy96100, Wjhonson, Wjstafford, Zarcadia, Zombie433, ÀrdRuadh21, 265 anonymous edits

A Bullet Is Waiting *Source*: http://en.wikipedia.org/w/index.php?oldid=533289008 *Contributors*: Dutchy85, GrahamHardy

A Death in the Family *Source*: http://en.wikipedia.org/w/index.php?oldid=526342974 *Contributors*: Ameliorate!, Arch dude, Aristophanes68, Astrowob, Bms4880, Bobo192, Calton, CyberSkull, Cybercobra, DCEdwards1966, Doniago, Dvyost, Easchiff, Emerson7, Erik9, GrahamHardy, Henry Merrivale, Hlmiller4, JLaTondre, Jack Merridew, Jask99, KhryssoHeart, Legiglass, Madmedea, MakeRocketGoNow, Mjb, MrDarcy, Notmicro, Orlady, P4k, PeaceNT, Pepso2, Pschmid1, Rms125a@hotmail.com, Sadads, ShelfSkewed, Smalljim, Spacedog7, Stubblyhead, Tassedethe, The bloomsbury group, Tklein27, TomRMorris79, TonyTheTiger, Ventur, 19 anonymous edits

A Little Night Music *Source*: http://en.wikipedia.org/w/index.php?oldid=531693010 *Contributors*: Agnosticraccoon, Ajd, Ajrocke, Amakuru, And1987, Angelic-alyssa, Aristophanes68, Aspects, Attys, BD2412, Bart133, Belovedfreak, Beyond My Ken, Bialytock&Bloom, Blazeorson, Bruxism, Camembert, Candyflossisnice, CestusHaberdasher, Chochopk, Chris the speller, ClaudiaVice, Colonies Chris, Conversion script, DESiegel, Darklilac, David Gerard, Daydream believer2, Deb, Donmike10, Dugwiki, Dybryd, Dyl, EarthLuau, Eggplantq, Emerson7, EoGuy, Erianna, Estudiarme, EthanHunt, ExpressingYourself, Flami72, FlashSheridan, Fproffs, France3470, Fratrep, FrontRowCentre, Fshepinc, Furryfratboy, Gmosaki, Gnat, Graham87, Gravidef, Guy M, Haerenia, Hephaestos, Inventm, Ipthief, Iridescent, Itxia, JDDJS, Jahlove1234, Jamesmarkhetterley, Jayfos, Jdlh, Jim10701, Jkluvs, JoanneB, JohnRogers, Kaihoku, Kaisersanders, Kbdank71, Keakealani, KikiJones6, KrakatoaKatie, Krylonblue83, Lane Wright, Lawikitejana, Lconnor, Legrenzi, Lfstevens, LilHelpa, LiteraryMaven, MLRoach, Magicpiano, Magioladitis, MarnetteD, Martianlostinspace, Matpe815, Maxpoto, MearsMan, Mercury McKinnon, Mhhutchins, Michael Bednarek, Motopera, MusicMaker5376, Nandt1, Nick, Nick Number, Nunh-huh, Ohnoitsjamie, Operettabuff, Orbicle, Patrickcolvin, Paulcaira, Peter land, Pstril, Purushakara, Rgoogin, Ridaderek, Robertgreer, Ron whisky, SDC, SFTVLGUY2, Sam, Sb1990, SeanMD80, Shetina, Skapur, Someone else, Squandermania, Ssilvers, Stageagent, Stevouk, StryoFome, Tenorcnj, TheRingess, Theatrefan2007, Thomprod, Tonyrex, Troutsneeze, Urbane Legend, Urcolors, Violncello, Warpedmirror, WereSpielChequers, Will Beback, WizardOfTheCDrive, Woohookitty, Wspencer11, Ybarkai, Zephyrprince, 194 anonymous edits

Academy Award for Best Actress *Source*: http://en.wikipedia.org/w/index.php?oldid=537902932 *Contributors*: *drew, 7, A2Kafir, AKR619, AKeen, Actryan, Adambro, Afterwriting, Agnosticraccoon, Aharmon1973, Ahseaton, Alan Liefting, Alan smithee, Alana Smithy, All Hallow's Wraith, Alyssa kat13, Amanda7061, Andland, Andre Engels, AniMate, Anthony Appleyard, Antofa, Aquintero82, Arfon-Illtyd, Arilicious, Aristophanes68, Asdfqwe123, Asianchick, Ason27, BD2412, BRG, Bbb23, Bearboir, Bebop, Bentogoa, Big iron, Birdienest81, Black Widow, Blacwainwright, Blanchardb, Blitz Lutte 2, BmtSon, BomBom, Bondcruz, Bovineboy2008, Brianwilsonisgod, Bryan Derksen, Buckeyebrain, Bzuk, CAWylie, CHill1045, Calaschysm, CanisRufus, Cardcapturs, CardinalDan, Carlos.e.valdivia, Cburnett, Chadmbol, Chowbok, Chris the speller, Chrishmt0423, Chrysalis, Chupon, Cinemaniac86, Cjc13, Clarityfiend, Classicaltorture, Clay70, Cmart514, Colonies Chris, Conversion script, Cop 663, Cornthwaite, Corvus cornix, Coulraphobic123, Countercouper, CowboySpartan, Cowlibob, Crboyer, Crumbsucker, Curero, DFS454, DVdm, Danbarnesdavies, Danny, DaveGorman, DeadEyeArrow, Derek Ross, Deskana, Diannaa, Dl2000, Dobie80, Dominicano1197, Donimo, DoodleHammer, DrKiernan, Drbreznjev, Drhaggis, Dsaichandan, E-Kartoffel, Eclecticology, EdGl, Edhed, Electric Storm89, Electrix, Elementalrain, Elliotbazz, Epbr123, Erintalley1, Estoy Aquí, Evil Monkey, Extraordinary Machine, Fabiom, Faithlessthewonderboy, Fastfission, FattieLuv2, Fcrozat, FilmExpert, Finlay McWalter, Flowerparty, Fratrep, Freakofnurture, FredR, Freefry, Frehley, Funnysheep, Fuzzy510, GFlohr, Gaius Cornelius, Gareth E Kegg, GcSwRhIc, Gemini86 618, Ghirlandajo, Gimmetrow, GluedToBatman, Goatasaur, GobBluthGambitDeadpool, GodfreyDaniels, Golbez, Gp2much, Gpbrown28, Graham87, Gtrmp, Guat6, Guppinchen, Gzornenplatz, Hannah797, Harley Hudson, Hayden5650, HesioneHushabye, Howardzzh, IJVin, Ianblair23, Ilampsurvivor5, Indopug, Ineverwonanoscar, Irk, J.delanoy, JDNeckers, JHunterJ, JLaTondre, JaGa, Jack Cox, JackofOz, Jackol, JamesAM, JamesBWatson, Japanscot, Jaranda, JavaTenor, Jbill007, Jeff G., Jeffreymcmanus, Jenolen, Jenoside85, Jihg, Jim10701, JimboB, Joel7687, Joelbert1124, John McDG, John Price, John Vandenberg, Johnny Assay, Joseph A. Spadaro, Joseph Dwayne, JustAGal, Justinp31233, Jzummak, Kamkek, Kaneshirojj, Karada, Karin127, Kbdank71, Kcordina, Kenmewku, Ketiltrout, Kickyandfun, Kilmer-san, Kingturtle, Kiss of dragon947, Koavf, Koyaanis Qatsi, Kraftlos, Kukini, Kurt Shaped Box, Kyle, KyndalC1, L1975p, LaVidaLoca, Legolas2186, Lekrecteurmasque, Les jolies choses, LiteraryMaven, Looxix, Lowellian, LtPowers, Luckscape, Lugnuts, Luke4545, Lurker, MK8, Maccoinnich, Magog the Ogre, Mantisia, MarkSweep, Martarius, Martin Linke, Martin TB, MartinP1983, Martinwilke1980, MaryLou, MegX, Megan1967, Mgmax, Migisigi, MikeWazowski, Mikomouse, MisterBadIdea, Misza13, Mklaus36, Mogism, MovieMadness, Movieguru2006, Mpo90, Mr Hall of England, MrDarcy, Mrbluesky, Mrceleb2007, Muriel Gottrop, Musdan77, NAD 0108, NTox, NWill, NYKenny, Nairobiny, Neddyseagoon, Nickfehr, Nilmerg, Niteowlneils, Nlu, NoSeptember, Noirish, Nora nettlerash, Nv8200p, OettingerCroat, Ohconfucius, Ohthelameness, Ojk007, Olivier, OneNamelessCat, Osarbu, Osgoode, OtterDW, Ouishoebean, Ozzieboy, PC78, Pantaallou, PatadyBag, Patstuart, Paul A, Paulancheta, Pegasus1138, Pegship, Pejorative.majeure, Peterwill, Piers Delcore, Pinnecco, Piotrpd, Plumphumps, Pm0110, Porlob, Prayer for the wild at heart, Preaky, PrincessofLlyr, Psychadelicboy33, Purplebackpackonthetrail, Quill, Qwerty200075, R'n'B, RBBrittain, Razzfan, Realdiamonds, Remember, Reywas92, Rfc1394, Rich Farmbrough, Richiekim, RickK, Ricky81682, Rjwilmsi, Rossrs, Rs09985, RyRo....LaCp, Ryulong, Rzf3, SDC, Sam Hocevar, Sara's Song, Schlockading, Schweiwikist, Scorpion0422, Senorbad, Sgfayeq, Shameless, Shanzwhaat, ShelfSkewed, Shortride, Shshshsh, Skier Dude, SlimVirgin, Smedpull, SnapSnap, Soliloquial, Spacejam2, Spangineer, SpeedoDan, SpuriousQ, StAnselm, Staffelde, SteveCrook, Stlsportsfan2316, Stofjas, Stoogetins, Stormie, Stymphal, Supertigerman, Sus scrofa, Sweetqt0428, TJ Spyke, TNAXXX, Tad Lincoln, Talia679, Tassedethe, Tata1711, Tbhotch, Ted Wilkes, Teeb, TerminatorSteve05, Textorus, That, TheMadBaron, Thefourdotelipsis, Theronp, Thisisaparadox, Titanic1916, Titodutta, Tkreuz, Tktru, TonyTheTiger, Toobevr1244, Trekphiler, Trickzakky, Tryptofeng, Ulric1313, Una Smith, Urcolors, Vaxent, Veggiegirl, Vidor, Vina, Volatile, WOSlinker, WadeSimMiser, Wafulz, Wallie, Walloon, Wapcaplet, Wendox34, Wgolf, WhatABoyWants, Wiki Raja, Wikipedical, Wikitanvir, Wildhartlivie, Willerror, Wknight94, Woohookitty, WoundedWolfgirl, WurmWoode, Xelaxa, Xezbeth, Xnuala, Y-take, YUL89YYZ, Yoursvivek, Zachyzz, Zannah, Zoe, Zoicon5, Zzyzx11, dt011nd4.san.rr.com, דוד, 1318 anonymous edits

Academy Award for Best Supporting Actress *Source*: http://en.wikipedia.org/w/index.php?oldid=535759934 *Contributors*: *drew, Actryan, Agnosticraccoon, Alan smithee, Alana Smithy, Alansohn, AldezD, Alexpon10, Altaïr, Amhershberger, Andre Engels, Arrest161, Art LaPella, Asianchick, Auntof6, Aussiegriff, BD2412, BRG, Babygirl89, Bakkouz, BaronLarf, Bebop, Belovedfreak, Big TT, Birdienest81, Blacwainwright, Blahthequah, BomBom, Bovineboy2008, BrightLights, BrotherFlounder, Bryan Derksen, Bwmodular, Caiaffa, CanisRufus, Casadesus, Catbar, Cburnett, Cgholson, Chowbok, Chris 73, Cinemaniac86, Cjc13, Clarityfiend, Classicaltorture, Colonies Chris, ConradPino, Conti, Conversion script, Cop 663, Coulraphobic123, Count de Ville, CowboySpartan, Crboyer, Cremepuff222, Curps, D6, DJRafe, Danny, Dante Alighieri, Daydream believer2, DeadSend4, DepressedPer, Disco dog23, Dl2000, Donald Albury, Drbreznjev, DuncanHill, E Kartoffel, E0kog, Eclecticology, EdGl, Editandlikeit, Ekabhishek, Elliottrainbow, Esprix, Esrever, Estrose, EvilCouch, Extraordinary Machine, Feudonym, FilmExpert, FishPhileo, FollowGuard, Fratrep, FredR, Fuzzy510, Gadfium, Gareth E Kegg, GcSwRhIc, Gea352, George Burgess, Gr8lyknow, GraemeLeggett, Graham87, Harland1, Headbomb, HesioneHushabye, Hut 8.5, IJVin, Ianblair23, Ineverwonanoscar, Infrogmation, Irk, Irregulargalaxies, JDNeckers, JLaTondre, JSydel, Ja92bs, JackO'Lantern, JackofOz, Jamdonaldson, JamesAM, Jaranda, Jeandré du Toit, Jeff3000, Jerzy, Jg325, Jogers, JordanDQ52, Joseph A. Spadaro, Josiah Rowe, JustAGal, Justinp31233, Jzummak, Kamkek, Kaneshirojj, Kbdank71, Kesla, Ketiltrout, Kickyandfun, Killer, Kollision, Koyaanis Qatsi, L1975p, Lacp Rp, Leanne, Lestatdelc, LiteraryMaven, LobitaMontoya, LtPowers, Lugnuts, MacStep, Mackerm, MarkSweep, Martin TB, Masonprof, MegX, Megan1967, Mgmax, Michael Snow, Migisigi, Mike M SA, MikeWazowski, Million Little Gods, Minesweeper, MisterBadIdea, MovieMadness, MovieNut14, Mr Hall of England, Mr link, Muriel Gottrop, MusiCitizen, Mwng, NWill, Nairobiny, Neddyseagoon, Neier, NeilHynes, NeilN, Nikkimaria, Niteowlneils, Nlu, Noirish, Norvy, Nues20, Nv8200p, Núria2, Paul A, Paulobrian, Pegship, Pejorative.majeure, PhantomS, PoliSciMaster, Prayer for the wild at heart, Preaky, Prodego, Psychadelicboy33, Quixoto, R'n'B, RBBrittain, Ravit, Rfc1394, Richiekim, Rick Block, RickK, Ricky81682, Rockhopper10r, Rogerd, Ron whisky, RossF18, Rossrs, Ryangibsonstewart, SDC, Schweiwikist, Scwlong, Senorbad, Shameless, ShelfSkewed, Shortride, Shshshsh, Singlepersian, SnapSnap, Spangineer, Squash, StAnselm, Stofjas, Stoogetins, Stormie, StrawIntoGold121, Tabletop, Talia679, Tassedethe, Tbhotch, Ted Wilkes, Theanthrope, Thefourdotelipsis, Theronp, Tony1, TonyTheTiger, Tyler, Ulric1313, Una Smith, Urcolors, Vesperholly, VitaminE, WOSlinker, Wadems, Wendox34, Wgolf, Wikipedical, Wikitanvir, Wikster72, Wildhartlivie, Woodyads, Woohookitty, Wricardoh, Yllosubmarine, Youlookfly, Yoursvivek, Zannah, ZeroJanvier, Zoe, Zoicon5, Zzyzx11, dt011nd4.san.rr.com, 512 anonymous edits

Adam and Evelyne *Source*: http://en.wikipedia.org/w/index.php?oldid=514084467 *Contributors*: A. Carty, Bovineboy2008, Clarityfiend, HawkOfDC, Hydeblake, Lord Cornwallis, Lugnuts, Rich Farmbrough, Tim1357, Wool Mintons, 6 anonymous edits

Affair with a Stranger *Source*: http://en.wikipedia.org/w/index.php?oldid=499494203 *Contributors*: Bearcat, JustAGal, Kollision, Neelix, Polisher of Cobwebs, Rich Farmbrough, Ronhjones, Skier Dude, Tassedethe, Tiptopper, TubularWorld, Whateverist, Woohookitty, Wool Mintons, 1 anonymous edits

Aida Foster stage school *Source*: http://en.wikipedia.org/w/index.php?oldid=501009383 *Contributors*: 1exec1, Bearcat, Bleaney, DavidCane, DonJay, Heysford, Le Deluge, LilHelpa, Tagishsimon, 1 anonymous edits

Androcles and the Lion (film) *Source*: http://en.wikipedia.org/w/index.php?oldid=537108780 *Contributors*: A. Carty, AguireTS, Bellhalla, Bovineboy2008, Cbrown1023, D'Ranged 1, Dazedbythebell, INS Pirat, Koavf, NickPenguin, Orbicle, Pegship, Polisher of Cobwebs, R'n'B, Sharnak, Treybien, Wool Mintons, 8 anonymous edits

Cage of Gold *Source*: http://en.wikipedia.org/w/index.php?oldid=524634829 *Contributors*: A. Carty, Draggleduck, Hazel75, Lord Cornwallis, Polisher of Cobwebs, Sayerslle, Tassedethe, TheMovieBuff, Treybien, 3 anonymous edits

December Flower *Source*: http://en.wikipedia.org/w/index.php?oldid=411852524 *Contributors*: Bradley0110, Motaros, Nymf, Sayerslle, Tim1357, Worldians, 1 anonymous edits

Demetrius and the Gladiators *Source*: http://en.wikipedia.org/w/index.php?oldid=537493184 *Contributors*: Bobet, Brazilian Man, Catamorphism, Cavarrone, Clarityfiend, D6, David Gerard, Davidatwikip, Destry, Drboisclair, Dsreyn, Dutchy85, Erik, Erik9, Girolamo Savonarola, Hmains, Hoverfish, Jared Preston, Jesster79, Joefromrandb, JosephMurillo, Kazuba, Kross, Kultoa, Kuralyov, Lockley, MarnetteD, MegX, Missourinez, Neddyseagoon, Nedrutland, Notmicro, Ohnoitsjamie, Orbicle, Pastor Kam, Polisher of Cobwebs, RHodnett, RJHall, Rojomoke, Sallyrob, Savolya, Signalhead, Sngnisfuk, Some jerk on the Internet, Steven J. Anderson, Supernumerary, Tagishsimon, Tassedethe, TheLastAmigo, TheMovieBuff, Thismightbezach, Varlaam, Wiki alf, 52 anonymous edits

Divorce American Style *Source*: http://en.wikipedia.org/w/index.php?oldid=534252772 *Contributors*: Beyond My Ken, Bovineboy2008, Bwmoll3, Cliff1911, Dutchy85, Freshh, JGKlein, JamesAM, Ldavid1985, MovieMadness, Polisher of Cobwebs, Sky Captain, Stetsonharry, Teófilo Moraes Guimarães, TheMovieBuff, Treybien, Voodoopoodle, Wool Mintons, 16 anonymous edits

Dominique (film) *Source*: http://en.wikipedia.org/w/index.php?oldid=507451760 *Contributors*: A. Carty, Bensin, Lachlan Foley, Nick Number, Rich Farmbrough, Skier Dude, Tim1357, Udar55, Wool Mintons, 1 anonymous edits

Désirée (film) *Source*: http://en.wikipedia.org/w/index.php?oldid=537164119 *Contributors*: A Nobody, Bovineboy2008, Carl Logan, David Gerard, Dryguy, Dudesleeper, Dutchy85, Erik, Films addicted, HDS, Jjjakegittes, Lugnuts, MachoCarioca, Neddyseagoon, Opera hat, Orbicle, P.D., Polisher of Cobwebs, Ricky81682, Rpab, Serbianboy, Sgeureka, Skippydogue, Studerby, Tassedethe, TheMovieBuff, Woodshed, Woohookitty, Wool Mintons, 6 anonymous edits

Footsteps in the Fog *Source*: http://en.wikipedia.org/w/index.php?oldid=537374196 *Contributors*: A. Carty, After Midnight, Andrzejbanas, Clarityfiend, ColumbiaClassics, Grutness, Joaquin008, Lord Cornwallis, Lugnuts, MER-C, Nigel45, Polisher of Cobwebs, Sayerslle, Steamroller Assault, Tassedethe, TheMovieBuff, Tim1357, Tjmayerinsf, 13 anonymous edits

Gene Simmons *Source*: http://en.wikipedia.org/w/index.php?oldid=536941436 *Contributors*: .:Jon-Mcroy:., 2602:306:CD2C:C80:C5AC:F20B:9685:20A9, 5 albert square, 757flyer, 75pickup, 78.26, AMC22, Acc78, Acdc25, Acdckid, Acroterion, Adater, Aericanwizard, Ahoerstemeier, Airforce87, Alansohn, Alexisjones1980, All Hallow's Wraith, Allen3, Alphathon, Amchow78, Amovrivs, Anand Karia, Anarkangel, Andre Engels, Andreasmperu, Andrew73, AndyPhillips, Anetode, Angel caboodle, Anger22, Angrykeyboarder, Ankit Maity, Ann Stouter, Anna Frodesiak, Anonymous from the 21st century, Anthropocentrism, Antonio Lopez, Antrophica, Armadillopteryx, Art1991, Aruton, Ashlux, Ask Alan, Aspects, AtTheAbyss, Atlant, Atropa vb, Aviados, Azraelelite, BBBNY, BGyss, Barefootguru, Barneca, Bashereyre, BeatlesBoy26, Belasted, BenFrantzDale, Bender235, Beno287, Betacommand, Beyond My Ken, Bhoeble, Bigsean0300, Bilderbear, Bindyree, Biosketch, Birdy541, Blanchardb, Blehfu, BloodyRose, Blue 22 hike, Boatsnhos, Bobak, Bobo192, Bogey97, Boing! said Zebedee, Bongwarrior, Bopash4, Borameer, Bossk-Office, BostonRed, Bou, Brandonha, Brekkbockrath, Brewcrewer, Briannewberry, Brianyoumans, Bricology, Bridgecross, BubbaHawk, Bucketsofg, Bwaddaz92, C.Fred, CJ King, CJAllbee, CWenger, Cacophony, Calmer Waters, CambridgeBayWeather, Cami Solomon, Can't sleep, clown will eat me, CanadianLinuxUser, CanadianPenguin, Canihaveacookie, CanisRufus, Captain Screebo, CarlosCoppola, Carlosguitar, CarmelitaCharm, Cat Parade, Cbarbry, Cbordiga, Cesarm, Ceyockey, Chadbryant, Charles Essie, Chase me ladies, I'm the Cavalry, Chawzon, Chochopk, Choij, Cholmes75, Chowbok, ChrisGualtieri, ChrisGuy, ChrisfromHouston, Christy747, Chuckiesdad, Cjmarsicano, Ckessler, Clarince63, Classicrockfan42, Clerks, Cogswobble, Colchester121891, Comicist, CommonsDelinker, Conical Johnson, Connormah, Coolhawks88, Courcelles, Cpl Syx, Crabman123, Crash Underride, Crazy Eddy, Crazytales, Crenner, Croat Canuck, Cromulent Kwyjibo, Crywalt, Csaenz12, CsikosLo, Cst17, Ctbolt, Cubs Fan, Cureden, Cyrus XIII, D'n, D6, D7maj, DBigXray, DFS, DL77, DRB 94 247, DRTllbrg, DVD Smith, Dakota Niko Carrie, DanielCD, Danielgrad, Danny, Dante Alighieri, Darthflyer, Dashwortley, Dave00327, Dave400, DaveJB, Davehart, David Koller, Davidscott12, Davshul, Dbalsdon, Dbone828, Dchagwood, Dealer Camel, Deanb, Deepred6502, Deflective, DerHexer, Derek R Bullamore, Derumi, Desimo86, Deuce1231, Diannaa, DigiBullet, Dillymachadlin, Dirkbb, Discospinster, Dismas, DiverDave, Djsonik, Dobie80, Doctorindy, Donmike10, Dorit, Doublefantasy80, Doug4422, DougsTech, Download, Dp462090, Dpodoll68, Dpoggeme, Dpscc, Dr.Who, Dracula790, Drag9955, Drbreznjev, Drmies, Drugyourlove, Drummer070, Ds13, Duggers, Dwc89, Dwdmang, Dylan620, E Pluribus Anthony, E tac, E2eamon, ER1969, ESkog, Eagle-eyedsteve24, EagleOne, East718, Eastlaw, Eatabullet, Edenc1, Edinborgarstefan, Eilbertn, Eino81, Ekw, El Capitaine, ElHornberg, Elcapitane, Elen of the Roads, Elf242, Epbr123, EpicFlame, Equilibrium Allure, Eran of Arcadia, Erebus555, Ericorbit, Escape Orbit, Esrever, EstebanF, Ethan C, EthanL*19934, Eumolpo, Evergreen 92, FMAFan1990, Fair Deal, Faith and infinity, Fallendevil006, Fat&Happy, Favonian, Finduilas 09, Fingerknöchelkopf, Fipplet, Firsfron, Flatterworld, FlaviaR, Fleela, Flewis, Fluffernutter, FrankRizzo2006, Frecklefoot, Frehley, Frehley72, Frontside, Fudoreaper, Furrykef, Fw5150, Fyyer, GB fan, GXIndiana, Gaius Cornelius, Garion96, Gary King, Gauss, GeneSimmonsFan, Genesthebest, Geni, Geniac, Ghiagirl, Gidonb, Giggy, Gil gillings, GinaDana, Glane23, GlassCobra, Goal2004, Godcthulha, Gogo Dodo, GoingBatty, Good Intentions, Gravebone57648, Greatrobo76, GregorB, Gregp22, Ground Zero, GroundZ3R0 002, Growing up stupid, Gtoomey, Gunmetal Angel, GuruzMedia, Gwernol, H Bruthzoo, HalfShadow, Hall Monitor, HannahPandolph, Happysailor, Harel, Harlem Baker Hughes, Heiny, Helen Davis, Hellosandimas, Hengist Pod, Historic98, Hmains, Hoalong, Hokiethug, Holiday56, Hoof Hearted, Hoponpop69, HordeFTL, Hotchoclate, Hubbbubbb, Hughsonj, Hulkrules22085, I dream of horses, I teh yuh, I'm not that crazy, II MusLiM HyBRiD II, INkubusse, Iaen, Ian Pitchford, Ian Rose, Ibbn, Icairns, Ilikeeggs1, Impaciente, Imperial78, Indon, Invisexec, Irakli88, Irishguy, Irk, IsaacAA, Isidore, Israeli Kiss Fan, It Is Me Here, Italianlover07, Ixfd64, IzzyVanHalen, J Moneu, J. Straub, J.delanoy, J04n, JC35, JNW, JRAROCKNROLL, JSmith9579, Jacksonrm, JamesBWatson, Jamesofur, Jamie, Jarjarbinks10, Jasonalvarado95, Jasonvomit, Jazz77, Jbl1975, Jcinzano, Jeffman52001, Jens kj, Jerky Chid, Jerryobject, Jerseyrose23, Jersyko, Jibbajabba, Jim1138, Jimig, Jivecat, Jjazwiecki, Jnlwriter, Joefromrandb, Johann110394, John Lake, Johnaaa, JohnathanK, JohnnyCalifornia, Johnpacklambert, Johnr roberts, Jonathanfu, Joshmt, Jprg1966, Jschnur, Juanvenus, Juiceterry, Julesd, Just another guy in a suit, Jwsvh, KISSman16, Ka Faraq Gatri, Kartano, Kate AandE, Kayla1183, Kazubon, Kbdank71, Kchishol1970, Kekslover, Kelly Martin, Kevinbrowning, Kingpin13, Kingturtle, Kintetsubuffalo, Kiss1234integrantes, Kissandcollide, Kissclassics, Kissforlife, Koavf, Kodiak666, Korny O'Near, Korrawit, Krakatoa, KrakatoaKatie, KrakenUO, Kristen Eriksen, Kross, Kvaks, Kwamikagami, Kww, Kylion, LEX LETHAL, LOL, Leenix, Lenks, Lequis, Leuko, Lhaggman, Liftarn, Lil Flip246, Limelight05, Lithium Dynamics, Llehctimdeer, Llort, LodeRunner, Lokifer, Longhair, LorenzoB, Lotje, Lots42, Luk, Luna Santin, MB412, Machsnell, Madhero88, Madtvmaster, Magellan Maestro, Mahanga, Mandragorae, ManfrenjenStJohn, Manuelle Magnus, Manway, Marc87, Marnen, Martarius, Martinasunshine, Marty jar, Masterofthemoon, Materialscientist, Matiasofalberta, Mayumashu, Mayur, McMarcoP, Mcouzijn, Mdawg728, Mdumas43073, Meegs, MegX, MegaSvensk, Mendaliv, Mercator79, Meryl-H, Metal Head 4 life, Metal Head Dave, Metallurgist, Metricopolus, MetsFan76, Mike Payne, Mike Rosoft, Mike Selinker, Mike Tv 2007, Mike V, Mike5995, Mikes1807, Mikeyasadie, Mindfreak14, Minimac's Clone, Mistakefinder, Mistereks, Misterrick, Mjeakman, Mk5384, Mmarci, Mnemnoch, Mo0, Mocean, Moeron, Moezzillas world, Momos, Mong Alcaraz, Mooncowboy, Moreschi, Moshgun, Motley Crue Rocks, Moxy, MrMisery, Mrmoocow, Mrsmurf, Mslaurel, Muj0, Mungo Kitsch, Mynameisphil, Mysdaao, Myspace69, MzMaihem, NERIC-Security, NYC2TLV, Nabla, Nakon, Nat Miller, Nathaniel R, NawlinWiki, Ndrly, Neltana, Neo139, Neoyamaneko, Neptunekh2, Nezzadar, Nibol, Nick Bond, NickBush24, Nicksharpe, Nightscream, Nihilkopf, Nikki829, Nite-Sirk, Njohnson09, NoisyJinx, Noozgroop, NotAnonymous0, Nymf, OCNative, Off2riorob, Ohconfucius, Ohe-ohe, Omega 13, Omegacc, Omergutman, Onias, OperaLuver, Optakeover, Orangemike, Organicmetal, Originals, Otr500, Otto4711, Ozzmosis, P989, Pakefield, Panda609, PatrikR, Patstuart, Paul August, PaulHammond, Paulchwd, Pauli133, Paulstanleyisawesome, Pawhite, Pbarnes1970, Pearldrummer1996, Pedro thy master, Penarestel, Pennsylvania-gal, Persian Poet Gal, Peter Fleet, Peter Karlsen, Petewithaw, PeteyWheaty, Pgrote, Phaedriel, Pharaoh of the Wizards, PhilHibbs, Philip Trueman, PhoenixAscendant, Pibby buddhism, Pickles27, Pierre1233, Pilotguy, Pink Bull, Pinkadelica, Pizzamaniac09, PlasticMan, Pnoble428, Pokerking34, Pokernikus, Porqin, Portillo, PowerSane, Preacher's Beard, Pristinegoal, ProveIt, Psych Dude 11, Psychobman, QuadrivialMind, QuasyBoy, QuiteUnusual, R'n'B, RCS, RMc, RadioMars, Raider Duck, Ralphwiggam75, Ramirez72, Randy bosworth, RandySavageFTW, RazorICE, Rdavid01, Reach Out to the Truth, Receptacle, Recognizance, Reconsider the static, Red dwarf, RedWolf, Reedy, RegentsPark, Regoli, Reisefre, Remy2038, ReneeCK97, Revan46, RexNL, Reywas92, Rfrigault, Rich4a1, Richard Arthur Norton (1958-), Rickholler, Ricky.zahnweh, Rjwilmsi, Robtj966, RockNWrite82, Rockercbar, Rocketrod1960, Rodhullandemu, Ronhjones, Rosenbluh, Ross.Hedvicek, RottweilerCS, RoyBatty42, Rrburke, Ruby.red.roses, Rug88, Runt, RyanGentry, Ryulong, SIbuff, SU Linguist, Safety Cap, SamBlob, Sammy1019, SamuelM555, Santaboy, Sapphireblaze9, Sarilox, Sarrus, Saturday, Savant13, Sbo, Scarian, Scarletpoet, Schmiteye, Scholz richard, SchuminWeb, Sdalmonte, Seanpaune, Seaphoto, Seb az86556, Sepguilherme, Ser Amantio di Nicolao, Sesu Prime, Sexecutioner, Shandy man, Shanes, ShelfSkewed, Shoeofdeath, Shreddedwheat79, Shrekkie45, SidP, SimmonsAXE, Simon Dodd, Sirtao, Sixtytwohundred, Sky Attacker, SkyWalker, Skysmurf, Slarre, SlayerXT, Slicknik13, SlimVirgin, SlubGlub, Slysplace, Smalljim, Smartse, Sneftel, Snigbrook, SoWhy, Solitaryxchild, Sonia, Soosim, Sorejax, Spartan, Spector Ray, Splash, SpongePappy, Squidward247, Sreifa, Srich32977, Sstteevvee, St.daniel, Staffwaterboy, Starlineinc, Steelerfanj, Steve2k2k3, Stevethefat, Stevewat, Stevey396, Stoopsklan, Struway, Stuart Clayton, Stupidlynamed, Sturm55, Stusutcliffe, Suffusion of Yellow, Sugar-Baby-Love, Summersavings2010, Superficiallove, SusieQ1961, Sword, Synchronism, Syntax Max, SynthesizedShredder, Sysy, THEN WHO WAS PHONE?, TMC1982, Takeaway, Takotah991, Tam001, Taranadair, Tasc, Tascha96, Taylordoucette, Tempodivalse, Tenebrae, Terrillja, Tfthompso, Tharsaile, The Ancient One99, The Earwig, The Elixir Of Life, The Red, The sock that should not be, The wub, TheBlackLodge, TheChimpanator, TheDorkKnight, TheFearow, TheMadBaron, TheRageDI, TheStarChild01, Thedarxide, Thefro552, Thejarpeople, Themoodyblue, Theopolisme, Thermeus, Theseanman66, Theserialcomma, ThuranX, Tide rolls, Tigger-ibby, Timc, Tinton5, Tiptoety, Tjmayerinsf, Tman125, Tmopkisn, Tmorrisey, Toglenn, Tohd8BohaithuGh1, Tombomp, Tomer T, Tommy2010, Tommyt, Tony1, Tork, Toscaesque, Total-MAdMaN, Tregoweth, Trencacloscas, TriangleBelow, Triona, Tromatic, Trusilver, Tsnsports, Tsonipeled, Twalls, Tweetsabird, UDScott, Ukbn2, Ukexpat, User101010, Utcursch, Valley2city, VasOling, Vcelloho, Vchimpanzee, Vegas949, Veritas Blue, Vianello, Vinney, Vivalaboosh, Vjamesv, Vox Humana 8', Vulturell, WLU, Walkiped, Walor, Ward3001, Wayward crumbs, Wdflake, Weefolk29, Werldwayd, Wether B, Whomp, Wickedflea, WikHead, Wiki alf, Wiki libs, Wiki-Wolf, WikiaPage, Wikipedia2006, Wikipediatrix, Wikipelli, Wikipoe, Wikirene, Wikiwatcher1, WildCowboy, William Avery, Willking1979, Wimt, WinTakeAll, Witchkraut, Witchwooder, Wmahan, Wolfgang wolfman, Woohookitty, Wtmitchell, Wyatt915, XDynamicz-, Xezbeth, Y2kcrazyjoker4, Yakamaro, Yamamoto Ichiro, Yankspizza, Yarl, Yasaminabobinarina, YesMapRadio, Yvesnimmo, ZacBowling, Zachlipton, Zahn, Zalgo, Zealander, Zileaafari, Zolkron, Zone46, ZooFari, Zrinschchuck, Zzuuzz, 키메라, 1852 anonymous edits

Guys and Dolls (film) *Source*: http://en.wikipedia.org/w/index.php?oldid=535102000 *Contributors*: AbelBergaigne, AlbertSM, Alloy, BD2412, Bays24, Beefjerkybutwhere'sthebeef, Before My Ken, Belovedfreak, Bevo, BillFlis, Billynomates009, Bovineboy2008, Brettalan, Cgersten, Clarityfiend, Darkking3, DatsMamaLuigi, Dave Andrew, David Gerard, Dbzsamuele, Deltabeignet,

Dpwkbw, Dr. Conehead, Dtgriscom, Dutchy85, Edlitz36, Emerson7, FMAFan1990, Flami72, Fuhghettaboutit, Gareth Griffith-Jones, Goustien, Hu12, Insanity Incarnate, Intelspy, J04n, JDDJS, JGKlein, James086, JamesBurns, JohnCD, Johnny Weissmuller, Jonjon893, Jonnybgoode44, Jpgordon, Jzummak, Kbdank71, Kintetsubuffalo, Koavf, Kostaki mou, Labalius, LeedsKing, Levineps, Lockley, Lou Crazy, Lugnuts, MMetro, MachoCarioca, Mandarax, Marktreut, MarnetteD, Masamage, Matilda, Mezzaluna, Mk5384, MusicMaker5376, Nickelodeon1995returns, Orbicle, Ozzieboy, Paul Mavis, Peterh5322, PhantomS, Phe, Pinkadelica, RHodnett, Rjwilmsi, Runt, SarahStierch, SchmuckyTheCat, Scieberking, Skymasterson, Softlavender, Spencer, Squids and Chips, Stevensanchezsiete, Storyliner, Strobilus, Tassedethe, Tim1357, Trivialist, Trotter, Upsmiler, WOSlinker, Wagexbabo, Wknight94, Woohookitty, Wool Mintons, Yenhsrav Keviv, 76 anonymous edits

Hugh Grant *Source*: http://en.wikipedia.org/w/index.php?oldid=537479039 *Contributors*: 21stCenturyGreenstuff, 66D, 7ofnine, A.K.A.47, AMittelman, Abenjoel13, Abhishek191288, Abu badali, Acalamari, Afarkas, Agricolae, Agrippina Maior, Alan Liefting, Alansohn, Ale jrb, Alessio990, Alex.muller, Alexgt, Algrene, All Hallow's Wraith, Allenf32, Allens, Alxeedo, Amaury, Ameliorate!, Amoammo, And we drown, Andromeda, Andy M. Wang, Angela, Angmering, Anthony Winward, Armyranger, Arthurian Legend, Ashley Pomeroy, Ashrafjaleel, Astorknlam, Augustus the Pony, AxelBoldt, Azzaazzaaron, B.D.Robertson, BIllyBoy66, Banaticus, Barneca, Bart133, Bdesham, Beckford14, Becki93, Belovedfreak, Benji1996, Bennmorland, BigClive, Bigar, Bilsonius, Blenda Lovelace, Blethering Scot, BloodDoll, BlueAzure, Bluewave, Bob Castle, Bobblehead, Bolwerk, Bongwarrior, Bovineboy2008, Bradley0110, Breakbackmountain, Breez, Brianyoumans, Bridgetlene, BrotherFlounder, Busillis, CE, Cabez, Can't sleep, clown will eat me, Carrie26, Catgut, Cavarrone, Ceeney, Cflm001, Cfsenel, Chaheel Riens, Charivari, Chick Bowen, Chris the speller, Ckatz, Classicfilms, Claudethecat, ClickRick, Conanfan1412, Confetti3, ConradPino, Cookiemonster67, Coolestpersonpersonever1, Coolkider, Cornellrockey, Count de Ville, Cr8tiv, Cube lurker, D6, DVdm, Da Joe, Daemonic Kangaroo, Danno uk, Danzella, Dareit, Darkieboy236, Darth Mike, Davebawx, David Wookie, DavidScobie1996, Davis 11, Ddball, DeadEyeArrow, Deb, Defiantdemon, Den fjättrade ankan, Denisarona, DerHexer, Dewey Finn, Diberri, Diliff, Discovery4, Djm237, Dobie80, Donama, Donmike10, Downwards, Dr. Blofeld, Drdevil44, Drmargi, Drw25, DuaneThomas, Dysepsion, E ponti, EALacey, Ecurran, Editor182, Egil, Eileenzzz, Electroguv, Ellsworth, Elvenscout742, Emyne8, Enauspeaker, Epbr123, Erasmussen, EricSerge, Ericoides, Esanchez7587, Escape Orbit, Esprit15d, Evil saltine, Excirial, ExpressingYourself, Exxolon, FCStaehle, Faithlessthewonderboy, Fanny bloggs, Fb75, Finlay McWalter, Fladrif, Fram, Frankie816, François, FredR, Fromgermany, Furrykef, Fvasconcellos, GB fan, GChriss, GWST11, Gaga's Monster, Gaius Cornelius, Garion96, Gary King, Gedge67, George cowie, Getontop13, Ghewgill, Ghostsofspain, Gikü, Gilliam, Gimmetrow, Goldstar012, Gonnym, Goomoo, Goosh2000, Grafen, Graham87, Great89, GreatWhiteNortherner, Greatjo, Gridge, Grunt, Guat6, Guitar Funk 101, Gunslinger, Gustav von Humpelschmumpel, Guyfromsomewhere, Guðsþegn, Gwernol, H1nkles, HJ Mitchell, Halsteadk, Hemanshu, Hintha, HornetMike, Hot totty, Hotbikerguy, Hutch y2k, Hypo, IJA, ITimmeh, IamNear, Iamtherealman, Ian Dunster, Ian-turner77, Idahugh, Ik.pas.aan, IkeDyson, Imroy, Indon, Ionutzmovie, Iridescent, Irishguy, Isaac Guard, Itzcuauhtli, J.Bogdanov, J36miles, JB1956, JGKlein, JRawle, Jaan513, Jack O'Lantern, Jake6293, Jauhienij, Jayen466, Jeanenawhitney, Jermtermfirm, Jerzy, Jevansen, Jihg, Jim Michael, Jim1138, Jjjsixsix, Jmcc150, Jni, JoanneB, Jogers, John KB, John McDG, JohnCenalover101, Johnatill, Johnelwaq, Jojhutton, Jon C., Jonnyskidmore69, Joshua Scott, Jpbowen, Jules1316, Jzummak, KF, Kaisershatner, Kakofonous, Kaleeyed, Katalaveno, Katefolsom, Kbthompson, Kesla, Khaosworks, Kingboyk, Kingpin13, KnightRider, Kolindigo, Kripkenstein, Krypticmind, Kuru, Larry laptop, Laygord, Layla12275, LeighMichelle75, Lemmiwinks900, Lexusuns, Lgrave, Lhynard, Liface, LittleOldMe, Littleolive oil, Liveupdate, Logical Cowboy, Logical Fuzz, Lolzhiz, Lord Pistachio, Louscones, Lova Falk, LoveActresses, Lrhea83, Lucas B. de Souza, Lumos3, Lupo, M2Ys4U, MBob, MER-C, MRSC, MacTire02, Magioladitis, Major Bonkers, Malcolm Farmer, Malo, Manfroze, Manupa, Marek69, Mark83, MarkM50, Markmel, Martarius, Martinp23, Marylandwizard, Materialscientist, Maximusveritas, Mayumashu, Mclauss, Mclay1, Mega4ever, Megawattbulbman, Mensurs, Mentifisto, Michael Devore, Mick aka, Microcell, MikeTempo, MilfordBoy991, Minutiaman, Mip1979, Miranda, Mirokado, Mirv, Misco, Mogism, Moncrief, Monty845, Moonraker, Morenooso, Mosmof, Mr Hall of England, Mr Stephen, Mslovelyday, MutterErde, Mwltruffaut, Mymanxcatisbald, Mythic Writerlord, N5iln, NCurse, Nabokov, Nakon, Nasarius, Nauticashades, Navhus, NawlinWiki, Nbdelboy, Nehrams2020, Nemobius, NewEnglandYankee, Nick, Nick Number, Nolady, Norm mit, Nues20, Numbo3, Nymf, O.Koslowski, Oanabay04, Obamamajuan, Od Mishehu AWB, Ohconfucius, Onebravemonkey, Onorem, Orange Suede Sofa, Orangutan, Orbicle, Ouro, Oxymoron83, P0lit0o, PaddyBriggs, Pakaran, Palefire, Pascal.Tesson, Paul A, Paulofthebakers, Pcb21, Peterwill, Philg88, Philip Cross, Philip Trueman, Pigsonthewing, Piki11, Pimdip, Pinethicket, Plasticup, Poeloq, Poisonclash, Pol098, Pollinator, PollyClaire, Polylerus, Posano, PrincessofLlyr, Professor Karen Smith, Dawn Fletcher Biographer, Puffin, Pundit, Quadell, Quantpole, Quantumphilosopher, Quentin X, Quill, Quintote, Quitegreat, Qxz, Qzm, R'n'B, RHodnett, Ragbin, RalphLee, Rangoon11, Ratchet865, RavenMaster7, Rd232, Reach Out to the Truth, Rebroad, Redefining form, Redrocket, RenamedUser01302013, Res2216firestar, Retroviseur, RexNL, RhysCumming, Rich Farmbrough, RichTTT, Risker, Rito Revolto, Ritto Revolto, Rjwilmsi, Rms125a@hotmail.com, Rnelson, Rob.ashwell, RobNS, Robert Merkel, Robma, Robth, Rodhullandemu, Rogerd, Rohithanda, Rojomoke, Ronhjones, Rossrs, Rousse, Rubywine, Rushbugled13, RyanGerbil10, Ryulong, SD6-Agent, SE7, SURIV, Safehaven86, SarekOfVulcan, Savolya, Sc147, Sc90, Scientizzle, Scoobycentric, Sebcastle, Sebids, Seminumerical, Sennen goroshi, Serendipodous, Sfan00 IMG, Sfmammamia, Shadowjams, Shakedown Bluff, Shannonbah, Shanverma, SharinganMan, SigPig, Simca-sama, SimonP, SimonSelle, SkyWalker, Smaines, Snakescool123, Soetermans, Somanyyoyo123, Souljafan07, Southdevonian, Sparkzilla, Spike Wilbury, Spondoolicks, Srikeit, Sry85, Staffel, Starswept, Stayinwonderland, Stephenb, Stevertigo, Stevo34, Storched, Stormcloak, Stratman07, Sugarcream, Supee, SuperHamster, Superm401, THEN WHO WAS PHONE?, Taalverslaafde, Tabercil, TakuyaMurata, Tariqabjotu, Teklund, Tesscass, Tetraedycal, Tgeairn, The JPS, The Magnificent Clean-keeper, The Rambling Man, The Thing That Should Not Be, The wub, TheThingy, TheTrojanHought, Theelusiveyak, Thorwald, Thw1309, Tide rolls, Timeineurope, Tinton5, Titocavalera, Tobby72, Tom Lougheed, Tom b 2, Tommy2010, Tommy23, Tony Sidaway, Tony1, TopDogIndahouse, Tovojolo, Tpbradbury, Trampikey, Trebor, Tresbon, Trident13, Trivialist, Troglodyto, Trynaus, Tumadoireacht, Tyrenius, Ume, Ummit, Unitsdrama4, Useight, Vanished 1850, Villa12564418, Violetriga, Violncello, Voidxor, VolatileChemical, Vulturell, WLU, WOSlinker, Wafflesrule101, Welsh, Werdnawerdna, Wertdunk999, Widr, Wiistrap, Wiki alf, WikiDan61, Wikipeterproject, Wildhartlivie, Wknight94, Woohookitty, Wool Mintons, Wordsaladdays, Wrathkind, Yamanbaiia, Yamla, Yorkshiresky, Yorricksfriend, Zackula, Zutopiaa, Æthelwold, Τασουλα, أنا أحبك, 988 anonymous edits

Hungry Hill (film) *Source*: http://en.wikipedia.org/w/index.php?oldid=536563054 *Contributors*: A. Carty, B3t, Lord Cornwallis, Philip Cross, RadioFan, Ribbet32, Sayerslle, Tim1357, WOSlinker, 2 anonymous edits

Mysteries of the Bible *Source*: http://en.wikipedia.org/w/index.php?oldid=528199120 *Contributors*: Angel David, Anyep, BD2412, Bearcat, CSWarren, Catneven, Cnlaw, Cyber4911, Dangerbugs77, Darth Sitges, Dekimasu, Dthomsen8, Eep², FleetCommand, Gaius Cornelius, GnuDoyng, Hugo999, Kintetsubuffalo, Mike hayes, Pegship, Pinkadelica, Pmcalduff, Reds0xfan, RyanChamberlyn, ShelfSkewed, Silverhorse, Splashen, StAnselm, Stephenchou0722, Steven J. Anderson, Tassedethe, Thekitehunter, Uncle G, VarietyPerson, WickerGuy, Woohookitty, 9 anonymous edits

National Board of Review Award for Best Actress *Source*: http://en.wikipedia.org/w/index.php?oldid=526574917 *Contributors*: Bovineboy2008, Colonies Chris, Dobie80, Euchiasmus, Ewlyahoocom, Frietjes, Kbdank71, Lquilter, Lugnuts, MegX, Movieguru2006, NWill, Nues20, PamD, ShelfSkewed, StAnselm, Tassedethe, Ulric1313, Vanthorn, Việt Chi, Xelaxa, 21 anonymous edits

New Milford, Connecticut *Source*: http://en.wikipedia.org/w/index.php?oldid=536942991 *Contributors*: 3Case, Acalamari, Adambiswanger1, Alansohn, Alexdank, Asarelah, BMenconi, Breffni Whelan, BuzyBody, CapitalE, Cosmok1, D6, Davej721, Dusmar, EJF, Elassint, Esurnir, FrenchManWGH, Greenshed, Guost, Harryboyles, Hmains, Howland3030, Hugh Manatee, Insomnivore, Jajhill, James086, Jim Douglas, Jmlinsa, JohnWBarber, Jse91, Juliancolton, JustAGal, Koavf, Kotosb, LakeBroker, Lakester10, Laurinavicius, Lightmouse, MJCdetroit, Maggiecattwo, Markvs88, Markymark4418, Mattpierce, Meanwellharry, MelbourneStar, Mild Bill Hiccup, Moges7, Newmilfordbull55, Nono64, Noroton, NortyNort, Nyttend, Parkwells, Patriotic Republican, Patsfan1234, Plasticup, Plutor, Polaron, RFD, Revmoran, Rhvanwinkle, Rich Farmbrough, Royalbroil, Rpgman456, Scanlan, Scottmt, Seanbagleyus, ShelfSkewed, Smt101, Smt10194, Soporaeternus, Spaghettig, Suffusion of Yellow, ThaddeusB, Thecoolman2011, Uifz, Veinor, VulcanTrekkie45, Waterboy6252, Zscout370, 153 anonymous edits

North and South (TV miniseries) *Source*: http://en.wikipedia.org/w/index.php?oldid=537681685 *Contributors*: 4meter4, 8th Ohio Volunteers, Abarrote, Acidburn24m, Alain Robert, Alandeus, Alicia4eva, Alro, Arcarius, Ary29, Barticus88, Beardo, Beetlecat, BlueWiz7, Bogsat, Boo1210, Bradley0110, Carinolamme, Chris the speller, ChrisCork, Colonies Chris, D6, DOHC Holiday, DStoykov, David Gerard, Deacon of Pndapetzim, Dewey Finn, DimTsi, Dobie80, Donfbreed, Donreed, Dr. Stantz, Drpryr, Dwanyewest, Emt1299d, Ezzex, Fish1941, Fred Bradstadt, Fred26, Fullerene, Godaiger, GoingBatty, Great Scott, GregorB, Grósznyó, Hockeychic9, Iceberg3k, J04n, JGKlein, JLemley1, Jay-W, Jbarco, Jennamccorcel, JessieGirl135, Jevansen, Jrcrin001, JustAGal, KdWiki, Kelly Martin, Ken Gallager, Kevin Myers, Kevinalewis, Kyleall, Kâlî, Le.Grand pensif, Mactographer, Maniago, Marc Shepherd, MarnetteD, Martarius, Mboverload, MonoAV, Muboshgu, Mulder1982, Mushrom, Nev9600, Nrswanson, Oneiros, PBP, Pegship, Pia Mark, Planetneutral, Prodego, PurpleMint, REStutes, RekishiEJ, Rfeezle, RicHard-59, Rjwilmsi, RobertG, Ryanmalik01, Satoriforsale, Sgeureka, Sioraf, Skapur, Sparsefarce, Stefanmg, TAnthony, Therese110, Tim Long, Twsx, Varlaam, Welsh, Woohookitty, Xihr, Zzyzx11, 342 anonymous edits

Ophelia *Source*: http://en.wikipedia.org/w/index.php?oldid=537894342 *Contributors*: @pple, ABF, Abra A., Abrech, Abubiju, Achnash, Adchelle, After Midnight, Alansohn, Alarbus, Alex Bakharev, Anazgnos, Andrei Iosifovich, Androstachys, AndyJones, Angie Y., AnneBoleyn1536, Asarelah, AshleyBarrett, Balthazarduju, BeSherman, Belovedfreak, Biruitorul, Boneyard90, Brad Rousse, Brandon Christopher, Bryan Derksen, CanadianCaesar, Capricorn42, Captain-tucker, Carrieia, Celithemis, Ceoil, Chase me ladies, I'm the Cavalry, ChirpingPenguin, Cinquay, Cireshoe, Ckatz, Cognition, Comicist, Cooperh, Counsell, Cowardly Lion, Crystallina, Curtangel, DSatz, Dan Guan, Darkskyz, David Gerard, DavidOaks, Deltabeignet, Dermieb, DionysosProteus, Dom Kaos, Drmies, Durova, Dwanyewest, Epbr123, Epolk, Erroneous01, Eugene van der Pijll, Ewen, Fateswebb, Feudonym, FrogTrain, Gherkins girl, Ghirlandajo, Gilliam, Glacialfox, Goatasaur, Graham87, Granpuff, Gscshoyru, H0n0r, Hadrianheugh, Haham hanuka, Hailinel, Hanoian, Hbdragon88, HiLo48, HisSpaceResearch, Hmrox, Im.a.lumberjack, Immunize, Irish Pearl, Ivan Štambuk, Ixfd64, J.delanoy, JamesAM, Janers0217, JanetteDoe, Jeff5102, JeffJo, John W. Kennedy, Juliancolton, JuneGloom07, Kakashi-sensei, Kbalter, Kbdank71, Kenneth M Burke, KimiWaPet2150, Kinaro, King Lopez, Kubigula, Kwiki, L. Clareton, Leftmostcat, Lethesl, Lianae, Lievfan666, Lizzysama, Lord Cornwallis, Louis Liang, MarmadukePercy, Marshall Williams2, Martarius, Martin451, MattieTK, Mau db, Mayfare, Mboverload, Mcenedella, MidnightWolf, Monado, Moshe Constantine Hassan Al-Silverburg, Musicaline, Myasuda, Naseem19, NawlinWiki, Netalarm, Nihthasu, Nskillen, Pablo X, Paul Barlow, Paul Erik, Peter Karlsen, Philapeter, Prolog, Propaniac, Pstuart, Rhanyeia, Richard Tuckwell, Rjwilmsi, Rmky87, Rosarinagazo, Roscelese, Rothsaj0, Rune X2, Rydra Wong, Sceptre, SchuminWeb, Scott3, Severinus, Shakespearediva, Shipleyguy, SluggoOne, So awful, SpaceFlight89, StAnselm, Stefanomione, Stevertigo, Stevouk, Stwalkerster, Surnólë, Tennyocelestia, Theelf29, Tiria, Tpb, Travelbird, Treybien, Ugajin, Ursamaj, Useight, VKokielov, Velella, Vlmastra, Warrington, WhisperToMe, Wik, Willthacheerleader18, Wrad, Writ Keeper, Xover, Zafiroblue05, Zoz, Zythe, Zzedar, 333 anonymous edits

Primetime Emmy Award for Outstanding Supporting Actress in a Miniseries or a Movie *Source*: http://en.wikipedia.org/w/index.php?oldid=535085473 *Contributors*: 2moms4life, After Midnight, Aibdescalzo, Alrofficial, Amadeus3000, Aquila89, ArkansasTraveler, Beausalant, Benson85, Blacwainwright, Bluejaylove, Dabomb87, Emerson7, FollowGuard, Gran2, JamesAM,

Johnakinjr01, Jonjon893, Jzummak, Kaneshirojj, Keybladeofhearts, LiteraryMaven, MarnetteD, Minnesotajohn29, NWill, Otto4711, PhantomS, Propaniac, Psychadelicboy33, Razzfan, Rburton66, ShelfSkewed, TUF-KAT, Taloson, Tassedethe, TonyTheTiger, Topbanana, Yllosubmarine, Zzyzx11, 35 anonymous edits

Stewart Granger *Source*: http://en.wikipedia.org/w/index.php?oldid=534436598 *Contributors*: A. Carty, Accubam, All Hallow's Wraith, All Scars, AlphaDolphin, Anthony Winward, Balgonie, Bender235, Bilsonius, Biruitorul, Bluetrellis, Bond007rh, Britmovieuk, Canavalia, Chris fardon, Clarityfiend, Cst17, D6, DagosNavy, DarkStar90, Darkieboy236, David L Rattigan, Dcrossle, Deb, Dl2000, Docu, Downwards, Dr. Blofeld, Drmies, Dutchy85, EmilyGreene1984, Ericoides, Excellentone, F W Nietzsche, Favonian, Foofbun, Francs2000, Ftord1960, GoodDay, Grstain, Gzornenplatz, Haphar, Hektor, Here2fixCategorizations, Hu12, Hullaballoo Wolfowitz, Huw Nathan, Ian Dunster, J JMesserly, JGKlein, JackofOz, Jaranda, Jay-W, Jennyarata, Jihg, John of Reading, Jpbowen, KVK2005, Kilo-Lima, Kross, Ksuwildcats, Kumioko (renamed), Lokifer, Lord Cornwallis, Lugnuts, MPeterHenry, MRSC, Mais oui!, Marktreut, MegX, MikeBriggs, Modernist, Monkeyzpop, Mr Instamatic, Nandt1, Neddyseagoon, NickelShoe, Noirish, OldSquiffyBat, Orbicle, Paul Barlow, Philip Cross, PhilipC, Plasticspork, Quasihuman, R'n'B, RegeEtLege, Rodhullandemu, Rossrs, SE7, Sam, SamuelTheGhost, Savolya, Sayerslle, Seanks, Ser Amantio di Nicolao, ShelfSkewed, Sngnisfuk, Spirit of 76.237.234.238, Steven J. Anderson, Tassedethe, ThaddeusSholto, Thismightbezach, Tinton5, Tjmayerinsf, Tovojolo, Unyoyega, Velpremus, Volatile, Vrenator, Wahkeenah, Winston00777, Wittkowsky, Woohookitty, Wwoods, Xn4, Zoicon5, Zundark, 86 anonymous edits

The Blue Lagoon (1949 film) *Source*: http://en.wikipedia.org/w/index.php?oldid=536304232 *Contributors*: A. Carty, Ajshm, AlbertSM, Andrzejbanas, Bluejay Young, DH85868993, Daisyabigael, Dl2000, DuncanHill, Dutchy85, Erik, Ezzex, Frecklefoot, Goustien, JaGa, Jay-W, Jt, Kitch, La goutte de pluie, Lady Aleena, Lord Cornwallis, MER-C, Mallanox, MarnetteD, Micromaster, Mike Selinker, MinghamSmith, Msw1002, Ndenison, Orbicle, Pegship, Philip Cross, Pjamescowie, Polisher of Cobwebs, Ragtimeacres, Reginmund, Rwxrwxrwx, SGJürgen, Sayerslle, SplendidPerformance, TheMadBaron, TheMovieBuff, Tim!, Tkynerd, Tuesdaily, Wool Mintons, 226 anonymous edits

The Clouded Yellow *Source*: http://en.wikipedia.org/w/index.php?oldid=509686525 *Contributors*: A. Carty, Andrzejbanas, BMedScience, Elsecar, Hairy poker monster, Iantresman, Lord Cornwallis, MinghamSmith, Nabokov, Pompey The Great, Sammyrice, Shadygrove2007, Sreejithk2000, Tim1357, 4 anonymous edits

The Dain Curse *Source*: http://en.wikipedia.org/w/index.php?oldid=517715964 *Contributors*: AAHoug, After Midnight, Amelianydia, Aristophanes68, Cliff1911, David Gerard, Deadlyhair, Dfconway, Gaius Cornelius, Gizzakk, Good Olfactory, GrahamHardy, GregorB, Groomtech, HairyWombat, Henry Merrivale, Hypnerotomachia, Jamesmorrison, Jaybrau, John, K1Bond007, Kellen`, Kevinalewis, Lady Mondegreen, Lectonar, Mdukas, Midnightdreary, Mr Frosty, NathanBeach, Norm mit, Pelagori, Sadads, Scanlan, Shallowgravy, Smee, Tassedethe, TheOldJacobite, 9 anonymous edits

The Dawning *Source*: http://en.wikipedia.org/w/index.php?oldid=518396638 *Contributors*: Blamelesslittle creature, DagosNavy, ExpressingYourself, GrahamHardy, Ground Zero, JForget, John, John of Reading, Kingstowngalway, Kollision, Millbanks, Nehrams2020, Ojevindlang, PamD, Paulinho28, Queenmomcat, R'n'B, Rnb, Tabletop, Tangerines, The JPS, Tim!, Treybien, Varlaam, Vitriden, 13 anonymous edits

The Drumhead *Source*: http://en.wikipedia.org/w/index.php?oldid=536736178 *Contributors*: Andrew Rodland, Avicennasis, BD2412, Briguy1978, Cbbkr, Cfeedback, Christopherwoods, Coinmanj, Comatmebro, DanLatimer, Dave-ros, David Gerard, Dekimasu, Diceman, Dposse, Drunkenpeter99, Dvp7, EEMIV, Ebehn, Emurphy42, Esrever, Fegor, GoingBatty, GoodDay, Hughcharlesparker, I do not exist, Jmorrison230582, Kchishol1970, Kevinkhu123, Koavf, Koweja, Krg005dc, LarryJeff, Lawikitejana, Ledzeppelin19, Lexiken, Lmoss77, Lord Hawk, Lquilter, Masem, Matthew, Mbp5125, Mcc1789, Morwen, Mr. Laser Beam, MsJonnyLenny, Mulad, Noformation, Oldag07, Onecuban, Pahuskahey, Polly, RFBailey, Randy.holland, Reavus, Seldumonde, Shabbs, Stile4aly, The Thing That Should Not Be, Thejadefalcon, Tim!, Tow, Trivee, Trivialist, Ultraexactzz, Western John, Wikidenizen, Worm That Turned, 64 anonymous edits

The Egyptian (film) *Source*: http://en.wikipedia.org/w/index.php?oldid=533794684 *Contributors*: -Majestic-, Adavidb, After Midnight, AlbertSM, Alensha, Andycjp, AnotherDomitian, BCtl, Bilsonius, Bluejay Young, Byoudou, Clarityfiend, Colonies Chris, Cybercobra, Darev, David Gerard, DavidRayner, Davidatwikip, Dpwkbw, Dutchy85, Epipelagic, Erik, Erik9, Euchiasmus, FFlixx7481, Grandpafootsoldier, HDS, Hmains, JGG59, Jg2904, Kizor, Kuralyov, Lisatwo, Matthew Dillenburg, MoRsE, MovieMadness, Nonexistant User, Ntsimp, Nutmegger, Ohnoitsjamie, Orbicle, Paul Barlow, Pegship, Pmarshal, Polisher of Cobwebs, Prof.Woodruff, Rbreen, Rjwilmsi, Savolya, T.E. Goodwin, Tad Lincoln, Tassedethe, Thefourdotelipsis, UncleBubba, Vlad b, Wedineinheck, Woohookitty, 68 anonymous edits

The Grass Is Greener *Source*: http://en.wikipedia.org/w/index.php?oldid=515321495 *Contributors*: A. Carty, Andrzejbanas, Bomkia, Cbrown1023, Cliff1911, Darev, Easchiff, Foofbun, Gilliam, Kitchawan, MinghamSmith, Orbicle, Polisher of Cobwebs, Quentin X, Sayerslle, Sreejithk2000, TheMovieBuff, Volatile, Wikiuser100, 15 anonymous edits

The Happy Ending *Source*: http://en.wikipedia.org/w/index.php?oldid=529338232 *Contributors*: Blubro, Bovineboy2008, Cburnett, Cgilbert76, Cliff1911, Curator2, Easchiff, GrahamHardy, Jdjudge, John K, Jonxwood, Kerowyn, Lord Cornwallis, Nehrams2020, Owen, RHodnett, Ricky81682, Sayerslle, ScottyBoy900Q, Ser Amantio di Nicolao, Tired time, Tovojolo, Treybien, Zoe, 5 anonymous edits

The Robe (film) *Source*: http://en.wikipedia.org/w/index.php?oldid=537686957 *Contributors*: ADWNSW, Adavidb, Aesopos, AlbertSM, Andycjp, Aradek, Auntof6, Bovineboy2008, Chris fardon, Chris the speller, Clarityfiend, David Gerard, Deanlaw, Delawaresky, Donfbreed, Drboisclair, Dutchy85, Easchiff, Ettrig, Freshh, Goustien, GreatWhiteNortherner, Gwguffey, HDS, Jevansen, Jonay81687, JosephMurillo, Koavf, Konczewski, Kransky, Krshwunk, Kultoa, LilHelpa, Lugnuts, MarnetteD, Martarius, Mcscott1st, Mellowdeigh, Merqurial, Necrothesp, Neddyseagoon, Nehrams2020, Nicholasm79, Ohnoitsjamie, Orbicle, Paul Magnussen, Phbasketball6, Philbertgray, Phunting, PickleM1, Plasticspork, R'n'B, Rjwilmsi, Sallyrob, Scanlan, Sgeureka, Sj, Sk4p, Sky Captain, Slrubenstein, Srajan01, StAnselm, SteveLaino, Steven J. Anderson, Tassedethe, The Video Game Master, TheMovieBuff, Thexper, VaneWimsey, XJ784, Ό οἶστρος, 82 anonymous edits

The Thorn Birds *Source*: http://en.wikipedia.org/w/index.php?oldid=536821907 *Contributors*: Adam Kidd, AlbertSM, AnakngAraw, AndreaMimi, AndrewAllen, Avia, Beardo, Ben King, Biasoli, Bobo192, Bookworm857158367, BrownHairedGirl, CanisRufus, Cherka, Chris the speller, Clarkk, Cocacola2008, CubsFan2006, DOSGuy, Daisybox, DaleCooper1888, Darklilac, Darorcilmir, David Gerard, DerHexer, Diamantina, Dickclarkfan1, Dl2000, Dobie80, Dobie80, Elagatis, Fabio Tirelo, Fayenatic london, Figaro, Froid, Gadfium, Georgann P, Girlwithgreeneyes, GrahamHardy, Great Scott, Grey Shadow, Guddug, Herve Reex, Jezzabr, Jgreenbook, Jlittlet, Jules68, Kevinalewis, Knerq, LGagnon, Liamdobrien, Lithistman, Longhair, Luciacadiz, Magdalena4ever, Miss Tabitha, Moondyne, MoondyneAWB, NawlinWiki, Noaa, NukeMTV, PatGallacher, Paul A, PaulVIF, Pb30, Philjfry, RevRagnarok, Reyk, Roberta F., Rodsan18, Rooh23, Sadads, Sam Hocevar, Smashville, Sunspro, Tarquin, The JPS, Tklein27, Vodnokon4e, Waggers, Wwoods, 109 anonymous edits

The Thorn Birds (TV miniseries) *Source*: http://en.wikipedia.org/w/index.php?oldid=537040926 *Contributors*: AlbertSM, Allens, Bender235, Bigar, Borowskki, Bovineboy2008, BrownHairedGirl, Bsilkey, Cadaques31, Chris the speller, Daftpunkboy93, Darev, Dravecky, Dwanyewest, Fabio Tirelo, Girlwithgreeneyes, Great Scott, Guddug, Hardy1956, Hiphats, Hugo999, Inwind, Jat1979, Jbill007, Jim Michael, Johnsp1, Jokes Free4Me, Liberatus, Logical Fuzz, Luciacadiz, Melodia, Menlee, Michael Hardy, Michael of Lucan, Moondyne, MoondyneAWB, NWill, Nikkimaria, PatGallacher, Raymondwinn, Robina Fox, Skitzouk, Skottyrock, Smallq, Tassedethe, The misha, Tomswife24, Tony00007, TonyTheTiger, Traceb77, Waggers, Wyn9, Xcharcoal, Youphoria, Zimin.V.G., Zundark, 69 anonymous edits

The Woman in the Hall *Source*: http://en.wikipedia.org/w/index.php?oldid=479058908 *Contributors*: Clarityfiend, Iantresman, Lord Cornwallis, Sayerslle, Tim!, Tim1357, 3 anonymous edits

They Do It with Mirrors *Source*: http://en.wikipedia.org/w/index.php?oldid=532022633 *Contributors*: 6afraidof7, Anne97432, Asdert, Avicennasis, CKarnstein, Cameron, ChKa, Chatzaras, Citius Altius Fortius, David Gerard, Daydream believer2, Fred Bradstadt, George Ho, Gil mnogueira, Good Olfactory, Grey Shadow, Hu, Hégésippe Cormier, IndulgentReader, Jtomlin1uk, Kevinalewis, Khazar2, NapoliRoma, Paul A, Pegship, Proxxt, Queenmomcat, RW153, Rangoon11, Rfc1394, Rms125a@hotmail.com, Sadads, Tantalizing Posey, Thomas Blomberg, Tim!, Tuesdaily, Wllted Youth, WikHead, Iøv, 32 anonymous edits

This Could Be the Night (film) *Source*: http://en.wikipedia.org/w/index.php?oldid=511779285 *Contributors*: Airair, Colonies Chris, Moviefan, Sreejithk2000, Tassedethe, Thefourdotelipsis, 7 anonymous edits

This Earth Is Mine (1959 film) *Source*: http://en.wikipedia.org/w/index.php?oldid=528476340 *Contributors*: 5th Avenue & 72nd Street, DeWaine, Dutchy85, Gaius Cornelius, GlennRay77, Hullaballoo Wolfowitz, JackofOz, Judesba, Khazar2, LilHelpa, Lockley, Lugnuts, MER-C, Markhh, Napa56, Pinkadelica, Ragtimeacres, Tassedethe, Teófilo Moraes Guimarães, TheMovieBuff, Timrollpickering, Tomas e, 1 anonymous edits

Turner Classic Movies *Source*: http://en.wikipedia.org/w/index.php?oldid=537960838 *Contributors*: -iNu-, 23skidoo, A.h. king, AEMoreira042281, AWeenieMan, AdamDeanHall, Adilive, Agmanuel, Ahasuerus, AlbertSM, Allisonok, Andymarczak, AnmaFinotera, AntL, ApprenticeFan, Armbrust, Aspects, Aszelan, AxG, Azumangal, B Touch, BNSF1995, Basketball110, Bearcat, Bencossette, BigCow, BilCat, Birdsong1954, Bizcallers, Bluejay Young, Bogsat, BoyRaisin2, Bravesbelle, C0re1980, Cab88, Chockyboy, Chris the speller, Cinemaniac, Compson1, ContiAWB, Cooksi, Cyzor, Dan69en, Danielk2, Danny, Davidbspalding, Deathawk, Dellhpapple, Derekbd, Dethme0w, DisambiguationGuy, Doc Strange, DoctorWho42, Dominicus Cerberus, Drpickem, ElSaxo, Empoor, Engineer Bob, Erik1980, ErratumMan, Escapay, Eugrus, FMAFan1990, Falcon8765, Femto, Freakofnurture, Frecklefoot, Freearmy, Fry1989, Fæ, Geniac, Ghat, Giraffedata, Gongshow, Grandpallama, Gta Ed, Guillu, Gwguffey, Hacker2000, Henry McClean, Heyrubengarcia, Hiphats, Hmains, Hmr, Hu12, Iam4Lost, Ido.f.cohen, Imroy, Infrogmation, J35u52012, JB82, JMyrleFuller, Janwillis, Jasmeet 181, Jason.cinema, JasonAQuest, Jeff schiller, Jengod, Jg325, Jj98, JoeTrumpet, Jol123, JustAGal, Kendal Ozzel, King Shadeed, Kross, Kurieeto, LBM, Lambertman, Laurentiu Popa, Lee M, Linkspamremover, Lokioak, Loren.wilton, MMuzammils, Magioladitis, Marcd30319, MarnetteD, Materialscientist, Matturn, Mdumas43073, MegX, Metropolitan90, Mfa fariz, Micuka, Mike Halterman, Mirmo!, Mlamarre79, ModusOperandi, Mogism, Morriswa, Motor, MrWeeble, Mrnovember, Mrschimpf, Muckraker, Mulad, Musimax, NEO-PAELEO, Nate Speed, Neitherday, Neptune's Trident, Nick Dillinger, NinjaTazzyDevil, Nua eire, Oahiyeel, Op47, Otto4711, Paralympic, Parthashome, PhantomS, Pharos, Platinum Star,

Quuxplusone, Raymond Cruise, Robomod, Rogerd, Rui Gabriel Correia, Ryanmalik01, Sam8, ShelfSkewed, Shikuesi3, Sj912, Sketchmoose, Some Person, Son of Somebody, Soxwon, SpongeSebastian, Stan weller, Stelian Dumitrascu, Sugar Bear, TMC1982, TPIRFanSteve, Tabletop, Tacoman12321, Tassedethe, The Ink Daddy!, The Little Blue Frog, TheREALCableGuy, TheRealFennShysa, TheValentineBros, Theherald1000, Thismightbezach, Tjmayerinsf, TomCat4680, Trakesht, Tregoweth, Trogga, Tvtonightokc, User92361, Vegan4Life, Vegaswikian, Viakenny, Warriorkoala, WayKurat, WikiPuppies, Wikievil666, Wikiuser100, Wilybadger, WizardDuck, Woohookitty, Wool Mintons, Xeno, YUL89YYZ, Ylee, Zisimos, 京葉車両セン ター, 鯨海, 435 anonymous edits

Uncle Silas *Source*: http://en.wikipedia.org/w/index.php?oldid=517539052 *Contributors*: Brian1979, Broken Claw, Ciaramcglacken, Clarityfiend, Colin4C, Danny, David Gerard, Djrobgordon, DoctorKubla, Dr Steven Plunkett, Good Olfactory, GrahamHardy, Henry Merrivale, Hohenloh, INeverCry, Italtrav, Jackyd101, John, Jslefanu, Kevinalewis, Lord Cornwallis, MagFlaherty, Natalie West, Ndorward, Quadell, Tesscass, Tim!, 20 anonymous edits

Uncle Silas (film) *Source*: http://en.wikipedia.org/w/index.php?oldid=517456443 *Contributors*: A. Carty, BD2412, DrKiernan, Lord Cornwallis, Skier Dude, Tesscass, WOSlinker, 4 anonymous edits

Young Bess *Source*: http://en.wikipedia.org/w/index.php?oldid=527507109 *Contributors*: Belovedfreak, Clarityfiend, Cooksey, David Gerard, Davidatwikip, Deb, Design, Dr. Blofeld, Dutchy85, Erik, Girolamo Savonarola, Gtrmp, Ilion2, John K, Lotje, Lugnuts, Marktreut, Necrothesp, Open2universe, Orbicle, Pegship, Rossrs, Savolya, Sonlui, TheMovieBuff, Tim!, Treybien, VladiMens, Will Beback, Wool Mintons, YUL89YYZ, 9 anonymous edits

Image Sources, Licenses and Contributors

License

Lightning Source UK Ltd.
Milton Keynes UK
UKOW012126130613

212205UK00005B/194/P